P9-DVC-796

DATE DUE

FE 10 '05			

DEMCO 38-296

BOLLINGEN SERIES LXXXV

Selected Works of Miguel de Unamuno

Volume 6

Selected Works of Miguel de Unamuno

Edited and Annotated by
Anthony Kerrigan and Martin Nozick

1. *Peace in War*
2. *The Private World*
3. *Our Lord Don Quixote*
4. *The Tragic Sense of Life*
5. *The Agony of Christianity*
6. *Novela/Nivola*
7. *Ficciones: Four Stories
   and a Play*

Miguel de Unamuno

Novela / Nivola

Translated, with an Introduction,
by Anthony Kerrigan

And with a Foreword
by Jean Cassou
Annotated by Martin Nozick
and Anthony Kerrigan

Bollingen Series LXXXV · 6
Princeton University Press

Printed in the United States of America by
Princeton University Press
Princeton, N.J.

Table of Contents

Introduction

Miguel de Unamuno's Non-Novels

> *If one dreams*
> *of dying,*
> *death is a dream.*

From Unamuno's last poem: *Cancionero*, no. 1755.

WHEN HE ESSAYED fiction, Unamuno did not write novels, exactly. And so the present volume is not so much a selection of *novelas* as it is of *nivolas*. And what are *nivolas*? First, they have no plot; or rather, their plot is existential, unknown to the author; plot makes itself up as it goes along, put together by the characters themselves; plot makes itself felt as it plotlessly becomes life-as-it-is-created, in this case by protagonists in a "fiction." And yet, in a fictional world, the existential moves are predestined. And there *is* an author, who can close the book on them, the protagonists, when he (He?) wants.

Our author did not believe in any genre of writing (or of living). And, if the critics insisted on judging his books according to the rules, he would invent his own genre, and did, changing existing names: he also invented *trigedias* and *drumas*. He was against classification in life or literature; he was against the idea of professional novelists, and even of professional readers (he was very Spanish); he was against "plots." In the case of his *Niebla*, translated as *Mist*, in calling it a *nivola* he was making use of the double play on the semi-assonance of *Niebla* and *novela*, thus inventing a nebulous genre indeed. And then, as had almost happened to Cervantes, and to Carlyle, and to Kierkegaard, whose characters took on a life of their own after their creators had imagined them, Unamuno found his imagined characters rising in revolt and getting out of hand. The book in which this first happens, our *Mist*, was written, it should be remembered, before and not after the dramatic *Six Characters in Search of an Author*, imagined by Pirandello: that is, *Mist* was published in Madrid in 1914, while *Six Characters* appeared in Rome (in print and on the stage) in 1921. Thus a historic moment in modern writing occurs when Augusto Pérez in *Mist* turns on Unamuno his maker and cries out: "I am to die as a creature of fiction? Very well, my lord creator, Don Miguel de Unamuno, you will die too! . . . God will cease to dream you. . . . Because you, my creator, my dear Don Miguel, you are nothing more than just another 'nivolistic' creature, and the same holds true for your readers. . . ." And the fictional entity argues with his maker that perhaps he as character has created the author rather than the other way around. Moreover, he threatens to kill Unamuno, for imagining him into existence and then willing him out of it. And this dialogue between author and character occurs seven years before the characters in the Pirandello play appear on stage, after being rejected by their creator, and attempt to dislodge the actors who merely represent them. After the play was produced in Paris in 1923, the echoes followed in Anouilh, Ionesco, and Beckett. For his part, Unamuno is most clearly echoed in Borges: "To dream that one exists . . . Well and good! That might be endured. But to be dreamt by someone else . . . !" The words are Unamuno's, but they might have been written by Borges. And the Argentinian has developed (in *The Circular Ruins*) Unamuno's thought as expressed by the protagonist Augusto Pérez as he muses on his life, wondering whether it may be no more than a novel, a *nivola*: "Perhaps all this is no more than God dreaming, or somebody else dreaming, whoever, and perhaps it will all evanesce as soon as He wakes?" And the Borgesian idea that Shakespeare and other creators tended to be not only everyman and all-men, but nobody, is a concept which begins with the Spanish mystics and carries through to Unamuno in such passages in *Mist* as where he speaks of "Hamlet, one of the protagonists who invented Shakespeare" and his "profoundly empty" phrase *To be or not to be* which is justified by the truth that "the more profound a phrase, the emptier it is," as the character Víctor Goti points out (he also writes a Prologue to the book in which he is a character: there is an index card on him in the Library of the University of Salamanca, recording his Prologue). This Víctor continues by saying that the greatest truth is certainly not *Cogito, ergo sum* but simply "$A = A$." And when Augusto Pérez says, "But that's nothing," Víctor counters: "That's exactly why it's the greatest of all truths, because it's nothing."

As a novel—or play: it has been performed as a play in Spain—*Mist* could stand re-writing, to make it live. In any case, it exists as a piece of *nivolistic* history.

* * *

In *Abel Sánchez* we have a barebones narrative of an obsession, one only. With an unclassical passion for immortality burning in one's soul, it is an easy step to greed and envy of a special kind: greed for immortality and envy for the immortality and fame of another. And here we have the record of Joaquín (Jo-Cain: Jehovah's Cain), who feverishly envies the unfairly favored Abel his easy fame and the possible immortality inherent in his painting, envies him from a driving desire to supersede and to himself live on. Even the Christian God is engaged in this struggle for eternal glory and survival: did He not create the world for His own greater glory? And not to struggle for immortality is not to be alive: "The physical eunuch does not feel the need to reproduce himself in the flesh, the spiritual eunuch does not feel the hunger to perpetuate himself." In the end, Unamuno could not pass judgment against his Cain. "In rereading my *Abel Sánchez* (he writes in the Prologue to the second edition) I have sensed the greatness of my Joaquín's passion and his moral superiority to all Abels. It is not Cain who is evil, but the Cainites. And the Abelites. The evil is in the petty Cainists, in the petty Abelists."

It could be objected that the monomaniacal Joaquín of our story is scarcely a real personage. In that case, then, he is a quintessential person, for there *are* people who live a love, or a hate, and whose whole life is their passion. More often than not the great dreamers, and creators, and players are monomaniacs —perhaps unfortunately.

Joaquín Monegro is no developing, evolutionary character, but a man obsessed with jealousy, who subsists on no other emotion. Later, Funes, the Memorious, or the Memorist, insomniac alter ego to Borges himself (in the memorial of the same name), has to do with nothing but his own memory. Since Joaquín and Funes are nothing but jealousy or memory, respectively, they are also almost nothing: further examples of Víctor Goti's intuition that "the more profound . . . the emptier."

*   *   *

As an obsessive, Unamuno begins with Juana la Loca. The obsession with Last Causes is a permanent symptom of Spanish madness (and madness seems definitely to have national forms: madness among the Japanese is altogether different from madness in Austro-Hungary), and the obsession is present from Mad Joan through Philip II among the titled, and, among spiritual brooders and meditators, from Teresa of Avila to Miguel de Molinos through to the paradox which was Miguel de Unamuno, the immortalist.

It would be hard to find a more obsessive tract than *How to Make a Novel*, wherein the novel is the narrator's obsession with his own death.

The decisive action begins along the Seine, which turns into a mirror. The protagonist, U. Jugo de la Raza (U for Unamuno, plus two of his family surnames which translate to Marrow of the Race: our author's full name actually included these surnames, in the form Jugo de Larraza) has bought a book to which he is instantly and fatally attracted, and almost at once reads: "When the reader comes to the end of this painful story he will die with me." The waters of the Seine had frozen into a hateful mirror (in modern Hispanic writing, mirrors are fearful, even hateful, to Unamuno, Pérez de Ayala, and Borges), and now the mirror breaks and spills over the pages and words of the fateful book. The protagonist hurries home, along the river. And he finds himself crossing le Pont de l'Alma—the Bridge of the Soul! And he is on the point of hurling himself into the Seine, into the mirror below.

How strange that James Joyce in Paris a few years

before, crossing the same Bridge of the Soul to go to his own birthday party—to a celebration of his birth! —a celebration planned to hail his body's birth and the birth of his fateful Book, *Ulysses*, on the same dark night, was accosted by a perfect stranger, a dark stranger from nowhere and whom Joyce had never seen, who hurled a curse at him—in Latin!—and damned him, and dubbed him "An execrable writer!" (whatever the words in Latin). It is reported that Joyce clutched the balustrade on this Bridge of the Soul, and nearly toppled (into the mirror below?). Encountering the dark stranger, Joyce turned pale. U. Jugo de la Raza "had to hold on to the parapet." And "He arrived home, his home in the house of passage . . . and there fell into a swooning trance."

No matter, for the protagonist survived the book which had unhinged him, his Book, but he wonders, in the last sentence of his novel proper: "And you, reader, who have come this far: are you alive?" Does he thus beg the question, or does he thereby postulate that there is no such question; does he not simply suggest that the question—or answer—is beside the point, suggesting, too, that we are all of us imbedded in a dream; or mirrored, perhaps?

The title in Spanish is *Cómo se hace una novela.* In titling it in just this way Unamuno engaged in a grammatical paradox: he placed an accent on the *Cómo* which makes it, automatically (as against *Como*, without an accent: *As, Like*) the introduction to a question, *How?* and then he deliberately omitted the (double) question marks of Spanish, ¿*Cómo* . . . ? , the "turned" (inverted) interrogation at the beginning and the "unturned" interrogation mark at the end. So that the title in the form he gave it could be read as *How to Write a Novel?* or *How Is a Novel Written?* or *How*

Write a Novel? or *How Is a Novel Made?* or, declaratively, *How a Novel Is Made*, or *The Making of a Novel*, or *How to Make a Novel*: we chose the last for title. It was published, integrally, not in Spain but in the Argentine, in 1927, after having appeared in French the year before (the French edition of 1926 is naturally lacking the additions made by Unamuno for the first Spanish edition). In 1950 an edition finally appeared in Spain. A good deal of political matter had been censored. Much furor was made—outside Spain—at the deletions, almost every word of which concerned the last king of Spain, Alfonso XIII, and his prime minister, Miguel Primo de Rivera. Unamuno had immured the pair in invective. The original, integral, text is given here, mostly for reasons of completeness (nothing of aesthetic value had been lost in the censoring; the censorship was motivated by politics, mainly nostalgic, since there was no attack on any contemporary institution, save the memory of the family of Primo de Rivera, whose son, José Antonio, much later was the founder of the Falange). The reader will find that Unamuno, in between vituperation, confesses his love for the monstrously all-too-human pair (the king and his prime minister). In his last years, Don Miguel is reported to have said (according to his oldest son and heir), "If I could have known what was to follow . . . I would have held my fire."

The implicit question of the title is answered by other implicit questions: How to Make a Novel is the same question as How to Make a Novelist and How to Make a Reader. Unamuno left the answer up to the reader of his book, and he appealed to that reader to answer. For they would have to answer the question together. And the last sentences of his added "Continuation" point out that by thinking and being, *making* himself think and be by *making* his antagonists think and be and by their *making* him do the same reciprocally he—and they—are *making* a novel: and to make a novel of oneself is to live, to be. "And that is how, reader, to make a novel, forever." Unamuno was a spiritual contender, his own antagonist, an *agonist*.

But, as before, he wondered, in that final question of his at the end of his novel of a novel (a book on the reading and reacting to a book found on a bookstall along the Seine by U. Jugo de la Raza), whether the greatest truth was not that everything—and we—are "nothing," or that the more profound a thing, "the emptier," wondering now anew, "And you, reader, who have come this far: are you alive?" Not just *still* alive, not *all* alive, but simply "alive?"

*   *   *

On March 26, 1927, in Hendaye, France, just before finishing this novel on how to make a novel (he finished the text proper at the end of May 1927, and the *Continuation* on June 17), Unamuno wrote an incandescent letter to Jorge Luis Borges, commenting on a recent essay by Borges on Quevedo, and ending with a litany on his own preoccupations at the time: "I keep going over and over in my mind the question of whether God will remember me always and whether these memories of God remember themselves or are aware of each other so that an eternity of eternities would be no more than a moment in time, under time, and the infinite circle its own center and the entire universe an atom, that is, 0, zero, and from these soundings and fathomings in the unfathomable mystery of *ex*isting and *in*sisting I come up sometimes with ferocious sarcasm, with a mockery fit only to hurl at the heads of my country's hangmen. . . ." And he concluded by offering Borges greetings from "your gratified reader, and—why not?—comrade and friend." The "0" in those lines is a nought, and Borges, years later, expanded this notion and, even more specifically, Unamuno's thought of "the infinite circle its own center," in his masterly history of this metaphor, "The Sphere of Pascal," dated Buenos Aires, 1951.

We have already called Unamuno an immortalist, a spiritual contender, an agonist. We might well add that he was a spiritual *conquistador*. A native Basque and a Basque-speaker, he had taken Castilian Spanish "by right of conquest," as he announced in the Spanish Parliament, and he would if he could take the kingdom of immortality by force, for "the kingdom of heaven suffereth violence, and the violent take it by force," as he tirelessly repeated, citing Matthew 11:12 as authority.

At the opposite end of the intellectual spectrum, a Viennese Jew eight years older than Unamuno, had written, in mid-career: "I am . . . not at all a man of science, not an observer, not an experimenter, not a thinker. I am by temperament nothing but a *conquistador*, an adventurer . . . with all the inquisitiveness, daring and tenacity characteristic of such a man." Thus Sigmund Freud, following the publication of *The Interpretation of Dreams* (his greatest work, he thought) in 1900. A few years later, Unamuno was to publish his dream book, *Mist*, in which all of life is seen as a dream where creators and created are such stuff as dreams are made on. Both writers were, as Freud noticed of himself, made to the measure of *conquistadores*. The *Zeitgeist* in which both contemporaries dreamed, before applied technological science and the unchallenged notion of progress blighted civilization, is elucidated by Freud's character-description, which succinctly encompasses two Europeans of utterly different bent and temper.

*　　*　　*

In summary: *Mist* (*Niebla*) was published in Madrid in 1914, again in 1928 in another edition, in still another edition in 1935, in Buenos Aires in 1939, and again in 1942; in Madrid again in the *Obras Completas* (*OC¹*) in 1951, in *Obras Completas* (*OC²*) in 1958, in the *Obras Completas* (Escelicer) in 1967. In the Austral paperback series, there had been twelve editions by 1968, issued either in Madrid or Buenos Aires. Among the translations, the Italian version was first, due to the vogue of Pirandello, and the resemblance of the earlier *Mist* to the Italian's work. The Italian translation appeared in Florence in 1922, but, surprisingly, the same year saw the appearance of a Hungarian version of *Mist* issued at Budapest: German translations appeared in Munich in 1926 and in Leipzig in 1933. A French version was issued in Paris in 1926. In 1928, there were four translations: into Dutch (Arnhem); into Polish (Warsaw); Swedish (Stockholm); and the first English version, by Warner Fite, was issued in New York. In 1929, there were translations into Rumanian (Bucharest) and a Serbo-Croatian version (Zagreb). A Latvian translation appeared (Riga) in 1935. In 1955 there was a second Italian version (Rome), by a new translator.

Abel Sánchez (*Abel Sánchez, historia de una pasión*) was published in Madrid in 1917, again in

1928, in Buenos Aires in 1940, and there was a remarkable and most helpful edition issued in New York—in Spanish, but with an Introduction in English, and a "Vocabulary" in both languages, in a most convenient "Dutch-door" arrangement at the bottom of the entire text—in 1947; this edition was the work of Ángel del Río and Amelia de del Río; much use was made of this edition by the present translator.

The first translation was put into German (Munich), 1925. There followed a translation into Dutch (Arnhem), 1927; into Czech (Prague), 1928; a second German version (Leipzig), 1933; into French (Paris), 1939; into Italian (Milan), 1953; there was a second Dutch edition, also in 1953; a new translation into Italian (Rome), 1955. The only previous translation into English was by the present translator and was issued in Chicago, 1956, under the title *Abel Sánchez and Other Stories*, with an Introduction by the translator, who here offers a more definitive version.

How to Make a Novel (*Cómo se hace una novela*) was first published, as indicated above: in France, 1926; in the Argentine, 1927; in Spain, 1950. The successive Spanish editions kept progressively restoring and printing more and more of the matter originally censored in 1950, so that by the time of the two Madrid editions of 1966 (there was even an earlier printing of OC^2 which contained the integral, original text), there was no longer any call for alarm from abroad about omitted passages: they were all, and continue to be, available in Spain in all their original and colorful (now sadly, nostalgically, dated) vituperation. The French version printed in *Avant et après la Révolution* (Paris, 1933), which contains all of Unamuno's additions to the first French edition of 1926, plus thirteen essays on various subjects, was usefully consulted in making the present version.

For some reason—perhaps some good reason—this novel of a novelist's Last End had never appeared before in English, though it was put into another foreign language before it appeared in Unamuno's Spanish. Except for the two translations into French (both by Jean Cassou: poet, art historian, Director of Paris' Musée d'Art Moderne, and Unamuno's half-Spanish intimate) there appear to have been no other versions in any other foreign languages—to date.

ANTHONY KERRIGAN

Palma de Mallorca
1974

Foreword

THE POSSIBILITY that a monologuist might also be a novelist is, in itself, a complete contradiction. But Miguel de Unamuno was nothing if not contradictory: contradictions made him what he was. And this fact is decisive. Unamuno had based his entire philosophy on the consciousness of his own being, and had concentrated all his energy on the resistance to death by the person who was himself: and so he could only truly express himself in a perpetual soliloquy. His every word, his correspondence, his entire work, all were soliloquy. The thinker and the man were fused in the vehement Don Miguel ceaselessly imposing himself on the world. How could he impose anyone else? Evoke another's persona? Live a discourse that was not his own but someone else's? Someone else's monologue? Other people's monologues? And consequently a dialogue, an exchange of dialogues? Nevertheless, Unamuno was a novelist, that is to say, a creator of characters.

The paradox is clarified if one considers his willful self-assertion, one aspect of which is his will to procreation. It is not enough merely to be oneself; the self has its own force, engenders action, moves and creates. In his will to procreation, Unamuno displays, not only his biological nature, but his peculiarly Spanish essence. For this will becomes a point of honor in the Spaniard. Spanish man takes pride in his virility, Spanish woman in motherhood. Whenever there was

talk of children in Don Miguel's presence, he would
be quick to declare, with an air of wild defiance, as
if it were a challenge, "I have eight." He was worried
by Don Quixote's being a bachelor. Of course, there
was Dulcinea . . . Dulcinea, the lady of Toboso, the
lady of Don Quixote's dream-thoughts. But he was
even more reassured by the real Dulcinea, the peasant-
maid Aldonza Lorenzo, a plump, good-looking wench,
the possible mother of any number of sturdy children. Here we touch one of the sensitive spots of the
Spanish "question." It constitutes the node of Federico
García Lorca's plays, in which all lands are barren
and all weddings bloody. And if the Spanish people
have made Saint Teresa of Avila one of their symbolic
figures, it is because she represents the Mother. And
she was celibate! There is no end to the paradox.
Along this road procreation remains desire.

Let us consider this critical, tragic, essential desire. Let us consider the mother. A mother gives birth,
and therefore every living creature must feel, in relation to her, like a child. But Unamuno balks, and
wishes to see in the mother figure the same procreative
quality he sees in himself. Spain is his mother. Good
enough. But she is also, and more exactly, his daughter. He has been created by her, but he, in his turn
has created her. He has created her daily as he has
created himself and his characters. And by creating
his characters he becomes their eternal creator and absolute master. Pirandello's characters wander through
limbo in search of an author. They are born of reality.
And they are still reeking of and throbbing with reality—a horrible reality, a truly dramatic horror—
which they claim to imitate, when they appear on
stage at rehearsals in an attempt to give flesh and
blood to the play, so at last it can be performed. But

then the really dramatic horror of the happening which they have experienced becomes a theatrically dramatic horror: it becomes the act of an author. They are the author's characters. And while they clamor for the author, they also rebel against him. The process is painful to them. Their reincarnation, their second birth, desired by them, is torture. Unamuno's characters, on the other hand, are born author's characters. They exist only through him and from the first moment, from their first appearance. They do not come from elsewhere to receive the breath of life, theatrical, novelistic life. He gives them this breath of life at the very beginning, as he brings them out of nothingness. And the only one among them who objects and seeks out the author in his study to demand justice, is made to listen to the authority of his law, which, when all is said and done, is the same authority and law to which he, the author, is subjected. What is this rebellious character demanding? The right to commit suicide? We understand that by this gesture he would prove his independence to the full. But his author cannot bring himself to accept this final demand. He will make his character die a natural death like everyone else, like—as he knows full well—himself.

Nonetheless, the character, while he exists, is master of his existence. In *Niebla*, Augusto Pérez is within his rights when he emphasizes the value of this existence. With customary penetration, Américo Castro, in a study of "Pirandellism" in Unamuno and in Cervantes ("Cervantes y Pirandello," in the book *Santa Teresa y otros ensayos*, Madrid, 1929), dwells on the second chapter of Part Two of *Don Quixote*, where the two heroes, knight and squire, are concerned with certain writings describing their adventures, which are said to be going the rounds. But how are their adventures described? With what degree of truth? Do these literary—imaginary—accounts conform to the reality of their being, the beings of Don Quixote and Sancho Panza? It is amazing that in his *Life of Don Quixote and Sancho*, Unamuno should have skimmed over this chapter so quickly and not have commented on it more fully. Of course, Unamuno's book as a whole is a commentary on that chapter; even more, Unamuno's entire *oeuvre*, particularly his novels, is a commentary on this theme.

And it is a commentary continually agitated by sharp contradictions. Why did Unamuno not pause at that passage in the *Quixote*? As we have just said, it is surely because he returns repeatedly to this precise passage throughout his book. His central theme is indeed that Don Quixote and Sancho are more real than Miguel de Cervantes, poor man. And if he does not allow his Augusto Pérez to rebel against him and shout "I want to live," and protest about his life and his right to terminate it himself by a voluntary act, that of suicide, if he does not allow this rebellion, he is, indeed, in the wrong. We must accuse him, then, of contradicting himself. His pride, and his jealous, creative despotism, cause him to be provoked at this protest, and make him condemn his character to the common fate, the common grave, to make him die when sovereign paternal authority commands it. This supreme dialogue in *Mist* achieves an overwhelming pathos precisely because it really is a dialogue. It is a dialogue between two characters as human as they could possibly be, human all-too-human, and thus liable to error and madness. Augusto Pérez admittedly, is presented to us as a most pathetic character. But Don Miguel, his creator, is no less pathetic for he defends his author's prerogative with a scornful sneer or with a tyrannical fury.

But let us concentrate on an Unamuno not yet transformed into a character in his own comedy, and playing the part of The Author. Let us think of Unamuno the author in objective reality. Unamuno who thinks according to Unamuno's philosophy, who thinks in an Unamunian way. In order to be true to himself, what must this Unamuno demand of his characters? What more than that they become in turn authors of themselves, that they create themselves, that they form themselves! A thousand obstacles block the way, the obstacles of life, of real life; other men's passions and their own. To create oneself, to author or make oneself in this world governed by all forms of domination and whim, of greed, absurdity, hate, envy—awful envy, Cainite envy—and all the ingenious, sordid combinations that society places in the way of our will to, and even more, in the way of our chance to create others, that is, to love. All these social combinations, all these artificial and self-centered strategies multiply the individual to infinity: there are countless ways of getting married and producing children, which are, equally, ways of destroying love. Society—systematic, theoretic, methodical—has established a rich repertoire of combinations. One of the most disastrous is, without a doubt, *a priori* reasoning, premeditated rationalizing, pedagogy. For human beings live and move in the realm of action, real work, real life! We live and move in the realm of the potential man, of the man who would be *nothing less than a whole man*! But do we wish to be a potential man or would we rather exhaust all the possibilities offered us by common legalistic reason, preconceived to prevent us from ever becoming that whole man?

Clearly, the world of Unamuno's dramatic characters is a dark one. In this it resembles other worlds in Spanish literature: those in which so-called realism prevails. And yet, Unamuno's world is a dramatic one. A dramatic action is played out there, and played out by characters. Its imaginary nature is affirmed from the first, altogether different from the express intention of describing reality affirmed by Balzac, Flaubert, or Pérez Galdós. But Unamuno's characters, brought forth from their creator's will and not from the reality of their time, accord with this reality during the period their author gives them to live, the time the author gives them to attempt to live and fulfill themselves. And this reality is cruel, atrocious.

But reality is always cruel and atrocious; the sight of it creates a bitter impression. To a greater or lesser extent this is the result achieved by all realistic art. But it appears that there is a greater-than-average bitterness to be found in certain examples of Spanish realism. Why? Because the author has purposely aimed at making the reader experience this bitterness. He has experienced it himself while writing the work. And the vitriol of pitiless sarcasm has infiltrated his writing from the start. We are gripped by this kind of taunting sarcasm in *La Celestina*. It permeates all the picaresque and Quevedo; it appears in certain pages of Galdós; and it sparkles in Unamuno's contemporary, Pío Baroja. And of course it is everywhere in Goya.

In the domain of cases and causes, of comic and tragic and tragicomic situations, Unamuno's imagination never runs dry. His is the imagination of the logician, the demiurgos who strips dramas down to the equation, the schema, the barest outline. Down to dialogue. But to pure dialogue, without any hint of décor or stage directions, tone of voice or facial expression, dialogue reduced to pure dialogue, dry, stripped and bare, brutal, primitive, striking. It is a dialogue in retaliation for a monologue. But in this dialogue form each of the adversaries reaches the zenith of individual self-affirmation.

Under this sign the characters lose nothing in pathos; on the contrary, they gain from this ease of representation, quick figures on a blackboard. They are presented in a situation from which varying consequences can ensue. And the author takes them out of this situation to push them into still another equally uncomfortable one. On a subsidiary plane, he invents other characters to live other cases, analogous or opposed, but just as likely to end up in ridiculous shambles, in some sorry fiasco. Is there cruelty in all this? Certainly there is, but it is cruelty combined with a strange tenderness, a father's tenderness: the tenderness of a frightfully lucid father who never laughs outright, but contains this laughter in a spasm which makes him all the fiercer. A fierce tenderness, therefore, but tenderness all the same. And is it not in the interests of love, out of love of love, which is action, work, and life, that Unamuno makes use of a farcical ferocity? This love is all the more admirable because it does not fulfill itself in effective procreation, but rather, as with the beloved, sublime *Tía Tula*, must confine itself to patterns of substitution or sublimation, and therefore evolves into a passion, a boiling point for love, and this passion reveals itself as pure will, pure spirituality. It is not possible to love on a higher plane than this, nor more intensely.

However much of a monologuist Unamuno was—
and he was an untiring, irrepressible monologuist
—let there be no mistake: the flame of love burned in
him, that is to say: he was a novelist, the author of
personae. Whence his heartfelt interest in others, his
vehement outpourings to others. These life-compan-
ions belonged to him, but they belonged less to his
creator's demiurgic empire than they pertained and
were an adjunct to the extraordinary tenderness he
showed as a man toward other men, a tenderness
which possessed him and which he communicated
totally. As potential animator of potential personae
(every friend was in the latter category), he intuited
the spark of life wherever it was to be found and the
sacred though slender chance of each one being
himself, oneself. Hence his forceful, highly emotive
use of the possessive of the first person singular in
connection with everyone for whom he cared. His way
of appropriating them was something which each one
—each of his friends, each of his personae—was
bound to accept with heartfelt consent. His appropria-
tion of them was at the same time the recognition of
their own existence, of their own free will, a hallmark
on their being alive for good or for ill—and they felt
it so with tender gratification! When he called his
friends, whoever they were, Pedro or Juan, "my Pedro, my Juan," he seemed to mean that he claimed
them—for their own good, in order to certify their
attempt to become themselves, to make their own
destiny.

* * *

Exile undermined his condition as father, his paternal role, his own claim to paternity. From his exile on,
Unamuno could no longer assume he was at home in
the universe, he could no longer say with any assur-

ance "my Universe." He was at a loss: cut off, disarmed, discountenanced. And thus he must have appeared to the curious public of Paris—more or less
aware of who he was—which received him in a city
as foreign to him as he was to it. Moreover, in that
year of 1924—when he was deported to Fuerteventura, escaped, and began his exile in France—people
were still not accustomed to the internments, banish-
ments, expulsions, emigrations which were to become
common currency of our century and make of existence, whether individual or collective, a matter of
chance. This precursor of the age's exiles was as surprising to others as he was himself surprised. I recall
an evening at the house of some friends. Everyone
gathered around Unamuno to hear that evening's
monologue: like every other evening's monologue it
was necessarily heavy-handed, maladroit, confused,
inadequate. . . . Next to me sat André Spire, observing Unamuno with an air of concerned melancholy;
at one point he whispered the half line from Victor
Hugo, first among exiles: ". . . *Oh! l'exil est impie.*"
Impious, yes, even ungodly: for it menaces everything
vital, everything personal, everything potentially active and decisive about a person, it menaces his will
to be. And therefore it affects his creative freedom, his
power to create others. Unamuno exiled could no
longer create personae; nor could he be the author of
his principal character, himself. Nor could he be
father to his daughter, Spain, for she had run away,
to languish in a tyrant's grip. His role as father was
abolished, and he was now merely a son; his daughter
Spain became his mother Spain, a wronged mother,
and he powerless to redress her wrongs. He could no
longer do anything for her nor with her. When the
Dictator's agents came to arrest Unamuno, his wife

had cried out: *"Hijo mío!"* "My son!" And with this cry from the depths of her being, the wife had become the mother. And not only the mother of the children which nature had given her but of the man she had loved, of the man she loved, the man who was her other self in day-to-day life on earth and whom she created each day just as he created her. But all creative action came to an end when he was no longer any more than a son.

As a result of this development he was constrained to face up to the fatality he shared with all men but to which he had always put up a frantic and paradoxical resistance: the inevitability of one's own disappearance. All of Unamuno's will to engender, all the originality of his thought, all his genius consisted in his admitting the inevitable and—battling against it. He had lived in struggle—agony—with this tragic sense of life.

To be a son, a child, to be a creature and not a creator, a creature who is nothing but a creature and who exists only to die, might have its own charm, a terrible melancholic but powerful enough charm. When he had had enough of Paris life, Don Miguel established himself in exile at Hendaye, at the very farthest reach of the French *pays basque* where it borders his own Spanish Basque country. From there, his senses strained to catch the sights and sounds across the frontier. He could clearly hear the bells of Fuenterrabía. His thoughts turned toward death. He began the first poem of his *Romancero del destierro*

If I should die here, in this green land . . .

From that time, he accepted death, the only act by which he could still express his connection with something alive—the memory of his origins, of his mother. In the poems he wrote as well as in those he read— and they were one and the same thing for a man who could do only by un-doing, create only by un-creating —he habitually underlined those passages which spoke of denuding oneself and of a return, a going back to primitive sleep, to the original nucleus, to the peace which is both beginning and end, to the mother and all that pertains to the mother: cradle, lap, womb. Whenever he read a poem aloud, whether one of his own or someone else's, he would underline this type of passage with a peculiar and particular gesture: he would cup his hand and open it out at the same time to indicate both receiving and gathering, a grace-ful gesture of pious solicitude; at the same time his voice would become more mellow and yet more somber.

In this retrospective state he wrote the novel which must inevitably be considered (a few later novellas are another matter) to be his last novel, a novelist's last novel. This novelist is his last character: the au-thor becomes his own final persona, namely, Don Miguel the author who has no further role to play, no other destiny to fulfill but the role and destiny of the man who must die. No longer his own father, he is his own son, and as such he begins to fade, to dimin-ish, to shrink. He becomes a *peau de chagrin*, a body of vexations, a chagrined spirit, a shrunken skin.

The idea for the book came to him one gloomy day during his exile in Paris. The Spanish title, *Cómo se hace una novela*, I changed in my French translation to *Comment on fait un roman*, his "How a Novel Is Made" into "How One Makes a Novel." I could have just as well called it *"Comment se fait un roman,"* but the Spanish reflexive is equivalent also to the French "*on*," which suggests a particular, individual, personal decision amidst the universal anonymity. The French "*on*" is everyone, and so in consequence is someone, Latin *unus*. Inasmuch as the key word is "Make," Unamuno would not have been adverse to the suggestion that the making of the novel was the work of someone, that the verb involved a subject. Still, the neuter, passive nuance suggested by the fact of the novel's "being made" is paradoxically and equally Unamunian. At this stage of his life as author, the last state of the deprivation of his creative powers, it was no longer he who wrote the novel, the novel of a novel, but rather it was the Novel itself which told How It Made Itself. And, How did It Make Itself? It Made Itself in the measure that the author, reduced to ghostliness, achieved annihilation.

At that time, when Don Miguel told me of his plans for the pathetic work, he did so with an air of imparting an appalling confidence; it was a note he struck often enough even when gossiping; on this occasion, however, such a panic-stricken air seemed more pointed and pertinent than usual. For in conceiving this story—whose point and finality was that of his own history, his own story—Miguel de Unamuno arrived at the terminal point of his own philosophy, the philosophy he had formed, lived, experienced, tested; he arrived at the end point of his thought as an existential thinker. Here we had a man who refused to accept death; we beheld, all of us, the spectacle of a man who all his life battled against death and, in the death struggle, the agony, with his tragic sense of life, was implacably bent on keeping his sense of immortality intact to the end, to the breaking point where the will despairs. But in his final period, caught in the wilderness of exile, in its disarray, it is no longer a matter of positive, creative struggle—but the reverse. It is this reverse that we must unavoidably take into account. In the measure that the story develops, in proportion to the effort expended by the author in relating it, the storyteller grows dim, exhausted, is diminished. In the end, soon enough, he will be annihilated.

If we accept my suggestion that all of Unamuno's later characters—for example, San Manuel Bueno— are supplementary, repetitive creations of an ever-flowing talent, or are mere episodic exceptions, we must then accept that the central character of *How to Make a Novel* is Unamuno's last creation. For Unamuno, creator of characters, himself identified with this last character to the point of dying whenever he dies. So that we should consider San Manuel Bueno a posthumous character. And Unamuno traced—or rather followed—the decline and fall of his last character until he himself was to all appearances breathing his last. Of course we must remember that his character was formed in the barrenness of exile, when he had lost, given up, his own fruitful paternity and become no more than a son. He was quite aware of all these circumstances, or his genius was aware of them, for he named this last character U. Jugo de la Raza, a name which begins with the initial *U* of Unamuno and goes on to combine the surnames of his maternal grandfather and paternal grandmother. Thus he reestablishes the maternal lineage, the side of the mothers. The play of words on *la Raza* (the race) whereby he deforms the equally Basque surname Larraza, only serves to stress his decline—accepted if not contrived—back to the merely filial condition. He is reduced to being the essence of the race; he becomes the source, the sensual marrow, the blood and seminal juice which can produce no more, a descendant who is no more than descent, pure descent, arrested in its flow, stanched.

The creator of characters, having died in the person of the character christened U. Jugo de la Raza, all that remained of Unamuno was the man of action. But in the given circumstances he had already been deprived of any and all means of action. His own history became that of a historical character, but at a time when there was no longer any history. Since Spain was no longer his daughter, he no longer had any influence over her, any hold on her. Spain was now only his mother, ill-treated, abused, dishonored, dispossessed, a docile captive. There was little hope that things might change. The only possible attitude for a historical personage without a history—Unamuno's fate—was one of protest.

He had taken up residence in a modest family pension, at 2, rue Lapérouse, in the Étoile quarter. I would visit him there, one of the regulars at his discussions, on his walks. I translated his writings: he would read me the pages as they came to life and I returned them to him translated, and he would give me what followed. In this way *The Agony of Christianity* and *How to Make a Novel* were written and translated, to be published in French before they were published in Spanish. The translation of the latter appeared in the *Mercure de France* dated 15 May 1926, with my study of the author titled *Portrait d'Unamuno*. I think about it today, since, as I have just shown, this work theoretically closed the cycle of novels, and its hero was the final, supreme character of the author. I intuitively expected that, all the same, there was still another possible character, but this time truly the final one: Unamuno himself. He himself, no longer incarnate in this twilight character, but he himself alive, real, not just the creator of characters but the creator of his whole work. Miguel de Unamuno, in flesh and blood, in short, a man, who can be portrayed. As it turned out, I had the right idea in including in the publication of *How a Novel Is Made* a *portrait* of the author. And in so doing, was I not following the spirit of Unamuno, according to which ideas, and moreover, all things, only have meaning and value when made man? You may analyze the *Critique of Pure Reason* and the whole Kantian system, but the efficacious and authentic effort lies in arriving at the same explanatory light by making the system live in "Kant the man." Somewhere I have spoken of this continual *anthropomorphization* which is Unamuno's philosophy. Nearly half a century later, I confirm that explaining Unamuno by portraying him was to conform to his obstinately humanistic philosophy. It would have been useless for me to bring the work of this foreign writer to the notice of the French public, who had only a very vague notion of him, by merely supplying them with a list of his books and a résumé of his philosophy. It would have been a useless undertaking to speak of this philosophy as philosophers would have spoken, to speak of these numerous novels, plays, essays, and poems as literary critics would. It would have been simply more *pedagogy*. But there was a possibility, a necessity even, and that was to give it the form of a descriptive portrait. I had to *portray* this philosophy, this literary creation, these novels. Or more exactly, I had to gather all this into a portrait which could be rightfully entitled, as I had entitled it, Unamuno.

And by so doing, I had stirred Unamuno to the quick. Since it was indeed his business to understand that henceforth only *he* remained.

After the disappearance of U. Jugo de la Raza in

the final pages of his prophetic novel, the central question could only be Unamuno himself, the creator of this last, imaginary character and of so many imaginary things, and figurehead of the whole vast output of the man. These works are only perceptible and real in the light of this figurehead. So my *Portrait of Unamuno* moved this impassioned man to comment on and argue about everything, as was the nature of his personal demon. He therefore wrote a reply to my *Portrait* and both our texts were published in the Spanish edition of *Cómo se hace una novela* which was, moreover adorned, enriched, spiced with many other observations.

Thus in his little Paris hotel room I would see him dying away from himself while he continued to dream of an impossible political future for his people, while he engaged in polemics, while he despaired. The perpetual soliloquy was continued without any imaginary, possible reply, or any surprising change. Then came the great chain of surprises: the fall of the dictatorship, the triumphal return of Unamuno to his liberated Spain, and later the fall of the monarchy and the establishment of the Republic. Other events followed, the last one being the height of tragic horror. History had become threadbare, then destroyed, not by wear and tear, but by a catastrophe. Miguel de Unamuno, historical character, and in this capacity, one of the most magnificent *personalizations* in Spanish history, was effaced by the Spanish Civil War, and thereupon disappeared into his abyss.

JEAN CASSOU

Paris
1970
1971

Mist

Prologue

DON MIGUEL DE UNAMUNO INSISTS on my contributing a prologue to this book of his, in which he recounts the lamentable life and mysterious death of my good friend Augusto Pérez. Since the wishes of Señor Unamuno are for me commands, in the full sense of the word, I can do no less than write it. For, though I have not succumbed to the Hamlet-like skepticism reached by my poor friend Pérez, who went so far as to doubt of his own existence, I am firmly persuaded that I lack what psychologists call free will. I am somewhat consoled by the thought that Don Miguel possesses no more free will than I do.

It will doubtless strike some readers as strange that I, a complete unknown even in the republic of Spanish letters, should be the one to prologue a book by Don Miguel, who is more advantageously known than I. A prologue customarily serves for a better-known writer to introduce a lesser-known one. But Don Miguel and I have decided to reverse this pernicious custom, inverting the terms so that the unknown should introduce the known. Books are bought, we assume, for the main body of the text rather than for the prologue, so that it is only natural that a young beginner like myself, wishing to make himself known, should ask a veteran man of letters, not for a prologue by way of presentation, but for the opportunity to prologue one of the master's works. This practice would at the same time solve one of the problems in the eternal dispute between the young and the old.

I am linked to Don Miguel de Unamuno by more than one tie. First of all, in this novel or *nivola* (and it should be made clear that it was I who invented this word) he quotes from the many conversations between myself and the ill-fated Augusto Pérez; he recounts the story of my son Victorcito's late birth; finally, it appears that I am distantly related to Don Miguel, my surname being the same as that of one of his ancestors, at least according to the very learned genealogical investigations of my friend Antolín S. Paparrigópulos, a famous man in the world of learning.

I am not at all certain what kind of reception Don Miguel's reading public will give this *nivola*, or what attitude they will take toward Don Miguel. For some time now I have been attentively following Don Miguel's campaign against public gullibility, and I have been astounded to learn how profound and candid that gullibility is. Following the appearance of a series of newspaper articles recently, Don Miguel received a number of letters as well as press clippings which confirmed the presence of a rich vein of ingenuousness and dovelike simplicity of mind still to be found among the public. Some people were shocked that our Don Miguel had said that Señor Cervantes (that other Don Miguel) was not entirely devoid of genius: they took it as a needless irreverence. Others were overcome by his melancholy musings on the falling leaves of autumn. Still others are stirred by his cry, "War against war!", a cry wrung from Don Miguel by the painful sight of seeing men die without being killed. Some of the provincial papers reprinted —because they recognized them as their own—that bag of un-paradoxical truisms which Don Miguel had collected from cafés, clubs, and gatherings, where they had gone bad from so much handling and which reeked of surrounding vulgarity. There were even guileless doves who were indignant because Don Miguel, the *logomachist*, sometimes spells Kulture— with a capital *K*—and then admits that, although he can claim some skill in the fortunate use of words, he is unable to make puns. For puns are the essence of artistic expression as conceived by the public, always ingenuous as to genius.

It is just as well that the ingenuous public seems not to have noticed some of the other peculiar practices indulged in by Don Miguel. For instance, his use of italics, when in some of his articles he underlines certain words chosen entirely at random, turning the manuscript pages upside down to make sure he does not see which words they are. When I asked him once why he did this, he answered, "How do I know? From sheer good humor! To cut a caper! Besides, underlined or italicized words annoy me, put me out of humor altogether. They're an insult to the reader. It's a way of calling him stupid, of saying 'Look here, my good man, pay attention: this means something!' I once advised a man to have all his articles set in italics, so that the public would know that he meant every word he said, from first to last. It's all a matter of pantomime in the field of writing: substituting gestures for what should be clear from intonation and emphasis. Look at how the ultra-right journals here overindulge in italics, small and large capitals, exclamation marks, every known typographical resource. All pantomime! Their means of expression is simple-minded, or rather, their view of the gullibility of their readers is simple-minded. And the point is that we must put an end to this gullibility."

I have sometimes heard Don Miguel maintain that humor, as it is generally known, true humor, has never taken root in Spain, nor will it easily do so in the foreseeable future. Those who are known here as humorists are either satirists or ironists, when they are not mere jesters. To call our Taboada a humorist, for example, is to misuse the word. And there is nothing less humorous than the harsh, even if transparently obvious, satire of Quevedo, in which the moral of the sermon is always apparent. "The only real humorist we have had in Spain is Cervantes," Don Miguel said once. "And if he were to raise his head again, how could he help but laugh at all those who became indignant when I suggested he was ingenious, and how could he help laughing at all those ingenuous simpletons who have taken some of his most subtle spoofing seriously? For it is clear enough that it was part of his burlesque of the books of chivalry—very serious burlesque—to parody their style; and that the passage 'Hardly had the rubicund Phoebus . . . ,' which some ingenuous Cervantists offer as a model of style, is nothing more than a genial caricature of literary Baroque. There is scarcely any point in speaking of the fashion of considering as idiomatic a passage like the one with which Cervantes starts a chapter, following one ending with the word 'hour,' where he begins: 'It must have been that of the dawn. . . .' "

Our public, like any public of little culture, is naturally wary, just as our people as a whole are wary. Everyone is on guard against letting anyone else take advantage of him, make a fool of him, put something over on him, "take" him in any way. In consequence, whenever anyone opens his mouth, everyone else wants to know, from the first instant, what he is up to, what he is getting at, and whether he is in earnest or is jesting. I doubt if the people of any other nation are so thoroughly upset as ours by any mixture of jest and earnest, of parody and truth. And what Spaniard can countenance any doubt as to whether or not something or somebody is serious? It is very difficult for the average suspicious Spaniard to understand that a thing may be said in jest and in earnest at the same time, as a joke and yet seriously, and both from the same point of view.

Don Miguel is fascinated with the idea of the *buffo*-tragic, and more than once he has told me he would not like to die without having written a tragic *buffo*-nade or a *buffo*-tragedy, a tragic farce or a farcical tragedy, not one in which the farcical or grotesque elements are mixed with the tragic, but one in which these elements are fused—and confused—into one. And when I observed that all this represented the most unbridled romanticism, he answered:

"I don't deny it. But putting names to things doesn't lead anywhere. In the twenty years I have spent teaching the classics I have never entertained the idea of a classicism as opposed to romanticism. Hellenism, they say, is a matter of distinguishing, of defining, of separating. Well then, my role is to un-define, to confound."

And the background for this attitude is the concept, or more than a concept, a sense of life which, however, I dare not label pessimistic, knowing as I do how Don Miguel loathes that adjective. His *idée fixe*—and on this point he is a monomaniac—is that if his own soul is not immortal, if the souls of all other men and even of all other things are not immortal, and immortal in the sense meant by the ingenuous Catholics of the Middle Ages, then nothing is worthwhile, nothing is worth the slightest effort. From the same source we have Leopardi's doctrine of tedium, following the demise of his most extreme deception,

Ch'eterno io mi credei

the illusion of thinking himself eternal. It is only natural that three of Don Miguel's favorite authors should be Sénancour, Quental, and Leopardi.

His rough and ready, his confounding humor not only wounds the sensibilities of all those who want to know from the first what the other person is getting at, but it also upsets countless others. People want to laugh, but to laugh as an aid to digestion and to counter their troubles; certainly not to provoke their vomiting up what they should never have swallowed and what could give them indigestion. And they have no real desire to digest their affliction. Don Miguel insists that if the point is to make people laugh, it should not be a matter of helping them to contract their diaphragms for easier digestion, but rather to provoke their vomiting up whatever they have gobbled down. The meaning of life and of the universe can be more clearly seen on an empty stomach—without sweetmeats or banquets. And he will not admit of any sweet-tempered irony or discreet humor, of any irony without bitterness or any humor without gall. He says that without gall there is no irony and without indiscretion no humor, or as he prefers to call it, no illhumorism.

The task he reserves for himself boils down to the disagreeable and thankless job of masseur, for he envisages himself giving the ingenuous public a rubdown, in an attempt to make it gradually and collectively more agile and subtle. He becomes furious when he hears it said that Spaniards, especially Southerners, are genial in either sense of the word. "Any people which is diverted by the bullfight and which finds variety and rewarding complexity in such a primitive spectacle betrays its own mentality," he claims. And he goes on to add that it would be difficult to find a more simple-minded, callous, or horny mentality than that of your *aficionado*. "Just try out some more or less humorous paradoxes on someone who has just been carried away by the sword-work of *Maestro* Vicente Pastor!" And he cannot stand the festival mannerisms of bullfight critics, those high-priests of word-games and kitchen-wit.

Now if we add to this approach his delight in playing with metaphysical conceits, we can understand why there are so many people who refuse to read him, some because he gives them a headache and others because they are mesmerized by the rule *sancta sancte tractanda sunt*, sacred matters should be treated sacredly, and thus they look askance at anyone taking liberties in certain areas. For his part he does not suffer such objections from the spiritual descendants of men who made mock of the most sacred matters in their own time, that is, of the most sacred beliefs and hopes of their brothers. If men have mocked God, why may we not mock Reason, Science, and even Truth? If men have uprooted our dearest and innermost vital hope, why not go the whole hog and confound ourselves just to kill time, to kill eternity, or just to get even?

It would be easy enough for someone to say that this book contains off-color, even pornographic passages. Don Miguel has asked me to say something on this head. He denies that any crudities to be found here are meant to pander to fleshly appetites, or that they have any other purpose than to serve as an imaginative point of departure for higher considerations.

His repugnance for all forms of pornography is well enough known. He is against it not only because of received moral conventions, but also because he considers erotic preoccupation a terrible drain, the most vitiating, on the intelligence. In short, writers of pornography, and even merely erotic writers, strike him as the least intelligent of men, unimaginative idiots in fact. I have heard him declare that of the three classic vices of wine, women, and gambling, the last two weaken the mind more than any wine: and it is well known that Don Miguel drinks nothing but water. "One can talk to a drunken man," he once told me; "he even says interesting things. But who can stand the conversation of a gambler or a ladykiller? The only thing worse is to talk bulls to an *aficionado*, the height of Spanish stupidity."

For my part I am not at all surprised at the evident relationship between the erotic and the metaphysical. I remember rightly enough that our European peoples began by being, as their literatures show, warriors and saints, developing later into eroticists and metaphysicians. The cult of the woman coincided with the cult of conceptual subtleties. In the spiritual dawn of our European peoples, in the Middle Ages, in short, barbarian society possessed a sense of religious, even mystic, exaltation alongside and accompanying a martial exaltation: the sword's hilt is a cross. But woman occupied a much smaller and very secondary place in that society's imagination. Concurrently, philosophical ideas as such, enveloped in theology, slumbered on in the cloisters. Eroticism and metaphysics developed together. Religion is martial, warlike. Metaphysics is erotic and voluptuous.

The religious instinct is what makes man bellicose,

combative, or perhaps it is belligerence which makes him religious. On the other hand, the metaphysical instinct, curiosity to know what is none of our business—original sin, in short—is what makes man sensual; or perhaps sensuality is what arouses, as it did in Eve, the metaphysical instinct, a longing to apprehend the knowledge of good and evil. Beyond lies mysticism, a religious metaphysics born of the sensuality of bellicosity.

This truth was well known to Theodota, the Athenian courtesan of whom Xenophon speaks in the *Memorabilia.* He records her conversation with Socrates, who enchanted her with his method of investigation, or rather of midwifery, his style of delivery at the birth of truth, and to him she proposed he become her procurer in the search for "friends": that he become her fellow-hunter, her *synthérates*, as the text puts it, according to Don Miguel, the professor of Greek, to whom I owe this highly colorful and revealing information. And all through that most interesting conversation between Theodota, the courtesan, and Socrates, the philosopher-midwife or maieutical philosopher, we clearly discern the intimate relation between the two professions: we see how philosophy in great good part is pandering and pandering is philosophy.

And if I have got it all wrong, it cannot be denied that the analogy is ingenious—and that's good enough.

I am not unaware, of course, that my beloved master Don Fulgencio Entrambosmares del Aquilón (whom Don Miguel enshrined in his *nivola* or novel *Amor y Pedagogía*) is not likely to concur on this distinction between religion and bellicosity on the one side and philosophy and eroticism on the other. I presume that the illustrious author of the *Ars magna combinatoria* will establish the bases for the following possibilities: a warlike religion and an erotic religion, a warlike metaphysics and an erotic metaphysics, a religious eroticism and a metaphysical eroticism, a metaphysical bellicosity and a religious bellicosity; in addition, there could be a metaphysical religion and a religious metaphysics, a bellicose eroticism and an erotic bellicosity; and even further, a religious religion, a metaphysical metaphysics, an erotic eroticism and a bellicose bellicosity. It all adds up to sixteen binary combinations, without counting the combinations of three, such as, for example, a metaphysico-erotic religion or a bellico-religious metaphysics. But I will not go on, for I possess neither the inexhaustible genius for combinations of a Don Fulgencio, nor the confusionist and indefinitionist passion of a Don Miguel.

There is much I would like to say concerning the unexpected end of the present narrative and the version therein given by Don Miguel of the death of my unfortunate friend Augusto—a version I consider erroneous. But it would scarce be proper to quarrel in a prologue with the subject of that prologue. Still, in duty to my conscience, I should record that I am utterly convinced that Augusto Pérez, in the course of acting out his proposal of suicide as outlined in our last interview, actually did commit suicide, in the flesh and not merely in idea. I believe that the proofs in my possession are authentic and support my opinion; they are such and so many that my opinion turns, in fact, into certainty.

With that, I conclude.

VÍCTOR GOTI

Post-Prologue

I WOULD BE more than willing to question some of the assertions made by Víctor Goti, my prologuist, but, since I am in on the secret of his—Goti's—existence, I had best assign him all the responsibility for what he says in his Prologue. Besides, since it was I who called on him to write it, undertaking in advance —that is, *a priori*—to accept whatever he said and in whatever form he said it, I cannot off-handedly now—*a posteriori*—reject it or even revise it. But neither need I let certain views of his stand without adding my own.

I am not sure of the legitimacy of publishing statements made in the confidence of friendship or of publicly revealing opinions not meant for the public, and in his Prologue, Goti has committed the indiscretion of making known certain judgments of mine which were not meant to be bruited about; in any case I never expected to see them publicly stated in the same rough and ready language I used in private.

Then, he claims that the "unfortunate" (yet why "unfortunate"? Well, all right, let us assume he was unfortunate), that the unfortunate, or whatever he was, Augusto Pérez committed suicide and did not die in the way I say he did, that is, in accord with my most utterly free will and decision. Such a claim only makes me laugh. There are opinions, of course, which are only good for a laugh. My friend and prologuist Goti would do well to tread softly when it comes to

questioning my decisions, because if he makes a nuisance of himself I will do with him what I did with
his friend Pérez: I'll let him die, or I'll kill him, just
like a doctor. Every reader knows that doctors are
caught in a dilemma: either they let the patient die
from fear of killing him, or they kill him from fear
of his dying on them. And I, too, am capable of killing
Goti if I could see he is going to die on me, or of letting him die if I should fear that I might have to kill
him.

I do not wish to prolong this post-prologue, now
that it has served me well enough to vouch for, as well
as point out the alternatives to, my friend Víctor Goti,
whose work I appreciate.

M. de U.

Prologue to the Third Edition

THE FIRST EDITION of this work of mine—mine alone?—appeared in 1914 under the imprint of *Biblioteca "Renacimiento,"* an entity since fallen victim to swindlers and their swindling. There was a second edition, apparently, in 1928, but I know of it only through bibliographical reference; I have never seen it, which is not so strange, for it was issued during the years of the Praetorian Dictatorship and I was in exile in Hendaye, avoiding even indirect support. When in 1914 I was thrown out—or rather de-caged—from my first rectorship of the University of Salamanca, I took up a new life, coincident with the outbreak of the World War which shook our country, even though Spain was non-belligerent. The War divided us into Germanophiles and anti-Germanophiles (Allied-ophiles, if you wish), along lines dictated more by our national temperaments than by the War's assumptions. This development set the course of our subsequent history up until the hypothetical revolution of 1931: the suicide of the Bourbon monarchy. At that juncture I felt trapped in the historic mist of our Spain, of our Europe, even of our human universe.

Now that I am offered the opportunity, in 1935, to reissue my *Mist*, I have reread it and, in rereading it, have redone it within myself, I have remade it: I mean, I have relived it. For the past does live: remembrance revives, it relives and remakes itself. It is a new work for me, as it will be, no doubt, for those readers who once read it and now reread it. Let them reread me in rereading my book. For one brief moment I thought to redo it, renovate it. But then it would have been another book. An *other*?

The "Other" plagues me! That Augusto Pérez of mine appeared to me in dreams twenty-one years ago (I was then fifty) after I had put an end to him, I thought, once and for all, and just as I was dreaming —repentant for having done away with him—of reviving him, and he asked me if I believed it possible to resurrect Don Quixote. I answered: "Impossible!" And he said: "Well, the rest of us creatures of fiction are in the same state." I asked: "But supposing I were to dream you again." He answered: "No one dreams the same dream twice. Whoever it is that you dream again, it will not be me you dream, whatever you think. It will be someone else, an Other." An Other? How this Other, an Other, has persecuted me and continues to persecute me! I found myself forced to write a tragedy called *The Other*. And as regards the question of resuscitating or resurrecting Don Quixote, I believe I did resuscitate Cervantes' Don Quixote— and so does everyone who contemplates and listens to him. I don't mean the scholars, of course, or the Cervantists. The hero is resurrected in the way that Christians resurrect Christ by following Paul of Tarsus. Thus history, or legend. And there is no other resurrection.

Creatures of fiction? Creatures of reality? Of the reality of fiction, which is a fiction of reality. One day I unexpectedly came upon my son Pepe, a child at the time, drawing a doll and muttering, "I'm flesh and blood! I'm flesh and blood, not paint!" And he had written the words down, under the doll. The scene

brought me back to my own childhood and I was remade myself. I saw, as if through the keyhole of a
door I couldn't open, myself as a child. I was almost
frightened by the reaction to what was in the nature
of a spiritual apparition. And then, not long ago, my
grandchild Miguelín asked me if Felix the Cat in the
children's tales was flesh and blood: if he were alive,
he meant. When I hinted, insinuated, that he was
pure story, storybook—dream or falsehood—he said:
"But a flesh and blood dream?" Here we have an entire metaphysics. Or meta-history.

I also considered amplifying the biography of my
Augusto Pérez, continuing the narrative of his life in
the other world, the other life. But the other world and
the other life are in this world and this life. All there
is, all that exists is the biography and the universal
history of somebody, some player or character whoever, and that specific character can be what we call
historic or literary or fictional. For a while I thought
to have my Augusto write his autobiography, where
he could correct my version of him and tell how he
dreamed himself. In that way I might have been able
to bring this story to two different conclusions—to be
printed in two columns, perhaps—so that the reader
could choose between them. But no reader would be
likely to accept this alternative, no one would tolerate
being pulled out of his own dream and plunged into
the dream of the dream, into the terrifying consciousness of consciousness—which is agonizing anguish.
No one wants his illusion of reality taken from him.
There is a story told of how a rural preacher once
spoke of Christ's Passion with such feeling that some
countrywomen were soon weeping loudly, whereupon
he exclaimed: "Stop your crying. All this took place
nearly twenty centuries ago. Besides, it may not have

happened in the way I've told you at all. . . ." And there are times when we might say: "Perhaps not at all. . . . Perhaps it didn't happen at all. . . ."

And I recall hearing a story of an archeological architect who planned to bring down a tenth-century basilica and, rather than restore it to what it had been, rebuild it from scratch—in accordance with how it should have been built and *not* how it actually was built. He would base himself, he said, on a plan he claimed to have found, a tenth-century architect's project. What kind of a plan was that? He seemed not to know that basilicas evolved by themselves, going beyond all the plans, forcing the hand of the builders. Much the same happens even with a novel, or with an epic poem or a drama: a plan is drawn up, and then the novel, or the epic poem, or the drama imposes itself, imposes its own laws upon the presumed authors, and takes over. Or, the agonists, the author's supposed creatures, impose themselves, take over. Thus did Lucifer and Satan, first, and then Adam and Eve, impose themselves upon Jehovah. And there you have, if not a proper novel, a *nivola*—or for that matter *opic* poetry or *opopoeia*, *an opic*, then, or a *trigedy*! For what Augusto Pérez had done to me was just that: impose himself upon me. But when it appeared, this obvious *trigedy* was seen for what it was only by my friend the Catalán critic Alejandro Plana. The rest of the critical pack wearily harried the notion of a *nivola*, that diabolic invention of mine.

The bright idea of calling it a *nivola*—not my bright idea, strictly speaking, but one which occurred in the manner recounted by me in the text of this book —was simply one more ingenuous piece of cunning designed to unnerve the critics. The book is a novel like any other novel which is a novel. That is, let it

be called or named such, since in this context to be is
to be named or called. For, what is all that talk about
the era of the novel having come and gone? Or of epic
poems if it comes to that? As long as novels out of the
past still live, the novel lives and will live and relive.
History is to redream history.

Before I set myself to dream Augusto Pérez and
his *nivola*, I had re-dreamed the Carlist War, of which
I was in some small way a witness during my childhood: I wrote my *Peace in War*, a historical novel, or
rather a novelized history, in accordance with the academic precepts of the genre, which is called realism.
I re-lived, at thirty, in writing this novel, what I had
lived at ten. I still re-live it in living present-day,
passing, ephemeral history: passing and remaining
history. Next, I dreamt my *Love and Pedagogy*
(which appeared in 1902), another tormenting tragedy. At least it tormented me. I thought that by writing it I would free myself of the torment and transfer
it to the reader. (And now, even in the present book,
there re-appears that tragicomic and nebulous *nivo-
lesque* Don Avito Carrascal who tells Augusto that
one learns to live only by living—just as one learns
to dream by dreaming.) Then came (in 1905) *The
Life of Don Quixote and Sancho, According to Miguel de Cervantes Saavedra, Explained and Expounded*. But not just explained and expounded, but re-
dreamt, relived, remade. And what if my Don Quixote
and my Sancho are not those of Cervantes? What of
that? The Don Quixotes and Sanchos who live in
eternity—which lies within time and not outside it,
all of eternity in all time and all of it in each moment
of time—do not belong exclusively to Cervantes nor
are they mine nor do they belong to any one dreamer
who dreams them, but they live and re-live as they

are dreamed by each dreamer. For my part I do believe that Don Quixote revealed to me intimate secrets
of his own which he did not reveal to Cervantes, especially regarding his love for Aldonza Lorenzo. And
then in 1913, before this *Mist* of mine, came *The
Mirror of Death*, a collection of short novels gathered
under the title of one of them. After *Mist* was issued,
Abel Sánchez was published in 1917: it was the most
painful experiment I ever carried out, for I plunged
my scalpel into the most terrible communal tumor of
our Spanish race. In 1921, *Aunt Tula* appeared, and
it was taken up by the Freudian circles of *Mitteleu-
ropa*, thanks to translations into German, Dutch and
Swedish. In 1927, there was issued, in Buenos Aires,
my autobiographical *How to Make a Novel*, a novel
itself; the excellent critic Eduardo Gómez de Baquero,
Andrenio by pseudonym, sharp and all as he was, fell
into the same kind of trap that surrounded the word
nivola and announced he hoped I would write a novel
on how a novel is made. Finally, in 1933, my *Saint
Manuel Bueno, Martyr, and Three Other Stories* was
published. Each title was a chapter in the same nebulous dream, a pursuit through the mist.

As of this date, early 1935, books of mine have
been translated, not at my instance ever, into fourteen
languages (that I know of): German, French, Italian,
English, Dutch, Swedish, Danish, Russian, Polish,
Czech, Hungarian, Rumanian, Serbian, and Latvian.
Of all the books rendered into foreign languages, the
most translated has been the present book, *Mist*. The
versions in other languages began in 1921, seven
years after the book's birth, with an Italian version:
Nebbia, romanzo, translated by Gilberto Beccari, with
a Preface by Ezio Levi. Then in 1922, into Hungarian: *Köd*, translated by Garády Viktor (Buda-

pest). In 1926 into French: *Brouillard*, in a series issued by *La Revue Européenne*, and in a version by Noémi Larthe. In 1927 into German: *Nebel, ein phantastischer Roman*, by Otto Buck (München). In 1928, there were three translations. Into Swedish: *Dimma*, by Allan Vought. Into English: *Mist, a Tragicomic Novel*, by Warner Fite (New York). And into Polish: *Mgła* (the l here traversed by an oblique line), by Dr. Edward Boyé (Warsaw). In 1929, into Rumanian: *Negura*, by L. Sebastian (Bucharest). In the same year, into Serbian: *Magla*, by Bogdan Raditsa (Zagreb). Finally, in 1935 into Latvian: *Migla*, by Konstantins Raudive (Riga). Ten translations in all, two more than the translations of my *Three Exemplary Novels and a Prologue*, which included *Nothing Less Than a Whole Man*.

Why, then, this predilection for *Mist*? Why has it "taken" in foreign places before other books of mine, this volume which the German translator Otto Buck called "a Fantastic Novel" and which the North American Warner Fite subtitled "A Tragicomic Novel"? Precisely because of the fantastic and the tragicomic. Early on, I guessed it would be thus, and said so. I wrote that this book I called a *nivola* would become my most universalized work: not my *Tragic Sense of Life* (in six foreign languages as of this date), because that book requires a certain philosophical and theological knowledge, less widespread than is commonly supposed. Given this fact, I was frankly surprised by that particular book's success in Spain, and still am.

And it could never have been my *Life of Don Quixote and Sancho* (three translations to date), for the simple reason that the original book by Cervantes is not as well known, is less popular, outside Spain—

and even within Spain—than our national literati suppose. And I would go so far as to say that works like that commentary of mine on Don Quixote contributes to making *Don Quixote* itself more and better known. In short, no other work of mine has proved of more universal interest than *Mist*. Is it because of its national character? My *Peace in War* has been translated only into German and Czech. The fact must be that the fantastic and tragicomic elements of my *Mist* are precisely those which speak and say something to the individual man who is the universal man, to the man above—and at the same time below—all classes, castes, social position, his being rich or poor, noble or plebeian, bourgeois or proletarian. All of which is a truism known to historians of culture, to the so-called learned community.

I suspect, I am afraid, that most of this Prologue, or Meta-logue, which some readers might well call an auto-criticism, has been suggested to me by Don (he deserves that title by now) Antolín Sánchez Paparrigópulos, who appeared to me all in one piece from out of the mist. He had already appeared in Chapter XXIII of the present work; but I was unable, as I dreamt and worked with him, to apply the exacting technique employed by the unforgettable and profound investigator himself. Ah, if only I had been able, following his own precepts, to undertake a history of writers who had thought to write but never did! It is to this caste, this breed, that our best readers belong: they are our collaborators and co-authors, or rather, our co-creators. They are the ones who, on reading a story, a narrative history, a *nivola* if you will, exclaim: "But I thought of this before! And I imagined it just this way! Why I've even known someone like this character here! I've had the exact same idea too! The same thoughts, everything!" How different these people are from those gross vulgarians, those abject slaves to reality, what they call reality, "true reality"! How different from those fools who think they are so lively, so awake, totally ignoring the fact that the only truly awake person is the one who knows he is dreaming—just as the only truly sane man is the one who knows he is mad. For: "Whoever does not confuse is confused." And whoever does not confound gets confounded, as Víctor Goti, my relative, said to Augusto Pérez.

This world of mine, this world of Pedro Antonio and Josefa Ignacia, of Don Avito Carrascal and Marina, of Augusto Pérez, Eugenia Domingo and Rosarito, of Alejandro Gómez, "nothing less than a whole man," and Julia, of Joaquín Monegro, Abel Sánchez, and Elena, of Aunt Tula, her sister, and her brother-in-law and nephews and nieces, of Saint Manuel Bueno and Angela—the angel—Carballino, and of Don Sandalio, and of Emeterio Alfonso and Celedonio Ibáñez, and of Ricardo and Liduvina, this world, all of it, is more real to me than the world of leaders and politicians like Cánovas, and Sagasta, and Primo de Rivera, and kings like Alfonso XIII, and the writers Galdós and Pereda and Menéndez Pelayo, and all the others I know and have known alive, and even though I have had dealings with some of them and with others still do. And it is in the world of the former, of the first-named that I will fulfill myself, be fulfilled and real-ized, if I am to fulfill and realize myself, in that world more than in the world of the second list, the list of public names.

And then as supporting fundament for these two differing worlds we have this other world of ours, substantial and eternal, where I dream myself and dream those who have been—and the many who still are—flesh of my spirit and spirit of my flesh; this world of consciousness without space or time, where the consciousness of my body is and lives and moves like a wave in the sea. The day I refused to commute my Augusto Pérez' death sentence, he argued back at me: "So you don't want to let me be myself, emerge from the mist, live, live, live at last, see myself, touch, listen, feel, hurt, be myself! So you won't have it? You want me to die a fictional being! I am to die as a creature of fiction? Very well, my lord creator Don Miguel de Unamuno, you will die too! You, too! And you will return to the nothing from which you came! God will cease to dream you! You will die, yes, you will die, even though you don't want to die. You will die, and so will all those who read my story, every one, every single one, without a single exception! They are all fictional beings too, creatures of fiction like myself! They will all die, each and every one!" How his words, prophetic and apocalyptic, have, for twenty years—during twenty years and through twenty years—how they have persisted in my mind! I hear them now in a low terrifying whisper, a piercing sound like the biblical voice of Jehovah! For not merely have I gone on dying through the years, under the weight of the years, continued to die, but so have my people: they have continued dying, and some have died on me. They were—and are—the people who made and dreamt me best. The soul of my body has gone from me drop by drop and, sometimes, in gushes. Those who assume that I live tormented by the anguish of my own individual mortality or immortality are altogether deceived. Poor fools! No, I live tormented by the mortality or immortality of everyone I have ever dreamed, of those I am dreaming now, of everyone who ever dreamt me or dreams me as I dream them. For immortality, like the dream, is communal or it is nothing. I can not recall a single person whom I ever truly knew—and truly to know is to love, even if one thinks one hates—and who died on me and whom I have failed to ask, speaking alone and to myself:

What are you now? What has become of your consciousness? What am I in your consciousness now? What has become of what once was?

And there you have the mist, the *nivola*, the legend, eternal life. . . . And the creative, dreaming word.

There is a visionary passage in Leopardi, the tragic dreamer of nausea, of ennui, a strikingly radiant vision, in the *Canticle of the Wild Cock*. A gigantic bird, taken from the Targum, a paraphrase of the Hebrew Bible in Aramaic, chants eternal revelation and calls on mortals to despair. And its visionary song ends as follows: "The time will come when this universe, and Nature herself, will be no more. And in the same way as of great kingdoms and empires of mankind, and their wondrous works, far-famed in other ages, there is now no sign nor any name; so of the whole world, and of the infinite vicissitudes and calamities of created things, no vestige will remain; but a bare silence, and a deepest stillness, will pervade the immensity of space. Thus this dread and wondrous mystery of universal life, before it has been declared or understood, will vanish and be lost."

No! Not so. For the canticle of the wild cock will remain and, along with it, the whisper of Jehovah. The Word, which was in the beginning and will be in the end, the spiritual Breath and Sound which gathers the clouds and brings form, will remain. Augusto Pérez threatened us all, all of us who have been and are I, all of us who form the dream of God—or, better, the dream of the Word—threatened us with having to die. Everyone goes on dying, they continue to die on me, in the flesh of space, but not in the flesh of dream, not in the flesh of consciousness. And therefore I say to you, readers of my *Mist*, dreamers of my Augusto Pérez and of his world, that this is the mist, the *nivola*, the legend, history, eternal life.

Salamanca, February 1935

I

AUGUSTO APPEARED at the door of his house and held out his right hand, palm downward; gazing up at the sky, he momentarily struck the posture of a statue. He was not taking possession of the external world, but merely observing whether or not it was raining. As he felt the fresh intermittent wet on the back of his hand, he frowned, not because the drizzle bothered him, but because he would have to open up his umbrella. It made such a fine line folded in its case! A folded umbrella is as elegant as an opened one is awkward.

It's unfortunate the way we must make use of things, thought Augusto. *Usage breaks down all beauty, destroys it. The noblest role of any object is that of being contemplated. How beautiful an orange still uneaten! Everything will be different in heaven, where our function will be reduced, or rather widened, to the contemplation of God and of all things in Him. Here, in this sorry life, we simply make use of God: we think of Him as an umbrella to protect us against all sorts of downpours.*

Following these meditations he bent over to roll up his trouser legs. He opened up his umbrella next and stood for a moment in thought. *And now where shall I go? Should I head toward the right or go to the left?* For Augusto was not so much a traveler through life as a stroller. *I'll wait until a dog comes along, and then I'll head out in the same direction.*

27

Just then, instead of a dog, a stunning young lady chanced to pass by, and, as if magnetized, and almost unconsciously, out went Augusto.

And so down one street and up another. Augusto went along not so much thinking to himself as talking to himself: *Now what can that boy there be doing stretched flat on the ground? Watching ants, of course! An ant, now, is one of your worst hypocrites! It runs about pretending to be working. Just like this loafer coming along now, charging ahead as if he were going some place, elbowing everybody else out of the way, and I'll bet he hasn't got a thing to do. What could he possibly have to do? Nothing at all! He's just a loafer. An idler like . . . No, I'm not an idler! My imagination never rests. The people who pretend to work are the idlers, the ones who do nothing but get all wound up and lose their minds, stifle all thought. Just look at this, for example, a ridiculous man rolling chocolate into bars there in the window, in public view. He's an exhibitionist, and an idler. What difference can it make to other people whether he's working or not? Work, work, work! All hypocrisy! As for real work, what about this cripple dragging himself along . . . ? And yet, how do I know anything about that?* And at this point Augusto addressed himself aloud to the cripple: "Forgive me, brother!" And immediately after he asked himself: *Brother? Brother in what way? A brother in paralysis? They say we are all children of Adam. Is this fellow, too, a child of Adam's? Hail and farewell! . . . Ah, now we have the inevitable automobile. Noise and dust! Where does it all lead, this cutting down of distances? The mania for travel comes from topophobia rather than from philotopia, from hatred for*

one place rather than from love of some other place.
The frenzied traveler is fleeing every place he leaves
behind and not really seeking the place he finds. Trav-
el, bah! . . . Damned nuisance, this umbrella! . . . And
now what's happening?

Augusto stopped before the door of a house into
which the striking girl he had been following had
disappeared. Mesmerized by her glance, he had simply wandered along behind her. He had scarcely realized until that moment that he had actually been following her. The concierge watched him out of beady,
malicious eyes; her searching gaze suggested the
course of action he must take. *This female Cerberus,*
he told himself, *is just waiting for me to ask her*
the name of the young lady I've been following and
whether or not she is married, and that's just what I
must do. Otherwise, I'd have to leave my task un-
finished, and that would never do. What's begun must
be finished. I hate imperfection! He felt around in his
pocket and found only a large coin, a five-peseta piece.
There was no possibility of getting it changed. He
would only lose time and miss his opportunity.

"My good woman," he began, his hand still in his
pocket, "could you tell me, confidentially and *inter*
nos, the name of the young lady who has just gone
in?"

"There's no secret to that, and there's no wrong
to it, sir."

"For that very reason . . ."

"Well her name is Doña Eugenia Domingo del
Arco."

"Domingo? It must surely be Dominga."

"No, Domingo. That's her surname, her first surname."

"In the case of a woman, then, that surname should be changed to the feminine ending. Otherwise, what becomes of concordance in gender?"

"I don't know anything about that, sir."

"Then tell me, tell me," said Augusto, two fingers still in his pocket, "how does it happen that she goes out alone like that? Is she married or single? Has she parents?"

"She's single, she's an orphan. She lives with an aunt and uncle."

"Mother's side or father's?"

"I don't know that now. I only know what I've told you. . . ."

"It's really plenty. Perhaps too much."

"She also gives piano lessons."

"Does she play well?"

"That much I don't know."

"Well, as I said, you know enough. And here's something for your trouble."

"Thank you, sir. Thank you indeed. Is there anything more? Can I be of service in some other way? Would you like me to take some word or message to her, to the young lady?"

"Perhaps . . . later. Goodbye for now."

"Count on me, sir, and trust to my absolute discretion."

Well now, Augusto began, as he addressed himself once more after he had taken his leave, *I've really gone and gotten myself mixed up with this good woman. I can't possibly leave it just like that, now. It wouldn't be honorable to back away. What would she say, that paragon and quintessence of a concierge? So . . . Eugenia Dominga, I mean Domingo, del Arco. Good enough. I'll write it down, so as not to forget. The art of mnemonics is no more than a matter of*

*keeping a notebook in one's pocket. As the unforget-
table Don Leoncio would say to me: Never put into
your head what you can put into your pocket. Still,
one could reverse it and say: Never put into your
pocket what you can put into your head. But wait,
what's the name of the concierge?*

He turned back.

"Oh, my good woman, one more thing."

"Whatever you wish to command."

"Your own name, what is your name, pray?"

"My name? Why . . . Margarita."

"Very well. Thank you once again!"

"You're quite welcome."

Augusto set off again, and soon found himself in
the Paseo de la Alameda.

The light rain had ceased, and he folded his umbrella and put it back in its case. He went to sit on a
public bench and found it necessary to spread a newspaper. Next he brought out a notebook and a fountain pen; he flourished the latter between his fingers
and mused: *A most worthy instrument. Without it,
I'd have to write down the young lady's name in pencil, and it could get erased. Will the memory of her
so easily be erased? And yet, what is she really like?
What is the sweet Eugenia like? I recall only her
eyes. . . . I can almost feel her eyes on me, touching
me. I was lyrically meandering and a pair of eyes
came along and bewitched me. Eugenia Domingo, yes
Domingo del Arco. I can't get used to her surname
being Domingo. No, I'll have to get her to change it
to Dominga. But then our children . . . Will the males
have to use the female Dominga as second surname?
And then, since they'll want to get rid of my own
absurd surname, the innocuous Pérez, reducing it to
the initial P., what will our first-born son and heir*

be called? Augusto P. Dominga? Oh, this won't do. . . . Where is all this leading me? What a fantasy! And he stopped to write down: "Eugenia Domingo del Arco, Avenida de la Alameda, 58." Just above this entry he had already written down the decasyllabic lines

From the cradle our sorrow and sadness
and from the cradle our joy and gladness . . .

There you are, Augusto pointed out to himself. *That Eugenia the piano teacher put an end to a fine beginning of a transcendental lyric. Now it's been interrupted. Yes, interrupted. For all a man can do is to search among the fragments of daily events, among the odd chances of fate, for some scraps to sustain his congenital joy or sorrow. Any given event gives rise to joy or sorrow in accordance with our innate disposition. And Eugenia, what of her? I must write her. But not here. I should write her at home. Or should I go to the club? No, I must go home. These things must be done at home, by the hearth. The hearth? My house is no hearth. It's more like an ashtray. Oh, Eugenia!*

And Augusto did go home after all.

II

WHEN HIS manservant opened the door . . .

Augusto was rich (his mother having died a scant six months before the insignificant events already outlined) and he lived alone with his manservant and the cook, who were both longtime servitors of the family, as well as the children of former retainers in the same house. The cook and the manservant were in fact married, but childless.

When his manservant opened the door, Augusto inquired if anyone had called in his absence.

"No one, *Señorito*."

The question was purely routine, and so was the answer, for no one ever called on Augusto at home.

Augusto entered his study and addressed an envelope:

Señorita doña Eugenia Domingo del Arco
E.P.M.

That is: *En propia mano*: Into her own hands. With a blank paper before him, he propped his head in both his own hands, rested his elbows on the desk and closed his eyes. *First summon her to mind*, he advised himself. He concentrated all his forces to bringing out of the darkness the luster of those eyes which had forced him to wander willessly behind them.

Since he had scarcely seen her, he had to conjure the figure of Eugenia up out of his imagination. As a result of his efforts, he evoked a vague figure of fantasy enveloped in dreamwear. And he himself fell asleep. He fell asleep because he had passed a bad night, a night of insomnia.

"*Señorito!*"

"What's that?" exclaimed the awakened Augusto.

"Lunch is served."

Who spoke? Was it the voice of the manservant, or his own appetite which the voice merely echoed? Psychological mysteries! murmured Augusto as he walked to the dining room.

He ate his ritual midday meal with a relish: a couple of eggs, fried, followed by steak and potatoes, finishing with a slice of Gruyère. He took his coffee in another room, sat back in a rocking chair, and lit a Havana cigar. *Ah, my Eugenia,* he sighed, and gave himself up to thinking of her.

Yes, my Eugenia, mine, the Eugenia I'm making up all by myself. Not the other one, the one of flesh and blood, not the one I saw pass by the door of my house, the chance apparition, not the concierge's Eugenia. Chance apparition, I said. But what apparition is not a chance apparition? What logic lies behind apparitions anyway? Perhaps the same logic that lies behind the chain of figures in the smoke from my cigar. Chance! Chance is the inner rhythm of the world. Chance is the soul of poetry. Ah, my chanceful Eugenia! My own humble, humdrum, routine life constitutes a Pindaric ode made up of the day's endless detail. Daily detail! Give us today our daily bread! Give me, Lord, the endless detail of every day! The only reason we don't go under in the face of devastating sorrow or annihilating joy is because our sorrow and our joy are smothered in the thick fog of endless daily detail. All life is that: fog, mist. Life is a nebula. And now suddenly Eugenia emerges from the mist. And who is she? Ah! Now I see it all: I have been looking for her for a long time. And while I was gazing about, she appeared just in front of me. Isn't that what is meant by "finding" something? When anyone finds an apparition, discovers the apparition one wanted, is it not because the apparition, responding to one's desire, comes to meet one? Did not America emerge for the meeting with Columbus? Didn't Eugenia emerge to meet me? Oh, Eugenia!

Augusto heard himself repeating her name aloud. Hearing a call, his manservant appeared at the door:

"Did you call, *Señorito*?"

"No, not you! . . . But: wait a minute. Isn't your name Domingo?"

"Yes, sir," replied Domingo, without showing any surprise that such a question should be put to him.

"And what's the reason for the name Domingo?"

"Because I'm called Domingo."

Augusto addressed himself: *Very well: we call ourselves whatever we are called. In Homeric times people and things had two names: the name given them by man and the one given them by the gods. I wonder what God calls me? And why shouldn't I call myself differently than I am called by other men? Why shouldn't I give Eugenia a different name from the one given her by others, from the name used by the concierge, for example? But what should I call her?*

He dismissed the servant, rose from his chair, went to the sitting room, took up a pen and then wrote:

"Señorita:

This very morning, beneath heaven's gentle rain, you yourself, a chance apparition, passed before the door of my house, where I live but which is no longer home. When I awoke I found myself before the door of your house, in which I do not know whether you have a home or not. Your eyes had carried me there, eyes burning like twin stars in the nebula of my world. Forgive me, Eugenia, and allow me to speak your sweet name as if I were a familiar. Forgive my lyricism. I live in a perpetual and infinitesimal lyricism.

"What more can I say? And yet I have so much to say, so very much more. I think it best to wait until we can meet and talk together. That is what I want now: that we may see each other and talk. That we may write one another, and learn to know each other. And then . . . Then, God and our hearts will tell us what to do!

"Will you then, Eugenia, sweet apparition in my day-by-day life, hear me, listen to me?

"Shrouded in the mist of my life, I await your reply.

Augusto Pérez"

As he signed his name he said to himself: *I like the custom of signing one's name with a flourish, just because it is so beautifully superfluous.*

Sealing the letter, he hurried out into the street.

He was murmuring to himself as he went down the Avenida de la Alameda: *Thanks be to God that I know where I am going and have someplace to go! Eugenia is a blessing of God. She provides a purpose and a goal for my wandering about. Now I have a house around which to make my rounds, and a concierge-confidante. . . .*

As he sped along, talking to himself in this fashion, he happened to pass right by Eugenia without even noticing her eyes' refulgence. The spiritual fog was too dense. Eugenia, however, noticed him and asked herself who could that young man with the apparent good bearing and air of well-being possibly be. She was not too clearly aware of why she had noticed him, but she was intuitively identifying him with the young man who had followed her that morning. Women are always aware of when they are being watched, even when the watcher does not quite see them, and they know when they are being seen, even when they are not quite looked at.

The two went on their separate ways, their souls slicing through the street's tangled spiritual web. For every street does form a web of tangled glances,

stares, and gazes of love and hate, of envy and desire, of disdain and compassion, of words of ancient
import become crystallized, of thoughts and aspira-
tions, all together forming a mysterious fabric en-
shrouding the souls of the passersby.

Augusto at last stood before the concierge, Margarita, and her smile. Margarita immediately took her
hands out of the pockets of her apron.

"Good afternoon, Margarita."

"Good afternoon, *Señorito*."

"My name is Augusto, my good woman. Augusto."

"Don Augusto," she replied.

"Not every name deserves a Don before it," he observed. "There is a chasm, an abyss, lying between
Juan and Don Juan, for example, and there is a difference between Augusto and Don Augusto. But, let
it be! Has the Señorita Eugenia gone out . . . ?"

"She just left, only a moment ago."

"Which way did she go?"

"That way . . ."

Augusto set out in that direction at once, but then
suddenly turned back. He had forgotten to hand over
the letter.

"Señora Margarita, please give this letter directly
into the fair hands of the Señorita Eugenia, if you
will."

"I will be glad to. . . ."

"But, directly into her hands, hands as much like
ivory as the keys of the piano she caresses."

"O, I understand! Just as on other occasions."

"On other occasions? What do you mean by other
occasions?"

"Surely the young gentleman does not think that
this is the first time I have handled a letter of this
type?"

"What type? How do you know the type of letter I have given you?"

"I knew it at once. It's just like the others."

"The others? What others?"

"You don't suppose you are the first suitor the Señorita has had . . . ? Not by a long shot. . . ."

"O! . . . But she's free right now, now, not spoken for now . . . ?"

"Now? No, sir, she has a kind of suitor, or perhaps he is only an aspirant for the post of suitor or sweetheart or something of the sort. . . . Or she may have him on trial. . . . Or perhaps he is a substitute. . . ."

"Why did you not tell me before?"

"Because you didn't ask me. . . ."

"That's true enough. . . . Nevertheless, please see that she gets this letter into her own hands. Do you understand? We'll fight for her! And here is another *duro* for you."

"Thank you kindly, sir."

Augusto had difficulty in tearing himself away: the nebulous, mundane conversation of Margarita was beginning to intrigue him. Was it not another good way of killing time?

As he moved away, Augusto talked on to himself: *We shall put up a battle! Yes, we shall fight! So she has another suitor, or aspirant to suitor . . . ? We shall fight!* Militia est vita hominis super terram: *the life of man on earth is warfare. My life now has a purpose. Now I have a conquest to carry out. O Eugenia! My Eugenia! You shall be mine! At least the Eugenia I created, my Eugenia, the one I formed from the passing vision of those eyes, from the conjunction of stars shining out of my nebula, that Eugenia, will be mine, whatever happens to the other Eugenia, the concierge's Eugenia, who can belong to anybody who-*

ever, for all I care! We shall fight! And I will win! I know the secret of victory. O Eugenia! My Eugenia!

By this time he was at the door of the Club, where Víctor was already waiting for him to begin their daily game of chess.

III

"You're a bit late today," said Víctor, "and you're always so punctual."

"I couldn't help it. . . . I had things to do. . . ."

"Things to do, you?"

"Do you think that only stockbrokers have to work? Life is more complex than you imagine."

"Or simpler than you think . . ."

"Anything's possible."

"In any case, let's play now. Your move!"

Augusto moved King's pawn two squares forward. Instead of humming bits of opera as was his custom, he was repeating Eugenia's name to himself and telling himself that she was the end-purpose of his life, the dulcet refulgence of twin stars in the mist, and repeating that he would do battle for her. He told himself that although there was sure logic in chess, it was also nebulous, fortuitous after all. *Is not logic also rather fortuitous? And as for the apparition of Eugenia, was it not perhaps somehow logical? Might it not be a move in some divine game of chess?*

"Just a moment, old man," Víctor interrupted Augusto's thought. "Are we not agreed that you can't take a move back? A piece moved is a piece played!"

"Understood, of course."

"Well, if that's your move, then I take your Bishop free of charge."

"True enough! I must have been distracted."

"Well, don't get distracted. If you play chess you can't be roasting chestnuts. And a piece moved is a piece played."

"To be sure. Irreparable!"

"That's the point of this game."

Augusto went back to addressing himself: *Why shouldn't one be distracted in playing a game? Isn't life a game? And why not take a play back, why be unable to do so? That's logic for you!* Alea jacta est! *The die is cast! Perhaps by now Eugenia has received my letter. What's done's done! As for tomorrow, it belongs to God! And as for yesterday, to whom does yesterday belong? O yesterday, treasure of the strong! Holy yesterday, matter and substance for our daily mist!*

"Check!" Víctor was interrupting Augusto's meditations once more.

"True enough . . . Let me see . . . How did I ever let things come to such a pass?"

"You were distracted again. If you weren't so distracted, you'd be one of our best players."

"Tell me, Víctor, is life a game or is it a distraction?"

"A game, play, is surely only a distraction."

"Then, what difference does it make how you get your distraction?"

"Well, if you're going to play, play your best."

"And why not play badly? Moreover, what does it mean to play well, or to play badly? Why should we not move these pieces in a different way from the way we do move them?"

"You, friend Augusto, noted philosopher, have taught me the thesis according to which we play."

"Well, now is the time to give you a startling piece of news."

"Out with it!"

"You'd better get ready to be staggered."

"I'm not one to be staggered in advance, *a priori.*"

"Well here goes. Do you know what's happening to me?"

"You're growing more and more distracted."

"It so happens that I've fallen in love."

"Bah! I already knew that."

"What do you mean you already knew it?"

"Of course. Quite simple. You've been in love *ab origine,* from birth. Congenital love-sickness."

"It's true enough that love is born at birth. . . ."

"I didn't say love. I said love-sickness. And I already knew, without your having to tell me, that you were infatuated, or better, smitten, or bitten. I knew it better than you yourself."

"But with whom? You can't know. Or tell me."

"You don't know that any more than I do."

"Listen, I'll tell *you.* Or . . . perhaps you're right. . . ."

"Didn't I tell you so? And if I'm not right, then tell me: is she a blonde or a brunette?"

"Well, the truth is I don't know. Though I seem to see her as neither one nor the other. I mean, her hair is more or less chestnut color. . . ."

"Is she tall or short?"

"I really can't say for sure. But she must be of middle height. But—what eyes! What eyes she has, my Eugenia!"

"Eugenia?"

"Yes, Eugenia Domingo del Arco, Avenida de la Alameda, 58."

"The *piano* teacher?"

"Yes, that's her. But . . ."

"Of course: I know her. . . . Check!"

"What!"

"Check!"

"All right. . . ."

And Augusto covered his King with a Knight. But he finished by losing the game.

As Víctor took leave of Augusto, he placed his left hand like a yoke around the back of his friend's neck and murmured: "So: Eugenita the pianist, is it? Very good, Augustito. You shall inherit the earth."

Emerging later alone, Augusto thought to himself: *Those awful diminutives . . . those terrible diminutives!*

IV

A s h e w a l k e d home, Augusto kept up a running monologue: *Why should the diminutive of a word make it a term of affection? Is it possible that love diminishes the beloved? And me, in love! In love, me! Who would have thought so . . . ? But, can Victor possibly be right in saying that I have been in love* ab initio? *Perhaps my love has preceded its object. Even more: perhaps my love called its object into being, extracted it from the mist of creation. If I move my Rook there, I won't be in check. Now, what is love anyway? Who can define love? Love defined is no longer love. . . . Damnation! Why in God's name does the Mayor allow such commercial signboards, such ugly letter-ing? That Bishop was badly played. . . . And how can I be in love if I do not, strictly speaking, know the girl at all? What's the difference? Knowledge, know-ing her, will come later. Love precedes knowledge. In any case knowledge kills love. As Padre Zaramillo taught me:* Nihil volitum quin praecognitum, *nothing is willed which has not first been known. But I've reached a contrary conclusion on my own:* Nihil cog-nitum quin praevolitum, *nothing is known which has not first been willed. To know is to forgive, they say. Not at all: to forgive is to know, rather. First love, then knowledge follows. . . . Now why didn't I see I was wide open to be checked? . . . What is necessary before something can be loved? First, a glimpse of the beloved. A glimpse: the intuition of love. A glimpse through the mist. Then focus follows, the clearer out-lines, the perfected vision, as the mist resolves into drops of water, or into sleet or snow or hail. Science is a hailstorm. No, mist! If only one were an eagle to be able to sweep through the clouds, through the lap and bosom of the cumulus, and see the sun through the mist, a luminary nebula! O eagle! And what must the eagle of Patmos have said to the owl of Minerva? Eagle which looks the sun in the face but sees nothing in the dark of night, escaped from the presence of St. John, meeting the owl of Minerva, which sees in the dark but cannot gaze on the sun, escaped from Olym-pus! Think of what they must have said to one an-other!*

Once more, deep in reflection, in his meditations, Augusto passed Eugenia in the street without seeing her.

He went on reflecting instead: *Knowledge comes after. But . . . What was that? I could swear that . . .*

a pair of mystically shining twin stars crossed my orbit just now. . . . Could it have been she? My heart tells me . . . But here I am, home!

He entered his house.

He went to his bedroom and the sight of his bed caused him to reflect anew: *Alone! To sleep alone! To dream alone! When people sleep together, they must dream together. Mysterious emanations must unite them, unite their minds. Or is it more likely true that the more their hearts are united, the more their minds are separated. Perhaps. Perhaps there is an inverse proportion to it all, two mutually adverse positions. If two lovers think alike, they feel in opposition to each other. If they participate in the same loving feeling, each of them will think differently, perhaps the opposite. A woman loves a man just so long as he does not think like her, that is, so long as he continues to think. . . . Ah, but there is the worthy married couple of the house. I'll go and look in on them.*

In the evening, before going to bed, Augusto often played a game of cards with his servant Domingo while the cook, Domingo's wife, looked on.

They began a game.

"Twenty in hearts!" Domingo called out.

"Tell me," parried Augusto, changing the subject without warning. "What would you say to my getting married?"

"A very good idea," said Domingo.

"It all depends," his wife, Liduvina, ventured, "on who you marry."

"Come now: didn't you yourself get married?" interjected Augusto.

"It all depends on who you marry, Señorito,"

"What do you mean, it all depends?"

"It's easy enough to get married, but not so easy to be married."

"That's a piece of popular wisdom, fountainhead of . . ."

"And as for the sort of person the Señorito's wife should be . . . ," added Liduvina, hurrying to cut off a fearsome monologue.

"What? What sort is she supposed to be? Tell me, woman, tell me at once!"

"Well, since the Señorito is so good . . ."

"O come now! Tell me what you mean, once and for all."

"You remember what the Señora used to say. . . ."

At this reverent reminder of his mother, Augusto laid his cards on the table, and his thoughts remained in suspense. Often had his mother, a gentle lady, daughter of misfortune, said to him: "I have not much longer to live, my son. Your father calls. Perhaps he needs me more than you do. As soon as I go, and you are alone, get married as soon as possible. Bring home, to this house, its proper mistress and lady. Our line of faithful servants merit our trust, but you must install a lady of the house, here, a mistress of your heart as well as your house, a mistress of your purse, of your larder, of your kitchen, and of your resolutions. Look for a woman who can govern, one who cares, knows how to care . . . and how to govern you."

"My wife will know how to play the piano," exclaimed Augusto, shaking himself free of his memories, of his nostalgia.

"The piano! What good is that?" asked Liduvina.

"What good is it? Why there's the beauty of it! It doesn't serve any purpose at all, and there's the charm: it's no good for a blessed thing. And I'm tired of everything useful. . . ."

"Of us, too?"

"No, not of your service, no! And besides, the piano actually does serve a purpose: it serves to provide harmony to a hearth, so that a hearth becomes more than a heap of ashes."

"Harmony, is it! Can you eat that?"

"Liduvina . . . Liduvina . . ."

The cook bowed her head before this gentle reproof. It was their set of manners.

"Yes, she will play the piano, for she is a piano teacher."

"Then she won't play it," affirmed Liduvina with insistence. "Else why should she get married?"

"My Eugenia . . . ," began Augusto.

"Ah, so her name is Eugenia and she is a piano teacher," ventured the cook.

"Yes. So . . .?"

"Is she the one who lives with her aunt and uncle on the Avenida de la Alameda, above the shop owned by Señor Tiburcio?"

"The very one. Do you know her then?"

"Yes . . . By sight . . ."

"Come now, Liduvina, you seem to know her better than that. Speak up. It's a question of my future and good fortune. . . ."

"She's a good girl, a good girl. . . ."

"Speak up, Liduvina . . . for the sake of my mother!"

"You should remember what the Señora counseled you. . . . Now, who's that in the kitchen? I bet it's the cat. . . ."

And the cook hurried out.

"Well, sir, shall we finish the game?"

Chapter IV

"You're right, Domingo, we can't leave the game like that. Whose turn is it?"

"Yours, Señorito."

"Then, here goes."

He lost that game, too, from sheer distraction.

As he went back to his bedroom he took up his monologue again: *Well now, everyone knows her— everybody except me! The true workings of love . . . Tomorrow! What shall I do tomorrow? Sufficient unto the day is the evil thereof.* And so to bed.

Once in bed he continued: *The truth is that I have been leading a weary, a tedious existence without knowing it . . . for two solid, mortal, years—ever since the death of my blessed mother. Yes, there is such a thing as unconscious tedium. Most of us, nearly all of us, are unconsciously bored. Tedium is the substratum of life, and it is from tedium that most games have been invented, games and novels—and love. Life's mist distills a bittersweet liquor which is tedium. All those insignificant events of the day, all those pleasantly distracting conversations which serve to kill time and to prolong life, what are they all but bittersweet tedium? O Eugenia, my Eugenia, flower of my life's unconscious weariness, be with me and attend me in my dreams, dream of me and dream in me!*

And thus he fell asleep.

H E S W E P T through the clouds, a shining eagle, his powerful wings pearled with drops of dew, bird-of-prey's eyes peering through the clouds, the upper mist, heart in a trance of cosmic tedium beneath a breast steeled by storms. About him stretched the silence of distance from the moving earth. Above him, at the zenith of the heavens, two twin stars emitting ineffable meaning.

The cosmic silence was rent by a strident cry: *The News!*

The light of day impinged upon Augusto.

Wrapping the blanket closer around him he communed: *Do I dream or am I alive? Am I eagle or man? What* News? *What will a new day bring? Has an earthquake swallowed Madrid? And why not Leipzig? O this damnable lyric association of ideas, this Pindaric disorder! The world is a kaleidoscope. Man alone is responsible for logic. Chance is the supreme art. Sleep! Sleep a little longer.*

And he turned over in the bed.

The News! Wine Vinegar! Wine Vinegar for sale!

And then the noise of a carriage, followed by an automobile. After that a noisy gang of boys.

Augusto complained to himself: *This is impossible! Life insists! And with life comes love. . . . And what is love? Is it not perhaps the distillation of all this? Is it not perhaps the juice squeezed from tedium? I must think of Eugenia. The time is right.*

He closed his eyes even more firmly in order to concentrate. To think?

But his thoughts dissolved, melted away, and his mind settled down to dancing a polka. The reason was simple: a hurdy-gurdy had been set down under his very window and the music played away. And Augusto's mind, in concert, was beating time, not thinking.

At last, when the final notes had died away, Augusto was able to resume his soliloquy: *Music is the quintessence of the world. Isn't my Eugenia musical? Every law is rhythmical, and rhythm is love. This divine morning, the virginal beginning of day, brings with it this discovery: love is rhythm. Mathematics is the science of rhythm, and music is the sensuous expression of love: the expression, merely, not the realization.*

He was interrupted by a tap at the door.

"Come in!"

"Did you call, Señorito?" Domingo inquired.

"Yes. My breakfast!"

He had rung, unaware of what he was doing, at least an hour and a half earlier than was his custom, and, once he had rung, he had perforce to ask for his breakfast, even if it was not time for it.

He continued his soliloquy: *Love quickens and sharpens the appetite. In order to love, one must live! Yes, and in order to live, one must love!*

He got up to eat his breakfast.

"What's the weather like, Domingo?"

"The same as always."

"You mean neither good nor bad."

"That's it!"

It was merely one of the manservant's theories they were discussing—for he, also, was theoretical.

Augusto washed, dressed, combed his hair, and groomed himself like a man with an objective in the world, now, overflowing with relish for life—though with a melancholy air, to be sure.

Once in the street, his heart began to beat violently. He admonished himself: *Be quiet! Of course, I knew her from before, I had seen her, I knew her for a long time. The image of her is nearly innate in me. . . . Mother mine, help me from heaven!*

Eugenia crossed his path. He saluted her with his eyes rather than with his hat.

He was about to turn and follow her, but restrained himself, his good sense prevailing. He also felt a strong desire to chat with the concierge.

And he also wanted to continue his soliloquy: *It's she, yes, it's she. The very same, the one I sought for years, even though I knew it not. And she sought me. By some preestablished harmony we were destined for each other. We are two nomads, complementary to one another. The family, now, is the true social cell. And I am no more than a molecule. Science is full of poetry! Mother, mother mine, behold your son, counsel me from heaven! Eugenia, my Eugenia . . . !*

He looked around him, lest he was being watched, and then he surprisingly—even to himself—embraced the air. He told himself: *Love is ecstasy. It takes us out of ourselves.*

He was brought back to reality—was it reality?—by Margarita's smile.

"Anything to report?" Augusto asked her at once.

"Not exactly, Señorito. It's still early for that."

"Didn't she ask you anything when you handed over the letter?"

"Nothing."

"And what about today?"

"Today? Yes. She asked me for your address, and whether I knew you or not, and who you were. She told me you had forgotten to write out your address. And then she gave me a message to pass on."

Chapter V

"A message? What was it? Don't hesitate to tell me."

"She said that if you came around again, I was to tell you that she was already engaged, that she had a fiancé."

"That she has a fiancé?"

"I already told you, Señorito."

"Never mind. We'll fight for her."

"Good enough."

"Will you promise to help me, Margarita?"

"Of course I will."

"Then we shall win!"

Augusto took his leave and walked over to the Alameda, so that he might stroll under the trees and submerge his strong emotions in the sight of the green and the sound of the lovemaking birds. His heart soon grew tender and the fugitive memories of his youth began to hold forth in his soul like nightingales.

The memory of his mother was like a sky shedding a dulcet dissolving light upon all his other recollections.

He scarcely remembered his father: a mythical shadow almost lost in the far distance, a blood-red cloud in a red sunset—sanguine because he remembered him bathed in blood from a hemorrhage, his face gone corpselike, a sight Augusto had witnessed as a very young boy. He could still hear the cry, resounding across such a great distance of time, of "My child!" a cry torn from his mother and rending the house, a cry which was directed indeterminately either at the dying man or at the child—it was impossible to tell. Augusto, in any case, had been petrified into incomprehension before by the mystery of death.

Shortly after, his mother, overcome with grief, baptized him in her close embrace with scalding tears,

51

as she chanted "My son! My son! My son!" He added his own tears to the baptismal water, clinging to his mother the while, not daring to turn his head away from the sweet obscurity of that palpitating breast and full lap, lest he encounter the all-devouring eyes of death.

Thus passed days of weeping and darkness, until the tears began to dry and the house to retreat from the gloom and come back into the light.

It was a warm, easy house. The light came in through the white flowers embroidered on the curtains. The armchairs held their arms wide open, like grandfathers made young by the years. The ashes of his father's last cigar had been left in an ashtray. A wedding photo of his parents hung on the wall. His father had been a tall man; in the photo he was seated, one leg crossed over the other, his boot-top showing; his mother stood beside him, one hand resting on his shoulder: her hand was finely made, not designed for grasping but for perching, like a dove.

After she became a widow, his mother came and went in silence, like a small bird; she wore only black; a wan smile had been left as sediment from the bitter tears of early widowhood; it played about her mouth and around her questing eyes. "I must live for you, only for you," she told the boy and, when he went to bed, he would take with him into his dreamworld a kiss still moist with tears.

Life passed as if it were only an unimportant dream.

In the evening his mother would read aloud to him, sometimes from the life of a saint, sometimes from a Jules Verne novel, or sometimes a simple robust story. From time to time she even managed a laugh, a silent sweet laugh which transcended ancient tears.

Eventually he entered secondary school, and his mother set herself the task of going over his lessons with him; she studied them along with him. She memorized all those strange names in universal history, and exclaimed in wonder at some of their deeds: "What terrible things men have done, what outrages!" She was particularly adept at mathematics. Augusto mused: *If my mother ever set her mind to mastering mathematics . . . !* He recalled, later, the interest she had shown in the development of an equation of the second degree. She looked into the subject known as psychology, but found this far less intelligible. "What a way to complicate matters! What an itch to make simple things difficult!" she would exclaim. She looked into physics and chemistry and natural science. She never liked the names given to animals and plants. Physiology horrified her, and she gave up going over her son's lessons with him. The mere sight of the plates depicting the heart and lungs recalled her husband's blood-soaked death. "Repulsive! Don't ever think of studying medicine," she told Augusto. "It's best not to know what goes on inside."

When Augusto graduated from secondary school, she embraced him and broke out in tears. She gazed at the down on his lip and murmured, "If only your father were alive!" Augusto, now become a big lad, was embarrassed to be made to sit upon her lap while she meditated on her dead past.

Then it was time for the university, its courses and comrades, and the mother's melancholy as her son began to take wing. "I exist only for you," she would say. "And who knows what woman you exist for. The ways of the world . . ." He received his degree in law and on the day he did so his mother gravely kissed his hand and whispered, "The blessing of your father upon you!"

His mother never went to bed before him, and always kissed him goodnight. He could not ever really stay up late therefore. And at whatever hour he awoke, his mother was the first person he saw. At table, if he did not eat something, she also refused the same.

Whenever they went out walking together, his mother kept silent, her thoughts on the past, while he thought only of whatever caught his eye by chance. She repeated everyday sayings, ancient yet always new. She often began with "When you get married. . . ."

If they chanced to pass a beautiful girl, even an attractive one, his mother watched Augusto closely.

And death came to her: slowly, gravely, sweetly. It was painless. It entered on tiptoe. It was somehow like a bird of passage. She was carried away in slow flight one autumn afternoon. She died with her hand in her son's hand, her eyes fixed on his. Augusto felt her hand growing cold, her eyes becoming fixed. He kissed her cold hand warmly and let it go; he closed her eyes. He knelt by the bed, and let the memory of all those uneventful years pass over him.

But now, today, he was walking in the Alameda, listening to the sound of the birds and thinking about Eugenia. She was said to be engaged. "What I fear, son," his mother used to tell him, "is your first encounter with a dangerous thorn on life's way." If she were only there, she would turn this first thorn into a rose!

Augusto told himself: *If she were alive, she would be able to solve this problem. It's no more difficult, really, than an equation of the second degree. It's much the same in the end.*

A faint moaning, as from an unfortunate animal, interrupted his soliloquy. He searched about in the bushes and found, in the middle of a thicket, a puppy weaving about in circles. Augusto conjectured: *Someone has left the poor pup to die . . . abandoned right after being born . . . they didn't have the courage to kill it.*

When Augusto picked it up, the pup began looking for a tit. He took it home, then, and began talking to himself: *When Eugenia finds out about this, she'll love this poor little animal, and think more of me for its sake. It's a very pretty little animal. Poor thing, how it licks my hand!*

"Domingo, bring some milk at once!" he said as soon as the door was opened for him at home.

"Oh, so now you've decided to buy a dog, Señorito?"

"I didn't buy him, Domingo. This dog is no slave. He's free-born. I found him in the open."

"Ah, he's a foundling!"

"We're all foundlings, Domingo. Now bring some milk."

Domingo brought some milk and a bit of sponge to make it easier for the dog to suck it. Augusto ordered a nursing bottle for the next feed. And then he christened the dog Orfeo, for some reason which remained obscure even to himself.

Orfeo, in any case, became the companion and confidant for Augusto in his soliloquies concerning his secret love for Eugenia.

He would address the pup in a low voice: "Listen, Orfeo, we have to fight for love. Now what shall I do? If you knew my mother . . . But you'll know about that when you get to sleep in Eugenia's lap. But what shall we do now?"

That day the noonday lunch was melancholy. His afternoon walk was melancholy. The daily chess game was melancholy. And his dreams that night were melancholy, too.

VI

A U G U S T O W A S passing number 58 on the Avenida de la Alameda, and he spoke to himself: *I must come to some decision. Things can't go on as they are.*

A woman appeared just then on one of the balconies of the second floor, precisely Eugenia's floor, and began to set a bird cage out in the sun; she was spare and gray-haired and as she leaned over to attach the cage to a nail she missed it altogether and the bird and cage came tumbling down the wall. She cried out in despair: "Pichín, my Pichín!" Augusto rushed to pick up the cage. A canary fluttered about in great agitation within.

Augusto carried the agitated bird up the stairs, his own heart fluttering to think of entering Eugenia's house. The lady of the bird cage was waiting for him.

"Oh, thank you, thank you, sir!"

"Not at all."

"O Pichín, my Pichinito! Come now, calm down. And sir, won't you come in?"

"With pleasure, thank you."

And Augusto entered Eugenia's home.

The lady of the house led him to the drawing room, and asked him to wait a moment while she put the canary in a safe place.

He was left alone, but a moment later an elderly man appeared, doubtless Eugenia's uncle. He wore dark glasses and on his head a fez. He sat down by Augusto and began a conversation in an unknown language (it later proved to be Esperanto):

His meaning was: "Do you not agree with me that, thanks to Esperanto, universal peace will soon be a fact?"

Augusto thought of taking flight, but was restrained by his love for Eugenia. The older man continued talking, still in the unknown tongue.

Augusto decided to speak up: "I cannot understand a word you are saying, sir."

The aunt reappeared in time to hear Augusto's complaint. "He must surely have been speaking to you in that awful jargon they call Esperanto." To her husband she said: "Fermín, this is the gentleman who picked up the canary."

"Well, now," said Fermín, "I don't understand you any better than you understand my Esperanto."

"My Pichín fell into the street when I went to sun him, and this gentleman was kind enough to bring him up to me." She turned back to ask: "What is your name, sir?"

"Señora, I am Augusto Pérez, son of the late widow of Pérez Rovira, whom you perhaps may have known."

"Of Doña Soledad?"

"Yes, Doña Soledad."

"O, but I knew her quite well. A model mother and a model widow. I congratulate you, sir."

"I am happy that the canary's fall, a lucky accident, brought us together."

"Lucky? Can you call such an accident lucky?"

"For me, yes."

"Thank you for the thought, sir," interjected Don Fermín. "Men and their affairs are guided by enigmatic laws, laws which men may nevertheless grasp in some measure. I, good sir, for my part have my own ideas about a good many things, about almost everything. . . ."

"Won't you please leave off that eternal refrain of yours," said the wife interrupting, and turning to Augusto: "How was it you were able to come so quickly and providentially to the rescue of my canary?"

"I shall be frank, Señora. The truth is that I was observing your house."

"This house?"

"Yes, Señora. You see . . . you have a charming niece and I . . ."

"That's enough said, sir. Now, now I see what you meant by a happy accident. And I also understand that even canaries may be providential."

"Which of us knows the ways of Providence?" chanted Don Fermín.

"Well, I know them, and that's that," exclaimed his wife. She turned again to Augusto: "The doors of this house are open to you . . . that's the least we can do! The son of Doña Soledad! . . . Besides, you can help me get rid of a silly idea that this girl has taken into her head to . . ."

"And what about her liberty?" Fermín broke in.

"You keep your anarchism to yourself, if you please, and be quiet."

"Anarchism?" exclaimed Augusto.

Don Fermín's face radiated happiness, and he murmured, in the mildest of voices:

"Yes, dear sir, I am an anarchist, a mystical anarchist. A theoretical anarchist only, of course; you understand, a theoretical anarchist. Never fear, friend," and he rested a hand gently on Augusto's knee. "I throw no bombs. My anarchism is purely spiritual. After all, my friend, I have my own ideas about practically everything. . . ."

For want of something better to say, Augusto timidly asked the aunt: "And are you an anarchist, too?"

"I? What a piece of nonsense! Imagine: no one in command, no one giving orders. If no one gives orders, who is going to obey? Don't you understand that it's all nonsense, an impossibility?"

"O men of little faith, who call impossible what . . . ," Don Fermín began.

The aunt interrupted him:

"Well, then, the bargain is sealed, my good Señor Don Augusto. You strike me as being a splendid person, well born, well educated, with a better-than-average income, more than respectable. . . . Now, now, don't try to thank me. From now on you are my candidate. . . ."

"It is a great honor, Señora!"

"Yes. We must make this young thing see reason. She's not a bad girl, of course, but likes to have her own way. Capricious. She was spoiled in her up-bringing. . . . Then, when the dreadful disaster struck . . . My poor brother! A catastrophe!"

"Catastrophe?" repeated Augusto.

"Yes, exactly. And since it is all a matter of public knowledge, there is no reason for me to conceal it from you. Eugenia's father committed suicide after a most unfortunate speculation in the stock market. He left her almost destitute. She was left a house, but so mortgaged that it consumes all her income. And the poor girl has insisted on saving money from her income as a teacher until she can pay off that mortgage. Imagine! She couldn't do it if she went on giving piano lessons for the next sixty years!"

At this point a generous and heroic thought was conceived in Augusto's mind.

"No, the girl is certainly not bad in any way. But it's impossible to figure her out."

"If all of you were to learn Esperanto . . . ," began Don Fermín.

"O, please spare us your universal languages! We don't understand each other in the languages we've got, so why bring in another?"

"But don't you believe, Señora," Augusto asked, "that it would be a good thing if there were only one language?"

"That's it! That's it!" Don Fermín cried out, beside himself.

"Yes, sir," the aunt answered firmly. "One single language: Castilian Spanish! And at most, one more, Babel, Asturian dialect, so that one could deal with maids, who are not rational beings."

Eugenia's aunt was from Asturias, and she had a maid, also Asturian, with whom she bickered in Babel, the Asturian dialect.

"So there is pure theory for you, my pure theory," added the aunt. "I don't think it a bad idea to have one language, you see. And as for my husband and his theories, he, for his part, is theoretically an enemy of marriage even."

Augusto stood up: "I fear I may perhaps be disturbing you. . . ."

"You cannot disturb us ever in any way," interposed the aunt. "And you are duty-bound to pay us a return visit. Moreover, I formally announce that you are my official candidate."

Chapter VI

As Augusto was leaving, Don Fermín came up close to him and whispered: "Think no more about it!"

"Why not?" asked Augusto.

"I have my presentiments, sir, my forebodings."

The aunt's last words were: "Remember, you are my choice."

Eugenia returned home and her aunt's first words were:

"Do you know who has been here, Eugenia? None other than Don Augusto Pérez."

"Augusto Pérez . . . Augusto Pérez . . . Ah, yes! And who brought him here?"

"My canary, Pichín."

"What did he come for?"

"What a question! He was chasing after you."

"After me, and brought here by the canary? Well, I don't understand that now. It would be better if you explained to me in Esperanto, like Uncle."

"He was in pursuit of you. And he is not at all bad to look at, as well as being decently educated, well turned out, a young bachelor. And, above all, rich, my girl, rich."

"He can keep his wealth. I work for my living, but I don't need to sell myself."

"Who said anything about your selling yourself, Miss Flare-Up?"

"Very good, Aunt. Enough said. Let's drop this nonsense."

"When you see him, my child, you'll change your mind."

"Hardly likely . . ."

"No one can say in advance what they will always do—or not do."

"The ways of Providence are mysterious," exclaimed Don Fermín. "God . . ."

"My good man! Now how does this mention of God
go with your anarchy? I've said it a thousand times. If
no one is to be in charge of things, why bring up
God?"

"My good woman! My anarchism, as I've told you
a thousand times, is mystical. God does not command, in the way of men. God himself is an anarchist.
He, too. God does not order so much as . . ."

"He obeys, I suppose. . . ."

"Exactly! You've said it: God has enlightened you.
Now come here!"

He seized hold of his wife, gazed into her eyes, then
blew lightly into her hair, displacing some snow-white
curls, and added:

"He Himself has inspired you! Yes, God obeys. . . .
He obeys."

"More theory, I assume. And as for you, Eugenia,
just stop this foolishness, and remember that here's
your chance, an opportunity."

"Well, I'm an anarchist, too. But not a mystic
one, like Uncle."

"We'll see about that . . . ," said her aunt.

VII

A U G U S T O , A T H O M E , was talking to his new pet,
as he gave it milk: "Listen, Orfeo. I've taken the decisive step. I've entered her house, her hearth, her sanctuary. Can you imagine what it means to take a decisive step? When the winds of fortune impel us along,

then every step is decisive. The steps we take are not even properly our own. We make our way through a wild, overgrown jungle without so much as a trail. We wend a way with our feet as we proceed haphazardly along. There are people who think they are following a star: I think I am following two, a twin star. And this star is simply the trajectory into the sky, a projection of chance.

"Yes, Orfeo, a decisive step! But tell me, what need is there for God to exist or the world or anything else at all to exist? What need is there for anything? Isn't the idea of necessity perhaps the supreme form Chance takes in our minds?

"Where did Eugenia come from? Is she a figment of my imagination, or am I a figment of hers? Or are we products of mutual creation, she from me and I from her? Is not all Creation the product of each single thing and each single thing the creation of all Creation? And what is Creation? What are you, Orfeo, and what am I?

"The thought has struck me often, Orfeo, that I do not exist. I'd walk down the street imagining that no one else could see me. Sometimes I imagined that no one saw me as I saw myself, and even though I thought I was conducting myself in a normal manner, I was in fact causing a scandal and people were laughing and making mock of me. Hasn't the same ever happened to you, Orfeo? Probably not, because you are so young and have no experience to speak of. And besides, you're a dog.

"Still, Orfeo, don't dogs sometimes imagine they are human, just as some humans think of themselves as dogs?

"What a life, Orfeo! Especially ever since my mother died. For me, every single hour strikes simply because it is pushed forward by the hours before it. I have never known a future, and now that I am on the point of catching sight of one, it seems about to turn into the past. Eugenia is already nearly a memory. The passing days . . . today, an eternal today which passes . . . slip by in a cloud of tedium. Today is like yesterday, tomorrow will be like today. Look, Orfeo, the ashes in my father's ashtray, my father's last ashes. . . . A revelation of eternity, awful eternity. A man is left alone and he closes his eyes to the illusion of the future and sees into the fearful abyss of eternity. Eternity has no future. When we die, death turns us about-face in our tracks, in our orbit so to say, and we begin the long trek back, toward the past, toward what once was. And so on without end, unraveling the skein of our destiny, undoing that infinity which an eternity has made of us, and we voyage toward nothingness without reaching it, for nothingness never was, nothingness never existed.

"Beneath the current of our existence, within it, flows a countercurrent: in one current we go from yesterday to tomorrow, in the other from tomorrow to yesterday. We ravel and unravel simultaneously. From time to time we get a whiff of the other world, we hear mysterious murmurs of its existence, of a world within our own world. The marrow of history is counterhistory, a quintessential counterprocess, a subterranean river flowing from the sea to the source.

"And now the twin stars of Eugenia's eyes shine in the sky of my solitude. They shine with the sheen of my dead mother's tears. They make me think that I exist. Dulcet illusion! *Amo, ergo sum!* And this love, Orfeo, is like the blessed rain which dissipates and condenses the mist of daily existence. Thanks to love I can feel my own soul take on shape, respond to my touch. My soul is sentient, feels pain, at its center. What is 'soul' in any case but love, sorrow made flesh?

"The days come and the days go and love remains. At the very heart of all things, the current of this world sweeps against the current of the other, and out of this sweeping contact arises the saddest and sweetest of sorrows, the sorrow of living.

"Look, Orfeo, consider the warp and woof, how the shuttle throws the thread back and forth, how the treadle goes up and down! And yet—where is the warp rod which rolls up the texture of our existence, where?"

Inasmuch as the dog—Orfeo!—had never seen a loom, it is not likely that he understood his master, though, gazing into his master's eyes, it may be that he intuited his meaning.

VIII

Augusto shuddered as if he were being stretched upon the rack. He felt an impulse to leap from his seat, pace furiously around the room in which he was sitting, brandish his fists, yell like a circus barker, forget himself in some excess. Neither of those present were capable of bringing him back to reality: neither Doña Ermelinda (Eugenia's aunt), nor her husband Don Fermín, the theoretical and mystical anarchist.

"As I was saying, Don Augusto," the aunt continued, "I believe it is best for you to hold on now, to wait for her. She can't be long. I'll call her in, and you two can become acquainted and that's the first step. All relationships of this kind must begin by the two parties becoming acquainted, isn't that so?"

"To be sure," said Augusto, like a man speaking from some other world. "The first step is to become acquainted."

"And as soon as she gets to know you the rest is clear."

"Not all that clear," objected Don Fermín. "The ways of Providence are always mysterious. . . . And as for the notion that in order to get married it is first necessary, or even advisable to know one another, I disagree completely, I disagree. . . . The only effective knowledge is knowledge *post nuptias*. I've told you before, my dear, the meaning of to know in the Bible. And believe me there is no knowledge more real and substantial than penetrating knowledge. . . ."

"Be quiet! Don't act the fool."

"Biblical knowledge, Ermelinda . . ."

The door bell rang.

"There she is!" the uncle cried out, interrupting himself and changing his tone to one of mysterious foreboding.

Augusto felt as if he had caught on fire: a bolt of lightning at his feet surging up through the top of his head and then beyond into space. His heart began to pound.

They heard the door open, and then some rapid, even steps, neatly rhythmic. Of a sudden, Augusto was calmed.

"I'll call her," volunteered the uncle, making as if to rise.

"No you don't!" cried out the aunt, and she called for the servant.

When the servant entered, she told her: "Tell Señorita Eugenia to come here!"

Complete silence reigned, a silence like that among conspirators. Augusto asked himself: *Will I be able to stand it? Won't I turn as red as a poppy or as white as a lily when her eyes shine through the doorway's space? Won't my heart burst?*

A slight rustle was heard, like that of a dove taking flight; a short, dry "Ah!" and the eyes of Eugenia appeared in the doorway, set in a face all freshness and life above a body which seemed to put no weight upon the floor; her eyes, those stars, seemed to lend a mysterious new light to the scene. Augusto was now grown altogether calm, affixed to his chair as if he were a plant which had grown there. He was almost vegetable in his self-oblivion, his absorption in Eugenia's irradiation.

He came to, came to himself, only when the aunt spoke and he heard her say: "This is our friend Don Augusto Pérez . . . ," Augusto reacted by getting to his feet and attempting to force a smile.

"Don Augusto Pérez, our friend, wishes to meet you."

"The man of the canary?" Eugenia asked.

"Yes, the man of the canary, Señorita," Augusto replied, as he came forward and extended his hand. The thought occurred to him that her hand would burn his when she touched him.

Nothing of the sort: a white cold hand, white as snow, cold as snow, touched his hand. Augusto felt instantly permeated by a fluid serenity.

Eugenia chose a place to sit down.

"And this gentleman . . . ," began the pianist.

This gentleman! thought Augusto, *this gentleman! . . . That's a bad sign! . . .*

"This gentleman" interrupted the aunt, "who by great good luck . . ."

"Yes, the canary's good luck."

"The ways of Providence are most mysterious!" the anarchist announced.

"This gentleman, as I was saying," the aunt continued, "through a fortunate chance has made himself known to us, and it turns out that he is the son of a lady whom I knew slightly but respected a good deal. He is a friend of this house, and now he would like to know you, Eugenia."

"Know her and admire her!" exclaimed Augusto.

"Admire me?" asked the pianist.

"Yes, as a pianist."

"Now, sir, really . . ."

"I am aware, señorita, of your great love of art."

"Art? What art? The art of music?"

"Naturally!"

"You have been misinformed, Don Augusto, deceived!"

Don Augusto! Don Augusto! Why all this Don? A bad sign, that word. Almost as bad as that "gentleman!" of hers. And Augusto ventured to say aloud:

"Don't you care for music?"

"Not a bit of it! You can take my word for it."

Ah, this Liduvina is telling the truth! After she gets married, with a man to support her, this girl won't touch the piano again. Aloud, he added:

"But of course everyone knows that you're an excellent teacher. . . ."

"As a professional, I do my best and, now that I must make my own living . . ."

"The idea of having to earn your own living . . . ," began the anarchist again.

"That's enough of that," his wife interrupted. "Don Augusto knows all the facts. . . ."

"All the facts? What facts are those?" asked the pianist with a show of pique and a move as if to rise.

"Yes. He knows about the mortgage. . . ."

"What!" exclaimed the girl, getting to her feet. "Now what is this all about? What is the reason for this visit?"

"I already told you, my dear niece, that this gentleman wished to make your acquaintance. . . . No need to get excited."

"But there are simply certain things that . . ."

"Please excuse your aunt, señorita," Augusto pleaded, as he, too, stood up. They all were on their feet in a moment. "Merely a matter of chance . . . For my own part I did not solicit any of the information about your self-sacrifice and love of work, or about the mortgage. I didn't pry this interesting information from your aunt. . . . I merely. . . ."

"Yes. You merely happened to bring in the canary a couple of days after having sent me a letter. . . ."

"I don't deny it."

"Well, sir, I'll answer that letter in my own time and way, and no one is going to force me. And now it will be better if I leave."

"Good! Good!" cried the anarchist. "That's integrity, liberty! There's the woman of the future! Women like this have to be won, friend Pérez, won!"

"Señorita! . . ." Augusto tried to get closer to the girl.

"You're quite right," said the pianist extending a hand as white and cold as snow, as before.

She turned her back and those eyes of hers, founts of a mysterious spiritual light. Augusto was overcome with a wave of fire. His heart pounded in his chest. His head seemed ready to come apart.

"Are you unwell?" cried Don Fermín.

"What a child, Lord, what a child!" exclaimed Doña Ermelinda.

"Wonderful! Majestic! Heroic! What a woman!" exclaimed Augusto.

"I agree," said the anarchist.

"Do forgive her, Don Augusto," the aunt went on. "Forgive her. That girl is a porcupine. Who would have thought it!"

"No, no! The truth is that I'm delighted with her! Why, this wild independence, which I lack, is most exciting for me! She's exactly the kind of woman I need. That kind and no other."

"Exactly!" cried the anarchist. "Now that's the woman of the future!"

"And what am I, then?" the aunt put in.

"You? You're the woman of the past! But that girl, why, she's the woman of the future. It was not in vain that she heard me talking day after day about the future society and the woman of the future. It has not been in vain that I have inculcated in her the emancipating doctrines of anarchism—without bombs!"

"Well now I think," said the aunt testily, "that she might well throw a bomb!"

"Even so . . . ," Augusto objected.

"Not that! Never!" the anarchist cried out.

"What's the difference?"

"Don Augusto!"

"I think," added the aunt, "that despite what just happened you should not give up."

"Of course not! All this only adds interest to the game."

"Press on, then! And you know that you have us on

your side, and that you can come and go from this house, which is your house, as often as you want, whether or not it suits Eugenia."

"Ermelinda, the girl never said she would be annoyed to have Don Augusto come here! . . . But, my friend, you must win her by force. When you get to know her, you'll see what she's really like. She's all woman, and you'll have to win her by force. You did want to get to know her, didn't you now?"

"Of course, but . . ."

"All right, then. Into the battle, my friend!"

"By all means. And on that note I'll leave you."

Before Augusto could get out the door, the anarchist uncle took him aside to make a suggestion:

"When you write the girl you must spell her name with a *j* and not with a *g*: Eujenia, not Eugenia. And the surname should be with a *k* and not a *c*: del Arko, not del Arco. Remember, Eujenia Domingo del Arko."

"But what's the reason for all that?"

"Because until that happy day when Esperanto becomes the one single language for all of Humanity, we must write Spanish phonetically. No more letter *C*! We must make war against every *C*! *Za, ze, zi, zo, zu* must be written with a *Z*, and *ka, ke, ki, ko, ku* sounds must be written with a *K*. And away with the *H*! *H* is the height of absurdity, of reaction, of authority, of the Middle Ages, of retrogression! Down with *H*!"

"So you're a phoneticist, too?"

"Why the 'too'?"

"Because you're an Anarchist, an Esperantist. . . ."

"It's all one and the same thing, good sir! Anarchism, Esperantism, spiritism, vegetarianism, phoneticism, it's all one and the same! Down with Authority!

Down with divisionary language! Down with vile matter! Down with Death! Down with the flesh! Down
with *H*! Goodbye!"

Once in the street, Augusto felt relieved of a burden; he even felt a surge of joy. He would never have
guessed at the reaction he now experienced after his
first meeting with the girl. Far from being depressed
by this first face-to-face encounter, he was intrigued
and excited by her manner. Suddenly now the world
seemed all the grander, the air purer, the sky more
blue. He seemed really to breathe anew. He heard the
echo of his mother's voice telling him to marry! All
the women he saw now seemed more lovely, some of
them raving beauties, and none were ugly. The world,
in short, was flooded by a mysterious light, one which
emanated from two invisible stars in the empyrean,
beyond the obvious blue vault. He felt the world in a
new way. For no apparent reason he found himself
speculating on the strangely erroneous popular notion that the Fall in the Garden of Eden was due to
sins of the flesh rather than to the attempt to taste
of the fruit of the Tree of the Knowledge of Good and
Evil.

And he went on to meditate on the old anarchist's
conviction that the only true knowledge was that understood by the Bible: that "to know" in the biblical
sense was the only true knowledge.

When he got home he took the puppy Orfeo in his
arms and told him: "Today is the beginning of a new
life. Don't you somehow realize that the world is
grander, the air purer, the sky more blue? When you
see her, Orfeo . . . Then you'll feel as sad about being
a dog and nothing more than a dog, as I do about
being a man and nothing more. And tell me, Orfeo,
how could you know anything since you can't sin,

since your knowledge is never sinful? Any knowledge which is not sinful is no knowledge at all, it isn't even rational."

When the maid Liduvina served his midday meal she stopped to gaze at him unexpectedly.

"What do you see?" asked Augusto.

"I think something has changed."

"Where do you get that idea?"

"Your face has an altogether different look."

"Are you sure?"

"Absolutely. And . . . what about the pianist?"

"O Liduvina, Liduvina . . ."

"I'm sorry. But I do think of your happiness!"

"Who knows what happiness is . . ."

"That's true enough."

And they both dropped their gaze, to look at the floor, as if the secret of felicity lay beneath it.

IX

THE NEXT DAY found Eugenia talking earnestly with a young man in the close quarters of a concierge's booth at the entrance to her building. The concierge herself had discreetly moved out to the door of the house to take the air.

"We can't go on like this any longer, Mauricio," the pianist was saying. "Especially after what happened yesterday."

"But didn't you tell me," said the man addressed as Mauricio, "that the silly fellow is a dreamer, with his head in the clouds. . . . ?"

"Yes, but he has money. And my aunt won't leave

me in peace about him. Besides, the truth is, I don't like being mean to anybody. Neither do I want to be constantly badgered."

"Send him packing!"

"I can't throw him out of my uncle's house. Suppose they want him there?"

"Don't pay him any attention."

"I'm not, and I don't expect to. But I have a feeling that the poor fellow will take to dropping around to honor us all with a visit whenever I happen to be there. I can't very well lock myself in my room and refuse to see him. Then, instead of declaring his intentions, he'd just become a martyr, a silent one."

"Let him!"

"No, I can't turn down a beggar—any kind of beggar. Especially those who beg with their eyes. And you should see the way he looks at me!"

"You mean you feel sorry for him?"

"Well, he worries me. The truth is . . . I might as well admit it, I do feel sorry for him."

"Are you afraid of something?"

"Don't be silly! I'm not afraid of anything or anybody. You're the only man for me."

"I was pretty sure of that," said Mauricio expansively. He placed his hand on Eugenia's knee and left it there.

"But you'd better make up your mind, Mauricio."

"Make up my mind to what, love?"

"What do you think? To our getting married once and for all!"

"And what are we going to live on?"

"I'll keep on working until you find something to do."

"You'll work?"

"Yes, at teaching my awful music!"

"Never! I'll never live off you and your work. I'll keep on looking. Meanwhile, we'll wait. . . ."

"We'll wait, and wait some more, and the years will slip away." Eugenia accompanied her words by beating her heel against the ground, the heel of the same leg on whose knee Mauricio had been resting his hand.

As his hand bounced up and down, he removed it from the cause of the bouncing. But then he began to play with one of her earrings, putting his arm around her neck to do so. Eugenia let him do as he wanted.

"Listen, Eugenia. If you like, you can go along with the game, and pretend to accept the chap."

"Mauricio!"

"Don't get mad, love! You're right!" By way of changing the subject he pulled her to him and kissed her, long and silently.

"Mauricio!"

Then he kissed her on the eyes.

"We can't go on like this!"

"Why? Is there something better? Do you think we'll ever have it better?"

"I'm telling you: we can't go on like this. . . . You'll have to find some employment. I hate music."

Obscurely, without any clear idea of it all, the girl felt that music was an eternal preparing, an eternal preparation for something which never quite takes place: an eternal initiation that never ended. She was weary of music.

"I'll look for work, Eugenia, I really will."

"You always say the same thing. And nothing ever changes."

"You don't mean to tell me that you think that . . ."

"The truth is you're really nothing more than a

75

layabout. And I'll be the one who'll have to find work for you. Of course men don't mind waiting . . . it's easier for you."

"That's what you think."

"That's what I think all right. And I'll tell you another thing. I don't want to have to look at the pleading eyes of young Don Augusto, the eyes of a hungry dog begging for . . ."

"What a way to talk!"

Eugenia stood up and pushed him away. "It's time for you to take a walk. Get some fresh air. You could use some!"

"Eugenia! If only you would care . . . ," sighed Mauricio in a feverish voice.

"It's you who has to learn to care. And now . . . you can begin by acting the man! Look for work, and make up your mind. If you won't work, I will. But make up your mind. Quickly. Otherwise . . ."

"Otherwise, what?"

"Nothing at all! But we've got to put an end to this!"

Without giving him time to reply, she quit the concierge's vestibule. As she passed the lounging concierge she told her:

"I've left your nephew in there. Pray tell him to make up his mind once and for all."

Eugenia went out into the street with her head held high. At that very moment a hurdy-gurdy launched into a furious polka. "Good God!" cried the anti-musical pianist and she fled rather than walked down the street.

X

Augusto felt a strong desire to confide in someone, and so he set out for the Club, to see his friend
Víctor. It was the day after his visit to Eugenia and,
by chance, at the same hour of the day as the anti-
musical pianist was putting the spurs to her slug of a
lover in the concierge's booth.

Augusto felt like a different man. The visit had revealed the valiant nature of the girl he pursued; her
very eyes had flashed with force; he felt as if his sensual spirit had been newly ploughed, as if a new
spring-source and fountainhead had been found within; his step was firmer, he breathed more freely.

His soliloquy revealed his new attitude:

*Now I have an objective, a purpose to this life of
mine. I will conquer this girl—or be conquered by
her: it's all the same. In love, to conquer is the same
as to be conquered. And yet . . . No! In this case to
be conquered would mean she would choose the other.
For there certainly is another. But is he another, an
"other"? To me? Because I may not exist at all, as
one. In which case there is no "other" about it. I am a
suitor, but he may not be one at all, because he has
already won the suit. The suit for the love of sweet Eugenia. Nothing more? No more than that . . . ?*

A woman passed close to him. Her body radiated
freshness, health, joy. His soliloquy was broken off.
He was carried along by her moving presence. Without thinking he followed her, and resumed his soliloquy:

*What a beauty! This one and the other, one and
another of them. Perhaps the other man is not a suitor
but one sought. And perhaps he does not react to her*

as she deserves. . . . But this girl now, she really is a beauty! What a lovely way to wave to someone as she just did! And the eyes! They're much like those others, Eugenia's! What a pleasure it must be to forget about life and death in those arms! To be rocked as on a sea of flesh! . . . As for the other man, the other . . . ! But the "other" man is not Eugenia's friend, he's not the one she loves. The other one is me. Yes, I'm the "other" one, I'm another!

As he was reaching this conclusion, the girl ahead of him turned into a doorway. Augusto stopped short and stood looking at the house. It was only then he realized he really had been following her. He recalled that he had been planning to go to the Club, and he set out again in that direction. He resumed his soliloquy:

How many beautiful women there are in the world! They're nearly all lovely! Thanks be to God. Gratias agimus tibi propter magnam Gloriam tuam! *We give thanks to thee for thy great glory! Thy great glory, Lord, is the beauty of woman! Good heavens! what a head of hair!*

Another girl, with a glorious head of hair! A serving-girl with a basket on her arm crossed in front of him. And he drifted behind *her*! Light seemed to nest in her golden hair. The strands seemed to be on the point of breaking away from her braid to scatter themselves on the clear air. And the face beneath the head of hair was all of it a sweet smile.

Augusto scarcely paused in his soliloquy as he followed the girl with the basket.

I am another, I am the other. But then there must be "other" women! "Other" women for an "other" man. But one like her, the unique and only one, none! All these others are mere imitations of the one, the unique, the sweet Eugenia! My Eugenia! Mine? Yes, I make her mine by thought and desire. The other man, that is, the one, may possess her materially, but the mysterious spiritual light of those eyes is mine. Mine, mine! But now, considering it well, doesn't this gold head of hair in front of me reflect a mysterious spiritual light as well? And are there perhaps two Eugenias instead of one, one of them mine and the other his? If that's the way it is, let him keep his and I'll have mine. Whenever I am overcome with sadness, especially at night, whenever I feel like crying for no reason at all, how sweet it would be to cover my face, my mouth, my eyes with all that hair, all that gold hair, and breathe the air through her perfumed hair! And yet . . .

He was suddenly drawn up short. The girl with the basket had stopped to chat with another one like her. Augusto hesitated an instant:

O there are so many lovely girls since I met Eugenia . . . . !

He turned away and set out for the Club once more, soliloquizing still:

If she insists on her preference for the other one, that is, the one, I know I have it in me to make a heroic gesture, a gesture of generosity which will cause astonishment. Whether she ever cares for me or not, the matter of the mortgage cannot be left untended!

He was startled out of his soliloquy by a burst of noisy joyfulness which seemed to fall from the sky. A bevy of girls, actually a pair, had burst into laughter, and they laughed like birds in a flowering tree. He fixed his beauty-thirsting eyes on the pair of loves and to him they seemed like a single twin-body. They walked arm in arm. He was possessed by a furious desire to detain them, to take them, each one by an arm, and go off with them wherever the wind of life blew.

Augusto walked behind the laughing couple and again told himself:

How many beautiful women I've seen since meeting Eugenia! The world has become a paradise! What eyes! What hair! What laughter! One blonde, the other brunette. Let me see now, which is which? I've gotten them confused one with the other! . . .

"Hello there! Are you awake or asleep?"

"Oh, hello, Víctor."

"I was waiting for you at the Club, but since you didn't show up . . ."

"I was just on my way there. . . ."

"Going the opposite way? You've lost your mind."

"Yes, you're right. But listen to me. I'll tell you the truth. I believe I've already spoken to you about Eugenia. . . ."

"The pianist? Yes, you have."

"Well, I've fallen madly in love with her, like a . . ."

"Like a madman. Go on."

"Yes, I'm mad for her. I saw her at home yesterday, on the pretext of calling upon her aunt and uncle. I *saw* her. . . ."

"And she *looked* at you. Is that it? And you believed in God?"

"It wasn't so much that she looked at me, but rather that she enveloped me in her gaze. And it wasn't that I believed in God but rather that I believed I was a god."

"By God, she hit you hard. . . ."

"And she wasn't exactly easy-going either. She came on rather wild. And now I'm a changed man. Every woman I see seems beautiful. Since I left the house not more than half an hour ago, I've been carried away by three, I mean four. The first one was all eyes, then one who was a head of glorious hair, and finally a pair who laughed like angels, one fair and the other dark. And I've followed all four of them. What do you make of it, now?"

"It's clear enough. Your great store of love lay dormant at the bottom of your soul. It was inert, lying there without movement, and along came Eugenia the pianist. She moved you, shook you up, and the wellsprings overflowed. And now you can't contain the flow, there's too much of it, and it spreads in all directions. When a man of your type falls deeply in love with a woman, he falls in love with them all."

"Well now, I thought it was just the opposite. . . . And yet, may I say, parenthetically as it were: Would you just look at that dark-haired girl now! She's bright night itself! Black does indeed absorb the most light! One can really feel the light hidden in her hair, behind the jet-black of her eyes. Let's follow her."

"Just as you like. . . ."

"As I was saying, I would have thought it was just the opposite: That when a man falls in love he concentrates all his love on one person, whereas before he spread his love among many, and that all others would then seem like nothing to him. . . . But look, just look at the glint of sunlight in that girl's black hair!"

"I'll try to explain what I mean. You were in love, unconsciously, of course, with woman in the abstract, and not with anyone concretely. When you first saw Eugenia, the abstract became concrete, and woman became one woman, and you fell in love with her, and from there, from her, you went toward all women, without leaving her, and you are in love with them collectively, with the genus woman. You've gone, then, from the abstract to the concrete and from the concrete to the generic, from woman to one woman and from one woman to all women."

"That's metaphysics for you!"

"And what is love but metaphysics?"

"Come now!"

"Especially in your case, since your kind of falling in love is purely cerebral, or as we say, in the head."

"That's what you think," exclaimed Augusto, piqued and put out of humor by the suggestion that his love was headwork, a suggestion that wounded him to the quick.

"And if you push me to it, if you drive me to tell the whole truth, I'll point out that you yourself are no more than a figment of imagination, a pure idea, a fictional being. . . ."

"You mean you think I couldn't possibly fall in love like everybody else . . . ?"

"I think you're really in love all right, but in your head alone. In other words, you *think* you're in love. . . ."

"But what does being in love mean except to believe that one is in love?"

"Ah, my friend, it's more complicated than you think!"

"What's the difference, then, between being in love and thinking that one is in love?"

"Look, we'd best drop the subject and talk of something else."

When he returned home that night, Augusto went on talking about it all to Orfeo:

"Look here, Orfeo, what's the difference between being in love and thinking that one is in love? Am I or am I not in love with Eugenia? Doesn't my heart pound and my blood run hot whenever I see her? Am

I not like other men? I must show them, Orfeo, that I'm just as good as they are!"

At supper he asked Liduvina:

"Tell me, how does one know when a man is in love, really in love?"

"What a strange question! Why do you ask?"

"Come now, tell me, how do people know?"

"Well, people know . . . when someone says strange things, when he talks odd and does odd things. When a man is gone on a woman, as they say, he's no longer his own man, no longer a man. . . ."

"What is he, then?"

"He's a . . . a thing, a little beastie. . . . A woman can do anything she wants with him, anything she pleases."

"In that case, when a woman falls in love with a man, is gone on him, as you said, can the man do anything he pleases with her?"

"It's not exactly the same. . . ."

"What! How's that?"

"It's all very hard to explain. But . . . are you in love, really in love?"

"That's what I'm trying to find out. But as regards doing and saying odd things, I haven't done or said anything very odd, it seems to me. . . ."

Liduvina held her tongue. And Augusto wondered: *Am I really in love?*

XI

THE NEXT TIME Augusto called at the house of Eugenia's aunt and uncle, the maid led him straight to the drawing room and said: "I'll announce you at once." Augusto suddenly felt abandoned, as if standing in a vacuum. He felt an overwhelming oppression, a sense of ridiculous solemnity. He sat down, and then stood up at once. He paced about the room, gazing at the paintings on the walls, a portrait of Eugenia among them. He felt like beating a retreat, running away. When he presently heard a light footstep, he felt an icy stab in his heart. His head felt as if it were lost in a mist. The door opened and Eugenia appeared. The poor man was forced to lean up against the back of the chair. Seeing him in this wan condition, Eugenia herself turned pale. She stood still in the middle of the room. When she again came forward she asked, in a low hoarse voice:

"What is the matter, Don Augusto? Do you feel ill?"

"No. It's nothing. I don't really know. . . ."

"Would you like something? Do you need anything?"

"A glass of water, perhaps."

The request provided an out for Eugenia, and she hastened from the room to fetch the water herself. The water shook in the glass, but the glass shook even more in Augusto's hand. He drank it down in one gulp, spilling some of it over his chin in the process, without taking his eyes off the pianist all the while.

"If you'd care for some, I'll have an herb infusion

made for you, camomile tea or linden. . . . What *was* the matter with you?"

"No, no, it was nothing. And thank you, Eugenia, thank you." And he applied a handkerchief to his wet chin.

"Well, then, do sit down." Once they had done so, she told him: "I was expecting you. I thought you would come back soon, and I told the maid to show you in even if my aunt and uncle were not at home. They often go out in the afternoon. I wanted to talk to you alone."

"Oh, Eugenia! . . ."

"Now let us proceed more calmly, more coolly. . . . I never expected you to be in such a state. I was frightened when I walked in here. You looked like a corpse."

"I was more dead than alive."

"We must come to some understanding."

"Eugenia!" He held out his hand, but quickly drew it back.

"It strikes me that you're still not in a frame of mind in which we could talk to each other quietly, like good friends. Let me see, I'll take your pulse."

The poor man now really was overcome. His heartbeat quickened, his face reddened. He could scarcely make out Eugenia's eyes behind a sudden red mist. He thought he was losing consciousness.

"Be compassionate, Eugenia! Think of me!"

"Please remain calm, Don Augusto."

" 'Don Augusto . . . don Augusto . . . don . . . don . . .' "

"Yes, my good Don Augusto, please remain calm and let us talk quietly and calmly."

"But . . . permit me—" and he ventured to take hold

of one of those white hands, cold as snow, with the tapering fingers designed to draw a flow of arpeggios from a keyboard.

"Just as you wish, Don Augusto . . ."

Augusto was inspired to raise those fingers to his lips and cover the cold hand with kisses which did little to fire her.

"When you are finished, whenever you are ready, we shall talk, Don Augusto."

"But, Eugenia, wait. . . ."

"Not at all. It is time for us to talk—formally." She took her hand away and proceeded: "I don't know what kind of expectations my aunt and uncle—or rather my aunt—have led you to conceive. But in any case it seems to me that you have been misled."

"How, how have I been misled?"

"They ought to have told you that I have a friend already to whom I am engaged."

"I know that."

"Did they tell you that?"

"Nobody told me. But I know."

"Then . . ."

"Eugenia: I make no demands on you, I want nothing. I ask for nothing from you. I would be happy merely to be allowed to come now and then so that my spirit might bask in the look of your eyes, so that I might drink in and lose myself in your very breathing. . . ."

"Come, come, Don Augusto. That will do. One reads those things in books. No more of that literature. I have no objection to your coming here as often as you like. You can see me and see me again, and you can talk to me and even—as you've seen just now—even kiss my hand. But the fact is I already have a suitor, a man I love and whom I expect to marry."

"Are you really in love with him?"

"What a question!"

"Just how do you know, what are the signs, that you are in love with him?"

"Have you gone mad, Don Augusto?"

"No, no, not at all. I only ask because my best friend has just told me that many people think they are in love without actually being so at all."

"He probably meant you. Isn't that so?"

"He said it about me, yes, but what difference does that make?"

"Because in your case it might well be true."

"Do you really think, Eugenia, do you really think I do not truly love you?"

"Not so loud, Don Augusto. Don't raise your voice. The maid will hear you. . . ."

"Ah, yes. True enough!" cried Augusto, as excited as before. "There are people who consider me incapable of true love . . . !"

"Excuse me a moment," said Eugenia, interrupting him, and she left the room, leaving him alone.

Presently she returned and, with the greatest composure asked: "Well, now, Don Augusto, have you calmed down?"

"Eugenia! Eugenia!"

Just then there was the sound at the front door and shortly Eugenia's aunt and uncle entered the room.

Eugenia spoke first: "Don Augusto came to pay us a visit and I opened the door myself. He thought he should come back later, but I told him to come in, that you wouldn't be long, and here he is!"

Don Fermín, the anarchist, spoke, issuing a proclamation: "The time will come when all social conventionalisms will have been abolished. I am totally convinced that all the walls around private property are nothing but a lure, an incentive for so-called thieves —when the real thieves are the ones behind the walls, the proprietors. No property is so secure as that without walls, property within reach of everyone. Man is born good, he is by nature good. Society corrupts him."

"O shut up!" exclaimed his wife. "I can't even hear the canary. Can you hear the bird sing, Don Augusto? A delight, that bird. You should have heard the canary I had when Eugenia used to practice the piano. The more crescendo on the piano, the louder the bird sang. In the end, that was what killed the little animal."

"Even the animals are victims of our vices," the anarchist pontificated. "The very animals that live with us have been uprooted from the blessed state of nature. Ah, humanity!"

"Did you have a long wait, Don Augusto?" asked the aunt.

"O not at all. No, a moment, like a flash . . . of lightning . . . Or it seemed something like that. . . ."

"Ah! Indeed . . ."

"Yes, indeed, aunt, it wasn't very long. Just long enough for Don Augusto to recover from a slight indisposition he seems to have gotten on the way here."

"What's that now . . . ?"

"O it was really nothing, nothing at all. . . ."

"I must leave you all, I have work to do," said Eugenia. She extended her hand to Augusto and quickly left.

"Well . . . and how is it all coming along?" the aunt asked as soon as the girl-pianist had quit the room.

"It?" . . .

"Your conquest! Your winning the girl, of course!"

"Not so well. Very badly in fact! She just told me she has a friend and means to marry him."

"Didn't I tell you, Ermelinda? Isn't that what I said?" said the uncle.

"No, no, and no again! Sheer madness! The idea of marrying *him!*"

"But, suppose she does indeed love him? . . ."

"That's the point I was trying to make," exclaimed the free-love anarchist. "Long live Freedom, sacred Freedom, freedom of choice!"

"No, no, and no again! Does anyone think that this little girl knows what she's doing? To think of rejecting you, Don Augusto, you! It simply won't do!"

"But, Señora, we must think of her. We must stop and reflect. . . . We cannot, we must not violate the will of a young woman like Eugenia. . . . It is a matter of her happiness, and we must think solely of her well-being, and even sacrifice ourselves so that she may fulfill herself. . . ."

"You mean you are ready to sacrifice yourself . . . ?"

"Myself, yes! I am most willing to sacrifice myself for the happiness of Eugenia, your niece. For my own happiness consists in her being happy."

"Bravo!" cried the anarchist uncle. "Bravo! Bravo! Done like a hero, like an anarchist! A mystical anarchist, that is!"

"An anarchist?" asked Augusto in wonder.

"Yes, an anarchist. By my definition anarchism consists precisely in each person sacrificing himself for the others and in finding his own happiness in the happiness of others, and . . ."

"O of course, Fermín. That's why you get into such

a state whenever your soup is served up to you ten minutes late!"

"Well, you know very well that my anarchism is theoretical. I strive for perfection but I'm not always able to . . ."

"Happiness is also theoretical," murmured Augusto ruefully, as if to himself. "And I have decided on an act of heroism. . . ."

"What is that?"

"Did you not tell me once, Señora, that the house which was left to Eugenia by her unfortunate father . . ."

"Yes, by my poor brother."

". . . is mortgaged in such a way that it takes all her inherited income?"

"Exactly."

"Well, I know what I have to do!" and he started for the door.

"But, Don Augusto . . ."

"Yes, I myself! I feel up to the heroic, and to sacrifice. And now we shall learn whether this Augusto which is me is in love only in his head, or whether his heart is not also involved, and whether he thinks he is in love without really being so! Eugenia has awakened me to life, to the true life and, no matter to whom she may be leagued, I owe her an eternal debt of gratitude."

He departed with solemnity: "Farewell!"

He had no sooner left than the aunt shrieked: "That girl!"

XII

O N E   D A Y the maid Liduvina announced the girl with the laundry.

"The girl with the laundry? Ah! Yes. Tell her to come in here."

She came in with a basket of clothes. Augusto kept quiet, and so did she, and the two looked at each other without moving. This had never happened before, and the girl felt a strange sensation of heat. In the many times she had come to this house before nothing of the kind had ever happened. It had always seemed as if the young master of this house never even saw her, a phenomenon which had piqued her, annoyed her, for she felt she knew her own merits, her own value and worth. Not even to look her over! Not ever to look at her as other men did! Not even once in a while to devour her with his eyes like the others! There were those who licked her eyes with their eyes—and her mouth as well, her whole face!

"What's the matter, Rosario? . . . Your name is Rosario, isn't it?"

"That's my name, all right."

"What's the trouble, then?"

"Why do you ask me that, Señorito?"

"I've never seen you get so red of a sudden. . . . And besides, you suddenly seem a changed girl."

"It's you who seem to have changed, a different man."

"It could be. . . . Come over here, would you?"

"O stop your joking, sir, and let's get on with . . ."

"Joking? Do you think this is a joke?" He went on, in a more serious tone: "Do let me look at you. Come closer."

"Haven't you seen me before?"

"That's true. But I never seem to have noticed how very pretty you are. . . ."

"Come now, Señorito, don't make fun of me. . . ." Her face, however, burned even more.

"Just now, your color is so vivid, a sun . . ."

"Please . . ."

"Come here. Come. You probably think I've gone mad. But it isn't so at all. The truth is I was mad before. I mean I was a fool before, a fool about every-thing, lost in a fog, completely blind. I've only just now had my eyes opened for me. You can see that for yourself. Think of all the times you've come to this house, and I've looked at you and not seen you. It's as if I hadn't been alive before. I was a fool, a fool! . . . What's the matter, little girl, what's the matter with you?"

Rosario had sunk or fallen into a chair. She hid her face in her hands and burst out crying. Augusto rose and closed the door to the room. He went over to the girl and put his hand on her shoulder. He spoke to her, then, in a very low voice, something like a warm moist breeze:

"What *is* it, my child, what's the matter?"

"When you say those things, you make me cry."

"You little angel! . . ."

"You shouldn't say such things, Don Augusto."

"Why shouldn't I? For the truth is that I *was* blind, a blind fool, as if I wasn't alive at all. Until a woman came along, you understand, another woman, and opened my eyes to it all, and now I can see the world, especially all you others, all you other women."

"That other woman . . . she must be bold. . . ."

"Bold? Do you know what you're saying, Rosario? Do you know what it means to be bold, to be a bad

92

woman? No, no, this woman is not that sort at all. She's an angel, like you. Still, she doesn't love me . . . she doesn't love me. . . ." His voice broke and his eyes filled with tears.

"Poor Don Augusto!"

"Yes, that's the truth. Poor Don Augusto! But look, Rosario, please drop the Don and call me Augusto. Let me hear you say it that way: Poor Augusto!"

"But, Señorito, I can't. . . ."

"Come now, just say Poor Augusto!"

"If you insist on it. . . . Poor Augusto!"

Augusto sat down again.

"Come over here!"

She stood up as if moved by a spring, or under hypnotic suggestion. She was breathing fast. He pulled her down onto his lap, pressed her to him and brought his cheek next to hers, which was burning hot. He began in a torrent:

"O Rosario, I don't know what is happening to me! I don't know what is coming over me! That woman you call bold, a bad woman, without even knowing her, has blinded me by making me see, by giving me my sight back. I did not live and now I do. But now that I live I realize what it means to die, now I know death. Now I must set up a defense against this woman, I must defend myself against her fateful gaze. Will you help me, Rosario, will you help me defend myself against her?"

The faintest of assents, a whisper from some other plane of being, a murmur of "Yes," was all the response.

"I no longer know what is happening to me, Rosario, nor what I'm saying or doing or thinking. I no longer know whether I am in love with that woman or not, with that woman you call bold. . . ."

"Don Augusto, I . . ."

"Not Don, just Augusto . . ."

"Augusto, I . . ." But she did not go on.

"Good enough. . . ." He closed his eyes. "You don't need to say anything. I'll go on talking to myself. That's the way it's been since my mother died. There's no one else to talk to really. I talk to myself, as if in sleep. I've never really known what it is to sleep together in the same dream, two people sleeping together in a dream. To sleep together, not just lying alongside each other while each one dreams his own separate dream, but really to sleep together, both in the same dream! Couldn't we sleep together, Rosario, dreaming the same dream together?"

"And what about that woman?" Rosario began, with tears in her voice as she lay in Augusto's arms.

"That woman, Rosario, does not love me. . . . She does not love me. But she has shown me, opened my eyes to the fact that there are other women. Because of her, through her, I've learned to see other women. And one of them might care for me. . . . Could you care for me, Rosario, could you love me?" And he pressed her wildly against himself.

"I think so. . . . I think I could love you. . . ."

"O, that's good, Rosario! Isn't it, Rosario?"

Just then the door opened and Liduvina appeared. She gasped at what she saw and quickly closed the door again. Augusto was even more discountenanced than Rosario. The girl merely stood up, smoothed down her hair with her hands, brushed herself off, and asked in an uneven tone:

"Shall we go over the account, sir?"

"Yes, of course. . . . But you'll come back now, won't you?"

"Yes, I'll be back."

"And you understand and forgive me?"

"Forgive you . . . what?"

"All that happened . . . a bit of madness. Do you forgive me?"

"I have nothing to forgive you for. What you should do is to stop thinking about that woman."

"What about you, will you think of me?"

"Well, now, I've got to go."

They settled accounts quickly and Rosario went off. She had no sooner gone when Liduvina appeared again.

"Weren't you asking me only the other day how to tell if a man is in love or not?"

"That's right enough."

"And I told you it was a matter of a person's doing or saying odd things. And so now I can tell you that you're in love."

"In love . . . with Rosario?"

"With Rosario nothing! . . . With that other one!"

"And now how did you decide that, Liduvina?"

"Simple enough. You've said and done with that girl what you never did with the pianist."

"You mean to say that you think? . . ."

"O no, I don't think or imagine you went so far as all that, but . . ."

"Liduvina!"

"Just as you wish, Señorito."

The confused Augusto went to lie down, his head in a turmoil. As he fell on to the bed he addressed Orfeo, who was lying there:

"This cursed business of sleeping alone, alone with a single, lone dream! The dream of one person alone is mere illusion, a mere appearance. The dream of a couple is a true dream, a reality. What is the real world but the dream we all dream together, the common dream?"

And then he dreamt.

XIII

O N E   M O R N I N G a few days later Liduvina appeared in Augusto's room to announce a young lady.

"A young lady?"

"Yes. Her. The pianist."

"Eugenia?"

"Yes, Eugenia. Apparently you're not the only one who's gone mad."

Augusto began to quake. He felt like an escaped criminal. He rose and dressed quickly. He quit the room ready for anything.

"I have learned, Don Augusto," Eugenia began solemnly and at once, "that you have bought my mortgage, and that it is in your possession."

"I have no reason to deny it."

"By what right did you do so?"

"By the right, Señorita, of any citizen to buy whatever he pleases if the owner is willing to sell."

"That's not what I mean. What I'd like to know is why you bought it?"

"Because it grieved me to see you dependent on a man who probably has little interest in you and who is, I suspect, a soulless speculator."

"You mean that you would rather that I be dependent on you, who are apparently more interested in me. . . ."

"O that's not it at all! Nothing of the kind, Eugenia! I am not trying to make you dependent on me in any way. You gratuitously offend me merely by suggesting such a thing. Look, I'll show you. . . ." Obviously agitated, he left her alone in the drawing room.

Presently he returned with a packet of papers.

"Eugenia, here are the documents, the security for your debt. Take them and do whatever you want with them."

"What do you mean?"

"I renounce all claim to anything. That was my reason for buying these papers."

"I knew it! That's why I said that your intention was to make me dependent on you. You want to tie me to you by gratitude. You want to buy me!"

"Eugenia, Eugenia!"

"You want to buy me! You want to buy, not my love —which can't be bought—but my body!"

"Eugenia, Eugenia!"

"And that's nothing short of infamy, dishonor, even if you won't admit it!"

"Eugenia, for the love of God! . . ."

"Don't come any closer! I won't be responsible for my actions in this room! . . ."

"In that case I will come closer. Hit me, Eugenia, if you want! Insult me, spit on me, do whatever you like!"

"You don't deserve anything from me!" And Eugenia stood up. "I'm going now, but I want you to understand that I do not, will not, accept your offer, your alms! I'll work harder than ever. I'll see that my fiancé—soon to be my husband—works too. And we'll make our own way. And as far as these papers are concerned, keep them, and keep my house."

"But won't you understand, Eugenia, I don't raise

any objections to your marrying the fiancé you mention!"

"Now what do you mean by that?"

"I didn't do what I did so that you would be bound to me by any gratitude or so that you would marry me! . . . I really do renounce my own happiness. Or rather, my happiness consists in your being happy. Nothing more. In your being happy with the husband of your choice! . . ."

"Ah, now I see your game! You are to play the part of the victim, you are to be the martyr! You reserve for yourself the role of hero! Keep the house, I tell you. It's a present from me."

"Eugenia, Eugenia!"

"That will do!"

And without another word or look that pair of fiery eyes vanished.

Augusto was stunned. He could not be sure that he existed. When he emerged from the mist of nonexistence, he rushed out into the street and walked aimlessly. He came to a church and went in, scarcely aware of what he was doing. It chanced to be St. Martín's, but as he entered he could make out only the subdued light of the lamp burning before the high altar. He breathed the darkness, and ancient odor of tradition perfumed by incense, a centuries-old hearth. Groping his way, he found a place to sit and slumped down on a bench. He felt mortally weary, and all the dark weight of the centuries pressed upon him. From out of what seemed a far-off distance he heard an occasional human sound, a cough. He thought of his mother.

Closing his eyes, he dreamt of the warm secret house, where the light entered through white flowers embroidered on the curtains. His mother came and went soundlessly, always dressed in black, a smile which was like sediment of tears. He dreamt of his life with her, under her care and protection, and he recalled her slow, unhurried, gentle, composed dying, and her departing at the end like a bird of passage quietly setting out on its long flight. He next thought of his finding Orfeo, and a whole series of images passed through his mind like a film.

Close by him a man was mumbling some prayers. He rose to leave and Augusto was led to do the same. At the holy-water stoup the man wet his fingers and then extended his hand to Augusto to partake and they both crossed themselves. They emerged from the church together.

"Don Avito!" exclaimed Augusto, as he recognized the other man.

"Augustito! You've recognized me. . . ."

"But, you . . . here, in a church!"

"Yes, me here. Life teaches us all, and death even more. They both teach us much more than science can."

"But, what about your son, the 'candidate for genius'?"

Don Avito Carrascal told him the woeful tale of his son, a fictive personage like himself. He concluded by saying: "You see, Augustito, how I have come to this. . . ."

Augusto remained silent and gazed at the ground. They walked along under the trees.

"Yes, Augusto, it seems to be true. Life is the only real schoolmistress to teach life. There's no pedagogy worth a hoot. One learns to live by living, by living only, and each one must begin all over again, from the beginning, first as an apprentice . . ."

"And what of the cumulative labor of generations, the legacy of centuries?"

"There are only two legacies: the legacy of illusions and the legacy of disillusions. Both of them meet where we just met, in the temple. . . . I am certain that you were brought there either by a great illusion or a deep disillusion."

"By both."

"Of course, by both of them. Illusion, hope, engenders disillusion, memory. And disillusion, memory, in its turn engenders illusion, hope. Science deals with reality, the present, and I can no longer live with any part of the present. Ever since my poor Apolodoro, my victim," and his voice choked, "ever since he died, that is, killed himself, there is no present possible, there is no science or reality worth a hoot to me. I cannot live except in recalling him or looking forward to him. And I have ended up going to the hearth and home of all illusions and all disillusions—the Church!"

"So that you've come to believe? . . ."

"How do I know! . . ."

"But don't you believe then? . . ."

"I don't know if I believe or if I don't believe. I know that I pray. I don't quite know what I pray. At nightfall there are a number of us saying the rosary. I don't know who the others are, and they don't know me, but we have a sense of solidarity, intimate communion with each other. And I've come to the conclusion that humanity has damned little need for geniuses!"

"And your wife, Don Avito . . . ?"

"Ah, my wife!" exclaimed Carrascal. Sudden tears gleaming in his eyes seemed to irradiate an inner light. "I discovered my wife! Up until the catastrophe I never knew her worth. I learned something of the mystery of life in the terrible nights following Apolo-doro's suicide, when I lay my head in her lap, the lap of the mother, and wept. She stroked my head and kept saying 'My poor son! My poor son!' She was never more a mother, never more than she is now. When I made her a mother—and I made her a mother merely to furnish the raw material for a genius—I never thought then that I would some day need her as a mother myself. And I never did know my own mother, Augusto, I never had a mother. I had no mother, I never knew what it meant to have a mother until the day my own wife lost her child and mine and felt herself then to be mother to me. You, Augusto, had the good luck to know your own splendid mother, Doña Soledad. If you hadn't, I'd urge you to marry as soon as you could."

"I knew my mother, Don Avito, but after all I lost her, and in the church I was recalling her just now."

"Well, if you wish to have a mother again, get married!"

"Whoever I married would never be my mother."

"True enough. But get married in any case."

"How, Don Avito, 'deductively' or 'inductively'?" Augusto was referring, in jest, to one of Carrascal's theories, a doctrine he had read about in the same book in which he had met Don Avito himself.

"You can forget about all that, Augusto. Don't re-mind me of all that tragedy, for God's sake! Still, if you want me to humor you, I'll tell you: marry in-tuitively!"

"What if the woman I love doesn't love me?"

"Marry a woman who loves you, even if you don't love her. It is better to marry and be won over to love than to marry and try to win your wife. Look for one who loves you already."

The image of the laundress's young daughter passed in a flash through Augusto's imagination. Augusto had already formed the illusion that the poor child was in love with him.

When Augusto finally took leave of Don Avito, he started off in the direction of the Club. He wanted to clear away the mist that enveloped him, to clear his head, and his heart, by playing a game of chess with Víctor.

XIV

AT THE CLUB, Augusto at once noted that something was amiss with his friend Víctor, who was irritably silent, and who lost one game after another.

"There's something wrong, Víctor, isn't there?"

"Yes, there is. A serious situation. I'd like to get it off my chest. It's a fine night. Why don't we go outside and I'll tell you about it?"

Víctor was Augusto's best and most intimate friend, although he was five or six years older than Augusto and had been married more than a dozen years, having married very young—as a matter of duty or conscience, according to the rumors. He and his wife had no children.

Once out in the street, Víctor began:

"As you know, Augusto, I was obliged to marry when I was very young. . . ."

"Obliged to marry?"

"Yes, don't pretend surprise; rumor reaches everyone. Our parents forced us to get married, mine and Elena's, when we were scarcely more than children.

And marriage was for us a kind of play, a game. We played at being man and wife. But it turned out later that it was all a false alarm. . . ."

"What was a false alarm?"

"Why, what they married us for. Exaggerated sense of shame, a false pregnancy of shame on the part of our respective parents. They had gotten wind of a little slip on our part which had caused a bit of scandal, and, without waiting to see what the consequences might be, if any, they married us off."

"They did the right thing."

"I wouldn't say so. In any case, as it turned out, neither the first slip nor any of a subsequent series of slips, post-marital slips, had any consequences."

"What do you mean by slips?"

"The word describes what we were doing. We were proceeding by slips. Slipping and sliding along. I already told you we were merely playing husband-and-wife. . . ."

"I'll be damned!"

"Now don't let your imagination go too far. We were still too young for perversity. We're still too young for perversions. But we certainly weren't thinking of founding a family. We were just a girl and a boy living together, carrying on a so-called marital life. Still, when a year passed and there was no fruition to the marriage, we began to fall out, to look at each other askance, to go in for mutual recrimination, even in silence. I found I couldn't accept the situation: apparently I actually wanted to be a father. Soon I was twenty-one, a man, and the fact of my being less than other men in this regard, less than any savage, who has a child punctually after nine months of marriage, or even before, was something I could not accept."

"But, it's no one's fault if . . ."

"Yes. However, even without saying anything to my wife, I was blaming her and thinking she was sterile and making me look ridiculous to one and all. I'm sure that at the same time she was thinking the same about me and even . . . I don't know. . . ."

"Even what? . . ."

"Oh, nothing, except that when one year passes and then another and another and a couple have no children, the wife begins to think the husband's to blame because he didn't come to matrimony in sound health and is the bearer of some disease. . . . The fact was that we acted like enemies. There was a devil in the house. It all blew up into a turmoil. Recriminations everywhere: 'You're no good!' followed by 'You're the one who's no good!' And all the rest of it."

"Was that the reason you went off by yourself to that sanatorium a few years after you were married, when we all saw that you were in a bad state of nerves?"

"No, that wasn't the reason . . . it was something worse that time."

They both fell silent. Víctor stared at the ground.

"Good enough. Don't tell me. I don't mean to pry into your secrets."

"Well, here goes, I'll tell you! The warfare with my wife finally drove me wild and I got to imagining that it was not a matter of intensity in lovemaking, or whatever you might call it, but a question of number, of times . . . you understand?"

"I suppose I do."

"And I set about eating like a trooper, gobbling everything I thought nutritious, all of it seasoned with every spice, especially those commonly thought to be aphrodisiacal. And I went for my wife like I did the food. . . . Then, naturally . . ."

"You fell ill."

"Naturally, as I was about to say. I came to my senses just in time, if I may put it that way, or I would have been done under. But I recovered in two ways: for I got back my wife as well as my health, and we gradually learned to accept the situation. Peace reigned in the house at last, and then even happiness. Sometimes we would allude to our solitude, but soon enough we became resigned and even used to it. In the end, we not only ceased bewailing the lack of a family but went so far as feeling sorry for people who did have children. We got so used to each other that each of us was the other's habit. Of course you wouldn't understand all that. . . ."

"No. The truth is I don't."

"Well, anyhow, I became my wife's habit and custom and she became the same for me. Everything became established and moderated in our house, as regular as the meals. At twelve noon, the soup was on the table. And every day we ate practically the same things, in the same order and quantity. By now, Elena hates any and all change, and so do I. We live by clock strokes."

"It reminds me of what our friend Luis says of the Romera couple: he calls them a bachelor husband and wife."

"Not bad. For no bachelor is as much of a bachelor or as set in his ways as a married man without children. But the paternal instinct had not died in me and, even less, the maternal instinct in her, and, to make up for the absent children, we adopted, or made a ward of, a dog. And then one day we watched

him die, a bone stuck in his throat, his eyes begging
for us to save his life. We were so horrified we never
had another dog or any other living thing in place of
the absent children. So now Elena has that collection
of dolls you've seen, those big things Elena dresses
and undresses."

"Those won't die on you."

"No, of course not. Everything was going along
fine. We were content. No babies crying to disturb
our sleep. I didn't have to worry about whether it was
to be a boy or a girl or what was to become of him
or her. . . . Besides, my wife has always been free for
me, no pregnancies or lactations to interrupt the
course of our lives. In short, we led a charmed life."

"Do you realize that a life like that resembles nothing so much as . . ."

"As a man and his mistress? Right? I agree. A marriage without children can easily turn into legalized
concubinage, very well ordered, very hygienic, relatively chaste. Husband and wife, both of them single
and both of them bachelors, but living as lover and
mistress. . . . Thus we spent eleven years, going on
twelve . . . But now, do you know what has happened?"

"No, how would I?"

"Can't you guess what's happened now?"

"Not unless it is that you've gone and got your
wife pregnant at this late date."

"Exactly! That's it. Just imagine! A disaster!"

"A disaster? But weren't you keen for some time
to . . ."

"For the first few years. But now . . . There's a
devil in the house again. And we're torn apart. Only
now each of us blames the other for the disaster, just

as years ago we used to blame each other for the sterility. . . . We've already begun to call him . . . No, I'd better not tell you. . . ."

"Well, don't tell me if you don't want to."

"We've already begun to call him the Intruder! And I've already dreamt of his dying on us some morning with a bone stuck in his throat. . . ."

"Atrocious!"

"Yes, you're right. Atrocious! And now, goodbye to all order, farewell comfort and custom! Only yesterday Elena had a fit of vomiting, one of those pleasantries associated with the condition we Spanish call 'interesting!' Some euphemism! Interesting, indeed! Did you ever hear of anything less interesting?"

"But she herself must be happy to feel herself becoming a mother."

"Happy? Just as much as I am! This is one of Nature's dirty tricks. Or perhaps Providence, or whoever, is making mock of us. If it had come, boy or girl whichever it's supposed to be, when we were expecting it, turtledoves that we were, full of vanity even more than paternal or maternal love, that would have been another matter. If it had only come when we were convinced that to be childless meant we were inferior to everyone else, then it would have been well and good, a godsend I suppose. But now! It's a mockery! If it were not for . . ."

"For what?"

"I'd give him to you as a playmate for your Orfeo!"

"Víctor, get hold of yourself! Don't talk nonsense. . . ."

"Nonsense, yes . . . I'm sorry. Still, does it seem right to you that after nearly a dozen years of a marriage which was going along beautifully, once we were cured of the ridiculous vanity of the newly wed, this should happen to us? We were so well-off, so sure of ourselves, so confident. . . ."

"Come, now. Calm down!"

"Yes, of course. But you don't know, you can't imagine the worst of it. My poor Elena is now convinced that she's cutting a ridiculous figure; she can't rid herself of the obsession that she's made to look utterly ridiculous!"

"Well now, I don't see how . . ."

"No, I don't see how either. But there it is! She feels ridiculous, and that's that! And the things she does make me fear for . . . the Intruder . . . or Intrudress."

"My God!" exclaimed Augusto in alarm.

"Wait, Augusto, don't imagine we have lost all moral sensibility. Elena is deeply religious and respects the intentions of Providence, even if she deplores them, and she is resigned to becoming a mother. And she will be a good mother, I don't for a moment doubt that. She will be a very good mother. But her fear of appearing ridiculous is so strong that she will go to any lengths to hide her condition, and she is capable of any kind of madness. I don't even want to think of it. . . . She hasn't been out of the house for a week. She says she's afraid of going out. She imagines that people would stop and stare at her on the street. She says we should leave town, and that if she's to take the air and the sun when her pregnancy is advanced, she can't do so where there are people who know her and who might meddle and go so far as to congratulate her, or pretend to congratulate her."

A brief silence set a seal on the woeful tale. Then Víctor drew the moral:

"So. Go ahead and get married, Augusto. Perhaps

the same kind of thing can happen to you. Go ahead and marry the pianist!"

"Yes, and who knows, I might find a mother for myself again, too," murmured Augusto, as if talking to himself.

"A mother, of course . . . for your children. If you happen to have any."

"Perhaps now, Víctor, you will find that your wife is also a mother to you."

"What I am going to find is that my nights will no longer be my own, or that I will lose . . ."

"Or win. Perhaps you will win back your nights and . . ."

"In any case, I don't know what's happening, to me or to us. I think that I'll eventually resign myself. But my poor Elena . . . Poor woman!"

"You see. You're already beginning to feel for her."

"Well, Augusto, you'd better think twice before you rush into marriage."

And they parted company.

Augusto walked home thinking of the contradictory lamentations he had heard from Don Avito and Víctor. He scarcely remembered Eugenia and her mortgage or even the laundress's daughter.

Orfeo jumped all over him as he entered the house, and Augusto at once felt the puppy's neck:

"Don't, for heaven's sake, swallow any bones, Orfeo. I don't want you to choke to death. I don't want you to die begging me for life with your eyes. . . . Just think, Don Avito, the educationalist, the theoretical pedagogue, has turned back to the religion of his forefathers—a clear case of heredity! His heritage, his inheritance! Meanwhile, Víctor cannot accept becoming a father. Don Avito can find no consolation for the loss of his child while Víctor finds no consolation for his having a child! . . . And Eugenia: what eyes! They flashed and burned like fire when she told me 'You want to buy me! You want to buy—not my love, which can't be bought—but my body! Keep my house! You can keep it!' Buy her body? Her body! Why, my own is already too much for me, it's enough and more than enough! What I need is soul. Soul, not body! A soul of fire, like the one which shows through Eugenia's eyes. Her body, yes, her body is splendid, grand, magnificent, divine. But her body is her soul, pure spirit, every part of it poetry, meaning, life, pure idea! I have too much body, Orfeo, because I lack soul. Or rather isn't it the other way around: I lack soul because I have too much body? I can see my body, touch it. But where is my soul? Do I have one at all? I could feel it barely breathing only when I had my arms around Rosario, when I had her on my lap, when she was weeping and I was weeping too. Those tears came from my soul, not my body. The soul is a source, a wellspring which only reveals itself in tears, then. There is no way of knowing one has a soul until the tears come . . . Ah, Orfeo, let's go to sleep. If we can. If they let us. . . ."

XV

"WHAT HAVE YOU done, child?" Doña Ermelinda asked her niece.

"What have I done? Just what you would have done in my situation! Anyone with any sense of shame would have done the same, I'm sure. Imagine his wanting to buy *me*!"

"Listen, child, it's better to have someone trying to buy you than trying to sell you. Take my word for it."

"Imagine trying to buy *me*!"

"That's not so anyway, Eugenia. What he did he did out of generosity. Rather heroic of him, too."

"Heroic? Well, I don't like heroes. Not those trying to play the part of hero, anyway. When heroism comes naturally, well and good! But when it's calculated, not at all! Trying to buy me! Me! I'm telling you, Aunt, I'll make him suffer for trying any such thing. That . . . that . . ."

"That what? Go on and finish your insult."

"That . . . dull fool. That insipid simpleton. I'll treat him as if he didn't exist. . . . He doesn't exist anyhow!"

"What are you talking about? Do you know what you're saying? Who are you talking about?"

"That . . . canary man! Do you really think, Aunt, that there's anything inside him?"

"His innards, I suppose. Viscera, guts."

"Guts? Do you really think he has any? . . . He's hollow, I tell you, I can see right through him. He's hollow."

"O come now, let's talk sensibly. Don't say or do anything foolish. Forget all that kind of talk. I think you ought to accept him. . . ."

"But I don't love him, Aunt. . . ."

"Now how do you know what that means? You have no experience in that line. You may know what a quaver is or a demisemiquaver, but as to knowing what love is. . . ."

"I believe you're talking for the sake of talking, Aunt. . . ."

"Now how would you know what it is to love, child?"

"But I do love . . . somebody else."

"Somebody else? Do you mean that layabout Mauricio, whose soul is so small it rattles about in his body? Do you call that love? You call him 'somebody else'? He's nobody. Augusto, I tell you, is your best hope. He's cultivated, rich, and a good man."

"He's so good that I don't love him. And that's why I don't love him. I don't like men who are good."

"I don't either, child, I don't either, but . . ."

"But what?"

"That's the kind of man one must marry. That's why they were born and that's why they're good— to make good husbands."

"But if I don't love him, how can I marry him?"

"How? By getting married! Didn't I marry your uncle? . . ."

"But, Aunt, didn't you? . . ."

"Yes, now I think I do, I believe I do. But when I got married . . . I don't know if I loved him. Listen, all that business about love is the stuff of books, something made up to furnish material for more books. Material for nonsense verse. The real, the positive factor is matrimony. The rest is music. . . ."

"Music?"

"Yes, music. You know well enough that music is good for scarcely anything except to live by teaching it. And now, if you don't take advantage of an opportunity like the one offered you, the road out of your purgatory is going to be good and long. . . ."

"What of it? I don't ask you and Uncle Fermín for anything, do I? And I earn my own living. Am I such a burden to you all?"

"Don't get so worked up. And don't go on like that,

or we'll really have a row. Nobody said anything about your being a burden. Everything I've said is for your own good."

"Of course, for my own good. . . . It was for my own good that Don Augusto Pérez performed his most manly action. So manly that he wanted to buy me. So manly. A man's kind of thing! Men, as I'm beginning to see, Aunt, are all of them a pack of beasts, coarse brutes without any sense of the fine points, any delicacy. They can't even do you a favor without insulting you. . . ."

"All men?"

"All of them! Real men, I mean."

"Ah! Real men!"

"Yes. Because the others, the ones who are not coarse, self-centered brutes and egotists, are not men at all."

"Well, what are they then?"

"I don't know for sure. Delicate fruits! Fags, probably."

"Some theories you have!"

"They're contagious in this house."

"You never heard a theory like *that* from your uncle."

"No, that's a theory I picked up on my own, from observing men."

"From observing your uncle, too?"

"No, not Uncle. He's not a man . . . in that sense."

"Then he's a fruit, a fag of some kind? Come now!"

"No, no, no! Not that either. Uncle is . . . well, he's Uncle. I've never thought of him as flesh and blood . . ."

"Well then, what do you think he is?"

"Just that . . . my uncle. Nothing more. Almost as if he didn't exist apart from that fact."

"That's what you think! But I can tell you, girl, that your uncle does indeed exist. I can vouch for that."

"They're all brutes. Didn't you hear what that barbarian Martín Rubio said to poor Don Emeterio a few days after Don Emeterio had lost his wife?"

"No, I don't think I did."

"Well, this is the story. It was at the height of the epidemic, you remember. Everyone was terrified, and I recall that you wouldn't let me out of the house for some time and that we boiled the water for drinking. Everybody avoided everybody else, and if someone wore mourning, he was treated as a carrier of the plague. Don Emeterio lost his wife, and a few days later he had to go out, wearing mourning clothes of course, and he ran into that barbarian Martín. That fellow kept his distance, when he saw the mourning outfit, afraid of infection, and he called out: 'What is it? Something happen at home?' And Don Emeterio confessed that he had lost his wife. 'How unfortunate! What . . . what happened?' 'She died in childbirth,' explained Don Emeterio. 'Ah! That . . . that's not so bad! Lucky man!' said Martín, and the scoundrel stepped up and shook his hand in congratulation. Did you ever hear of anything more manly and chivalrous! There was a manly act! They're nothing but brutes, coarse beasts. . . ."

"Better they be brutes than layabouts like your Mauricio! That nobody has made you lose any good sense you ever had. I don't know how. According to what I hear and from pretty good sources too, there's no question of his really being in love with you at all. . . ."

"But I am with him, and that's enough!"

"And do you think, now, that he, that fellow, is

really a man? If he were, he would have found work and a solution to your problems a long time ago."

"Well if he's not a man, I'll make him one. It's true he's everything you say, but perhaps that's why I love him. In any case, after Don Augusto's heroic and manly behavior—his trying to buy me—I'm all the more determined to stake everything on one throw of the dice and marry Mauricio."

"And what are you going to live on, silly girl?"

"On what I earn! I'll work harder than ever. I'll give lessons to people I turned down before. In any case, I've given up the house. I've made a present of it to Don Augusto. It was only a whim to try and keep it anyway. It's only because I was born in it. Now that I'm free of the burden of house and mort-gage, I'm also free to work more. When Mauricio sees me working so hard for both of us, he'll get busy himself, if he has any sense of shame, that is. . . ."

"And suppose he hasn't?"

"In that case, he'll have to be dependent on me. I'll support him!"

"Lovely! The piano teacher's husband!"

"So be it. He'll be mine. And the more dependent he is on me, the more he'll belong to me."

"He'll be yours, all right—just like a dog might be. And *that*, my girl, is called *buying* a man!"

"And didn't your manly candidate just now try to buy me with his money? Why should it be any more strange that I, a woman, should want to buy a man with my work?"

"That sounds like what your uncle calls femi-nism."

"I don't know about that, and I don't care to know. But I can tell you, Aunt, that the man who can buy me hasn't yet been born. Buy me—*me!*"

At this point, the maid came in to announce that Don Augusto was waiting to speak to the Señora.

"Him? Why doesn't he go away? I don't want to see him. Tell him that I've told him all I want to say to him."

"Think it over, child, think it over calmly. Don't get so excited. You simply haven't understood Don Augusto's intentions."

When Augusto talked to Doña Ermelinda a bit later, he began by asking her to accept his explanations. He had been deeply moved: Eugenia had simply not understood his intentions. For his part, he had formally cancelled the mortgage on her house, which now stood legally in her name, free of all encumbrance. If she persisted, obstinately, in refusing it, in refusing to accept the income from it, he could not accept it either. In such an eventuality, the income would be lost, without immediate benefit to anyone. However, it would go on being deposited to the owner's account. Further, he wanted it known that he formally renounced any claims to Eugenia and desired only that she might be happy. He was even willing to seek a good position for Mauricio, so that they would not have to live off his wife's income.

"You have a heart of gold!" cried Doña Ermelinda.

"All we need now, Señora, is for you to convince your niece of my real intentions. I ask her to forgive me, if I have been impertinent in meddling in her affairs. But I think there is no use in brooding on what's been done. If she will allow me, I offer to be best man and sponsor at her wedding. After the ceremony, I'd plan on embarking on a long voyage."

Doña Ermelinda called the maid, and told her to ask Eugenia to step in, for Don Augusto wished to speak to her.

"The Señorita has just gone out," replied the maid.

XVI

"You're impossible, Mauricio," Eugenia was telling her boy friend in the concierge's vestibule, "completely impossible, and if you don't change . . . pull yourself together and get some sort of work so that we can marry, I'll do something terrible."

"And what will that be, my sweet?" as he caressed the back of her neck, twirling a curl around one of his fingers.

"Look, if you like we'll get married anyway and I'll go on working for both of us."

"And what will people say about me if I go along with that?"

"What do I care what people say?"

"Look here, this is serious!"

"Yes it is. It doesn't matter in the slightest what people say. All I'd like to do is to put an end to this situation as soon as possible . . ."

"Is it as bad as that?"

"It certainly is, very bad. And if you don't make a decision soon I'll do something. . . ."

"What will you do?"

"I'll take up Augusto's offer."

"To marry him?"

"No, that no! His offer to recover my property for me."

"Well, go ahead, darling, do it! If that's the answer and there's no other . . ."

"And you have the cheek to . . ."

"There's no cheek involved! This chap Augusto doesn't seem all there and if he's bent on this whim of his why should we stand in his way?"

"So, in fact, you . . ."

"Of course, darling, of course!"

"A man, after all is said and done."

"Not as much as you'd like, if I go by your standards. But come closer. . . ."

"Please, Mauricio, stop that. I've told you a hundred times not to be so . . ."

"So affectionate . . ."

"No, not that, not to be so coarse! Be still. If you really want to win me, you'd best pull yourself together and get some honest-to-goodness work. The rest you know. Let's see if you can't use your head. The last time you had your face slapped. You won't forget that, will you?"

"How well I remember! Look, darling, do it again! Here's my face for you."

"Don't be too keen. . . ."

"Go to it, then."

"I won't. I don't want to give you the satisfaction."

"Nor any other!"

"I told you to stop acting so coarse. And I'm telling you again that if you don't look sharp and find work, I'll take up Augusto's offer."

"Well, Eugenia, do you want me to tell you the truth, the whole truth, cross my heart?"

"I do."

"I adore you, ever so much. I'm mad about you, but marriage frightens me, overwhelms me. Temperamentally I'm a born idler, I'm not denying it, and what really upsets me is the idea of work. And

I can well imagine that with marriage there will be children. I suppose you'll want children. . . ."

"Well, that's the limit!"

"I'll have to work, really work, because living isn't cheap. And as for your working, never, never, never! Mauricio Blanco Clará cannot live off a woman. But maybe there's a solution which won't involve my working, nor you; there's always a way. . . ."

"Tell me. I want to know. . . ."

"Well, then, my little one, will you promise not to be offended?"

"Go on, tell me!"

"From what I've heard and know, this poor fellow, Augusto, is a wretched devil, and a bit off, I don't know, a . . ."

"Go on!"

"You won't be offended?"

"I told you to go on!"

"Well, as I was saying, he's fated to be. . . . And perhaps the best thing would be not only to accept his offer to help with your property but that you . . ."

"What, then? Go on."

"That you also marry him."

"So that's it?" and she stood up.

"Take him for a husband and as he's a poor fool, well . . . then everything will right itself. . . ."

"What do you mean by that?"

"Well, he foots the bill and we . . ."

"We what . . . what about us?"

"Well, we'll . . ."

"That's it. I've heard enough. . . ."

And Eugenia stalked out, her eyes blazing: "What monsters, what animals!" When she reached home, she locked herself up in her room and burst into tears.

Then she fell victim of a fever and had to take to her bed.

Mauricio was taken aback briefly, but he quickly came to, lit a cigarette, and went out. He tossed off a flirtatious remark to the first pretty girl who came his way. And that night he talked with a friend about Don Juan Tenorio.

"Don Juan is not really a believable character," Mauricio said. "He can only be imagined on stage."

"Coming from you, Mauricio, who pass yourself off as a Tenorio and big woman seducer!"

"Me! A seducer! That's so much fiction, Rogelio!"

"And how about the pianist?"

"Bah! Do you want to know the truth, Rogelio?"

"Let's hear it!"

"Well, out of a hundred liaisons, more or less respectable liaisons, and the one you're alluding to is respectable, well, out of a hundred such affairs, in about ninety the woman is the seducer, the man the seduced."

"Do you mean to say you haven't been the aggressor, in the case of the pianist?"

"I have not. I am not the aggressor, rather the opposite way around."

"You seducer!"

"Have it your way, but she really is the seducer. I simply put up no fight."

"It doesn't matter one way or the other in this instance."

"But it seems the affair is coming to an end and I'll be free again. Free of her, that is, because I can't answer for another woman taking me as fair game. I'm so weak! If I'd have only been born a woman. . . ."

"But how is it coming to an end?"

"Because I've made a mess of it! I actually wanted

our affair to go on, rather to really begin, you know what I mean, but without any complications or enormous commitments. . . . Well, there you have it. Naturally, she's going to give me the sack. She wanted to take me over completely, body and soul."

"She will, too!"

"Who knows? I'm such a weakling! I was born to be kept by a woman, in a dignified way, of course, and if not that, well nothing!"

"And what do you mean by 'a dignified way,' if I may ask?"

"That's impossible to answer! Certain things defy definition!"

"True enough!" Rogelio answered, with real conviction, and then added: "And if she drops you, then what?"

"Well, I'll have some time off, until another woman comes along to take me over. It has happened so many times already . . . ! But this Eugenia! She never gave an inch, and always managed to keep a respectable distance—as pure as pure can be. There's no one purer than Eugenia and I really went overboard for her. She'd have ended up doing whatever she liked with me. But now, if she drops me, I'll feel awful, but I will be free."

"Really?"

"Free for another woman, that is."

"I think you'll make it up with her."

"Never can tell! But I have my doubts, because she has something of a temper . . . and today I insulted her, I really did."

XVII

"Do you remember, Augusto," said Víctor, "That fellow Don Eloíno Rodríguez de Alburquerque y Álvarez de Castro?"

"You mean the one who worked as a civil servant, the big woman-chaser, especially the cheap ones?"

"The very one, the same fellow. Well, he married!"

"Some bag of bones for a woman to drag about!"

"But the marvelous part is the way he got married. Just listen to this. You know that Don Eloíno Rodríguez de Alburquerque y Álvarez de Castro, in spite of his string of surnames, scarcely had enough to die on, neither more nor less than his Government salary. Besides, his health was completely broken."

"Such a life he led!"

"Well, the miserable wretch was suffering from a cardiac disorder from which there was no hope of recovery. His days were numbered. He had just pulled through a tight spot, which had led him to death's door—and to marriage—and then . . . well, the whole thing blew up. It happened that the poor fellow was going from one boarding-house to another and finally had to leave all of them, because at four pesetas a day he couldn't expect delicacies and gourmet dishes in exquisite sauces, and he was ever so exacting. And not all that clean. So, he wandered from place to place, when he finally met up with a landlady well on in years, older than he, who, as you well know, must have been nearer sixty than fifty. This venerable woman was widowed twice: her first husband was a carpenter who committed suicide by throwing himself from a scaffolding to the street below, and she refers to him occasionally as *her* Rogelio. The second fellow was a sergeant in the carabineers, and he left her a small sum, which brings in a peseta a day. And into this situation appears our man Don Eloíno, who is living at the house of the twice-widowed lady, and he decides to fall ill, but very ill, so ill it seemed he wouldn't pull through, that he'd just die. First they called in Don José to attend him and then Don Valentín. But he just went on dying! His sickness required so much attention and nursing, and not always of the pleasantest nature, to be sure, that it monopolized all of the landlady's time. Naturally, the other tenants were threatening to leave. And so we have Don Eloíno who could not pay much more than he was already paying and the twice-widowed landlady telling him she couldn't keep him at her house, as it was ruining her business. 'But, for heaven's sake, Señora, take pity on me!' he apparently said to her. 'Where can I go in this condition? Who will have me? If you throw me out, I'll have to die in hospital! . . . For the love of God, take pity on me, for the few days I have left!' He was convinced he was dying, and very soon, to boot. But the landlady quite naturally felt that her house was not a hospital. She made a living from her rooming-house business and that business was being ruined by his presence.

"About this time one of his fellow civil servants hit upon a brilliant idea to save the situation. He said to him: 'There's only one way, Don Eloíno, for you to get this good woman to keep you in her house while you go on living.' 'And what way is that?' he asked. 'First of all,' his friend told him, 'I'd like to know how ill you think you are.' 'Well, I think I've only a short time to go. Perhaps not even long enough for my family to get here to see me alive.' 'So you think you're that badly off?' 'I feel I'm dying. . . .' 'Well, if that's how it is, then there's only one way you'll get your good woman from throwing you out into the street, which will result in your having to go into hospital.' 'Yes, and what is it?' 'Marry her.' 'Marry her? Marry the landlady? Me, a Rodríguez de Alburquerque y Álvarez de Castro! You must be jesting!' It seems the incident was disastrous, for he nearly expired in the act."

"It's what you might have expected."

"As soon as Don Eloíno recovered from the initial shock, his friend made it clear that by marrying the landlady he'd be leaving her thirteen *duros* a month as a widow's pension, of which no one would benefit otherwise, as it would be taken by the State if there was no claimant. You see . . ."

"Yes, my dear Víctor, I know of several friends who have married just to prevent the State from grabbing up the pension. That is what's known as civic virtue!"

"But if Don Eloíno turned down the idea with such indignation, just imagine what the landlady had to say about it!"

" 'Marry? At my age, and for the third time, marry that corpse? How disgusting!' Nevertheless, she had a word with the doctor and was assured that Don Eloíno had but a few days to live. She said, 'To tell the truth, thirteen *duros* would suit me fine,' and she finally agreed to the proposal. Then the priest, the good Don Matías, a saintly creature, was called in to put the final touches to the business of convincing the dying man.

" 'Yes, of course I'll help,' said Don Matías. 'The poor man!' " And he succeeded in persuading Don Eloíno.

"Then Don Eloíno sent for Correita, with whom he wanted a reconciliation, for they had quarreled, and he asked him to be a witness at his wedding. 'You don't mean you're getting married?'

" 'Yes, Correita, I'm marrying my landlady, Doña Sinfo! A Rodríguez de Alburquerque y Álvarez de Castro, just imagine! So she'll take care of me for the few days left to me. . . . I don't even know if my family will get here in time to see me alive, . . . and she's doing it for the pension, the thirteen *duros*.' And they say that when Correita went home and told the story to his wife, Emilia, she, as was to be expected, exclaimed:

" 'But, you're a fool, Pepe! Why didn't you tell him to marry Encarna? (Encarnación was the serving-maid, neither young nor good-looking, whom Emilia had brought by way of a marriage dowry to their household.) She would have taken as good care of him as that other woman for the thirteen *duros* a month.' And it's rumored that Encarna added: 'You're right, Señorita, I would have married him and nursed him for the short time he has left, for his pension.' "

"Well, Víctor, I think you've made all this up."

"Well, I have not. Certain things can't be invented. The best is still to come. Don Valentín, the doctor who stepped in after Don José, told me that one day when he was visiting Don Eloíno he met Don Matías, decked out in his priestly vestments, and he thought he had come to administer Extreme Unction, but he was told that he was there to perform the wedding ceremony, not the final rites. Later on when he returned to see the patient, the newly married landlady —for the third time no less—accompanied him to the door and asked him in an anxious, contrite way, 'Tell me, Don Valentín, will he live? Is he going to live?'

" 'No, Señora, of course not, it's a matter of days. . . .'

" 'Then, he'll die soon?'

" 'Yes, very soon.'

" 'You're certain he will?'

"How monstrous!"

"And that's not all. Don Valentín left orders that they should give the sick man nothing but milk, and only a little at a time, but Doña Sinfo told another boarder:

" 'Not at all! I'll give him anything he wants! Why take away the few pleasures left to him if he has such a short time to live . . . !' But when an enema was ordered, she said: 'An enema? How awful! For that decrepit creature! Never! If it had been for one of my other husbands, whom I married out of love, it would have been different! But him, an enema! Never!' "

"This is all too incredible."

"Not at all. It is historically factual. Don Eloíno's family, a brother and sister, arrived at that point, and the brother, overwhelemed by the horror of it all said, 'Imagine my brother, a Rodríguez de Alburquerque y Álvarez de Castro marrying the landlady of a rooming house on the Calle de Pellejeros. My brother, the son of a former High Court Judge from Zaragoza, Za-ra-go-za, marrying a . . . Doña Sinfo!' He was beside himself.

"Meanwhile, the widow of the suicide victim and newly married bride of the hopelessly sick Don Eloíno, was thinking: 'Let's see what happens now. Since we're all related I suppose they'll go off without paying their board, which is my bread and butter. Ah, it's clear . . . !' However, they did pay up—the sister's husband paid—but they managed to walk off with a gold-topped cane, the dying man's."

"Well, did he die?"

"Yes, but some time later. As a matter of fact he improved quite a bit. And the landlady's comment was: 'Don Valentín's to blame for this. He knew how to handle this sickness. Don José, the first doctor, was better. He didn't know a thing and if Don José had been in charge, the old fool would have been dead by now and I'd be free of this nuisance.' Doña Sinfo, apart from the children of her first marriage, had a daughter by the second, the carabineer. Not long after Don Eloíno married, he said to the girl: 'Come here and let me kiss you, for we are father and daughter now.'

" 'She is not your daughter, just your god-daughter!'

" 'Step-daughter, my dear woman, she is my step-daughter, not my god-daughter. Come here . . . I'll see you inherit. . . .'

"And it's known the mother grunted: 'The old scoundrel only did that to get his hands on her! Have you ever seen . . . !'

"Eventually the inevitable rupture took place. 'This was all a hoax, nothing less than a hoax, Don Eloíno. I married you on the condition that you would die, and soon, at that. There's some trick here! I've been hoodwinked, fooled.'

" 'So have I, my dear woman. And what would you have me do? Die just to please you?'

" 'That was the agreement.'

" 'I'll die yet, señora, sooner than you think and sooner than I'd care to. . . . A Rodríguez de Alburquerque y Álvarez de Castro!'

"Then they quarreled over the price of board, a few

cuartos, more or less, and she ended by getting him to leave.

" 'Good-bye Don Eloíno, God bless!'

" 'God bless, Doña Sinfo!'

"Finally, the third husband of this lady died and she was left the widow's pension, which worked out at 2.15 pesetas a day, apart from the 500 pesetas which were set aside for funeral expenses. Naturally, she did not use these pesetas for that purpose. She had a couple of Masses said for him, out of remorse, and also out of gratitude for the widow's pension."

"Heavens, the things that happen!"

"Things that one can't invent, not possible to. I'm gathering data on this tragicomedy, this funeral farce. I originally thought of turning it into a one-act play, but thinking it over, I've decided to interpolate it somehow, in the way Cervantes interpolated certain tales into *Don Quixote*, into a novel I'm writing to keep me from worrying over my wife's pregnancy."

"Don't tell me you've decided to write a novel?"

"What do you think I should do?"

"What is the plot, if you don't mind telling me about it?"

"There is no plot, or rather, the plot will unfold. The plot is going to create itself."

"How will that happen?"

"Well, you see, one day when I didn't really know what to do, but felt an urge to do something, a deep yearning, a gnawing of phantasy, it was then that I decided to write a novel. But I determined to write it as life itself, without knowing what will happen next. I sat down, took out paper and started by setting down the first thing that crossed my mind, without thinking about what would happen next, without any plan. My fictional characters will create themselves by the way they act and talk, especially in the way they talk. Their personalities will develop gradually. And sometimes their personalities will be not to have any personality at all."

"Like mine."

"I don't know. We'll see. I'm simply letting myself be carried along."

"And are you using psychological techniques? Description?"

"Whatever comes out in the dialogue, especially the dialogue. Most important is that the characters talk, a good deal, even if they say nothing."

"Elena must have suggested this to you?"

"Why?"

"Once she asked me for a novel to while away the time and I remember her saying she wanted it to be mostly dialogue and very precise."

"That's true. Whenever she reads a novel full of endless description, tirades, or anecdotes, she shouts: 'Padding! Padding! Nothing but padding!' The only part that isn't padding is dialogue. It's as easy to let loose a tirade during the course of a dialogue, you know."

"Why should that be?"

"Because people like conversation for its own sake, even if nothing is said. Some people can't sit through a half-hour speech though they can babble three hours away in a café. That's the charm of conversation, to talk for the sake of talking, disjointed and fragmentary talk."

"The monotonous sound of a speech also bores me. . . ."

"Of course, there's satisfaction in talk, live talk . . . Especially when it doesn't seem as if the author is saying things just to say them, not imposing his personality on us, his devilish ego. Even though every-thing my characters say I'm really saying myself . . ."

"Up to a certain point . . ."

"What do you mean by that?"

"Well, you start by thinking you're leading the characters around with your own hand, when you suddenly discover that you're being led around by them instead. Often enough, it's the author who be-comes the toy of his own creations. . . ."

"Perhaps, but in this novel I've decided to include everything that's happening to me, whatever it is."

"Well, it won't be a novel."

"No, that's true . . . it will be a *nivola*.

"And what is a *nivola*?"

"I once heard a story from Manuel Machado the poet, brother to Antonio, that he brought a sonnet to Eduardo Benot, to read out loud. It was written in Alexandrian verse or some other unusual way and when Eduardo Benot heard it, he said:

" 'But this isn't a sonnet!'

" 'No, sir, it is not,' Machado admitted, 'it's not a sonnet, it's a *sonite*.'

"Well, that's how it is with my novel. It won't be a novel, but a . . . What did I call it? A *navilo* or *nebulo* . . . no, not that, a *nivola*! That's it, a *nivola*! Then no one can say I'm violating the rules of the novel form. I'm inventing the form, the genre, and to in-vent a genre is no more than calling it something new, and I'm laying down the laws I want for it. And there'll be plenty of dialogue!"

"But when one of the characters is by himself?"

"Then we'll have a soliloquy. And to make it seem more like dialogue I'll bring in a dog as a sounding board."

"Víctor, I have the feeling you're inventing . . ."

"That's possible."

After they parted company, Augusto went along talking to himself.

And what is my life? A novel? Nivola? *Just what is it? Everything that happens to me and to everyone around me, is it reality or fiction? Perhaps all this is no more than God dreaming, or somebody else dreaming, whoever, and perhaps it will all evanesce as soon as He awakes? And perhaps that's why we pray to Him and sing canticles and hymns to Him, so as to keep Him asleep, to rock the cradle of dreams? Isn't the entire liturgy of all religions an assuaging of God's dream, so He won't awake and stop His dream of us? Ay, my Eugenia! My Eugenia! And my Rosarito . . .*

"Hello, Orfeo!"

The dog had run to greet him and leapt about trying to climb on to him. He took the animal up and it began to lick his hand.

"Sir," the maid said, "Rosarito is waiting for you here with the ironing."

"And why didn't you take care of it?"

"I don't know. . . . I told her you wouldn't be long and if she wanted to wait . . ."

"But you could have taken care of it, as usual. . . ."

"Yes, but . . . you understand. . . ."

"Liduvina! Liduvina!"

"It's best you take care of it."

"I'll see her, then."

XVIII

"Hello, Rosarito!" Augusto shouted, no sooner he saw her.

"Good afternoon, sir," the girl said in a steady, clear voice, and her expression matched her voice.

"How come you've not settled the bill with Liduvina as you usually do when I'm not at home?"

"I don't know! She told me to wait. I thought you wanted to tell me something. . . ."

Is this ingenuousness or not? Augusto reflected, and he stood aloof briefly. There was a moment of embarrassed, uneasy silence.

"I'd like you to forget what happened the other day. Don't give it another thought. Do you understand?"

"All right, as you like. . . ."

"Yes, that was pure nonsense, madness! I didn't really know what I was doing . . . or saying, as I do now," and he moved closer to the girl.

She waited quietly, as if resigned to her fate. He sat down on the sofa and called her: "Come over here!" He instructed her to sit on his knees, as on the other occasion, and lingered long gazing into her eyes. She did not yield before his glance, but her whole body trembled like a leaf.

"You're trembling, my little one . . . ?"

"No, no, it's not me. You seem to be . . ."

"Don't tremble, calm down."

"Don't make me cry again."

"Come, come. I know you want me to make you cry. Tell me, do you have a boyfriend?"

"What a question . . ."

"Tell me, do you?"

"Boyfriend . . . not exactly!"

132

"Hasn't some young fellow about your own age approached you yet?"

"You see, sir . . ."

"And what did you tell him?"

"Certain things can't be . . ."

"Very true. And tell me, are you in love with each other?"

"Heavens, sir, but . . . !"

"Look, if you start crying, I'm leaving."

The girl rested her head on Augusto's chest, to conceal herself and stifle her sobs, as she burst into tears.

This little baby is going to faint, Augusto decided, as he stroked her hair.

"Calm down! Quiet!"

"And that woman?" Rosarito asked holding back her sobs, her head still buried in his chest.

"Oh, so you're still thinking about her? Well, that woman has finally turned me down completely. I've never won her affection and now I've lost her for good!"

The girl lifted her forehead and stared directly into his face, as if to discover whether or not he was telling the truth.

"Are you trying to deceive me?" she whispered.

"Why would I want to do that? Ah, it's clear now. So that's it. And didn't you tell me about your boyfriend?"

"I said nothing. . . ."

"Calm down!" and with that he set her down on the sofa, stood up, and began to pace up and down across the room.

When he glanced at her again, he saw that the sorry creature's expression had altered and that she was quaking. He suddenly realized she felt unprotected, alone there on the sofa, facing him from a distance, like a criminal before a judge. He thought she would keel over.

"It's true!" he said. "The closer together we are the safer we feel."

He sat down again, set her on his lap and enfolded her in his arms. He held her close to his chest. The sad creature raised an arm to his shoulder, as if to support herself on him, and again hid her head on his chest. Hearing his heart pound, she took fright.

"Do you feel all right, sir?"

"Whoever does?"

"Would you like me to order something for you?"

"No, no. I know what my trouble is! I must go on a trip." After a pause, he added: "Will you join me?"

"Don Augusto!"

"Leave off calling me 'Don!' Will you go with me or not?"

"As you wish. . . ."

A mist clouded over Augusto's mind. His blood began to throb in his temples and he felt a pressure on his chest. To overcome it, he started to kiss Rosarito on her eyes, which she had to shut. Suddenly he stood up and said:

"Leave me! Leave me! I'm afraid!"

"Afraid of what?"

The girl's absolute composure unnerved him even further.

"I'm afraid. I don't know of whom. You, me, I don't know! Anybody! Maybe Liduvina! Listen, leave, go away! But you'll return, won't you? You will?"

"Whenever you say."

"And you'll go with me on the trip, won't you?"

"Whatever you say . . ."

"Go away now!"

"And that woman . . ."

Augusto hurled himself at the young girl, who had stood up, seized her and pressed her against his chest. He put his dry lips to hers, and without actually kissing her, he held her for a spell, their mouths together. Suddenly he broke free and shook his head, and then, releasing her, he said:

"Get out! Go!"

Rosarito left immediately. Hardly was she out of the room, when Augusto, exhausted as if he had been running, threw himself on his bed, turned out the light and fell into a soliloquy:

I've been lying to her and to myself as well. It's always that way! Everything is phantasy, nothing but phantasy. As soon as a man speaks he lies, and if he talks to himself, that is, insofar as he is conscious that he thinks, he's lying to himself. The only truth lies in the physiological side of life, the physical. Speech is a social product and was created for the purpose of lying. I've heard a philosopher of ours say that truth is also a social product, something everyone believes in, and by believing in it, we finally come to understand each other. The real social product is the lie itself.

Suddenly he felt his hand being licked, and he called out: "Oh, so you're here, Orfeo? Well, since you don't talk you don't tell lies, and I don't even think you're ever on the wrong track; you never even lie to yourself. But, since you're a domestic animal, some of men's ways must have rubbed off on you. . . . We men do nothing but lie and give ourselves airs. Words were invented for exaggerating our feelings and impressions—probably so we'd believe in them . . . words and speech and all the other conventional means of expressing ourselves, such as kissing, embracing. . . . Every one of us does nothing but act out his role in life. We're all so many characters in a drama, mere masks, actors! No one really suffers or enjoys what he's saying or trying to express, but probably believes he is suffering or enjoying something. If it were not so, no one would be able to live. At heart we're all so passive. And so am I right now, playing out my drama as both actor and audience. The only pain that really kills is physical pain. The only truth is the physiological man, the man who doesn't speak, and so doesn't lie . . ."

He heard a knock at the door.

"What is it?"

"Aren't you going to have supper tonight?" Liduvina asked.

"Of course! I'll be there in a minute."

And then I'll sleep, as I do every night, and she'll sleep, too. Will Rosarito sleep? Perhaps I upset her spiritual peace? And that unaffected way of hers—is it innocence or slyness? Maybe there's nothing as sly as innocence, or perhaps nothing as innocent as slyness? Yes, of course, I've always suspected that down deep there's nothing more than . . . more than . . . How should I put it? There's nothing more cynical than innocence. Yes, that quiet way she gave herself up to me, that's what was frightening, and I can't say what frightened me, yet I daresay it was nothing but innocence. And what about her saying, "And that woman?" Was it jealousy? Possibly jealousy? No doubt in every burgeoning of love there is jealousy. It's jealousy which reveals love to us. No matter how much a woman is in love with a man or a man with a woman, they never realize it fully, never tell themselves they are, that is, they don't really fall in love, until the moment he sees her looking at another man or she sees him eyeing another woman. If there were only one man and only one woman in the world, and nobody else, it would be impossible for them to fall in love. Besides a third party is always essential: La Celestina, and Celestina is society, the go-between. El Gran Galeoto! And lucky for that! Yes, the Gran Gale-oto! Even if it were only for the language. And so all this thing about love is just one more lie. And the physical side? Well, the physical part of it is not love nor is it worth the bother! And that's why it's truth. "Come now, Orfeo, off to supper. That is unquestionably a truth!"

XIX

Two days after this Augusto was informed that a lady wished to speak to him. He went out to receive her and discovered it was Doña Ermelinda. To Augusto's "What are you doing here?" she replied, "Since you did not want to call on us again . . . !"

"I'm sure you must understand, señora, after what happened to me the last couple of times I went to your house, once with Eugenia by herself and the other time when she didn't want to see me, that I ought not return. I held by what I've said and done, but I can't return there."

"Well, I'm here on a mission for Eugenia. . . ."

"For Eugenia?"

"Yes. I really don't know what has happened with her and her boyfriend, but she won't hear a word about him, she's in a fury, and the other day when she came back home she locked herself in her room and refused to have supper. Her eyes were ablaze from having cried, with those tears that scald, you know what I mean, tears of anger. . . ."

"Oh, so there are different kinds of tears?"

"Of course. There are tears that revive a person, give relief, and there are scalding tears that strangle. She wept and wouldn't eat. And then she kept on repeating that refrain of hers of how all men are brutes, monsters, nothing but brutes. And for the past few days she has been sulking about with a terrible long face, in a devilish frame of mind. That is, until yesterday, when she called me to say she was sorry for everything she had told you, that she had gone beyond the limits of politeness and had been unfair with you and besides, she was well-aware of the upright and noble nature of your intentions, and it's not that she'd like you to forgive her for having said you wanted to buy her, but to have you know she doesn't think any such thing. And it was this above all else that she stressed. She says that more than anything else she wants you to believe that if she actually did say that, out of burning spite, she didn't mean it. . . ."

"I don't think she does."

"Then, after that, she requested that I ascertain in a diplomatic way, of course . . ."

"And the best diplomacy, my dear lady, is the lack of it, especially with me. . . ."

"Afterwards she asked me to find out whether you'd be put out if she did actually accept the gift you offered of her own house, without any obligation. . . ."

"What do you mean by 'without any obligation'?"

"Come, now, I simply mean her accepting the gift as a gift and no more."

"That is exactly how I offered it, so how else can she accept it?"

"She says she's prepared to accept your generosity

as a mark of good faith and proof of her sincere sorrow for what she said, but it must not imply more. . . ."

"Enough of that. It seems that now, but unwittingly so, she's insulting me again."

"Unintentionally, of course . . ."

"There are times when the worst insults are those unintentionally inflicted on another."

"I don't understand. . . ."

"It's quite clear. For instance, I was once at a gathering, where one of the people there didn't even so much as greet me. As I left, I muttered about this slight to a friend and he said: 'Don't take it so hard, for he hasn't done it on purpose. He didn't even realize you were there.'

"To that commentary, I answered, 'That's really what makes it a piece of rudeness. It's not that he didn't greet me, but that he wasn't even aware of my existence.'

" 'It wasn't intentional. He's very distracted . . . ,' my friend justified.

"And then I said: 'The greatest boorishness underlies those acts known to be unintentionally committed. And the rudest insult of all is to be absented-minded with others.' That, my dear woman, is the same as what is known as unintentional forgetfulness, as if it were possible to forget something intentionally. Unintentional forgetfulness is usually no more than rudeness."

"What is all this leading up to?"

"To this, señora: After begging my pardon for her slighting remark about my gift and for feeling she was being bought and would have to show some sort of gratitude, I don't really know what she means by accepting it 'without any obligation.' What obligations is she talking about?"

"Don't get so nervous about it."

"What do you mean I shouldn't get so nervous! Is this girl trying to make mock of me? Am I a mere toy for her?" and as he said this he thought of Rosarito.

"Good heavens, Don Augusto . . . !"

"I've already told her that the mortgage is paid off, there is no more mortgage, and if she doesn't want to take the responsibility of her own house, that's her decision. And whether or not she thanks me matters not one iota."

"But don't get angry, Don Augusto! She only wants to make up with you, so you can be friends again . . . !"

"Of course, now that war has broken out between her and the other fellow. Isn't that it? Before I was the *Other*, and now I'm the *One*. Isn't that how it is? Now she's trying to land me, eh?"

"But I've said no such thing!"

"No, but I can guess it."

"Well, you're completely wrong. Because just after my niece said everything I've just told you, I suggested that now she had quarreled with that lazy no-good boyfriend of hers, she should try and win you as—you know what I mean. . . ."

"Yes, that she should win me back . . ."

"Exactly! Well, she told me emphatically that she wanted no such thing—no, no, and no—that she regarded you highly as a friend, but she did not want you as a husband and did not care to marry anyone she wasn't in love with."

"And she'd never manage to be in love with me, isn't that so?"

No, she didn't say that much."

"Come, come, señora, this is just more diplomacy. . . ."

"What?"

"Of course! You came here not only for me to forgive this . . . this young lady, but also to see if I wouldn't consent to court her once again. Isn't that how it is? A little pact, no? And she'll resign herself to her fate. . . ."

"I swear to you, Don Augusto, on my mother's sacred honor—may she be in heaven—that . . ."

"Don't forget the second commandment: Thou shalt not swear. . . ."

"Well, I'll swear that it's you who are forgetting yourself now, unintentionally of course, forgetting who I am, Ermelinda Ruiz y Ruiz."

"If it were as you say . . ."

"I tell you it is just as I say," and she uttered these words with such emphasis, there was no room for doubt.

"Well, then . . . tell your niece that I accept and deeply appreciate her explanations and that I'll continue to be a loyal and noble friend, but only that. Nothing but a friend, that is all . . . and you needn't tell her that I am *not* a piano on which she can play footloose and fancy free and that I am *not* a man to be dropped today and picked up tomorrow and that I am *no* substitute or vice-boyfriend, that I am no second fiddle. . . ."

"Don't work yourself up like that!"

"No, I am not getting worked up! Just tell her that I'll be her friend."

"And you'll come and see us soon?"

"Well . . . that . . ."

"You know the poor girl won't believe me and she'll be hurt. . . ."

"You see, I'm thinking of taking a long trip, far away."

"But before you go, come and say good-bye. . . ."

"All right, we'll see. . . ."

They parted company. When Doña Ermelinda arrived back home and recounted the conversation to her niece, Eugenia said to herself: "There's another woman. No doubt of it. Now I must have him."

As for Augusto, once alone he started to pace up and down the room telling himself: *She wants to play me along, to play me like a piano . . . she drops me, she picks me up again, and then she'll drop me once more . . . I was to be held in reserve. . . . She can say what she wants, but what she's really after is to get me on my knees, perhaps to take her revenge or make the other fellow jealous and twist him around her little finger. As if I were a puppet, a dupe, a Little Mr. Nobody. But I have a personality, too, yes I do, I am I, myself! Yes I am. I am I, myself! And I owe that to Eugenia. Why deny it? It was Eugenia who brought my instinct for love to the fore, but now that it's awakened, evoked, I no longer need her. There are plenty of women around, more than enough.*

At this juncture he could do nothing but smile. He recalled a certain remark Víctor had made when their newly married friend, Gervasio, announced his intention of going to Paris with his wife for a brief visit. It was then Víctor said: "You're taking a woman to Paris? That's like carrying codfish to Scotland or coals to Newcastle!" Augusto had been vastly amused by it all.

And he went on telling himself: *There are plenty of women around. And how attractive that sly innocence or innocent slyness of Rosarito! That new version of the Eternal Eve! What a charming creature she is! Eugenia led me from the abstract to the concrete, but Rosario has taken me to the generic, and there are so many appealing women, so very many.*

. . . So many Eugenias and Rosarios! No, nobody is going to play around with me, least of all a woman! I am I, myself! My soul might be small but it is mine! Feeling his ego in a state of ecstasy, as if it were expanding, swelling up, he decided to go out; the house had become too narrow, too contracted for him. He needed space to give vent to his ego.

No sooner had he stepped out into the street, with the sky overhead, and people coming and going, each one bent on his own task or caprice and none of them conscious of him (unintentionally, of course), nor paying him any attention (probably because they didn't know him), than he felt his ego, that I of "I am I!" diminish, grow progressively smaller, folding up in his body, seeking a tiny corner to huddle into, so as not to be seen. The street was like a film and he felt as if he were becoming part of it, perhaps a shadow or phantom. Losing himself in the crowd of bustling humanity, who neither knew him nor noticed him, had the same effect as having a bath in open country, a vault of sky above, the winds blowing from all points of the compass.

Only when he was by himself was he conscious of who he was. Only then could he say, perhaps to convince himself, that "I am I, myself!" When he was thrown among the masses, lost in the plodding, indifferent crowd of humanity, he did not have any realization of himself.

At this point he came to the tiny hidden garden in the secluded plaza of the peaceful quarter where he lived. The plaza was a quiet backwater where a few children always played, as no trams and few other vehicles traversed this spot. And some old men sat around the plaza during the sweet sunny autumn afternoons. After the north wind blew, the leaves of the dozen or so secluded chestnut trees swept about the flagstone walks or covered the wooden benches, which were always painted green like the color of new leaves. Those domesticated, city trees, originally from the Indies, correctly lined up and regularly watered during dry spells by a system of canals, spread their roots under the flagstones of the plaza. Those captive trees that awaited the rising and setting of the sun over the rooftops, those caged trees that perhaps yearned for the far-off wilderness, had a special mysterious appeal for Augusto. Birds sang among the branches; and they were also city creatures, the sort that learn to flee from children and occasionally draw near the old men who bear offerings of bread crumbs.

How often he had sat there by himself, alone on one of the green benches of the plaza, watching the blaze of a setting sun over a rooftop or sometimes a black cat atop a chimney, profiled against the gold fire of a splendid sunset sky. Meanwhile yellow autumn leaves rained down, broad as the leaves from a grapevine, like mummified, paper-thin hands, over the tiny garden-borders and potted plants at the center of the plaza. And children continued to play among the dry leaves, sometimes playing the games of gathering these very leaves, unaware of the sunset's blaze.

When he reached that peaceful plaza after his meeting with Doña Ermelinda and sat down on a bench, first clearing the bench of the dry leaves, for it was autumn, he found some little boys playing nearby as usual. One of them pushed another up against the trunk of one of the chestnut trees from the Indies, and he said:

"You've been a prisoner here. You were held by robbers. . . ."

"It happens . . . ," the other little fellow began angrily . . . and the first boy broke in and said:

"No, but *you* weren't *you* then. . . ."

Augusto did not want to hear any more, and so he went to another bench. And he said to himself: *We adults play the same games. You are not you! I am not I! And those poor trees, are they what they're supposed to be? Their leaves fall earlier, long before their fellow chestnuts in the woods, and they become skeletons which cast their silhouetted shadows across the walks under the light cast by the electric streetlamps. A tree lit up by electric light! How strange! What a fantastic sight when a tree top is lit up metallically in the springtime by a streetlamp! Especially here where there are no open breezes to rock their branches. These wretched trees that haven't even had the pleasure of a black night in the country, a moonless night, under a mantle of twinkling stars! The men who planted each of these trees here must have said to them: "You're not you!" and so they put them behind night lights . . . to make sure the trees would not sleep. These wretched night-owls of trees! No, no, they'll not play about with me as they have with you.*

He rose and started to walk the streets like a sleepwalker.

XX

WOULD HE TAKE a trip or not? He had already announced it: first to Rosarito, without really knowing what he was saying, but just to say something, or more as a pretext for finding out if she'd join him, and then to Doña Ermelinda, to prove to her . . .What? What was he trying to prove by telling her he was about to go on a trip? Anything whatever! But now he had committed himself twice by having said he was going on a long trip. And as he was a man of character himself, did he also have to prove that he was a man who kept his word?

Men who keep their word or promises first say one thing, then think about it and finally act on it, no matter how it works out. Men who keep their word neither deviate from or retract what they once said. And he, Augusto, had said he was going on a long, distant trip.

A long, distant trip! But why? What for? How and to where?

The servant interrupted his speculations by saying a young lady was there to see him.

"A young lady?"

"Yes," Liduvina said, "I think it's . . . the pianist!"

"Eugenia!"

"The very one."

He was taken aback. A quick wave of annoyance flashed across his mind and he thought of sending her away, by having Liduvina say he was not at home. To himself he said: *She's come to take me as her prey, to play with me as if I were a puppet. She wants to make a game of me, a substitute for the other chap.*

Then he thought better of it and said: *No, I have to put up a show of strength.*

"Tell her I'll be right there."

He was fascinated by her temerity. And inwardly he said: *I have to admit she's every bit a woman, a real individual. What spirit! What determination! And what eyes! But she's not going to get me to yield. She'll not overawe me.*

He found Eugenia still standing, as he walked into

146

the drawing room. He motioned for her to sit down, but before she did so, she exclaimed: "They've hoodwinked you the same way as they have me, Augusto!" With that Augusto felt totally disarmed and was rendered speechless. They both sat down and were silent momentarily.

"Yes, Augusto, it is exactly as I said: they've fooled you as regards me, just as I've been fooled as far as you're concerned. And there is no more to say."

"But, Eugenia, we have already spoken to one another about this."

"Never mind, don't bother yourself with what I said. The past is past."

"Yes, so it is, and it can't be otherwise."

"You know what I mean. And I don't want you to interpret my acceptance of your generous gift in any other way than the way it is."

"That's how I feel. I don't want you to attribute anything to my gift except what was intended."

"So, one loyalty for another. And now, since we should speak as frankly as possible, I must tell you that after everything that has happened and after everything I've said, I couldn't, even if I wanted, try to repay your generosity in any other way than with my deepest gratitude. And as far as you are concerned, I think . . ."

"Exactly, as far as I'm concerned, after what has happened, and after your remarks at our last meeting and after what your aunt said to me and after the conclusions I drew, I couldn't put a price on my generosity, even if I wanted to."

"Then we are of one mind about this?"

"Of course."

"And so we'll be able to be friends again, good friends, true ones?"

"Certainly."

Eugenia stretched out her delicate, snow-white hand, with its tapering fingers designed to dominate a keyboard, toward Augusto and he held it in his, which was trembling.

"Then, my friend, we shall be good friends, even if this friendship for me . . ."

"What are you saying?"

"Perhaps in the view of those . . ."

"What is it? Tell me!"

"Well, after some recent experiences, painful ones, I've now renounced certain things. . . ."

"Don't be so vague, señorita. It's no good telling me by half-measures."

"All right, then, I'll make everything crystal clear. Do you think it is easy after what has happened for anyone to approach me with certain hopes or intentions? All our acquaintances know that you've paid the mortgage on my inheritance, made me a gift of it, so how can anyone approach me now?"

This woman is a devil, Augusto thought, and he stared down at the floor, not knowing what to say. The moment he raised his eyes he saw that Eugenia was drying a furtive tear.

"Eugenia!" he cried in a quivering voice.

"Augusto!" she whispered, overcome.

"And what should we do about it?"

"No, no, nothing! It is Fate, nothing but Fate. We are mere toys in the hands of Fate. It is a piece of bad luck!"

Augusto rose from his armchair and went to sit beside Eugenia on the sofa.

"Eugenia, for heaven's sake, don't play around with me like this! Fate, you make your own Fate, you and no one else. You're the one who pulls me this way and that way, whirls me about like a spinning top. You're driving me mad. You make me break my strongest resolutions. You unhinge me and I can't even call my ego my own."

He put his arm around her and drew her close against his chest. She calmly removed her hat.

"Yes, Augusto, it is Fate that has brought this upon us. Neither you nor I is capable of being untrue or disloyal to ourselves. It must never appear as if you were buying me off, as I once said in a moment of confusion, nor can I act as if I were using you as a substitute, a second fiddle, or a second choice, as you put it to my aunt, merely by trying to reward your generosity. . . ."

"But why should all this acting one way or another matter to us? In whose eyes are we to be judged?"

"In our own."

"But why, my dear Eugenia?"

He pressed her to him again and covered her forehead and eyes with kisses. Their breathing could be heard.

"Stop that! Stop!" she said, as she smoothed her hair and rearranged herself.

"No, no, you . . . you . . . Eugenia . . ."

"It cannot be, no . . ."

"You don't love me then?"

"Loving . . . who knows anything about love? I don't know. . . . I'm not sure of anything."

"And what about now, this . . . ?"

"This is a . . . a momentary piece of bad luck! Brought about by repentance . . . I don't know. These things have to be put to the test. And besides, didn't we agree we'd be good friends, nothing more than friends?"

"Yes, but . . . what about your so-called sacrifice?

What did you mean when you said that now you've accepted my gift and we're friends, only friends, no one will consider marrying you?"

"That doesn't matter! I've come to a decision about that."

"Perhaps because you've split up with . . . ?"

"Perhaps . . ."

"Eugenia! Eugenia!"

Someone knocked at the door at that moment and Augusto, flushed and quivering, shouted hoarsely: "Yes, what is it?"

"Rosario is here!" Liduvina answered.

Augusto went white.

"Ah!" Eugenia exclaimed, "I'm in the way here. She . . . Rosario is waiting for you. Now do you see how we can only be friends, good friends, very good friends?"

"But Eugenia . . ."

"But Rosario's waiting for you . . ."

"When you turned me down, Eugenia, when you told me that I wanted to buy you off and that you actually loved someone else, what else was I to do? I had learned to love through you and . . . Perhaps you don't know what spite means or what it means suddenly to discover there's no haven for your affection?"

"Come, come, Augusto, give me your hand. We'll see each other again, but remember what is past is past."

"No, no: The past is not past. No, not at all!"

"All right then, but Rosario is waiting. . . ."

"Good heavens, Eugenia . . ."

"Well, there's nothing odd about that. After all, at one time there used to be someone waiting for me

. . . Mauricio . . . We'll see each other again. And we'll be true to ourselves."

She put on her hat and stretched out her hand, which Augusto lifted to his lips and covered with kisses. She left and he accompanied her to the door. He watched her for a moment as she walked elegantly down the staircase, with a sure step. From a lower landing she looked up and bade him farewell with a glance and a wave of the hand. Augusto turned and went into his sitting room. When he saw Rosario standing there, the basket of ironing in her hand, he said curtly, "And how are you?"

"Don Augusto, I think that woman is deceiving you. . . ."

"And what does it matter to you?"

"Anything that has to do with you matters to me."

"What you're trying to say is that I'm deceiving you. . . ."

"That really doesn't matter to me."

"Do you mean to say that after all the hopes I've filled you with you're not jealous?"

"If you only knew, Don Augusto, how I was brought up and the kind of family I come from, you'd understand that even though I'm young, I'm beyond jealousy. People like us . . ."

"Quiet!"

"As you wish. But I'll tell you again: That woman is deceiving you. If it weren't so I wouldn't say it. If you really loved her, if she were truly to your taste, how could it matter to me if you married her?"

"Really? Are you telling the truth?"

"I really am."

"How old are you?"

"Nineteen."

"Come here," and he took her shoulders in both hands and brought her face to his and stared into her eyes.

And it was Augusto who changed color, not Rosario.

"To tell the truth I don't understand you."

"I know that."

"I don't know what this is all about. If it's innocence, slyness, or mockery, or plain perversity . . ."

"It is only affection."

"Affection? But why that?"

"Do you want to know why? You won't be insulted if I tell you? You promise?"

"Go ahead, tell me."

"Well then, because . . . because you're a poor unhappy man. . . ."

"You, too, say this?"

"As you like, but have faith in me, trust me . . . trust Rosario. I'm more loyal than . . . than Orfeo!"

"Forever?"

"Yes, forever!"

"Whatever happens?"

"Yes, whatever happens."

"Yes, you, you're the real person . . . ," and he lunged forward as if to clutch her.

"No, not now, when you're calmed down. And when . . ."

"Say no more. I understand."

And they took leave of each other.

When he was alone Augusto began his soliloquy: *Between the one and the other they're going to drive me out of my mind . . . I'm no longer myself. I've lost my I, my ego.*

As Liduvina served dinner, she commented to Augusto, "I think the Señorito ought to go into politics or something like that. It would distract you from all this."

"And how did you happen to think of that?"

"Because you're better off distracting yourself than having someone do it for you. You can see for yourself. . . ."

"Good enough. Call your husband, and when I finish eating, tell him I'd like to play a game of cards with him—to distract me."

As they were playing, Augusto suddenly dropped the cards on the table and asked:

"Tell me, Domingo, when a man is in love with two or even more women at the same time, what should he do?"

"That depends."

"Depends on what?"

"It depends on whether or not he has plenty of money and plenty of nerve; if he has, he can marry them all, and if he hasn't, he better not marry any."

"But, Domingo, the first is not possible!"

"With enough money anything is possible!"

"And if the women find him out?"

"They won't care."

"You mean a woman doesn't care if some one else is depriving her of some of her husband's affection?"

"She'll be satisfied with her share, if he doesn't put a limit on the money she's allowed to spend. What bothers a woman most is when a man tells her how much she can spend on food, on clothes, and everything else, including her luxuries. But if he lets her spend what she likes . . . Now, if there are children . . ."

"What about that?"

"That's the real source of jealousy—children. One mother can't stand another mother or possible future mother. It's the mother that can't stand having her own children slighted for another child or for another woman. But if there are no children involved and no limits on what is spent on the table, or the wardrobe, or the pomp and circumstance, well then, in that case, he's helping her out, ridding her of some of the nuisance. . . . Besides if a man has one wife who is expensive and another who isn't, the expensive one will hardly notice the other one's existence. And, moreover, if the wife who doesn't cost him anything also happens to bring something in . . . if he brings the expensive wife money from the other one, well then . . ."

"Then, what?"

"Well, in that case, everything's for the asking. Believe me, señorito, there are no female Othellos. . . ."

"Nor male Desdemonas."

"That's possible!"

"But the things you say . . ."

"Before I married Liduvina and came to work here, I worked in some grand places. You might say I did my apprenticeship there."

"But what about the people in your walk of life?"

"In our walk of life? We can't allow ourselves certain luxuries."

"What do you mean by luxuries?"

"Oh, the things you see in movies and theaters and read in novels."

"But, Domingo, there are few of those so-called crimes of passion, crimes committed out of jealousy, in your walk of life."

"Bah, that's because that scum go to theaters and read novels. If they didn't . . ."

"And, if they didn't?"

"Well, all of us like to act out a role and no one is

ever the person he thinks he is, but the person other people make out of him."

"Domingo, you're a philosopher."

"That's what my last employer called me. You know, I think Liduvina has the right idea, you ought to go into politics."

XXI

"Y E S , Y O U ' R E R I G H T ," Don Antonio was telling Augusto that afternoon at the Club, as they talked by themselves in a corner. "You're right. There's a painful mystery in my life, excruciatingly painful. You must have guessed something. The few times you've visited my poor home, if it can be called that. Surely you noticed . . ."

"Yes, something peculiar . . . Some sort of melancholy in the atmosphere that aroused my . . ."

"Despite my children, those poor children, it must have seemed a childless home, even a house bereft of husband and wife. . . ."

"I can't say. I don't know."

"We came from far away, very far, in flight, but there are certain things that can never be forgotten. They mysteriously surround you and invade your entire existence. My sad wife . . ."

"Yes, your wife's face reveals a life of . . ."

"Of martyrdom—you can say it. Well, my dear friend, I don't know exactly why, perhaps out of some hidden sympathy, but you've been the person who has shown us the greatest feeling and understanding. So once more, to get the illusion that I'm freeing myself of a burden, I'm going to pour out my misfortunes. The woman who is the mother of my children is not my wife."

"I gathered that, but if she's the mother of your children, if you live as man and wife, then she is your wife."

"No, you see, I have another wife, a legitimate one. I'm married all right but not to the woman you know. And the mother of my children is also married, but not to me."

"Ah, a double . . ."

"No, a quadruple affair, as you will soon see. I was wildly in love when I married, head over heels in love, with a withdrawn, reticent woman who said little, but who always seemed to want to say much more. Her gentle, heron-blue eyes were so soft they seemed to be sleeping and only awoke occasionally, as if to spark forth a flame. And everything about her was like that. Her heart, her whole soul, her body, they all seemed to be asleep normally, but then suddenly they would come alive as if electrified, only to fall back to sleep soon again, once the lightning flash of life had passed. And what a life! It was as if nothing had ever been, as if everything that had happened was past recollection. It was always as if we were beginning life anew, as if I were forever courting her to win her love. We became engaged to one another in one of those epileptic-like moments and I think she finally said yes at the altar in another one of those attacks. I was never able to get her to tell me she loved me— or did not love me, for that matter. How often I asked that question, before and after our marriage, and she always answered, 'There are certain things one doesn't ask; it's ridiculous.' On other occasions she would say that the verb 'to love' was obsolete and was only used in the theater or in books, and if I had ever written 'I love you' to her in a letter, she would have thrown me out without another thought. For more than two years we lived together in this strange state of marriage and every day I set about to woo or win that sphinx. We had no children. Then one day she did not return and I went insane. I searched everywhere. The following day I found out in a brief, curt note that she had gone away, very far away with another man. . . ."

"And you didn't suspect anything before? You hadn't anticipated anything?"

"Nothing! My wife would usually go out by herself, to her mother's, to friends, and I was totally without suspicion because of her very peculiar coldness. I never fathomed a thing about that sphinx! The man she fled with was also married, and he not only was married, and he not only abandoned his wife and a little girl for my wife, but he managed to take along all of his wife's fortune, which was only normal since he had always done with it as he pleased. In other words, he not only abandoned his wife but he robbed and ruined her as well. And in the curt, cold letter that I received from my wife there was a reference to the condition in which the thief's wretched wife had been left. I call him a robber but perhaps it was he who was robbed! Robber or robbed . . . who knows! For days I neither slept, nor ate, nor relaxed. I did nothing but roam the most distant streets of the city in which I lived. I was about to yield to the lowest, most evil vices. When my grief abated and I thought it over, I recalled that other miserable victim, the wife who was left destitute, bereft of affection and robbed of her fortune. I thought that in all good conscience, since my wife was the cause of her misery, I was duty-bound to go to her and offer her financial assistance, since I had been lucky enough to have been born rich."

"I can imagine the rest, Don Antonio."

"It does not matter, I'll tell you the rest. I went to see her. You can imagine what our first meeting was like. Both of us cried out our misery to one another. I said to myself: 'And her husband has left her to go off with *my* wife?' To tell the truth, I felt a certain inward satisfaction, something intangible, as if I had known how to select a wife better than he and that somehow he had recognized this fact. Later, his wife confessed to me that she had reacted similarly, though the roles, of course, were reversed. I offered financial help, whatever she might need, and at first she turned my offer down. 'I'll go to work to keep alive and support my daughter,' she told me. But I insisted, persisted, until she finally accepted my help. I suggested she become my housekeeper, that she come and live with me, provided we moved abroad, far from our native country, and after much thought, she also accepted that."

"Of course, once you lived together . . ."

"No, that came later, some time later. It was the result of having lived together and, of course, a certain feeling of vengeance, spite, I don't exactly know what. Actually, I was less taken with her than I was with her daughter, the unlucky daughter of my wife's lover. I developed a deep love for her, an intense paternal love, the same love I feel for her now. I love her as much as, or perhaps more than, I love my own children. I would gather her into my arms, hold her close and cover her with kisses, crying the whole time. And the child would say, 'But why are you crying, Papa?' I had taught her to call me 'Papa' and to think of me as such. And when her poor mother saw me crying, she would also cry, and our tears would sometimes mingle over the blonde head of the daughter of my wife's lover, the thief of my happiness.

"One day I learned that my legitimate wife had become a mother, and on that day my whole being rose in revolt. I suffered as I never had before and I thought I would go mad, kill myself. I had never experienced jealousy until then, the most brutal jealousy possible. My soul's wound, which had seemed to have healed, was opened and bleeding . . . it bled fire! I had lived with my wife, my real wife, for more than two years, and nothing, and then that thief . . . ! I had decided that my real wife had finally awakened, totally so, and that she was now living life at white heat. The woman I was living with suspected something and asked me, 'What's the matter?' I told her to forget it, not to bother, but in the end I poured out my heart and she shook with emotion as she listened. I think she must have caught my sickness, my furious jealousy. . . ."

"And, of course, after that outpouring . . ."

"No, it came about later, in a completely different way. One day when both of us were together with the little girl, who was on my knees and to whom I was telling stories, and nonsense rhymes, kissing her the while, her mother approached and also began to caress her. And then the little darling put one of her hands on my shoulder and the other on her mother's, and said to us: 'Papa . . . Mama, why don't you bring me a little brother to play with, like all the other little girls have, so I won't be alone?' We blanched and exchanged a glance which laid our souls bare, and to conceal our embarrassment, we started to kiss the little girl and one of those kisses strayed. . . . That night, between tears and outbursts of jealousy, we spawned the first brother to the daughter of the thief of my happiness."

"What a strange story!"

"And our love, if that's what you can call it, was arid and mute, full of fire and fury, without sweet speech and tender words. My wife, or rather the mother of my children, because she—and not the other legal one—is my wife, this woman, I say, is a woman of charm, perhaps even beautiful, but she never fired me with desire, despite our having lived together. And even after it reached this stage, which I've just described, I never thought I was too much in love with her, until something happened which proved the opposite.

"After one of her deliveries, the birth of our fourth child, she fell so ill, so terribly ill, that I thought she was dying. She had lost so much blood, she was as white as wax, her eyes shut. I thought I was losing her. I went crazy. I was as white as she, and my blood ran cold. I took refuge in a corner of the house, where no one could see me and fell to my knees and begged God that I be killed before letting that saint of a woman die. I cried and pulled my flesh and scratched my chest until blood ran. It was then that I realized how closely linked I was with the mother of my children. When she regained consciousness and was out of danger, smiling with her return to life, I whispered to her something which I had never whispered before, which I have never said since. And she went on smiling, for a long while, staring up at the ceiling. And I put my mouth to hers and wrapped her bare arms around my neck and tears fell from my eyes to hers. And she said: 'Thank you, Antonio, thanks, for me, our children, for all of them . . . for her, for Rita. . . .' Rita is our oldest daughter, the child of the thief . . .

no, no, our daughter, my daughter. The thief's child is someone else, the daughter of someone who was once called my wife. Do you understand everything now?"

"Yes, and much more, Don Antonio."

"Much more?"

"Much, yes! In other words you have two wives."

"No, I have only one wife, only one, the mother of my children. The other one is not my wife, I don't even know if she is the wife of her child's father."

"But all this melancholy around you. . . ."

"The law is a melancholy matter. And love that is born and bred on someone else's tomb, like a plant nourishing itself on the decay and putrefaction of another plant, is still sadder. Crimes, yes, other people's crimes brought us together. And perhaps that makes our being together a crime? They violated what wasn't to be violated. And perhaps it was for us to join the loose ends, the 'violated' ends?"

"And you never heard any more about them?"

"We didn't want to. And now our Rita is a young lady and one fine day she'll be getting married . . . using my name and only my name, of course, and the law can take the high road. She's my daughter and not that thief's. I brought her up."

XXII

"WELL, HOW DID you greet the Intruder?" Augusto was questioning Víctor.

"I would never have believed it! Up till the eve of his birth, we were still irritated beyond belief. And even while he was fighting his way into the world, Elena was hurling insults at me. You can't imagine. 'You're to blame for all this,' she kept saying. And then, 'Get out of here! get out of my sight! Aren't you ashamed to be here? If I die it will be your fault.' And then: 'This is it. There'll be no more. This is the end!' But then he was born and everything changed. It's as if we had just awoke from a dream, as if we had just gotten married. I've gone blind, completely. This baby has rendered me sightless. So much so, that even though everyone says Elena has become completely transformed because of the pregnancy, that she is nothing but skin and bones, and looks ten years older, I find her younger, more delectable, fresher, and even more appealingly plump than before."

"That reminds me of the tale of the pyrotechnician I heard in Portugal."

"What is it?"

"You know that in Portugal the whole business of fireworks, pyrotechnics, is a truly exquisite art. Whoever's not seen fireworks in Portugal can't imagine what endless possibilities they contain. And what names they give them, good heavens!"

"But what's the story?"

"I'm getting to that. It happens that in a small Portuguese village there was a pyrotechnician or *fogueteiro*, as they say there, whose wife was a stunning creature, his pride and joy, his heart's comfort. He was wildly in love with her, but even more than his love for her there was his incredible pride. He delighted in making the rest of mankind's mouth water, so to speak, and he showed her off, as if to say, 'Do you see this woman? Does she appeal to you? Well, she's mine and nobody else's! You can all go fly a kite!' He was forever contemplating his wife's beauty and superb qualities and he even went so far as to say that she was the inspiration of his loveliest pyrotechnical creations, she was his muse. On one of these occasions when he was preparing a display, with his gorgeous wife at his side for inspiration, the powder caught fire and there was an explosion. Both husband and wife were carried out unconscious, and both were seriously burned. A large part of his wife's face was affected, as well as her breast and she was left hideously disfigured. Luckily, the *fogueteiro* was completely blinded by the accident, so that he never saw his wife's terrible disfigurement. And he continued to be as proud as ever of his wife's beauty, raving to one and all. They'd walk side by side—she leading him now—and he still maintained his challenging, arrogant style, as if to say, 'Have you ever seen as stunning a woman?' And everyone, knowing what had happened, took pity on the poor man and praised his wife's beauty."

"So, wasn't she still beautiful in his eyes?"

"Probably more than before, as your wife is for you since the arrival of the Intruder."

"Don't call him that!"

"It was your invention."

"Yes, but I don't want anyone else to call him that."

"This often happens. A nickname you give someone in particular sounds quite another way when you hear another person mouth it."

"Yes, and they say that no one knows his own voice."

"Nor face, for that matter. I, for example, know that one of the things that most horrifies me is to look in the mirror when I'm alone, when there's no one else to see me. I begin to doubt my own existence and imagine myself a dream character, a fictional creature; when I look in a mirror I see myself as some other person, another I."

"Then stop looking at yourself."

"I can't help it. I'm obsessively introspective."

"You'll turn into an Indian fakir and end up staring at your own belly button."

"And I think if someone doesn't know his own voice or face, neither can he possibly know what really belongs to him, as if it were part and parcel of himself."

"His wife, for instance."

"Exactly. I have the feeling it must be impossible to know the woman one lives with and who eventually becomes part of oneself. Have you ever heard what one of our greatest poets, Campoamor, has said about this?"

"No, what did he say?"

"Well, he said that when a man marries, if he has made a true love match, he can't touch his wife's body at first without becoming passionately fired with carnal desire, but as time goes on, after he becomes accustomed to his wife, he gradually discovers that it's exactly the same thing to touch his wife's leg as it is his own. But, by the same token, if his wife's leg had to be amputated, it would be as painful as if it were his own."

"That is certainly true. You've no idea how I suffered during the baby's birth!"

"But she suffered more."

"Who knows! And now that she has become part of me, of my being, I place little importance on people saying she has become ugly or misshapen, just as a person isn't aware of his own aging or his own ugliness or disfigurement."

"Don't you really think a person is aware of the fact he's growing old and ugly?"

"No, I don't, even if he says so. Of course, only if it's a gradual process, but if something suddenly happens, then . . . But as for feeling yourself grow old, not at all. What you really feel is that everything around you is growing old or perhaps growing younger. And that's the only thing I feel now. You know what parents usually say, as they point to their children: 'Just look at them! They're beginning to make us feel old!' To see a child grow up is the sweetest and most excruciating experience, I think. Don't marry, Augusto, don't marry if you want to enjoy the illusion of eternal youth."

"And what will I do instead? What will I do to fill my days and nights?"

"Become a philosopher."

"Isn't marriage the best, perhaps the only school of philosophy there is?"

"Heavens no! Has it never struck you how many philosophers have been bachelors? And great philosophers to boot! Not even counting those who were monks in orders, we have Descartes, Pascal, Spinoza, Kant. . . ."

"I don't want to hear about bachelor philosophers!"

"And how about Socrates? Don't you recall how he sent Xanthippe, his wife, away on the day he was to die, so as not to be agitated?"

"I don't want to hear about that either. I can't bring myself to believe that Plato's discourse was anything but a novel. . . ."

"Or a *nivola* . . ."

"Whatever you like."

He suddenly broke off his conversation with Víctor and took his leave.

A beggar approached him in the street and said: "Alms for the love of God, sir, for I have seven children . . . !"

"You'd have done better not to have had them!" Augusto replied in a temper.

"I would like to see what you would have done in my shoes," the beggar replied. "What do you expect us poor to do if we don't have children . . . to serve the rich?"

"You're right," Augusto answered. "And as you're a philosopher as well, take this!" and he handed him a peseta, which the good fellow pocketed at once to spend in the nearest tavern.

XXIII

A U G U S T O   W A S distraught. It was not only that he felt pulled apart, drawn inexorably to both Rosario and Eugenia, but he also felt himself falling in love with almost every woman he saw. His proclivity to love was growing stronger instead of waning. He was beginning to see ominous signs in everything.

"Get out of here, Liduvina, for God's sake. Leave me alone. Go on, get out!" he shouted to his servant.

And no sooner was she out of sight, when he would lean his elbows on the table, and rest his head in his hands. He would tell himself:

This is awful, really awful! Even without realizing it I'm falling in love, even with Liduvina! Poor Domingo! Ay, there's no question of it. Despite her age, her fifty years, she's still a handsome woman, and that well-rounded body of hers is really something. And when she comes out of the kitchen with her sleeves pulled up, those juicy plump arms of hers . . . Heavens, this is insane! And her double chin and the fleshy folds in her neck! This is awful, absolutely awful!

"Come here, Orfeo," he continued, grabbing the dog, "What should I do? How should I protect myself from all this until that time I decide to marry? Now I know! A brilliant idea, illuminating, Orfeo! I'll turn this woman question, which is driving me crazy, into a subject for investigation. What do you think of my devoting myself to the study of feminine psychology? Yes, that's it, and I'll write two papers or monographs, since they're all the rage now: one will be called *Eugenia* and the other one *Rosario*, with the subtitle *A Study of Women*. Now, just what do you think of that idea, Orfeo?"

And he decided to consult with Antolín S.—which stood for Sánchez—Paparrigópulos, who was also carrying on a study of women, but women in literature and not living, breathing females.

Antolín S. Paparrigópulos was known as a scholar, a young man destined to bring glory to his country by elucidating its forgotten splendor. If the name of Antolín S. Paparrigópulos did not yet echo in the circles of the ebullient younger generation, who strove for public notice through the power of noise, it was because he was in possession of a truly deep sense of power, that is, patience. His awe of the public and his own self-respect kept him from making his scholar's debut, until he was completely prepared and certain of the ground he was treading.

Far from seeking an ephemeral reputation with flash-in-the-pan ideas, built upon the ignorance of others, or by indulging in scholarly clownishness, he aspired to perfection in every single one of his literary projects, insofar as perfection was humanly possible, and above all he tried not to exceed the limits of common sense and good taste. Rather than sound off-key just to have himself heard, he wanted to reinforce, with his well-disciplined voice, the glorious symphony of everything authentically national and thorough-bred Castilian.

Above all else, his intelligence was crystal clear. His clear-headedness was truly spectacular, sparklingly transparent, and without a shadow of mistiness or nebulosity. His thoughts were always recorded in a precise Castilian, untainted by the influence of hideous northern fogs, and without a trace of the decadence natural to Parisian boulevards—in a perfectly pure Castilian. And because of his clear Castilian his thought was profound and solidly grounded. His thought derived nutriment from the soul of his race and people, and from them his spirit drew sustenance. Hyperborean mists were perhaps adequate enough for fortified beer drinkers, but certainly not in our glorious Spain, with its magnificent sky and strong earthy wines of Valdepeñas. He fashioned his philosophy after the ill-starred Becerro de Bengoa, who, after labeling Schopenhauer an odd duck, decided his ideas would not have crossed his mind, nor would he have been such a pessimist, had he drunk Valdepeñas instead of beer. He also asserted that neurasthenia was brought about by not tending to one's own affairs and the cure for it was donkey slops.

In the last analysis, S. Paparrigópulos was of the persuasion that everything was form, more or less interior form, and that the universe itself was a series of kaleidoscopic forms, each fitting neatly into another, and it was because of form that such a plethora of great works survived through the centuries. S. Paparrigópulos elaborated his ideas with an elegance worthy of the Renaissance artists, constantly perfecting the language in which he was to fashion his future writings.

He had not wavered in his fortitude in the face of periodic outbreaks of neo-romantic sentimentalism and he had stood his ground vis-à-vis the devastating, faddish interest in these matters known as "social questions." He was convinced that the prime social question was not meant to be solved here on earth, that there would always be the rich and the poor, and no change in that situation could be hoped for, except what was wrought by the rich in the form of charity, and, as for the poor, only resignation could mitigate their troubles. And so he kept his spirit aloof from petty disputes that were conducive to nothing worthwhile and took refuge in the purest realms of immaculate art, beyond the hustle and bustle of passion, where man could find a comforting haven in which to escape life's disillusionments. Moreover, he loathed sterile cosmopolitanism, which merely overwhelmed man's spirit by charging it with impotent dreams and enervating Utopias. He adored and idolized his Spain, which was as much disparaged as it was unknown to some of her children! This Spain which was the source of raw material for his writings, the Spain upon which his future fame rested!

He devoted his powerful spiritual energy to an examination of the intimate life of our people in their history, and his labor was as selfless as it was thorough. He strove for a resuscitation of our collective past, that is, the revival of what was contemporary at the time our great-grandparents lived. Fully aware of the deception others had endured by attempting to accomplish this aim through the process of pure phantasy, he had decided to search and scour every type of ancient tome and memoir, so as to build his structure of scholarly historic science upon unshakable foundations. There was no event in the past, however insignificant, that did not have an invaluable worth from his point of view.

He knew it was indispensable to learn to see the universe in a drop of water. The paleontologist could reconstruct the whole animal with a single bone, and for an archeologist all that was necessary to restore an entire ancient civilization was the handle of a pot. At the same time he remembered how important it was not to view the stars with a microscope or microorganisms with a telescope, as professional humorists and clowns would have us confusedly imagine. But even though he knew that a brilliant archeologist only needed the handle from a pot to restore a period of art buried in the limbo of oblivion, for him it was not enough. In his modest opinion he did not consider himself a genius, and so he preferred two pot handles instead of one, in fact, the more handles the better, and if there were a choice he would choose the whole pot over a single handle.

His motto was, "Ground gained in extensity is lost in intensity." He was well aware that an entire philosophy could be expounded in the most specialized piece of writing or in the most limited monograph. And he believed, above all else, in the marvelous results achieved by the division of labor and the enormous progress made in the sciences by the selfless legion of frog-butchers, word-hunters, date-detectives, and teardrop-collectors of all classes.

Most tantalizing to him were the complicated and

arduous problems of our literary history, such as the question of Prudentius's birthplace, although lately it had been rumored about that Paparrigópulos was devoting himself to a study of Spanish women of past centuries as a result of having been rejected in marriage.

It was precisely in those works of a seemingly insignificant nature that his perspicuity, sound judgment, discernment, incredible historic intuition and critical penetration were most advantageously perceptible. His qualities had to be judged by his adherence to the concrete, the living, and not the abstract, such as pure theory. Every dissertation of his was a complete course in inductive logic, a scholarly monument as great as Lionnet's work on the willow caterpillar, and above all a proof of what is meant by the rigorous love of sacred Truth. He spurned ingenuity as if it were the plague and he believed that only by habituating ourselves to respect the divine Truth in its smallest manifestation, could we render due homage to Truth in the greatest sense.

He was involved in a popular edition of the apologues of Kalilah and Dimnah, with an introduction concerning the influence of Indian literature upon the Middle Ages in Spain. If only he had gotten it as far along as necessary for purposes of publication! The mere reading and knowledge of it would have had beneficial effects. The masses of people would have abandoned taverns in favor of that knowledge, and the pernicious doctrines which expounded impossible economic measures would have become unpopular. The two works of the greatest magnitude that Paparrigópulos had planned were a history of obscure Spanish writers, that is, those writers that were not included in ordinary histories of literature, or were only mentioned in passing, because of their assumed un-importance. In that way he would rectify the injustice of the age, an injustice that he not only feared but also deplored. The second work would consist in re-storing those authors whose works have been lost, with a record of their names, and with luck, the titles of their works. He was also about to take on the his-tory of still another class of writers: those who had thought about writing but had never reached the point of putting pen to paper.

To best achieve his projects, Paparrigópulos, after first nourishing himself on the vital marrow of our national literature, had immersed himself in foreign literature. As this was a laborious process for him, since he was slow in foreign languages, and learning them required time that he needed for more important pursuits, he had recourse to a remarkable method, which he had acquired from one of his distinguished masters. He would read the main critical works and literary histories published in foreign parts, whenever they could be found in French translation. As soon as he had seized the gist and general assessment of the most renowned critics as regards this or that author, he would riffle through the pages in a trice to satisfy his conscience. At the same time he would feel free to refashion the opinions of others without prejudicing his own scrupulous integrity as a critic.

It was clear, then, that S. Paparrigópulos was not just some young and erratic literary hobo who wan-dered aimlessly through the realms of thinking and phantasy, occasionally setting off a fugitive spark. Not at all. His tendencies were fundamental and rigorous: he was a man with a purpose. If there seemed to be no high points in his studies, that was because every-thing was a high point, in the same way as the high-altitude plateau-land of the vast, sun-speckled Castilian prairies, which throbbed with nourishing golden grain.

Ah, if only Providence would bestow on Spain many Antolín Sánchez Paparrigópuloses! With their help we would all become masters of our store of traditional riches, thereby reaping more abundant harvests. When Paparrigópulos strived—and he still does, since he is still living and involved in preparing his works —to pierce the earth with his critical plough, even if only a half-inch deeper than those who had preceded him in this field, it was so the grain might grow more lushly, the kernels fatter, the flour more exquisite, so we Spaniards might feed upon a finer and less costly spiritual bread.

We have just stated that Paparrigópulos is still involved in the preparations of his work for publication. And Augusto had heard, through the grapevine, about his studies on women, though at that time he had published nothing and has published nothing to date.

There is no lack of scholars, other scholars, who, with the generosity characteristic of their species, have spotted Paparrigópulos and are already envious in advance of the fame which awaits him, and so attempt to belittle him. One of them says that Paparrigópulos is like the fox who rubs out his tracks with his tail and leaps this way and that so as to throw the hunter off his trail. In that way no one can guess where the fox has gone to trap the hen. Actually, if he is guilty of some single sin it is the sin of leaving the scaffolding still up after the tower has been built, thereby preventing us from admiring the structure or of even seeing it. Another scholar refers to him disdainfully as a chef, as if a fine cuisine were not a supreme art in itself! Still another accuses him of being nothing but an interpreter, an adapter of ideas culled from foreign parts, but this scholar forgets that when Paparrigó-pulos refashions these ideas in his precise, pure, and limpid Castilian, he makes them his own and also Castilian, not too different from the way Padre Isla made Lesage's *Gil Blas* his own. Still another ridicules him by saying that his principal strength lies in his profound faith in the general ignorance, totally forgetting that it is faith which moves mountains. But the supreme injustice of these rancorous people, whom Paparrigópulos has never harmed, stems from the obvious fact that Paparrigópulos has still not published a thing, and all the begrudgers who snap at his heels are talking out of mere hearsay and to hear the sound of their own voices.

And so it is not possible to write about this unique scholar with any attitude other than that of quiet serenity, and without any *nivolistic* flourishes.

This was the man, I mean to say scholar, who came to Augusto's mind, for he was aware that Antolín was devoting himself to the study of women, fictional women, of course, the least dangerous kind, and to women in the past, who are less dangerous to the student himself than those living around us today.

It was to Antolín then, the lonely scholar who studied women in books, since he was too shy to seek them out in real life, and because he desired revenge for this shyness, that Augusto rushed for counsel.

He had scarcely explained the purpose of his visit when the scholar interrupted him:

"My poor Señor Pérez, how I pity you! Do you really wish to study women? Pure drudgery . . ."

"But you yourself are studying them. . . ."

"One must make great sacrifice. Study for the sake of study—obscure, patient, and silent study—is my *raison d'être*. But as you know, I am a modest, lowly laborer in the realm of thought. I gather and classify material for others who will later know how to work that material to some advantage. All human endeavor is collective, and if it is not collective it is neither solid nor durable. . . ."

"What of the masterpieces of great geniuses? *The Divine Comedy*, the *Aeneid*, a Shakespearian tragedy, a Velásquez painting . . . ?"

"They are all collective endeavors, much more than anyone imagines. *The Divine Comedy*, to take one example, was brought about by a whole series of . . ."

"Yes, I know about that."

"And as concerns Velázquez . . . By the way, do you know Justi's book on Velázquez?"

To Antolín the main and practically the only good in the great masterpieces of man's genius was to bring about critical works or commentaries. The great artists, poets, painters, musicians, historians, philosophers were born solely for purposes of biography and commentary by scholars and critics. Any passage or phrase culled from a great writer is meaningless until a scholar quotes it and cites the work, edition, and page number. All of the talk about the solidarity of a collective effort was no more than another name for envy and impotence. Paparrigópulos belonged to that ilk of commentators on Homer, who, if Homer himself was brought back to life and entered their offices chanting his *Iliad*, would heave him out again for having disturbed them in their search for words occurring only once in the dead texts of Homer's poems.

"Well, then, what is your opinion of feminine psychology?" Augusto asked.

"That kind of question is so vague, so generic and abstract that it lacks any exact meaning for a humble researcher like me, my friend, who is neither a genius nor cares to be one."

"You don't even care to be one?"

"No I do not. It's a bad business. And naturally your question lacks exact meaning for me. To answer it would require . . ."

"Yes, of course, like that colleague of yours who wrote a book on the psychology of the Spanish people, and since he too was a Spaniard, who lived among Spaniards, the only thing that occurred to him to say was this fellow says such-and-such, the other says this-or-that, and to finally compile a bibliography."

"Ah, a bibliography! Now I know . . ."

"No, please don't go on, my friend, just tell me as simply as you can what your idea of female psychology is."

"Then we would have to start by asking a preliminary question and that is whether or not a woman has a soul."

"Good heavens!"

"It does no good to reject the question like that."

Augusto wondered if the scholar himself had a soul. And then:

"All right, then, let's talk about what there is instead of souls in women and what happens there. What about that?"

"Do you promise not to tell anyone what I'm going to say? I know you won't. You're not a scholar."

"What do you mean by that?"

"I mean that you're not the type ready to rob a man of the last thing you heard him say and make out it was your own."

"But what is all this?"

"O, my dear friend, a scholar by nature is a petty thief, a pickpocket. I can tell you because I'm one myself. We scholars go around relieving each other of little ideas that we've formulated so as to keep another scholar from getting ahead of us."

"That's understandable. The owner of a warehouse watches over his stock more zealously than the man who owns the factory. Just as the water in a well has to be saved and husbanded and not the water's source."

"Perhaps that's it. Well, since you're not a scholar and promise to keep my secret until such time I choose to make it public, I will tell you what I've discovered in the work of an obscure, practically unknown Dutch writer of the 17th century. It's an incredibly interesting theory concerning women's souls."

"What is it?"

"This writer says—in Latin—that even though all men have souls, the same does not hold for women, that women have one and the same soul, in other words, a collective soul, something like Averroes' activating agent of understanding, which is spread among all women. And he goes on to say that the differences observable in an individual woman's way of feeling, thinking, and desiring results from bodily distinctions, which can be ascribed to race, climate, diet, and for that reason are insignificant distinctions. Women, according to this author, are similar one to the other, far more than men are, and that is because all women together are one and the same creature. . . ."

"So that's it. That explains why when I fell in love with one woman, a chain reaction was set up, and I immediately fell in love with all the rest."

"Of course! And then this extremely interesting and almost unknown gynecologist says that women have much more individuality, but far less personality than men. Each woman feels more herself, more a finished creature, more of an individual, than any man, but at the same time she feels that she lacks depth, content."

"Yes, yes, I think I fathom his meaning."

"And for that reason, my friend, it's all the same whether you analyze one woman or several. The problem is to delve deeply into the woman you've chosen to study."

"Wouldn't it be more fruitful if I chose a few, so as to make a comparative study? Comparative studies are very much the fashion now, as you know."

"True, true, science is nothing if not a way of comparing one thing to another. But as far as women go, that method is unnecessary. If you know one, well, you know them all, that is, you know quintessential Woman. Besides, 'Ground gained in extensity is lost in intensity.' "

"Yes, of course, and I prefer to devote myself to an intense cultivation of women, rather than an extensive one. But there must be at least two for that purpose, at least two. . . ."

"Two, never, not at all! If you're not satisfied with studying one woman, which I think is the best procedure, and a big enough project, then there must be three at least. No conclusions can be drawn from two subjects."

"How come?"

"It's perfectly clear. Two lines cannot surround a given area. The simplest polygon is a triangle. At least three . . ."

"But a triangle lacks depth. The basic polyhedron is a tetrahedron and that means four lines at least."

"But not two, never! If there must be more than one, then there must be three at least. But I counsel you to delve deeply into one."

"I intend to do that."

XXIV

O n t h e w a y back home, after the interview with Paparrigópulos, Augusto mused:

So now I'll have to give up one of the two women or find a third. Nevertheless, for the purpose of my psychological study Liduvina could easily do as the third subject, for a purely theoretical point of comparison. Well, then, now there are three: Eugenia, who speaks to my imagination, my head; Rosario, who speaks to my heart; and Liduvina the cook, who speaks to my stomach. Head, heart, and stomach, the three forces of the soul, which other people call intelligence, feeling, and will. We think with our heads, feel with our hearts, and love with our stomachs. All this is obvious, but now . . .

And now, he proceeded, *I have a brilliant idea! I'm going to pretend that I want to assume my role as Eugenia's suitor again. I'll try wooing her to see if she'll accept me as her fiancé and future husband. Of course, this will be only by way of testing her, a purely psychological experiment. I am quite sure she'll turn me down. That's to be expected! She couldn't act otherwise. After all that has transpired, after everything she said at our last encounter, I am certainly no longer eligible. I'm fairly sure she's one of those women who stands by her word. But, one minute, do women have a word to keep or stand by? Do women, I mean Woman, with a capital W, that unique woman shared among millions of other female bodies, more or less beautiful, rather more beautiful than less, is that Woman necessarily obliged to keep her word? All this ado about keeping one's word might very well be a masculine attribute. No, no, that's not possible. Eugenia could not possibly consider me eligible simply because she's not in love with me. She's not in love with me and furthermore she has agreed to my gift. And now that she has accepted my gift and is reaping its benefits, why should she love me?*

But, then what if she retracts her previous words and says Yes to me, and accepts me as a fiancé and future husband? Every possibility has to be considered. And what should I say if she does take me back? That will be a mess! She'll land me with my own hook! This would really be the case of the angler angled! But it can't be, no! But if it were? Well, then, there would be nothing for it but resignation. One must also know how to be resigned to good fortune. Resignation to happiness may be the most difficult thing of all to learn. Didn't Pindar say that all of Tantalus' troubles stemmed from his inability to absorb his happiness? True, happiness must be absorbed! And if Eugenia says Yes to me, if she takes me back as her suitor, then . . . Well, then psychology has won out! Long live psychology! But no, what am I thinking about? She won't have me, she can't. She'll turn me down, even if it's only to prove her point. A woman like Eugenia won't have her arm twisted. When Woman faces up to Man in a contest to prove who is the tougher and more tenacious in their intentions, she, Woman, is capable of anything. No, she won't have me!

"Rosario is waiting for you."

Liduvina, with those few emotionally charged words, interrupted Augusto's train of thought.

"Tell me, Liduvina, do you think women stand by what they've once said? Do you women know how to keep your word?"

"That depends."

"That's your husband's refrain. Give me a straight-forward answer and not the kind women usually give. Women rarely answer the question asked, but rather the question they imagined was going to be asked."

"And what did you want to ask me?"

"That when you women have once given your word do you stand by it?"

"Now that depends on the word."

"What do you mean by that?"

"It's quite clear. Sometimes you give your word in order to keep it and other times you don't. No one is fooled because it's all taken for granted."

"All right, enough of that. Tell Rosario to come in."

When Rosario came into the room, Augusto asked her:

"Tell me, Rosario, do you think a woman should keep her word once she has given it?"

"I can't remember having given you my word about anything."

"That's not what I mean. I just want to know if a woman should keep her word or not, once she has given it."

"Ah, you're talking about the other woman, aren't you?"

"Never mind about her. What do you think?"

"Well, I don't understand these matters."

"It doesn't make any difference!"

"Well, if you insist, I think it's best not to give your word about anything."

"But if you've already given it?"

"Well, you shouldn't have then."

Augusto said to himself: *It's clear that I'll get no-where with this little wench. But now that she is here*

I'm going to put my psychology into action and carry out an experiment.

"Come over here, sit down!" and he offered his lap.

The girl obeyed docilely and without a change in expression, as if it were a foregone conclusion. Augusto, on the other hand, was a bit startled and didn't quite know where to begin his experiment. And as he could say nothing, he decided to act. He pressed Rosario tight against his throbbing chest and covered her face with kisses. Meanwhile he kept saying to himself: *It looks like I'm going to lose the necessary sangfroid for my little psychological investigation.* He suddenly stopped what he was doing and seemed to regain his composure. He released Rosario a bit and said to her:

"But don't you know I love that other woman?"

Rosario did not utter a word. She simply stared at him and shrugged her shoulders.

"But do you or don't you know that?" he insisted.

"What difference does that make to me now?"

"What do you mean by 'What difference does it make now?' "

"Well, right now it doesn't. I thought you were making love to me right now and in love with me, too."

"I think I am!"

And then the unexpected happened, something that Augusto had not anticipated in his psychological experimentation on Woman. Rosario suddenly put her arms around Augusto and began to kiss him. He scarcely had time to collect his thoughts: *Now I'm the subject of the experiment. This little lass is making her own study of masculine psychology.* And not fully aware of what he was doing, he found himself caressing Rosario's legs with his trembling hands.

Suddenly Augusto stood up, lifted Rosario up bodily and threw her on to the couch. She let him do it, but her face was flushed. Augusto pinned her down with his two hands and gazed into her eyes.

"Don't shut your eyes, Rosario, don't, for heaven's sake! Open them. That's the way . . . more, more. Let me see myself—so tiny—in them."

Looking at himself reflected in her eyes as in a living mirror, his first throb of ecstasy waned.

"Let me see myself there as I would in a mirror. I'm so tiny. Only then will I get to know myself. . . . Seeing myself reflected in a woman's eyes."

The mirror was looking back at him in a peculiar way. Rosario thought to herself: *This man is different from other men. He must be crazy.*

He drew away from her abruptly, looked himself over, felt himself to see if he really existed, and finally announced:

"Now, Rosario, you must forgive me."

"Forgive you for what?

Rosario's tone of voice conveyed more fear than any other emotion. She felt like bolting, and she said to herself: *When someone begins to act this way and to say strange things, I don't know how it will all end. This man could kill me in a fit of madness.* And tears welled up in her eyes.

"You see, Rosario?" Augusto said. "Yes, forgive me, forgive me. I didn't know what I was doing."

And then she thought: *What he doesn't know is what he forgot to do!*

"And now, you must go! Leave!"

"Are you throwing me out?"

"No, I'm trying to protect myself. I am not throwing you out, no! God help me! If you insist, I'll go away and you can stay here, so you can see for yourself that I am not throwing you out."

He's definitely not all right, she thought to herself, and she felt a wave of pity for him.

"Go, please go, and don't forget me," and he held her chin, and stroked it with affection. "Don't forget me, your poor wretched Augusto."

He embraced her and kissed her mouth long and hard. As Rosario left, she glanced at him with bewilderment and fear. No sooner was she gone, when Augusto thought: *She must think I'm despicable. No doubt of it. Totally despicable. I've behaved ridiculously, absolutely ridiculously. How should she, poor thing, know about these psychological matters?*

If Augusto had been able to fathom Rosario's train of thought at that moment he would have despaired further. Because the simple girl was thinking to herself: *That will be the day when I come back to go through what I've gone through for the other woman's benefit. . . .*

Augusto felt a surge of excitement again. It began to dawn on him that opportunity never knocked twice. Self-anger was setting in. Not quite knowing what he was doing, and by way of whiling away the time, he summoned Liduvina. When she appeared, so well-rounded and composed, smiling devilishly, he was overwhelmed by an extraordinary sensation, which caused him to order her out: "Get out, leave, hurry up!" And he himself dashed out to the street. For one moment, he had feared he would lose control and even leap at Liduvina.

When he was finally in the street he calmed down. A crowd of humanity is like a forest: it gives each person his proper place and perspective.

Am I out of my mind? Augusto wondered. *Is it pos-*

sible that while I think I'm walking normally down the street like an ordinary citizen, whatever that may be, I'm actually going through circus contortions and pantomime, and even gesticulating wildly? And perhaps these people passing by, without even deigning to look at me, or at most, glancing at me, are in reality all staring or laughing at me or pitying me? And maybe even this idea is madness? Am I really insane? And, in the last analysis, what if I am? A man with a kind heart, sensitive, and good who doesn't go mad is a real scoundrel. A man who's not off in the head is either an idiot or a rogue. And that doesn't mean idiots and rogues don't run the risk of madness, too.

What I did to Rosario was absolutely ridiculous. What could she possibly think of me? But after all, what difference does it make what a girl like that thinks of me? Poor thing! But the innocent way she gives herself up! She is completely physical, a perfectly physical creature. Absolutely physical, not a speck of psychology to her. It's a waste of time trying to use her as a guinea pig for psychological experiments. At most, she'd only serve for an experiment in physiology. But psychology, especially feminine psychology, is it really anything but physiology, or perhaps physio-psychology? Do women have souls? To carry out experiments in physio-psychology I'd have to possess some technical knowledge. I never had a laboratory course and, besides, I have no equipment. And this requires equipment. Am I, then, really mad?

After unburdening himself with these street-musings, as he strolled amidst the bustling multitude, who were indifferent to his problems, he began to feel less perturbed and returned home.

XXV

Augusto decided to call on Víctor. He wanted to cuddle the couple's belated child, so as to revive his flagging spirits, to contemplate the new-found happiness of that household, and also, in passing, to consult Víctor about the state of his own mind. When they were finally by themselves, he said:

"What about that novel, I mean . . . oh yes, your *nivola* you were writing? I imagine that now your baby has appeared on the scene you've dropped it."

"Well, then, your imagination is off. Just because of the baby, just because I am a father now, I've gone back to it. It's a way of giving vent to my overflow of happiness."

"Would you like to read me a bit?"

Víctor brought out the manuscript and began to read random passages to his friend.

"But Víctor, you have become a changed person!" Augusto exclaimed.

"Why do you say that?"

"Because there are passages that verge on the obscene and even go beyond the obscene."

"Obscene? Not at all. There are fairly crude parts, but nothing obscene. An occasional nude, but never anyone undressed. It's realism. . . ."

"Realism, yes, and besides . . ."

"Cynicism, perhaps?"

"Yes, cynicism."

"But cynicism is not pornography. These crude passages are a way of stimulating the imagination, in order for it to be able to examine the reality of things more perspicaciously. These crude parts are . . . are pedagogical. That's it, pedagogical!"

"As well as slightly grotesque . . ."

"I won't deny that. I have a taste for buffoonery."

"Which is basically rather dreary."

"Exactly. I only enjoy lugubrious jokes, black humor. Laughter for its own sake horrifies me. It's terrifying. Laughter is merely the groundwork for tragedy."

"Well, your vulgar buffooneries cause a hideous reaction in me."

"That's because you're a solitary type, Augusto. You know that I mean by solitary, a species of hermit. I write these things as therapy. No, no, I don't write them for any reason except for my own amusement, and if the people who read them are also amused then I am satisfied. But if I also happen, by chance, to put someone on the road to recovery, some solitary, double-solitary, creature like you, with my writing . . ."

"Double?"

"Yes, you suffer from a solitude of body and a solitude of soul."

"On that subject, Víctor . . ."

"Yes, I know what you're going to say. You've come here to consult me about your state of mind, which has been rather disastrous for some time now. Really disastrous, wouldn't you say?"

"Yes, that's true."

"I guessed as much. Well, look here, Augusto, get married and do it soon."

"But with which one?"

"Don't tell me there are more than one."

"And how have you happened to guess that too?"

"Quite simply. If you had asked, 'But, with whom?' I would not have thought there was more than one, assuming there was only one. But when you ask, 'With which one?', it is understood that you mean which of the two, or three, or ten, or x-number of women."

"Yes, that's so."

"Well, get married then, marry any one of the x women you happen to be in love with, marry the one closest to hand. And don't think about it too much. You know I married without thinking about it. We were married off, so to speak."

"But it happens that I've just begun some experimental studies in feminine psychology."

"The one and only psychological investigation on Woman is marriage. The man who is not married can never hope to investigate the psychology of the soul of Woman. The one and only laboratory of feminine psychology or gyne-psychology is marriage."

"But there's no way out of marriage! It's forever."

"There's no way out of any experimentation that is real. Anyone who takes up some aspect of experimentation, but still leaves a way to get out of it, by not burning his bridges behind him, will never discover anything. Never trust a surgeon who hasn't amputated one of his own limbs, or turn yourself over to a psychiatrist who isn't crazy. Get married, then, if you want to learn something about psychology.

"Which means that bachelors . . ."

"Which means that what bachelors know is not psychology, it is metaphysics, pure and simple. To wit: beyond physics and beyond nature.

"And where is that?"

"Well, just about where you are now."

"Am I in the realm of metaphysics? But, my dear Víctor, I am not beyond nature, but really still on this side of it."

"It's all the same."

"What do you mean it's all the same?"

"Yes. This side of nature is the same as beyond nature, just as outer space is the same as this side of space. You see this line I'm drawing here, well, extend it in both directions into infinity and the ends will meet. They'll join together in infinity, where everything eventually meets and unites. Every straight line is ultimately a curve of a circumference with an infinite radius, which comes together in infinity. So, ultimately, this side of nature is the same as the other side. That's perfectly clear, isn't it?"

"No, I'd say it is perfectly obscure, recondite."

"Well, if it's so obscure, get married."

"Yes, but . . . I'm so torn with doubt!"

"So much the better, my little Hamlet. You doubt, therefore you think. You think, therefore you are."

"Yes, to doubt is the same as to think."

"And to think is to doubt, nothing but that. One believes something, knows something, imagines something, all without a shadow of a doubt. Neither belief, nor knowledge, nor imagination presupposes doubt. In fact doubt destroys them, but it is impossible to think without doubting. And it is the doubt that is inherent in faith and knowledge, converting their static, inert, dead qualities into dynamic, restless, living thought."

"And what about imagination?"

"Well, there is some doubt there. I'm usually dubious about what I must make my characters in my *nivola* do and say, and even after I've made them do and say certain things I'm dubious if I did the right thing, if it was truly in keeping. But, I let it go! Yes, yes, there is room for doubt when it comes to imagination, for that is really thought."

While Augusto and Víctor were carrying on this "nivolistic" conversation, I, the author of this nivola, *that you have in hand and are reading, dear reader, I*

*was smiling enigmatically as I watched my "nivolistic"
characters pleading my case and justifying my method. Meanwhile I told myself: "How far these unhappy
creatures are from suspecting that all they are doing
is justifying my manipulation of them! Just as when
a man searches for reasons to justify himself, he is, in
actual fact, only searching to justify God. And I am
the God of these two wretched 'nivolistic' devils."*

XXVI

AUGUSTO MADE his way to Eugenia's home, prepared to perform his final, definitive psychological experiment, although in his heart he feared she would
reject him. He met her on the stairs on the way up to
her house, as she was leaving to go out.

"Oh, so you're here, Don Augusto?"

"Yes, I am, but as you're on your way out, I'll let
it go for another day. I'll come back."

"No, don't go. My uncle is at home."

"No, Eugenia, I'm not here to see your uncle. I
came to see you. We'll leave it for another day."

"No, not at all, we'll both go up. It's best to strike
when the iron is hot."

"But if your uncle is at home . . ."

"Heavens! He's an anarchist! We won't even tell
him we're there."

And she insisted that Augusto go upstairs with her.
Poor Augusto, who had started out a bit pretentiously
in his role of scientist and experimenter, began to feel
like the object of experimentation instead.

When they were alone in the living room, Eugenia,

still wearing her hat and dressed for the outdoors, said to him:

"Well, now, let's hear what you have to say."

"Well, it's . . . ," and Augusto could only stutter.

"Well, what is it?"

"I cannot get any rest, Eugenia. I have gone over everything we said the last time we spoke a thousand and one times, and, try as I may, I cannot resign myself docilely. I simply can't. I cannot resign myself!"

"And what can't you resign yourself to?"

"Well, to this, Eugenia, to this!"

"And what is 'this'?"

"That we'll be nothing more than friends . . ."

"Nothing more than friends! Does that seem so paltry a thing to you? Or would you rather that we were something less than friends?"

"No, of course not, Eugenia."

"Well, what is it?"

"Good heavens, don't make me suffer like this."

"The only person making you suffer is yourself."

"But I cannot resign myself. I simply cannot!"

"Well, what is it you want?"

"I want . . . I want us to get married."

"I'll hear no more of that. It's all over."

"It must first begin before it can be over."

"And what about your promise?"

"I didn't know what I was saying. . . ."

"And how about that girl, Rosario?"

"O, for heaven's sake, Eugenia, don't bring her up! Forget her!"

Eugenia then stood up and removed her hat, set it on a little table, and sat down again. And in a deliberately solemn manner she declared:

"Well, Augusto, now that you, who are after all is said and done, a man, don't feel compelled to keep your word, I, who am a mere woman, don't feel I should have to keep mine. Besides, I'd like to set you free from Rosario and all the other Rosarios or Petras, who are bound to enmesh you. Compassion accomplishes what gratitude for your generosity could not, or indignation for what happened between Mauricio and me—you see I'm being open with you. Yes, Augusto, you worry me, make me sad. Deeply so!" and as she told him this, she patted his knee lightly with her right hand.

"Eugenia," and he held out his arms to embrace her.

"Ah, careful now!" she insisted, as she withdrew out of his range.

"But last time . . ."

"Yes, but last time was different!"

The experimental psychologist mused: *I am acting the guinea pig in this drama.*

"Yes," she continued, "certain liberties may be granted to a friend who is nothing but a friend, but it would be impossible to do the same in the case of a . . . how should I put it? . . . a . . . fiancé."

"But why not? I don't understand."

"Once we're married, Augusto, I'll explain everything to you. However, now you must behave."

It has all been decided for me, Augusto thought, and he felt like the perfect example of a guinea pig.

"Now," Eugenia added, as she got to her feet, "I'm going to call my uncle."

"What for?"

"To give him the news, of course!"

"Yes, naturally!" Augusto assented, astonished.

Don Fermín was there in a second.

"Look, Uncle, here is Don Augusto Pérez, who has come to ask my hand in marriage. And I have agreed to marry him," Eugenia announced.

"Marvelous! Marvelous!" Don Fermín cried. "Come

here, my dear, and allow me to embrace you! Marvelous!"

"Do you think it's so marvelous, Uncle, that we're going to be married?"

"No, not exactly that, what is really marvelous, what really takes my fancy, what really captivates me is the way in which this whole affair was resolved. The two of you alone, without any third parties. Long live anarchy! And it's a real pity that in order to carry out your intention you have to submit to authority. . . . Of course, in the inner tribunal of your consciousness you need not submit to authority. Pure formality, of course, simply *pro formula*. For I know you already consider yourselves man and wife. In any case, I alone, in the name of the God of Anarchy pronounce you man and wife. And that's all that's needed. Marvelous! Marvelous! As of now, regard this house as your own."

"As of now . . .?"

"I'm sorry. This has always been your house. My house . . . mine? The house I inhabit was always yours, it has always belonged to all of my brothers. But from now on . . . well, you know what I mean."

"Of course, he understands you, Uncle."

Just then, someone knocked at the door and Eugenia called:

"It's my aunt!"

As she entered the drawing room and took account of the situation, she exclaimed:

"So it's all done! I figured as much!"

Augusto thought to himself: *Why, if I'm not the perfect guinea pig! They've landed me all right!*

"You'll stay to dinner with us, to celebrate the event," Doña Ermelinda said.

"What else!" the wretched guinea pig let slip.

XXVII

IT WAS THE START of a new life for Augusto. He spent practically every day at his fiancée's house studying, not psychology, but aesthetics.

And Rosario? Well Rosario did not return to his house. Someone else brought back the ironed clothes on the next occasion. He scarcely dared ask why Rosario no longer came with the clothes. Why should he bother if he already guessed the reason? And this scorn of hers, for it was nothing but scorn, he understood perfectly, and instead of hurting him, it filled him with a certain pleasure. *That was all right. He would receive his just reward, by having Eugenia.* And Eugenia continued her, "Careful, now, keep your hands to yourself!" But her charms were many!

Eugenia rationed out her presence with him, only her visual presence, to be sure, but this whetted his appetite all the more. Once he said to her: "I feel like writing some lines of poetry to the beauty of your eyes!"

And she answered, "Why don't you?"

"But to do that, you should play the piano for me. Hearing you through music, through *your* piano music, would inspire me."

"But you know that I've stopped giving lessons, thanks to your generosity, and I haven't touched the piano since. I can't stand it. It never gave me anything but trouble!"

"That doesn't matter, Eugenia. Play for me anyway, so I can write my poetry."

"All right, but just this once!"

Eugenia sat down at the piano and while she played Augusto wrote the following:

My soul soared far from my body
in the lost mist of my spirit,
lost among the sound of your music
which some call music of the spheres;
and my solitary body remained
soulless and sad, wandering the face of the earth.
Though born to travail side by side,
life did not materialize this way,
for he was matter pure and simple
and she a spiritual creature through and through,
constantly striving for completion, my sweet Eugenia!
But from your sparkling fountains of eyes
a brilliant light lit up my path,
and took hold of my soul and carried it
back from a hazy heaven to a dubious earth,
planting it well in my body, and from then on,
and only then, do I love, my Eugenia!
Your eyes are two blazing nails
that have fired my body to my soul,
and cause my blood to surge with feverish dreams,
to transform my ideas into flesh.
If this light in my life were snuffed out,
my Spirit and matter unyoked,
I would wander lost in celestial mists
and in the voracious dark Hell of the deep.

"What do you think of my verse?" Augusto asked, after she had read the lines through.

"Like my playing, not very musical, or not at all. And those words 'some call' . . ."

"Yes, that's to make it more personal. . . ."

"And what about 'sweet Eugenia'? That's really rubbish!"

"What? You call yourself rubbish?"

"In this poem, yes! And then it all seems very, very . . ."

"Oh, yes, very *nivolistic*."

"What's that?"

"Nothing but a private joke between Víctor and me."

"Well, look here, Augusto, I won't want any private jokes in my house once we're married. Neither private jokes nor dogs. And so you better start thinking about what you're going to do with Orfeo. . . ."

"But Eugenia, good heavens, you know the way I found the poor animal! Besides, Orfeo's my trusty confidant! All my solitary speeches are addressed to the little thing. . . ."

"Well, when we get married, there won't be any solitary speeches in my house. That dog's the limit."

"Goodness, Eugenia, at least until we have a child . . ."

"If we have one, you mean."

"Of course, if we have one. And if we don't, why not a dog? Why not a dog, for it has been rightly said that if a dog had money, it would be man's best friend."

"No, if dogs had money they wouldn't be any kind of friend to man. That I'm sure of, and since dogs don't have money that explains their friendship to men."

On another occasion Eugenia said to Augusto:

"Augusto, listen here, I have to speak to you about something important . . . very important, and I beg you to forgive me in advance if what I say to you . . ."

"Good heavens, Eugenia, speak up!"

"You remember my fiancé . . . the one I had before . . ."

"Yes, Mauricio."

"But you have no idea why I sent that scoundrel packing. . . ."

"I don't care to know."

"That's in your favor. Well, I had to get rid of that layabout, that ne'er-do-well, but . . ."

"You mean to say he's still pursuing you!"

"Yes, still!"

"Ah, if I lay my hands on him!"

"No, no it's not that. He's still after me, but not for the reason you think. It's something else."

"What is it? Tell me!"

"There's no reason for alarm. His bark is worse than his bite."

"Well, then, you must follow the counsel of the old Arabic proverb: 'If you stop for every barking dog on your path, you'll never reach your destination.' It doesn't help to throw stones. Pay no attention to him."

"I think there's an even better way of eliminating him."

"And what is that?"

"To carry crusts of bread in our pockets and throw them to the barking dogs, as they rush out, for they're only barking out of hunger."

"And what do you mean?"

"I mean that Mauricio is not trying to do anything but get me to help him find some kind of employment, a way of making a living, and he says he'll leave me in peace, and if not . . ."

"If not . . ."

"He threatens to pursue me in order to bring me down. . . ."

"The rotter! The filthy scoundrel!"

"Don't get so worked up. I think our best course of action is to get him out of our way by securing him some sort of employment, as far away as possible. Besides, as far as I'm concerned, he's worthy of some bit of compassion because he is what he is, he's really like a . . ."

"Perhaps you're right, Eugenia. I think I'll be able to arrange everything. Tomorrow, I'll speak to a friend of mine and I think we'll be able to get him the job he needs."

And, as it turned out, Augusto was able to find him employment and see to it that his assignment was good and far away.

XXVIII

ONE MORNING Liduvina announced there was a young man waiting to see Augusto. When he heard it was Mauricio, he pulled a long face. His immediate reaction was to send him away without hearing the fellow out, but he was vaguely drawn to him, as he had once been Eugenia's fiancé, and apparently he had loved her, and perhaps still did, in his own way. And he most likely knew certain intimate details of the woman who was going to be his wife, more than he, Augusto, did himself. That man who . . . Ah, yes, there was something that linked them.

"I've come here, sir," Mauricio began obsequiously, "to thank you for the great favor you've extended to me, through Eugenia's kind intervention, . . ."

"You need not thank me, sir, but I hope now you'll not continue to harass my future wife."

"But I've not troubled her in the slightest!"

"I know exactly what I'm talking about."

"Since she turned me out, and I think she acted sensibly in doing so, for I'm hardly the man for her,

I've done as best I could to lick my wounds, and certainly to respect her decision, of course. If she has said otherwise . . ."

"I beg you not to mention again the woman who is going to be my wife, and please do not suggest that she has in any way deviated from the truth. Comfort yourself as best possible but leave us alone."

"I will do that. I wish to thank you both once more for the favor you have granted me by securing this employment. I'm going to take the job and comfort myself any way possible. In any case, I'm considering taking a young girl along with me."

"What difference does that make to me, my dear sir?"

"Well, I think you know her. . . ."

"What is this? Are you trying to make a fool of me?"

"No, no, not at all. Her name's Rosario and she irons clothes in a shop. . . . I think she used to deliver your clothes. . . ."

Augusto blanched: *Does he really know all about everything?* This unnerved him even more than the previous suspicion that Mauricio had been more intimately connected with Eugenia than he. However, he quickly recovered his composure and shouted:

"And why are you coming around here with all this gossip?"

"It seems," and Mauricio droned on, as if he had not heard a word, "that those of us who have been thrown over ought to be allowed to commiserate with one another."

"But what are you getting at? What do you mean by all this?" Augusto pondered the possibility of strangling the man in the same room that had served as a backdrop for his last outburst with Rosario.

"Don't get so excited, Don Augusto, please don't. I didn't mean anything. She . . . the one you don't want me to mention, loathes me, threw me over, and now I've met this poor little girl, who is also despised and . . ."

Augusto could no longer contain himself. First he went white and then flushed fiery red. He stood up and took hold of Mauricio. He threw him into the air and then on to the sofa, without really clearly knowing what he was doing, as if he were going to choke him. But when Mauricio found himself on the sofa, he said with icy indifference:

"Come here now, Don Augusto, look into my eyes and see how tiny you are. . . ."

Poor Augusto felt himself going to pieces. All the strength ebbed from his arms, and the room itself was dissolving into mist before his eyes. *Am I dreaming?*, he wondered, and he suddenly discovered Mauricio directly in front of him, smiling foxily:

"O, I didn't mean anything, really. I'm sorry. It was a kind of frenzy. . . . I don't even know what I did exactly. . . . I didn't even realize. . . . Thanks again, many thanks. Thanks to both of you. Good-bye!"

No sooner had Mauricio left when Augusto called Liduvina.

"Tell me, Liduvina, who was with me here?"

"A young fellow."

"What did he look like?"

"But do you need me to tell you that?"

"Was there really someone here with me?"

"Señorito!"

"No . . . no . . . Swear to me that someone was here with me and tell me what he looked like. . . . Tall, blond . . . With a moustache, rather on the heavy side, with a long nose? Was he here?"

"But are you feeling all right, Don Augusto?"

"I wasn't dreaming?"

"Not unless both of us were dreaming. . . ."

"No, both of us couldn't have been dreaming the same dream at the same time. And that's when we know that something is not a dream, precisely when it's not one person's dream alone. . . ."

"Well, don't trouble yourself any more. Calm down! The young man you were talking about was here."

"And what did he say as he left?"

"He didn't say anything to me as he left. I didn't even see him. . . ."

"And do you know who he is, Liduvina?"

"Yes, I know. He was the fiancé of . . ."

"That's enough. And now do you know who he's courting?"

"That would be knowing too much."

"You women know so much that you don't pass on to us. . . ."

"True, but on the other hand, we don't seem to be able to learn the things meant to be taught us."

"Very good, but tell the truth, Liduvina: Don't you really know whom he's going with, that . . . that fellow?"

"No, but I can imagine."

"How?"

"By what you're saying."

"All right, call Domingo now."

"What for?"

"To find out if I'm still dreaming or not, and if you're really his wife, Liduvina, or if . . ."

"Or if Domingo is also dreaming? But I think I have a better idea."

"What's that?"

"Call Orfeo."

"You're right. He doesn't dream!"

Shortly after Liduvina left, the dog came into the room.

"Come here, Orfeo," his master commanded. "Come here! You poor thing! So few days remain for us to be together! She doesn't want you in the house. And where will I send you? What will I do with you? What will happen to you without me? This may kill you, I know! Only a dog is capable of dying when he finds himself without his master. And I've been more than your master—your father, your God! No, she doesn't want you in the house. She wants to take you from me! Is it possible that you, the veritable symbol of loyalty, would upset her household? Who knows the answer? Perhaps a dog discovers, surprises a person's most intimate thoughts, at least the thoughts of the people he lives with, and even though he keeps silent . . . And I have to get married. There's no other way. Otherwise I'd never awake from this dream and I must awake.

"But why are you looking at me like that, Orfeo? You look as if you're crying without tears. . . . Do you want to tell me something? I can see you are suffering at not being able to speak. I was too quick in thinking you didn't dream! You're definitely dreaming me now, Orfeo! Why is it that we men exist as men only because there are dogs, cats, horses, oxen, sheep, and all sorts of animals, especially domesticated ones in the world? Without domesticated animals which we men have employed in order to unload the brutishness of life, would man have attained his humanity? If man hadn't domesticated the horse, wouldn't half of our race now be dragging the other half on their backs? Yes, it is to you we owe our civilization. And to women, too. But maybe women are just another species of domesticated animals. And if there were no women would men be men? O, Orfeo, someone is coming into this house in order to drive you out!"

And Augusto hugged the dog against his chest. And the dog, meanwhile, really looked as if it were crying, as it licked Augusto's chin.

XXIX

EVERYTHING WAS now ready for the wedding. Augusto had wanted it to be an intimate, discreet affair, but his future wife preferred a celebration with flourish and fanfare.

The nearer the day came, the more warmly did Augusto desire to take certain small liberties and intimacies. But Eugenia kept herself even more guarded than before.

"But, Eugenia, in a few days we'll be one and the same, man and wife."

"That's exactly why. We must begin by respecting each other."

"Respect . . . respect. . . . Respect doesn't exclude the possibility of warmth and affection."

"You *would* think that! You're a man through and through!"

And Augusto detected something odd, something strained in her manner. Sometimes it seemed as if she were trying to avoid his glance. And then he would recall his mother, his poor mother, and how she yearned for her son to marry well and be happy. And now, on the verge of marrying Eugenia, he was more than ever tormented by what Mauricio had said about going off with Rosario. He was riddled with jealousy, a raging jealousy, and he was furious with himself for having passed up an opportunity and for the ridiculous position he was put in as regards the girl. To himself he said:

Now they'll have a good laugh on me, and Mauricio will get a double guffaw out of it: by leaving Eugenia he has managed to pawn her off on me, and, on top of it, he is stealing my Rosario. And there were moments when he felt a violent urge to break off his engagement with Eugenia and stride into battle for Rosario, to snatch her out of Mauricio's arms.

"And what about that sweet thing, that Rosario, what have you ever done with her?" Eugenia asked a few days before the wedding.

"And why are you reminding me of her now?"

"If you don't care to think about it, I won't say any more."

"No, it's not that . . . but . . ."

"Well, I remember how she interrupted us once when we were together. Haven't you heard anything about her since?" and she gave him a piercing look.

"No, I haven't heard about her since then."

"You don't happen to know who's taking her out these days, do you?" And she turned her look away from Augusto and stared into space, beyond him.

A series of strange presentiments crossed his mind, and he wondered if she suspected something. Then he said:

"Why, do you know something about her?"

"Me?" she answered, feigning indifference, and she looked at him again.

A mysterious cloud floated between them.

"You've probably forgotten her by now. . . ."

"But why do you insist on talking about that little nothing of a girl?"

"How do I know! Well, to change the subject, what does a man feel when someone else takes over the woman he was after and steals her away?"

When Augusto heard this, he felt his blood rush to his head. He was seized with a desire to dash out and bring back Rosario, as a prize, and then say to Eugenia: "Here she is . . . mine and not . . . *your* Mauricio's!"

There were only three days till the wedding. Augusto left his fiancée's house in a thoughtful mood, somewhat concerned. He could scarcely sleep that night.

No sooner had he risen on the following morning, when Liduvina came into his bedroom.

"There's a letter here for you, sir. It was just delivered. I think it's from Señorita Eugenia. . . ."

"A letter from her? How come? Leave it here and go!"

Liduvina left the room and Augusto began to quake. He felt his heart contract with a peculiar unnerving agitation. He thought of Rosario and Mauricio. But he did not want to touch the letter. He examined the envelope with terror. He got out of bed, washed, dressed, ordered breakfast and gobbled it down. *No, I don't want to read it here*, he decided. He went out of the house and repaired to the nearest church and opened the letter. He thought: *Here I'll have to control myself for I don't know what my heart* . . . The letter read:

"Dear Augusto: By the time you read this I'll be with Mauricio on my way to the town where he has his new job, thanks to your generosity. And also because of your generosity, I'll be able to live off my property, which in addition to Mauricio's salary, will enable us to live together rather comfortably. I won't beg your forgiveness, because after all this, I am sure you'll be more than convinced that I would have never made you happy, and even less, you would not have made me happy. I'll write again once you get over the initial shock, and I'll explain why I'm doing this now, and in this fashion. Mauricio thought it would have been better if we had left the same day as the wedding, after leaving the church ceremony, but his plan was too complicated and it seemed to be unnecessarily cruel. And as I've said before, I hope we'll remain friends.

Your friend,
Eugenia Domingo del Arco

P.S. Rosario didn't come along. She stayed behind and you'll be able to find some solace in her company."

Augusto fell limply on to a bench. After a short while, he knelt and began to pray.

When he left the church, he thought he had become calm, but it was that terrible calm before a storm. He turned toward Eugenia's house and there he found her poor uncle and aunt totally distraught. Their niece had not returned the night before and had communicated her decision by letter. Eugenia and Mauricio had departed by train at nightfall, shortly after her conversation with Augusto.

"What are we to do now?" Doña Ermelinda asked.

"What is there to do but bear it?" Augusto answered.

"It's an outrage. This sort of behavior should not go unpunished. It should be held up as an example of . . . of . . . ," Don Fermín exclaimed.

"What are you saying, you, the anarchist?"

"What does that have to do with it? There are certain things one doesn't do. To lead a man on that way!"

"Well, she didn't lead the other fellow on," Augusto said indifferently, and then was terrified by his own indifference.

"But she'll get around to it. She'll fool him, too, without a shadow of doubt."

Augusto felt a thrill of diabolic pleasure at the thought of Eugenia's eventually deceiving Mauricio. *But not with me*, he murmured to himself, so quietly he could hardly hear himself.

"Well, I'm sorry about what has happened and even worried for your niece, but I must take my leave now."

"I'm sure you understand, Don Augusto, that we . . . ," Doña Ermelinda started.

"Of course I do! But . . ."

The visit could not be dragged out any longer. After a few words of farewell, Augusto left.

As he went down the street he began to feel terrified of what was happening to him, and even more of what was not happening to him. His apparent indifference, his calm reaction at being struck down by this act of supreme deception, made him doubt his own existence. To himself he said:

If I were really like other men, if I had a heart— if I were even human, if I truly existed—how would I be able to endure this blow with the indifference I've displayed?

And unconsciously he began to touch and pinch himself to see if he felt anything.

Suddenly he felt a tugging at his leg. It was Orfeo, who had come out to meet him and comfort him. Strangely enough, when he saw Orfeo he felt enormously happy. He picked up the dog and said: "Cheer up, Orfeo, cheer up! Let's both of us cheer up! You're not going to be driven out of the house. We're not going to be separated! We'll live and die together. Some good comes out of every disaster, no matter how big the disaster or how tiny the good, or vice versa. You, Orfeo, you're loyal! I suppose, one of these days, you'll find a love-mate, but you won't leave home for that reason, or abandon me. You're loyal, Orfeo. And, look here, so you won't ever have to leave, I'll bring a love-mate home for you. Yes, I'll bring one home for you. I wonder, now, did you rush out to comfort me in my suffering, or did you just happen to meet me on your way back from a visit to your bitch? In any case, you're the loyal one, and nobody will drive you from my house. No one will ever separate us."

He entered the house, and once inside, the storm in his soul that had been disguised as a calm, was unleashed. A wave of passion was unleashed, passion which ran the gamut of bitterness, jealousy, fury, fear, hatred, love, pity, scorn, and, above all, shame, a monumental shame, and an awful awareness of his ridiculous position.

"She has finished me off!" he told Liduvina.

"Who has?"

"She has."

He locked himself in his room. And as he visualized Eugenia and Mauricio, he also pictured Rosario making a fool of him. He thought of his mother. He threw himself on the bed, bit the pillow, and found there was not even anything he could say to himself. His soliloquy had run dry. He felt as if his soul had been shriveled up. Then he burst into tears, and he wept and wept. His thoughts finally evaporated into a fit of silent weeping.

XXX

Víctor found Augusto sunk in the corner of a sofa, his head lowered, staring beyond the floor under his feet.

"What's all this about?" he asked, as he raised his hand to Augusto's shoulder.

"And do you ask me this? Don't you know what has happened?"

"Yes, I know what's happened on the surface, that is, what she has done to you. What I don't know is what is going on inside you. In other words, I don't know why you're in such a state."

"I can't believe it. It's incredible!"

"All right, so one love, say love A has flown the coop. There's still love B, C, D, and so on, or any X number of loves yet to be discovered."

"This is no moment for jokes."

"Quite the opposite, this is precisely the moment for joking."

"It's not that this lost love pains me so much. It's the awful way I've been made to look ridiculous, the infinite trickery of it. They've mocked me, scorned me, ridiculed me, made a laughing stock out of me! I suppose they wanted to prove . . . I don't know what exactly, perhaps they wanted to prove I don't exist."

"What luck!"

"Don't make jokes, Víctor."

"And why shouldn't I joke? You started by trying to turn her into a guinea pig and, instead, it is she who has transformed you into the guinea pig. So now you can begin to act the guinea pig."

"I beg you to stop. . . ."

"Stop joking? Well, I'll joke anyway. Jokes were made for moments like this."

"But your humor is so caustic, so corrosive."

"But one has to be caustic . . . to corrode. And it's also necessary to confuse. Above all to confuse, to confuse everything. To confuse sleep with being awake, fiction with reality, the true with the false. To confuse everything in one all-encompassing mist. A joke that is not corrosive and confusing isn't worth the bother. In tragedy, the child laughs, while in comedy, the old man cries. You wanted to be a guinea pig and so you've turned into one: well, accept the situation, and become a guinea pig."

"What do you mean?"

"Experiment on yourself."

"Yes, you think I ought to commit suicide."

"I am not saying either yes or no to that idea. It would be one solution, but not the best."

"Then perhaps I should seek those two out and kill them."

"Killing for the sake of killing is an extravagance. It makes sense as a cathartic, a way of purging yourself of hatred, which simply corrodes the soul. More than one rancorous creature rid himself of his rancor, and finally felt pity and even love for his victim, once he satisfied his hatred. An evil act is a way of liberating oneself from an evil passion. It is the law which creates sin."

"Then, what am I to do?"

"Haven't you ever heard that in this world of ours there is nothing to do but to devour or be devoured?"

"Yes, either make a fool out of others or be the fool yourself."

"No, there's still a third possibility, and that is to devour yourself, to make a fool of yourself. Devour yourself! The man who devours, enjoys himself, but he can't help thinking of the end of all his pleasure, and that turns him into a pessimist; the man who is devoured suffers, and he can't help looking forward to the end of his suffering, and so he becomes an optimist. So devour yourself, and since the pleasure of devouring yourself will be confused with the pain of being devoured, one neutralizing the other, you'll achieve a perfect equanimity of spirit, in other words, ataraxia. Then you'll be merely a spectacle for yourself."

"And that it should be you, you, Víctor, who comes here to tell me this . . . !"

"Yes, Augusto, it is I."

"Well, at one time you didn't think in this . . . in this corrosive way."

"That was before I became a father."

"And becoming a father means . . . ?"

"Becoming a father for anyone who isn't completely mad or a liar, is the most terrible kind of awakening possible. What sense of responsibility! I'm the one entrusted to hand down the perennial legacy of humanity to my son. Just to meditate on the mystery of paternity is enough to drive you mad. And the fact is that if most parents don't go stark raving mad, it's because they're fools . . . or they're not parents. Rejoice, then, Augusto, and don't forget that in having managed to escape marriage, you've also avoided becoming a father. I told you to marry, but I never told you to become a father. Even marriage is an experiment . . . a psychological experiment. Paternity on the other hand, is also an experiment but . . . pathological."

"But I've become a father, Víctor!"

"What in the world do you mean? What do you mean you've become a father?"

"Yes, my own! I've the feeling I've really been born, born for the first time. Born to suffer and born to die."

"Yes, of course, the second birth, the true awakening, is to be born with the painful consciousness of ever-returning death. But if you've become your own father, then you've also become your own son."

"It doesn't seem possible, Víctor, in fact, it's really incredible that in spite of what has happened to me and what *is* happening to me, and after what she has done to me, I can still listen to this subtle sophistry of yours, this intellectual play on concepts, these macabre jokes . . . and what's worse . . ."

"What's that?"

". . . I'm distracted by it all! It makes me furious with myself!"

"That's play-acting, Augusto, our own play-acting, performing for ourselves in the inner forum, on the stage of our own consciousness, where we are both actor and audience. Sometimes during a painful scene, when we act out our pain, it suddenly doesn't seem quite right, and we feel like bursting into laughter. And it is just at that moment we most feel like laughing! Play-acting, yes, the comedy of pain!"

"And do you think play-acting based on pain can bring one to the point of suicide?"

"You mean the comedy of suicide!"

"But one really dies!"

"Still it's play-acting!"

"Then, what is actually true, real? What is it we truly feel?"

"But who said play-acting wasn't actually real or true or capable of making people feel real emotion, for that matter?"

"Well, then . . . ?"

"I think that everything is the same, one and the same, that it is essential to confound and confuse, Augusto. And whoever does not confound gets confounded."

"As well as the person doing the confounding."

"Perhaps."

"Well, what then?"

"Well, this: All this talk and wordplay is just a way to while away the time!"

"Well, those who indulge in it are simply whiling away the time!"

"And so are you. Have you ever thought of yourself as more interesting in your own eyes than right now? How can a man be sure he has arms or legs if they don't hurt him?"

"I agree, but still what am I going to do now?"

"What must you do? Right now you're the center of a drama or a novel! Isn't it enough to be the center of a . . . *nivola*! What is there to do? Do you think it's such a minor role to be here talking this way? Everyone is obsessed with action, but really it's all only pantomime! When they say a play has a lot of action, what they really mean is that the actors are making grand gestures and strutting about, fighting imaginary duels and leaping about and . . . well, it's all pantomime, just pantomime! On the other hand, there are also plays in which everything's talk. As if to talk were not action. In the beginning was the Word . . . and the Word was made flesh . . . and through the Word all things were made. Just imagine, for instance, that some 'nivolist' were tucked away behind the wardrobe, transcribing everything we said in shorthand, and suppose he were to publish it all later for his readers. It's possible his readers would say that nothing is going on here, and yet . . ."

"Oh, Víctor, I assure you they wouldn't say that if they could see into me!"

"Into whom? Into you or into me? We don't have anything inside. And they really would say nothing was going on here if they could see inside of *themselves*, of themselves, the readers. The soul of a protagonist of a novel or drama or *nivola* has no inside except what's given him by the . . ."

"Yes, by the author."

"No, the reader."

"Well, I assure you, Víctor . . ."

"Don't assure me of anything. Devour yourself, for that's the only sure thing there is."

"I'm doing just that. I've already begun. I started like a shadow, a piece of fiction. For years I've wandered about like a phantom, like a puppet fashioned out of mist, without believing in my own existence, imagining myself a creature of phantasy invented by a hidden genius for his own solace or catharsis. But now, after what has been done to me, after this mockery, this ferocious mockery, now yes, now I know I can feel, touch. Now I no longer doubt my own existence."

"It's all play-acting, nothing but play-acting!"

"How?"

"But it's all there. For instance, the man who plays the part of the king begins to think he is king."

"But what are you driving at?"

"I merely want to take your mind off yourself. Besides, what if a 'nivolist' were concealed here, as I said before, listening to our words and transcribing them for future publication—well, in that case, the reader of the *nivola* might begin to doubt of his own flesh and blood body, if only for a fleeting moment, and would believe that he, too, were a 'nivolistic' character like ourselves."

"And why would he do that?"

"To save himself."

"Yes, I have heard it said that the most liberating effect of art is that it makes one forget one's own existence. There are people who wade through novels just to take their minds off themselves, to forget their troubles. . . ."

"No, that isn't it. The most liberating effect of art is that it makes one doubt of one's own existence."

"And what is it to exist?"

"You see, now you're on the road to recovery. You're beginning to devour yourself. The proof is in your last question. '*To be or not to be!*' said Hamlet, one of the protagonists who invented Shakespeare."

"Well, Víctor, as far as I am concerned this '*to be or not to be*' has always seemed a profoundly empty phrase."

"The more profound a phrase, the emptier it is. There is nothing more profound than a bottomless well. Tell me, what you would say is the greatest truth?"

"Well, one minute, now let's see. . . . What Descartes said: 'I think, therefore I am.' "

"Not at all. The profoundest truth is that $A = A$."

"But that's nothing."

"That's exactly why it's the greatest of all truths, because it's nothing. But do you think that Descartes' twaddle is all that incontrovertible?"

"Just so . . ."

"Well, then, did Descartes say it or didn't he?"

"Yes, of course he did!"

"Then, it is not true. For Descartes was never anything but a creature out of fiction, an invention of history, since . . . he neither existed . . . nor did he think, for that matter!"

"Who, then, uttered that famous statement?"

"No one at all said it. It was something said by itself."

"Do you mean, then, that the man who was and who thought was simply the famous maxim itself?"

"Of course! It's the same as saying that to be is to think and what does not think does not exist."

"That's perfectly clear."

"So don't think, Augusto, don't think. But if you insist upon thinking . . ."

"What then?"

"Devour yourself!"

"Do you mean I should commit suicide . . . ?"

"I don't want to meddle in that matter. Good-bye!"

Víctor departed, and left Augusto bewildered, and lost in thought.

XXXI

THE UPHEAVAL in Augusto's soul finally ended in an awful calm. He had decided to kill himself. He wanted to put an end to that self, which had been the source of all his trouble. But before carrying out his decision, it occurred to him, just as it occurs to the shipwrecked man to grasp at the flimsiest plank, to discuss the whole thing with me, the author of this story. At that time, Augusto had read an essay of mine, in which I had made a passing reference to suicide and this, along with some other things of mine he had read, had apparently made such an impression on him, that he did not want to leave this world without making my acquaintance and conversing with me for a while. And so he came to Salamanca, where I have been living for over twenty years, to call on me.

When he was announced I smiled enigmatically to myself and had him come into my study. He came in like a phantom, looked at an oil painting of me which hangs over my bookcase, and then, at a gesture from me, he sat down in front of me.

He started by talking to me about my literary pursuits, especially the quasi-philosophical ones, and displayed a fair enough knowledge of them, which, I must admit, pleased me. In short order, he began to tell me his life story, replete with all its miseries. I interrupted him to say he could spare himself the bother, since I was as well-versed in the vicissitudes he had endured as he was himself. I proved this to him by bringing up particulars of a very private nature, which he had considered to be most secret. His eyes revealed genuine terror, as if he were looking at a monster. I thought I noted a change in his color and expression. He even seemed to be trembling. He was spellbound.

"It doesn't seem possible," he kept repeating. "It doesn't seem possible! I would never believe it if I didn't see it with my own eyes. I don't know if I'm awake or dreaming. . . ."

"Neither one nor the other," I replied.

"I can't figure it out, I simply cannot," he added, "but since you seem to know as much about me as I do myself, perhaps you've guessed the reason for my visit."

"Yes," I said, "you (and I emphasized the *you* with all the authority I could muster), you are crushed by all your miseries, and have concocted this devilish idea of committing suicide, and before actually doing it, motivated by something you've read in one of my recent essays, you've come here to discuss it with me."

The poor man shook like quicksilver, staring at me as if he were possessed. He made an effort to stand, perhaps to flee from me, but he could not manage it. He could not gather the necessary strength.

"No, don't make a move!" I ordered.

"Do you mean . . . Are you . . . ," he stammered.

"I mean that you're not going to commit suicide, even if it's what you most want."

"What!" he shouted, when he found himself so flatly rebuffed and repudiated.

"Yes, now, just think, what is the essential quality demanded for a man to kill himself?" I questioned.

"The courage to do it," he answered.

"No," I told him, "It's first necessary he be alive."

"Of course!"

"Well, you are not alive!"

"I'm not alive! Have I died, by any chance?" and he began, without realizing it, to touch himself.

"No, my dear Augusto," I answered him. "I already told you that you were neither awake nor dreaming, and now I want to tell you that you're neither alive nor dead."

"Explain this to me once and for all, for heaven's sake! Tell me everything," he implored nervously. "Because, given the things I'm hearing and seeing this afternoon, I fear for my sanity."

"Very well, the truth, my dear Augusto, is this," I told him in my gentlest voice, "you cannot kill yourself because you are not alive, and because you are not alive, neither are you dead, because you do not exist. . . ."

"I don't exist!" he shouted.

"No, you don't exist any more than any other creature of fiction exists. You are not, my poor Augusto,
anything more than a figment of my imagination and
of my readers' imagination, when they eventually read
this story of your fictitious adventures and mishaps
that I have invented for you. You are a mere protagonist in a novel, or *nivola*, whatever you'd like to call
it. Now you're privy to your secret."

Upon hearing this, the poor man sat looking at
me for a while with a penetrating stare, one of those
stares that seems to pierce your own gaze and goes
even further. Then, he glanced again at my portrait
over the books, and his color returned and his breathing became more regular. He gradually pulled himself together, mastered himself, and with his elbows
on my round brazier table, to which he had drawn
close, directly opposite me, his head in the palms of
his hands, he suddenly looked at me with a smile in
his eyes and said to me slowly:

"Look here, Don Miguel . . . are you sure you're not
mistaken and everything that's happening to me is the
exact reverse of what you think and have told me?"

"What do you mean by the exact reverse?" I asked
him, alarmed at seeing him taking control of his own
life.

"Could it not possibly be, my dear Don Miguel,"
he added, "that it is you and not I who are a creature
out of fiction, the person who actually does not exist,
who is neither living nor dead? Could it not possibly
be that you are a mere pretext for bringing my story
to the world . . ."

"What nonsense!" I exclaimed, somewhat irascibly.

"Please don't get nervous, Señor de Unamuno," he

retorted. "Keep calm. You have brought to light certain doubts about my existence. . . ."

"Doubts! Not at all!" I blurted out. "I have made it absolutely clear that you have no existence outside of the novel I have invented."

"Very well, then, but don't be so put out if I, in turn, doubt your existence instead of my own. Let us get to the heart of the matter. Aren't you the person who has stated, not just once, mind you, but several times, that Don Quixote and Sancho are not only real people, but more real than Cervantes himself?"

"I cannot deny it, but my meaning . . . the sense of it was . . ."

"All right, let's leave the meaning or sense of it to one side, and we'll discuss something else. When a man is asleep and inert, dreaming his dream, what really exists, he as the consciousness that dreams or the dream itself?"

"And what if he dreams that he, the dreamer himself, exists?" I answered with another question.

"Well, in that case, my friend Don Miguel, I'll ask you still another question. How does he exist, as a dreamer who dreams himself or as a creature dreamed by himself? And take heed, by carrying on this discussion with me you are already ascribing recognition of my existence, independent of yourself."

"No, no, not at all." I said with alacrity. "I depend on discussion; without discussion I am not alive, and when there is no one outside of me to question or contradict me, I invent somebody inside to do it. My soliloquies are dialogues."

"Perhaps the dialogues you concoct are actually soliloquies."

"That's possible. But I repeat, you do not exist outside of me. . . ."

"And I am also going to repeat something: I suggest that it's you who do not exist independent of me and all the other characters that you think you've invented. I am certain Don Avito Carrascal and the great Don Fulgencio would agree. . . ."

"Don't bring Don Fulgencio into it. . . ."

"All right. But you shouldn't ridicule them. And let's go back. What do you think about my suicide plans?"

"Well, since you only exist in my imagination, I repeat, you shouldn't—nor can you, for that matter—do anything except what I'll have you do, and I'll be damned if I'll let you die that way, I simply will not have it. And that's that!"

"All this about 'I'll be damned if I'll let you die that way,' Señor de Unamuno, is very Spanish of you, but very offensive. And besides, even supposing your peculiar theory that I do not exist—and that *you do* exist—and that I am no more than a creature out of fiction, a figment of your novelistic imagination, or 'nivolistic' imagination, even then I should not succumb to your 'I'll be damned if I'll let you die that way,' which is your special quirk. For even those so-called creatures out of fiction have their own inherent logic. . . ."

"Come now, I've heard that before."

"But that's absolutely the case. A novelist or playwright just can't do anything he fancies with a character he creates. Nor can a creature out of a novel do anything a reader might not expect of him, in accordance with the basic precepts of art. . . ."

"That might apply to a character in a novel. . . ."

"Well, then?"

"But a character of a *nivola* . . ."

"Let's stop this foolishness. It goes against the grain and it also hurts me to the quick. I have my own character, whether or not you gave it to me or I simply had it—and you can think what you like about that and I'll do likewise—and I also have my own way of acting or *being* and my own inherent logic, and right now this logic bids that I kill myself. . . ."

"You can think what you like, but you're still wrong."

"How am I wrong? And what am I wrong about? Just show me where I've gone wrong. Since the knowledge of oneself is the most difficult knowledge to come by, I may very easily have gone wrong and suicide might not be the most logical solution to all my adversity. But you must prove it to me. And though this knowledge of oneself is difficult, my dear friend Don Miguel, there is still another kind of knowledge which does not seem to be any less difficult."

"And what is that?" I asked.

He observed me with a sly, enigmatic smile on his face, and he spoke deliberately:

"Well, even more difficult than self-knowledge for the novelist or playwright is the knowledge of the characters he has created or thinks he has created."

These notions of Augusto's were beginning to unnerve me, to try my patience.

"And I insist," he added, "even though you have endowed me with being—fictitious being, to be sure —you cannot, just like that, just because you feel like it, and just because you say, 'I'll be damned if I'll let you die that way,' you cannot keep me from committing suicide."

"That's enough, that will do!" I cried, and I struck the table with my fist. "Keep quiet! I'll have no more of your insolence! And from one of my own creatures! Since I've had my fill of you and, besides, I no longer know what more there is for you to do, I have decided right here and now that you will not commit suicide, but that I shall kill you instead. You're going to die very soon. Very, very soon!"

"What?" Augusto cried, thunderstruck. "You're going to let me die, make me die . . . kill me?"

"Yes, I am going to make you die."

"Never! Never! Never!" he screamed.

"Ah!" I said, watching him with a mixture of pity and rage, "So you were ready to kill yourself and you won't have me kill you? You were about to take your own life and you resent my doing it for you?"

"But it's not the same thing."

"Actually, I've heard of similar cases. I heard of a man who went out one evening with a revolver, intending to kill himself, when he was suddenly assaulted by some thieves. They attacked him and he defended himself, and in the fracas, he ended up killing one of the thieves, while the others fled. He felt that he had bought his own life at the cost of another man's, and so renounced his original intention."

"That's understandable," Augusto observed. "The question was to take somebody's life, to kill a man, and once someone was killed, why should he kill himself? Most suicides are simply cases of frustrated homicide. Men kill themselves because they haven't the courage to kill someone else."

"Now I understand you, Augusto. You mean to say that if you had the courage to kill Eugenia or Mauricio, or both of them, you wouldn't think of killing yourself. Is that it?"

"Well, it wasn't exactly them I had in mind. No!"

"Whom *did* you have in mind?"

"You!" and he looked directly into my eyes.

"What!" I shouted, as I got to my feet. "You

thought to kill me! You, of all people, killing me?"

"Sit down, Don Miguel, and don't get so excited. Or do you think that it would be the first case of a creature out of fiction, as you refer to me, doing away with his maker, the one who breathed him into fictitious life?"

"This is too much," I said, pacing back and forth across my study. "This has gotten out of hand. This couldn't happen except . . ."

"Except in *nivolas*," he finished my sentence for me, in a malicious drawl.

"That's enough. I've had just enough from you! This is about as much as I can put up with. . . . You came here to consult with me and you end up discussing *my* existence. Have you forgotten that I have every right in the world to do anything I damned please with you? Yes, just as I say, I can do anything I damned please, anything that comes into my head."

"Don't be so Spanish, Don Miguel!"

"On top of everything else . . . that. Why you nitwit! Well, I am Spanish! Spanish by birth, education, language, profession, and calling. I am Spanish in both body and soul. Spanish before and after, through and through. Spanish is my religion and the heaven in which I want to believe is a celestial, eternal Spain, and my God is a Spanish God, the God of Our Lord Don Quixote, a God who thinks in Spanish and said in Spanish 'Let there be light!' '*Sea la luz!*' and his Word was a Spanish Word. . . ."

"Very well, but what now?" Augusto interrupted me, bringing me back to reality.

"And so you've taken it into your head to kill me . . . me! Am I to die at the hands of one of my creatures? I'll not put up with this another minute. And to punish you for your insolence and your wild, extravagant, ruinous, anarchist doctrines, which you have brought around here, I've decided to pass a death sentence on you. As soon as you reach home you're going to die. You shall die, I hereby pronounce it, you shall die!"

"But, good God . . . ," Augusto shouted, in an imploring tone of voice, quaking and white with fear.

"No sense invoking God. You shall die!"

"But I want to live, Don Miguel, I want to live, live, live. . . ."

"Weren't you thinking of killing yourself?"

"But, if that's the way you feel, I swear I won't kill myself. I will not take this life that God or you have given me. I swear it to you. . . . Now that you want to kill me, I want to live, live, live. . . ."

"Some life!" I exclaimed.

"Yes, whatever it is. I want to live, even if I'm made butt of more mockery, even if another Eugenia or another Mauricio wrench my heart out. I want to live . . . live . . . live. . . ."

"It's no longer possible. It cannot be."

"I want to live, I tell you, to live and to be myself, myself. . . ."

"But what if that self can only be what I decide it to be?"

"I want to be myself, myself! I want to live!" and his voice became tearful.

"It cannot be . . . it cannot be. . . ."

He fell to his knees, imploring and shouting:

"Don Miguel, for God's sake, I want to live, to be myself."

"It cannot be, my poor Augusto," I told him, as I took one of his hands and brought him to his feet, "it cannot be! It's already written. It's in the books. Your fate is sealed and you cannot live any longer. Anyway,

I don't know what else there is for you to do. For instance, God, when He no longer knows what to do with us, kills us. And I can't forget that it crossed your mind to kill me. . . ."

"But, Don Miguel, if I . . ."

"It doesn't matter. I know what I'm about. And I'm really worried that if I don't kill you quickly, you will eventually kill me."

"But didn't we agree . . . ?"

"It cannot be, Augusto, it simply cannot be. Your time has come. The words are already written and I cannot retract them. You're going to die. And I can't imagine what your life is worth to you now. . . ."

"But . . . for God's sake . . ."

"There is no 'but' or 'God' about it. Leave now!"

"So you won't let me be myself?" he said to me. "So you won't let me be myself, emerge from the mist, live, live, live at last, see myself, touch, listen, feel, hurt, be myself! So you won't have it? You want me to die a fictional being! I am to die as a creature of fiction? Very well, my lord creator, Don Miguel de Unamuno, you will die too! You, too! And you'll return to the nothingness from which you came! God will cease to dream you! You will die, yes, you will die, even though you don't want to. You will die, and so will all those who read my story, every one, every single one, without a single exception! They are all fictional beings, too, creatures of fiction like myself! They will all die, each and every one! It is I, Augusto Pérez, who tells you this. I, Augusto Pérez, a creature of fiction like yourselves, who are as 'nivolistic' as you. Because you, my creator, my dear Don Miguel, are nothing more than just another 'nivolistic' creature, and the same holds true for your readers, just as it does for Augusto Pérez, your victim. . . ."

"Victim?" I cried.

"Yes, victim! To create me only to let me die! Well, you're going to die, too! He who creates creates himself, and he who creates himself, dies. You'll die, Don Miguel, you will die, and so will all those who imagine me, they too will die. Let us begin to die, then!"

This supreme effort in his passionate striving for life—or yearning for immortality—left poor Augusto totally exhausted.

I urged him to the door. He walked out with his head lowered, and he began to touch himself in wonder, as if he were already wary of his own existence. I wiped away a furtive tear.

XXXII

THAT EVENING Augusto left this city of Salamanca, whither he had come to visit me. He left with a death sentence hanging over him, and he was finally convinced that it would no longer be feasible, try as he may, to commit suicide. With the thought of his death uppermost in his mind, he struggled to prolong his journey home, but a mysterious magnetism, an inner force impelled him on. It was a melancholy trip for him. He spent his time in the train counting the minutes, but literally counting them: *one, two, three, four. . . .* All of his troubles, the forlorn dream of his love adventures with Eugenia and Rosario, the whole tragicomic story of his frustrated marriage, had been driven from his memory, or more likely, had been evaporated into mist. He scarcely felt any contact with the seat he sat upon or even the weight of his own body. *Could it be true that I do not really exist?* he wondered. *Is he right when he says that I'm no more than a figment of his imagination, a purely fictional creature?*

Lately his life had been overwhelmingly sad, painful beyond belief, but it was even sadder and more painful to think that all of it had been no more than a dream, and not even his dream, but my dream. Nothingness was more horrific than all of his suffering, his pain. To dream that one exists . . . well and good! That might be endured. But to be dreamt by someone else . . . !

And why must it be that I do not exist? Why? he wondered. *Let's assume it's true that this man has invented me, dreamt me, fashioned me out of his imagination—but still, don't I live in the imagination of other people, for instance, those people who read this story of my life? And if I live that way, in the phantasy-life of some people, isn't that reality, that which is common to several minds and not just to one? And if I come to life out of the written pages in which the tale of my fictitious life is contained, or rather from the minds of those who read them, of you who are reading them at this moment, why should I not exist, then, as an eternal soul, eternally painful and sad? Why?*

The poor fellow could not relax. The plains of Castile passed before his eyes, sometimes lined with oak groves, and at other moments, with copses of pines. He pondered the snowy peaks of the sierras, and in a kind of visual retrospection, he could see the faces of his companions in life shrouded in mist, and meanwhile, he himself felt dragged along to his death.

He reached his house and knocked. Liduvina, who

came to open the door, went pale at the sight of him.

"What's wrong, Liduvina? What are you afraid of?"

"Good heavens! You look more dead than alive. . . . Your face is out of another world. . . ."

"I've just come from another world, Liduvina, and I am going back to another world. I am neither dead nor alive."

"But have you gone mad? Domingo! Domingo!"

"Don't call your husband, Liduvina. I am not mad, no. And as I said, I am not dead—although I'll die shortly—but neither am I alive."

"But what in heaven's name are you talking about?"

"Simply that I do not exist, Liduvina. I am a creature out of fiction, like a character out of a book. . . ."

"Fiddlesticks! This is stuff and nonsense out of books! You must get some good food in you. Undress and get into bed and forget this. . . ."

"But, Liduvina, do you think I exist?"

"Come, come, stop all these high jinks. You'll have some supper and go to bed! And tomorrow will be another day!"

Augusto mused: *I think, therefore I am.* Then he thought further: *Everything that thinks is and everything that is, thinks. Yes, everything that is, thinks. I am, therefore I think.*

He really did not feel like eating, but out of habit and his usual custom of yielding to the entreaties of his loyal servants, he asked for a couple of soft-boiled eggs, nothing more, something light. But as he ate, a strange, voracious appetite took hold of him, a mad fury to eat more and more. And he demanded two more eggs and then a steak.

"That's it, eat," Liduvina told him. "This must all come from weakness. A man who doesn't eat dies."

"And so does the fellow who eats, Liduvina," Augusto commented dejectedly.

"Yes, but not out of hunger."

"And what's the difference if you die of hunger or anything else?"

And then he thought: *But, no, no! I can't die. Only a person who is alive, who exists, can die, and since I don't exist, I can't die. I am immortal! There is no immortality like that which belongs to someone who was never born and does not exist. A creature out of fiction is an idea, and an idea is always immortal!*

"I am immortal! Immortal!" Augusto shouted.

"What did you say?" Liduvina asked, as she rushed into the room.

"I said, bring me some . . . let's see . . . some ham, some cold cuts, *foie gras*, whatever there is. I'm really ravenous!"

"This is how I like to see you. Just like this! Eat up! He who has an appetite is in good health and he who is in good health lives!"

"But, Liduvina, I am not alive."

"What are you talking about?"

"Just that, I am not alive. We immortals are not alive, and I am not alive, I am beyond being alive. I am super-alive. I am an idea! An idea, pure and simple!"

He began to wolf down the ham. And then he wondered: *But if I eat, how can I not be alive? I eat, therefore I exist! No doubt of it.* "Edo, ergo sum." *What can be the reason for this voracious appetite? And then he recalled from his reading how men condemned to death, in the last hours, as they awaited their execution in the death house, spent all their time eating. It was something I never could fathom,* he thought. *The other thing that Renan talks about in* "L'Abbesse de Jouarre" *is understandable. It's perfectly understandable. A couple condemned to die should feel, just before dying, the instinct to survive by reproducing themselves . . . but to eat! Still, the body continues to put up a battle. And when the soul learns of its imminent death it either becomes sad or becomes exalted, but the body if it is sound of wind and limb, develops a wild appetite. Even the body takes cognizance of these things. Yes, it is my body which is protecting itself. I eat voraciously, therefore I am on the verge of death!*

"Liduvina, bring in some cheese and cakes . . . and fruit. . . ."

"You're overdoing it. It's too much. You're going to do yourself some harm."

"Well, wasn't it you who said that he who eats lives?"

"Yes, but not like this, the way you're eating now. And you know the saying: 'Food killed more than Avicena healed.' "

"Food can't kill *me*."

"And why not?"

"Because I am not alive. I do not exist. I've already told you that."

Liduvina went to get her husband. "Domingo, it seems the señorito has gone mad. He's saying the most peculiar things. Things out of books . . . about how he doesn't exist . . . and I don't know what else."

"What's all this, señorito?" Domingo said, as he came into the room. "What's the matter?"

"Ay, Domingo," Augusto answered in an unearthly voice. "I can't help myself, but I am terribly afraid to go to bed!"

"Well, then, don't."

"No, no, I must. But, I can't even get to my feet."

"I think you had better walk off your supper. You've eaten too much."

Augusto tried to stand up.

"You see, Domingo, you see? I can't. . . ."

"Naturally, having stuffed yourself so much."

"Quite the opposite, a bit of ballast helps keep a man on his feet. It's because I don't exist. Look, a while ago during my supper, it was as if everything I ate went tumbling from my mouth into a bottomless barrel. Liduvina is right when she says that the man who eats, lives, but the man who eats the way I've eaten tonight—out of despair—doesn't exist. I do not exist. . . ."

"Come, come, let's not be silly. Have a coffee and liqueur to help settle your supper and then we'll take a walk. I'll go with you."

"But don't you see, I can't get up."

"That's true."

"Come, let me lean on you. I want you to sleep in my room tonight. We'll put a mattress out for you and you can keep watch."

"It will be better if I don't lie down at all. I'll just sit down in an armchair. . . ."

"No, no, I want you to lie down . . . to sleep. I want to know you're sleeping—to hear you snore would be even better."

"Whatever you like . . ."

"And now, bring me a piece of paper. I have to write out a telegram, which you will send as soon as I die. . . ."

"But . . . señorito, good heavens!"

"Do as I say!"

Domingo obeyed and brought the paper and ink-stand. Augusto wrote:

"*Unamuno*

Salamanca

It has all turned out as you said. You have had your way. I am dead.

Augusto Pérez"

"As soon as I'm dead, send this, won't you?"

"Just as you say," the servant answered, to humor his master.

Both of them went to the bedroom. Poor Augusto was trembling so violently that he could not even manage to undress by himself.

"You'll have to undress me!" he told Domingo.

"But, what is the matter with you? It's as if you've seen the devil! You're as white and cold as ice. Should I call the doctor?"

"No, no, it won't help."

"We'll warm the bed. . . ."

"What for? Don't bother! Undress me completely. Take off every last stitch of clothing. I want to be exactly as when my mother brought me into the world. . . . The way I was when I was born. . . . If I ever was born . . ."

"Don't say such things!"

"Now, lay me down. I want you to do it, for I can't move."

Poor Domingo, who was in a state of terror, put his master to bed.

"And now, Domingo, I want you to recite into my ear, slowly, the *Pater Noster*, the *Ave Maria*, and the *Salve*. That's the way . . . slowly . . . very slow-ly . . . ," and then after he had repeated them to himself, he said: "Now, take my right hand, pull at it. It's as if it weren't mine, as if I had lost it . . . now help me to make the sign of the cross . . . like that . . . like . . . This arm must already be dead. . . . Look and see if you can feel my pulse. . . . Now leave me, leave me and I'll try to sleep a while . . . but cover me up, cover me up well."

"Yes, it's best you sleep," Domingo said, as he tucked the blankets around him. "This will all pass, if you get a good sleep. . . ."

"Yes, if I sleep it will all pass. . . . But tell me, have I ever done anything but sleep? Anything but dream? Hasn't all of this been nothing but mist?"

"Everything's all right. Stop worrying about these things. These are all things out of books, as Liduvina says."

"Books . . . things out of books. . . . And what isn't, Domingo? Before there were books, in one form or another, before there were stories, words, thoughts, was there anything else? And when there are no more thoughts, will there be anything left? Things out of books! And who isn't something out of a book? Domingo, do you know Don Miguel de Unamuno?"

"Yes, I've read something about him in the papers. They say he's a bit strange and spends his time acting the truth-teller, telling truths that are all beside the point."

"But do you know him?"

"How could I know him?"

"Because Unamuno is also something out of a book. . . . We all are. . . . And he'll die, yes, he'll die, he'll also die, even if he doesn't want to, he will die. And that will be my vengeance. He doesn't wish to let me live? Well, then, he will also die . . . die, die, die!"

"Very well. Let's forget this Unamuno now and let him die when God wills it. Meanwhile, you should get some sleep!"

"To sleep . . . to sleep . . . to dream . . . To die . . . to sleep . . . to sleep . . . perhaps to dream! I think, therefore, I am: I am, therefore I think. I do not exist! I do not exist. . . . O dear Mother of God . . . Eugenia . . . Rosario . . . Unamuno . . . ," and he fell asleep.

But in a few minutes he sat up in bed. He had turned ashen and was panting for breath. His eyes were shadowy black and aghast, staring as into deepest darkness, and he screamed:

"Eugenia, Eugenia!"

Domingo rushed to his side. Augusto's head fell onto his chest. He was dead.

When the doctor reached the house he first thought Augusto was still alive and talked of bleeding him or applying poultices, but very soon the terrible truth dawned on him.

"It was some sort of heart condition . . . a cardiac failure," the doctor said.

"No, sir," Domingo declared. "It was a case of indigestion. He had just eaten an enormous meal. He ate like a lion, something he didn't ordinarily do, in fact had outgrown, as if he wanted to . . ."

"Yes, as if to make up for what he wouldn't eat in the future. Isn't that it? Perhaps he had some premonition . . . his heart . . ."

"Well, I think," Liduvina interrupted, "I think it was all in his head. It's true he over-ate terribly this evening, as if he didn't know what he was doing and all the time he was saying one insane thing after another. . . ."

"What sort of insane things?" the doctor asked.

"That he did not exist and other things of that nature . . ."

"Insane?" the doctor muttered, as if he were talking to himself. "Who knows if he existed or not? Certainly he himself didn't. Each one of us knows less than anyone else about our own existence. . . . We only exist for others. . . ."

And then in an audible voice, he added:

"The heart, head, and stomach are all one and the same thing."

"Of course, they are all parts of the body," said Domingo.

"And the body is one and the same thing."

"Naturally."

"And even more than you think . . ."

"Do you know, sir, just how much I think . . ."

"Of course, and I can see you're not stupid."

"At least, I don't consider myself so, doctor, and I fail to understand people who take everyone they happen to meet for a fool, unless he doesn't prove the opposite."

"Quite, but as I was saying," the doctor proceeded, "the stomach manufactures the juices which constitute the blood, the heart carries them to the brain and the stomach, so they may function, and the head governs the activity of the stomach and the heart. And so this man Don Augusto has died because all three functions have failed, in other words, the whole body, the synthesis of his vital functions, has failed."

"Well, if you ask me, I think," Liduvina butted in, "that someone suggested to my master the idea that he was going to die, and he simply upped and died. And if a man is bent on dying, he'll die."

"Of course!" the doctor agreed. "If a man didn't think he was going to die he probably wouldn't die, even if he were in his final death throes. But once he feels the slightest suspicion that he has no choice but to die, then he is lost."

"What happened to my master was nothing more nor less than suicide. To sit down and eat the way he ate, especially in the state he was in when he arrived home, is suicide. Suicide, pure and simple. It all turned out as he willed it!"

"Troubles perhaps . . ."

"Yes, and a lot of trouble at that! Women!"

"I see, yes, I see! Well, there is nothing left to do but make the funeral preparations."

Domingo was weeping.

XXXIII

WHEN I RECEIVED the telegram bearing the news of poor Augusto's death, and when I learned of the attendant circumstances, I began to wonder whether I had acted correctly on the afternoon of his visit, when he had come to tell me of his plan to commit suicide. I wondered if I should have said what I did. I even repented of having killed him. I went so far as to think that he was right and that I should have let him have his way, let him commit suicide. The thought of resuscitating him even crossed my mind.

"Yes," I said to myself, "I'm going to resuscitate him and then let him do whatever he takes it in his mind to do, to commit suicide, if that is his particular fancy." And with this thought in mind, I fell asleep.

A short time after I had fallen asleep, Augusto

appeared in my dreams. He was completely white, cloud-white, and he was silhouetted by the rays of a setting sun. He looked at me hard and said:

"I am here again!"

"What have you come for?" I asked him.

"To take leave of you, Don Miguel, to take leave of you until eternity. I've also come to order, rather command . . . not request, mind you—but to command that you write the *nivola* of my life and adventures."

"It is already written!"

"I know it's written. But, I'm also here to inform you that your idea of bringing me back to life, so that I'll later be able to take my own life, is pure nonsense. And even more, it is impossible. . . ."

"Impossible?" I exclaimed. (All this, of course, was my dream.)

"Yes, impossible. The afternoon we spent talking together in your study—remember?—when you were wide awake and not like you are now, sleeping and dreaming, I said that we creatures out of fiction, to use your own terminology, have our own inherent logic and that it is simply not possible for the man who invents us to try and do what he damn well feels like doing with us. Do you remember?"

"Yes, I do."

"And now surely, no matter how Spanish you are, you don't really feel like doing a damn thing. Isn't that so, Don Miguel?"

"No, I don't feel like doing a thing."

"No, a man who sleeps and dreams doesn't really feel like doing a single thing. And you and your fellow countrymen are sleeping and dreaming—dreaming that you'd like to do something, but that's not really the case."

"You may thank God that I'm sleeping," I told him, "for if I weren't . . ."

"It doesn't matter. Concerning that notion of yours to resuscitate me, I must tell you it is not feasible, that you cannot do whatever you like, even if you want to, even if you dream that you want to. . . ."

"But, my dear man!"

"Yes, it is the same for a creature out of fiction as it is for a man of flesh and blood, which you specify is a man of flesh and blood and not fictional flesh and not fictional blood. You can bring him to life and you can kill him, but once you've killed him, you cannot . . . no, no, you cannot resuscitate him. To make a mortal man of flesh and blood, an earthly man, who breathes the air around him is easy, too easy unfortunately. . . . To kill a mortal man, a flesh and blood man, who breathes the air around him, is also easy, too easy unfortunately. . . . But to resuscitate him? That is impossible!"

"True enough, it is impossible!" I agreed.

"Well, the same thing, exactly the same, happens in the case of those you call creatures out of fiction. It is easy to give us life, perhaps too easy, and it is easy, ridiculously easy, to kill us, . . . but to resuscitate us? There is no one who has really resuscitated a creature out of fiction, a creature who has really died. Do you think it's possible to resuscitate Don Quixote?" he asked me.

"No, it is not possible," I answered.

"Well, all the rest of us creatures out of fiction are in the same position."

"And if I should happen to dream you again?"

"You don't dream the same dream twice. When you dream some person that you think is Augusto Pérez, it will be someone else. And now that you are asleep

239

and dreaming and perfectly aware of it, and I am also aware that I am a dream, now I would like to tell you something again, something that made you so nervous when I said it to you the last time we were together. Look here, Don Miguel, it is quite possible that you may be a creature out of fiction, someone who does not really exist, who is neither living nor dead. . . . It may very well be that you are the mere vehicle or pretext for my story, and other stories like mine, to be used to disseminate those stories throughout the world. And then when you are dead, it will be we, your creatures, who keep your soul alive. No, no, don't be upset! Even though you sleep and dream, you are still alive. And now, farewell!"

And he evaporated into a black mist.

Later I dreamt that I was dying, and at the moment I was breathing my last breath, I awoke with a vague pressure on my chest.

And that is the story of Augusto Pérez.

Funeral Oration
by Way of Epilogue

When the hero or protagonist dies or gets married, it is customary, at the end of certain novels, to give an account of the fate of the remaining characters. We will not follow that custom, and therefore offer no account of whatever happened to Eugenia and Mauricio, to Rosarito, to Liduvina and Domingo, to Don Fermín and Doña Ermelinda, to Víctor and his wife, and to all the others whom we saw around Augusto. We are not even going to describe their feelings or what they thought about the strange and singular manner of his death. We will make only one exception, in favor of the one who felt Augusto's death most deeply and sincerely: his dog Orfeo.

In the true sense, Orfeo found himself to be an orphan. He had no sooner scented his master's new state, his death, than a dark mist invaded his canine soul and spirit. He had already chanced on other deaths, had gotten the scent of dead dogs and cats; he himself had harried an occasional rat to death. He had even scented the odor of dead human beings before. But he had assumed his master was outside mortality. Augusto was a god. Now, his fundamental beliefs were undone, his faith in life and in the world was shaken, and an immense desolation took over.

Crouched at the feet of his dead master, the dog mused, and the following impressions, more or less, passed through his head:

My poor Master! Poor Master!—He's gone! He's dead! He's gone and died on me! Everything dies! Everything, everything! Everything goes and dies on me! And it's worse for everything to die on me than for me to die on everything. My poor master! This cold white bulk lying there with the scent of rot already on it is not my master. No, no more. Where has my master gone? Where is the man who used to caress me, who used to talk to me?

Man is a strange beast! He is never aware of what is in front of him. He pats and caresses us without our knowing the reason why and not because we nuzzle him, and the more we give in to him, the more he demands, the more he punishes us. There is no way of knowing what he wants, even if he knows himself. He never seems interested in what he's got in hand. He doesn't even see what he's looking at. It's as if he was thinking of another world. Of course, if there's another world for him, then this one doesn't exist.

And then he barks, or talks, in a pretty complicated fashion. We used to howl, all dogs howled, until he came along, and then we learned to bark, to please him by our imitation. But even then we couldn't get to understand each other. We can really understand man only when he howls, too. Whenever a man howls or shouts or yells threats, then we can understand him well enough. That's because then he's not thinking about that other world of his. But he barks in his own special way, in any case, that's his talk, and he's used it to invent things that don't exist, forgetting to pay attention to what does exist. As soon as he can find a name for something, he forgets about it, he can't even see it. He's happy just to hear the name of the thing or to see it written down. His language is good for lying, for inventing whatever isn't, and for getting everything confused. Everything he does is only a way of talking to other men or to himself. He's even infected dogs with his habit of talking.

He's just a sick animal, really. He's always sick! He's well only when he's asleep, and then, not always: sometimes he talks even in his sleep! And that kind of sickness has spread to us, too. He's infected us in so many ways!

And he has the gall to insult us! For instance, he uses the word cynicism, which means curlike, to be like a cur, a dog, after all, in order to describe mean and brazen disbelief. As if he, the most brazen hypocrite of all animals, had the right to do any such thing! It's his language has made him a hypocrite. In fact, hypocrisy should really be called anthropism, humanism, if brazenness is to be called cynicism. And he's tried to make us dogs into hypocrites, that is, actors, performers, fakes! That is what he does to us dogs, who joined him of our own free will, as partners in the hunt, by mutual agreement, and did not need to be forcibly domesticated or broken, like the bull or the horse! We flushed the game from cover for him, flushed prey from its cover, and he hunted it down and gave us our part. Our association was born in a social contract.

And he has paid us back with outrage and abuse. He has tried to make monkeys of us, performing dogs, in truth. Performing dogs are made to resemble man to the point where they can stand and walk around on their two hind legs, and perform farces dressed up in costume. All very indecorous! Those silly dogs are said to be the "smartest," the most "human" of all dogs, the "wisest." Some wisdom! That's what men call wisdom: to play out farces and walk around on one's hind legs!

Besides, the dog that stands on two hind legs exhibits his privates most brazenly, like man, and most cynically, as they *say. The dog does just what man did when he first stood up and became a vertical mammal, and immediately felt shame, because he was soon covering his exposed parts. I've heard that their Bible tells them that the first man, that is, the first of them who began to walk about on two legs, was ashamed to appear naked before his God. So they invented clothing, to cover their sex. But since both male and female began by dressing alike, they couldn't tell each other apart, they couldn't always make out each other's sex, and a thousand atrocities and outrages took place, atrocities of a human kind, although* they *like to use the words like bitchy, and currish, and cynical, suggesting atrocities of a doglike nature. If we are any of those things, it is they who have made us so, and that is our hypocrisy. Cynicism in a dog is pure hypocrisy, just as in man hypocrisy is cynicism. We have infected and contaminated each other.*

Yes, men and women at first dressed alike, and, since they got all mixed up and couldn't tell each other apart, they had to invent different kinds of clothes and carry some sign of sex on their clothing. Those pants of theirs are a simple consequence of standing up on their hind legs.

And what a strange beast he is, man! His mind is never where it should be, that is, it's never on what he's doing. And he talks in order to lie. And he puts on clothes!

Poor Master! Presently they'll bury him in a place they have reserved for such purposes. The way men keep and store their dead, without letting dogs or crows pick at them! In the end all that is left of them anyway is a few bones, just like any other animal in the world! Imagine, storing the dead! An animal that speaks, wears clothes, and stores its dead! Poor man!

Poor Master! He was only a man, yes, he was no more than a man, only a man! But he was my master! And, without realizing it, he depended so much on me: even without realizing it, he owed me so much! He talked and talked and talked to me, and my silence and my nuzzling had much to say to him and to teach him too. "Can you understand me?" he would ask. Yes, I understood him all right. He went on talking in any case. He was really talking to himself. He also talked to the dog in himself. I kept alive his so-called cynicism.

A dog's life he led, and that's the truth! And that was a dirty dog's trick they pulled on him, those two. Or rather, a real piece of humanism. Real manliness on the part of Mauricio, a real bit of womanishness on the part of Eugenia! My poor Master!

And here he lies, cold, white . . . all dressed up, true enough, but unable to speak to himself or to me. You have nothing to say to your Orfeo, and Orfeo has nothing to tell you with his silence.

My poor Master! What will become of him now? Where is it, whatever it was in him that made him talk and dream? Perhaps up there in the pure air, the high plateau of the good earth, the pure world of pure color, Plato's world, which men call divine; on that superior terrestrial plane from which precious stones fall, where the pure and the purified dwell, quaffing air and breathing the aether. There, too, dwell the pure dogs, the one that accompanies Saint Humbert the Hunter, Saint Dominic's dog with the torch in its mouth, and Saint Roch's. Saint Roch is the one the preacher pointed out in a painting and said: "There you have him, Saint Roch, dog and all!" Up there, in *the pure Platonic world, the world of incarnate ideas, of pure dog, dwell the truly cynical dogs. And there my muster must be!*

I feel my soul becoming purified from contact with death, with this purification of my master. My own soul seems to rise toward the mist into which he was at last dissolved, the mist out of which he emerged and into which he disappeared. I can feel the dark mist descending.

Orfeo, a dog, scents the dark mist descending. His tail signals furiously, and he leaps toward the master.

Master! Man, poor man!

Shortly thereafter, Domingo and Liduvina picked up the poor dog, dead at its master's feet, purified at last like him and like him shrouded in the black cloud of death. Domingo was deeply moved and he wept. It would be hard to say whether he wept for the death of Augusto only or for the death of the little dog, too. Most likely he wept, in his simple way, to see that stunning manifestation of faithfulness and loyalty. And he murmured, once again:

"And there are people who say that no one dies of grief!"

FINIS

Abel Sánchez

The Story of an Obsession

On the death of Joaquín Monegro there was found among his papers a memoir of the dark passion which had devoured his life. Fragments taken from this *Confession* (the title he gave his memoir) have been interspersed in the following narrative. These fragments serve as a commentary, by Joaquín Monegro himself, on his affliction: they are put in italics.

The *Confession* was addressed to his daughter.

I

ABEL SÁNCHEZ and Joaquín Monegro could neither of them remember a time when they had not known each other. They had known each other since before childhood—since earliest infancy, in fact; for their nursemaids often met, and so the two infants met even before they could talk. They had each gone on to learn about each other as they learned about themselves. And thus they had grown up, friends from birth, brought up almost as brothers.

On their walks, in their games, in their mutual friendships, it was always Joaquín, the more willful of the two, who seemed to initiate everything and dominate everything. Still, Abel, appearing to yield, really always did as he pleased. The truth was that he found not obeying more important than commanding. The two almost never quarreled. "As far as I'm concerned, it's whatever you want . . . ," Abel would say to Joaquín, who would become exasperated; for by this "whatever you want . . . ," Abel managed to convey a certain disdain for the argument.

"You never say no!" Joaquín would burst out.

"What's the use?"

"Well, now," Joaquín began one day when they were with some schoolmates who were ready to go for a walk, "this fellow"—pointing at Abel—"doesn't want to go to the pine grove."

"Me?" yelled Abel. "Why wouldn't I? Of course I do. Just as you want. Let's go!"

"No! It's not what I want. I've told you that before. It's not what I want. The fact is you don't want to go!"

"I do, I tell you!"

"In that case *I* don't want to."

"Then I don't either."

"That's not fair!" By now Joaquín was screaming. To the other boys he yelled: "Either go with him or come with me!"

And they all went with Abel, leaving Joaquín to himself.

When Joaquín in his *Confession* commented on this event of their childhood he wrote:

Already Abel was, unconsciously, the agreeable one, and I the disagreeable one, without my knowing why this was so any better than he did. I was left alone. Ever since childhood my friends left me to myself.

All during their secondary school studies, which they pursued together, Joaquín was the grind, the hunter hotly in pursuit of prizes. Joaquín was first in the classroom, Abel was first outside it, in the school-yard among the boys, in the street, in the country, and whenever they played truant. It was Abel who made everyone laugh with his jokes and wit; most celebrated were the caricatures he drew of their teachers. "Joaquín is much more diligent, but Abel is quicker . . . if he really made up his mind to study. . . ." And this prevailing judgment on the part of his classmates, of which Joaquín was fully aware, served to poison his heart further. He was even tempted to neglect his studies to try to excel the other in the other's own field. But he managed to tell himself: "Now what do they know about it. . . ." And he remained true to his own nature. Besides, however much he tried to surpass Abel in facility or wit, he was unsuccessful. His jokes were ignored, and he was thought to be rather dry. "You're really macabre," Federico Cuadrado would say to him, "those jokes of yours would go well at a wake."

The two of them finished school. Abel decided to be an artist and went to art school. Joaquín entered medical school. They saw each other frequently and compared their progress in their respective studies. Joaquín was intent on proving to Abel that medicine, too, was an art, even a fine art, one which allowed of poetic inspiration. On the other hand, Joaquín sometimes inveighed against the fine arts, "enervators of the will," and extolled science, which "elevated, fortified, and expanded the spirit with Truth."

"The truth is that medicine is not exactly science either," Abel said once. "It is simply an art, a skill based on the sciences."

"But I don't intend to dedicate myself to the profession of curing the sick."

"A very honorable and useful profession. . . ."

"Yes, but not for me," interrupted Joaquín. "It may be as honorable and useful as you like, but I detest such honorableness and usefulness. Making money by taking a pulse, looking at tongues, and writing some kind of prescription is for others. I aspire to something higher."

"Higher?"

"Yes. I hope to open new pathways. I expect to devote myself to scientific investigation. The glory of medicine belongs to those who discover the secret of some disease, not to those who apply the discovery with greater or lesser luck."

"It's a pleasure to see you in this idealistic frame of mind."

"Well now, do you suppose that only you people, the artists, the painters, dream of glory?"

"Wait now, no one said that I dream of any such thing. . . ."

"No? In that case why have you taken up painting?"

"Because, if one is successful, it's a profession full of promise. . . ."

"What does it promise?"

"Well, now, it promises . . . money."

"Throw that bone to some other dog, Abel. I've known you ever since we were born, almost. You can't tell that to me. I know you."

"And have I ever tried to deceive you?"

"No, but you deceive without trying. Despite your air of not caring about anything, of acting as if life were a game, of not giving a damn, you're really terribly ambitious."

"Ambitious, me?"

"Yes, ambitious for glory, fame, renown. . . . You always were, you have been since birth, even though you conceal it."

"Wait a bit, Joaquín, and tell me something. Did I ever dispute your prizes with you? Weren't you always first in your class, the fellow most likely to succeed . . . ?"

"Yes, but the little cock of the walk, the boy everybody humored, was you. . . ."

"And what could I do about that?"

"Do you want me to believe that you weren't seeking that kind of popularity?"

"Now, if *you* had sought it . . ."

"If *I* had sought it? I despise the masses!"

"All right, all right. Spare me the speech and the

nonsense, and save yourself the bother. It would be better if you talked about your girl friend again."

"My girl friend?"

"Well, your little cousin, then, whom you'd like to make your girl friend."

For Joaquín was, in fact, laying siege to his cousin Helena and was burning with the fire of his intense and jealous nature in these amorous overtures. And he unburdened himself—the inevitable and salubrious unburdening of the embattled lover—to his friend Abel.

How his cousin Helena made him suffer!

"Every time I see her I understand her less," he would complain to Abel. "That girl is like a sphinx to me."

"You know what Oscar Wilde, or whoever, said: every woman is a sphinx without a secret."

"Well, Helena seems to have one. She must be in love with someone else, even though the other person doesn't know it. I'm certain she's in love with someone else."

"Why do you think so?"

"Otherwise I can't explain her attitude toward me."

"You mean that because she doesn't want to love you, want you as a lover . . . for as a cousin she probably loves you. . . ."

"Don't mock me!"

"Well, then, because she doesn't want you for a lover, or more exactly, for a husband, she must be in love with someone else? Nice logic!"

"I know what I'm saying."

"Yes, and I understand you, too."

"You?"

"Don't you claim to be the one who understands *me*

best? Why is it surprising if I claim to understand you? We met at the same time."

"In any case, I'm telling you that this woman is driving me mad. She'll drive me too far. She's playing with me. If she had said no from the beginning, it would have been all right; but to keep me in suspense, telling me that she'll see, that she'll think it over. . . . These things can't be thought over, coquette that she is!"

"She's probably studying you."

"Studying me? Her? What is there about me to study? What *could* she study?"

"Joaquín, Joaquín, you're underestimating yourself and underestimating her. Or do you think that she has only to see you and hear you to know that you love her, in order to surrender herself to you?"

"Oh, I know, I've always repelled people. . . ."

"Come, now, don't get yourself into that state. . . ."

"It's just that this woman is toying with me. And it's not honorable to play this way with a man who is loyal, open, above-board. . . . If you could only see how beautiful she is! And the colder and more disdainful she grows, the more beautiful she becomes! There are times when I don't know if I love her more or hate her more. . . . Would you like me to introduce you to her . . . ?"

"Well, if you . . ."

"Good, I'll introduce you."

"And if she likes, if she wants it . . ."

"What?"

"I'll paint her portrait."

"That's wonderful!"

But that night Joaquín slept badly, envisioning the portrait and haunted by the idea that Abel Sánchez, the guileless natural-born charmer, the one who was humored in everything, was going to paint Helena's portrait.

What would come of it? Would Helena, too, like all their mutual friends, find Abel the more endearing? He thought of calling off the proposed introduction, but, since he had already promised . . .

II

"WHAT DID YOU think of my cousin?" Joaquín asked Abel the day after the two had been introduced. Abel had broached the matter of the portrait to Helena, and she had been extremely flattered.

"Well, now, do you want the truth?"

"The truth at all times, Abel. If we told each other the truth always, this world would be Paradise."

"Yes, and if everyone told himself the truth . . ."

"Well, the truth then!"

"The truth is that your cousin and future fiancée, perhaps wife, Helena, seems to me to be a peacock. . . . I mean a female peacock, a peahen. . . . You understand what I mean . . . ?"

"Yes, I understand you."

"Since I don't know how to express myself well except with a brush . . ."

"And so you'll paint this peahen, this female peacock, strutting about, her little head . . ."

"As a model, she's first-rate! Really excellent, my friend! What eyes! What a mouth! A full-lipped pouting mouth . . . eyes which do not quite look at you . . .

and what a throat! Above all, what a complexion! And I hope you're not offended. . . ."

"Offended?"

"I tell you she is the color of a wild Indian, or, better still, of a wild animal. There is something of the panther about her, in the best sense, and she is so totally indifferent to it all, so cold."

"So cold!"

"Anyway, old man, I expect to paint you a stunning portrait of her."

"Paint me a portrait? You mean paint *her* a portrait."

"No, the portrait shall be for you, even if it is of her."

"No! The portrait will be for her."

"All right then, for the two of you. Who knows . . . Perhaps it will join you together."

"Well, now, of course, since you go from being a painter to being a . . ."

"Whatever you like, Joaquín, a go-between if it will help, as long as you stop suffering. It's painful for me to see you in that state."

The painting sessions began, the three of them meeting together for the occasion. Helena would take her seat, solemn and cold, in an attitude of disdain, like a goddess borne along by destiny. "May I talk?" she asked on the first day, and Abel answered her: "Yes, you can talk and move about; it's better for me, in fact, if you do move about and talk. That way the features take on life. . . . This will not be a photograph, and besides I don't want you like a statue." And so she talked and talked, but without moving very much, careful of the pose. What did she talk about? The two men were not aware. Because both of them devoured her with their eyes; they saw her, but they could not take in what she said. . . .

And she talked and talked, considering it a sign of good manners not to remain silent; and, whenever possible, she taunted Joaquín.

"Are you having any luck getting patients, my dear cousin?" she would ask.

"Do you really care about that?"

"Of course I care about it. You think I don't. . . . Imagine . . ."

"No, I can't imagine."

"Since you take so much interest in me, I can do no less than take interest in your affairs. And besides, who knows . . ."

"Who knows what?"

"All right, let's drop the subject," Abel interrupted. "Neither of you do anything but scold."

"It's natural," Helena said, "Between relatives. . . . And besides, they say that's the way it begins."

"The way what begins?" Joaquín asked.

"That's something you should know, since you started it."

"What I'm going to do now is finish!"

"Well there are various ways of finishing something, cousin dear."

"And various ways of starting."

"Doubtless. Tell me, Abel, do I disturb the pose with this *badinage*?"

"No, no, on the contrary. This *badinage*, as you call it, adds expression to your look and gesture. But . . ."

Within a couple of days Abel and Helena were addressing each other familiarly; on the third day, Joaquín, who had wanted it this way, missed the painting session.

"Let me see how it's going now," Helena said getting up to stand before the portrait.

"What do you think?"

"I'm not an expert and besides I'm not the one to judge whether or not it's like me."

"What? Don't you have a mirror? Haven't you looked at yourself in it?"

"Yes, but . . ."

"But what . . . ?"

"Oh, I don't know. . . ."

"Don't you see that you're quite stunning?"

"Don't try to flatter me."

"Well, then, we'll ask Joaquín."

"Don't mention him to me, please. What a bore he is!"

"Well, I must mention him."

"Then I'm going. . . ."

"No, listen! You're treating that fellow very badly."

"Oh! So now you're going to plead his case for him? Is this business about the portrait just an excuse?"

"Look, Helena, it isn't right for you to act this way, toying with your cousin. He's something after all, he's . . ."

"Insufferable!"

"No, he's engrossed in himself, he's proud, stubborn, full of his own importance, but he's also good, honorable in every respect, intelligent; he has a brilliant future in his profession; he loves you passionately. . . ."

"And suppose I don't love him . . . ?"

"Then in that case you should discourage him."

"And haven't I discouraged him enough? I'm tired of telling him that I think he's a good fellow, but for that very reason, because he does strike me as a good fellow, a good cousin, a good 'coz'—and I'm not using the word nastily—I really don't want him for a suitor and for everything that comes later."

"But he says . . ."

"If he has told you anything else, Abel, he hasn't told you the truth. Can I send him packing or forbid him to speak to me since he is, after all, my cousin? Cousin! What a joke!"

"Don't be so mocking."

"The fact is I can't. . . ."

"Moreover he suspects something else. He insists on making himself believe that since you don't want to love him, you are secretly in love with someone else. . . ."

"Has he told you that?"

"Yes, he has told me just that."

Helena bit her lips, blushed, and was silent for a moment.

"Yes, he told me that," Abel repeated, letting his right hand rest on the maulstick he was holding against the canvas; he was gazing steadily at Helena, as if he wanted to find a meaning in some feature of her face.

"Well, if he insists . . ."

"What . . . ?"

"He'll succeed in having me fall in love with someone else. . . ."

Abel painted no more that afternoon. And the two became lovers.

III

ABEL'S PORTRAIT of Helena was an overwhelming success. There was always someone standing before the gallery window where it was exhibited. "Another great painter among us," people said. And Helena made a point of passing near the place where her portrait was hanging in order to hear the comments, and she strolled through the streets of the city like an immortal portrait imbued with life, like a work of art—or a peacock with tail spread. Had she perhaps been born for just this?

Joaquín scarcely slept.

"She's worse than ever," he told Abel. "She's really playing with me now. She'll be the death of me."

"Naturally. She's become a professional beauty. . . ."

"Yes, you've immortalized her. Another Mona Lisa!"

"And still, you, as a doctor, can do more, you can lengthen her life. . . ."

"Or shorten it."

"Don't act so tragic."

"What am I going to do, Abel, what am I going to do . . . ?"

"Learn to have patience. . . ."

"And then, she has told me certain things from which I gather you told her of my feeling that she is in love with somebody else. . . ."

"It was in order to help your cause. . . ."

"To help my cause. . . Abel, Abel, you're working with her . . . the two of you are deceiving me. . . ."

"Deceiving you? In what way? Has she promised you anything?"

"And you, has she promised *you* anything?"

"Is she your mistress, perhaps?"

"Is she already *yours* then?"

Abel kept quiet, and blushed.

"You see," exclaimed Joaquín, trembling and beginning to stammer, "you see?"

"See what?"

"Will you deny it now? Are you brazen-faced enough to deny it to me?"

"Well, Joaquín, we have been friends since before we knew each other, almost brothers. . . ."

"And a brother is to be treacherously stabbed, is that it?"

"Don't get so furious. Show some patience. . . ."

"Patience? And what has my life been if not a continuous show of patience, continuous suffering? . . . You, the most attractive, the most pampered, the constant victor, the artist . . . And I . . ."

Tears sprang from his eyes and cut short his words.

"And what was I to do, Joaquín, what did you want me to do?"

"Not to have courted her, since it was I who loved her!"

"But it was she, Joaquín, it was she . . ."

"And naturally, it is you, the fortunate one, the artist, the favorite of fortune, it is you the women court. Well, now you have her. . . ."

"She has me, you mean."

"Yes, the female peacock, the professional beauty, the Mona Lisa, now she has you. . . . You will be her painter. . . . You will paint her in every pose and every light, clothed and unclothed. . . ."

"Joaquín!"

"And so you will immortalize her. She will live as long as your paintings live. Or rather not *live*—for Helena doesn't live. She will endure, endure like marble, the marble of which she is made. For she is made of stone, cold and hard like you. A mass of flesh!"

"Don't get into such a rage."

"Oh, I shouldn't get into a rage, you think, I shouldn't be enraged? This is an infamous piece of work you've accomplished, a low, vile trick."

He felt weak and disheartened, however, and grew quiet, as if words with which to match the violence of his passion failed him.

"But stop and consider," Abel said in his most dulcet voice, which was also his most terrible. "Was I going to make her love you if she doesn't want to love you? She doesn't think of you as her . . ."

"No, of course not, I'm not attractive to any woman; I was born already condemned."

"I swear to you, Joaquín. . . ."

"Don't bother with oaths."

"I swear to you that if it were up to me alone, Helena would be your beloved now, and tomorrow she would be your wife. If I were able to give her up to you. . . ."

"You'd trade her to me for a mess of pottage, is that it?"

"Trade her, no! I would give her up freely and would be more than happy in seeing you both happy, but . . ."

"I know, she does not love me, and she does love you, isn't that it?"

"That's true."

"She rejects me, who wanted her, and wants you, who rejected her."

"Exactly. Although you won't believe me, it's I who was seduced."

"Oh, what a way of putting on airs! You nauseate me!"

"Airs?"

"Yes. To play the role of the one seduced is worse than playing the seducer. Poor victim! Women fight over you. . . ."

"Don't exasperate me, Joaquín. . . ."

"You? Exasperate *you*? I tell you this is a vile trick, a piece of infamy, a crime. . . . We are through with each other forever!"

But then later, changing his tone, and with fathomless sorrow in his voice:

"Have pity on me, Abel, have pity. Can't you see that everyone looks at me askance, that everyone is against me. . . ? You are young, fortunate, indulged; there are more than enough women for you . . . Let me have Helena; you can be sure I won't be able to love another. . . . Let me have Helena. . . ."

"But you can have her. . . ."

"Make her listen to me; make her acknowledge me; make her understand that I am dying for her, that without her I can't live. . . ."

"You don't know her. . . ."

"Yes, I know you both! But, for God's sake, swear to me that you will not marry her. . . ."

"Who spoke of marriage?"

"Ah, then all this is only to make me jealous? It's true that she is nothing but a coquette . . . worse than a coquette, a . . ."

"Be quiet!" roared Abel.

His voice had been such that Joaquín remained silent, staring at him.

"It's impossible, Joaquín; one cannot have any dealings with you. You are impossible."

And Abel turned and walked away.

I passed a horrible night—Joaquín wrote in the *Confession* he left behind—*tossing from one side of* the bed to the other, biting the pillow at times, and getting up to drink water from the washstand pitcher. I ran a fever. From time to time I drowsed off into bitter dreams. I thought of killing both of them, and I made mental calculations—as if it were a matter of a drama or novel I was creating—planning the details of my bloody vengeance, and I composed imaginary dialogues with the two of them. It seemed to me that Helena had only wanted to affront me, nothing more; that she had made love to Abel to slight me, but that in reality—pure mass of flesh before a mirror that she was—she could not love anybody. And I desired her more than ever and more furiously than before. During one of the interminable half-waking, half-sleeping spells of that night I dreamt that I possessed her beside the cold and inert body of Abel. That night was a tempest of evil desires, of rage, of vile appetites, of futile wrath. With daylight and the weariness of so much suffering, reason returned to me and I understood that I had no right whatsoever to Helena. But I began to hate Abel with all my soul, and, at the same time, to plan the concealment of this loathing, which I would cultivate and tend deep down in my soul's entrails. Loathing, did I say? I did not yet want to give it a name. Nor did I care to understand that I had been born predestined to bear the weight of hatred upon me and its seed within me. That night I was born into my life's hell.

IV

Abel spoke to Helena, "Joaquín disturbs my sleep. . . ."

"Joaquín? Why should he?"

"I wonder what will happen when I tell him we plan to be married. . . . Still, he seems to have quieted down and more or less resigned himself to our relationship. . . ."

"He's a fine example of resignation!"

"The truth is that what we did wasn't altogether fair."

"What? You, too? Are women supposed to be like animals, to be handed round and loaned out and rented and sold?"

"No, but . . ."

"But, what?"

"Well, it was he who introduced me to you, so I could paint your portrait, and I took advantage. . . ."

"And that was well done! Was I, by any chance, engaged to him? And even if I had been! Everyone must go his own way."

"Yes, but . . ."

"But what? Are you sorry after all? Well, as far as I'm concerned. . . . Even if you were to leave me now, now that I'm promised to you and everyone knows that you will ask permission to marry me one of these days, even then I wouldn't want Joaquín. No! I'd want him less than ever. I would have more than enough suitors, more of them than I've fingers on my hands, like this"—and here she raised her two long hands with their tapering fingers, those hands which Abel had painted with so much love, and she shook her fingers so that they fluttered.

Abel seized her two hands in his own strong ones, raised them to his lips, and kissed them. And then her mouth. . .

"Be quiet, Abel!"

"You're right, Helena, we must not undermine our happiness by thinking of what poor Joaquín feels and suffers on account of it. . . ."

"Poor Joaquín? He's nothing but an envious wretch!"

"Still, Helena, there are states of envy. . . ."

"Let him go to the devil!"

After a pause filled with black silence:

"Well, we'll invite him to the wedding. . . ."

"Helena!"

"What harm would there be in that? He's my cousin, and your best friend; it's even his doing that we know each other. And if you don't invite him, I will. He won't come to the wedding? So much the better! He will come? Better than ever!"

V

WHEN ABEL told Joaquín of his impending marriage, the latter said:

"It had to be. Each to his own."

"Now, you must understand. . . ."

"Yes, I understand; don't think I'm demented or a wild man; I understand; it's all right; I hope you will be happy. . . . I can never be so again. . . ."

"But Joaquín, for God's sake, in the name of everything you love most . . ."

"That's enough. Let's not speak of it any further.

Make Helena happy, and may she make you happy, too. . . . I have already forgiven you. . . ."

"Have you truly?"

"Yes, truly. I want to forgive you. I will try to make my own life."

"Then I will venture to invite you to the wedding, in my name. . . ."

"And in hers too? . . ."

"In hers too."

"I understand. I will go in order to heighten your happiness. I'll go."

As a wedding gift, Joaquín sent Abel a brace of magnificent damascened pistols, worthy of an artist.

"They're for you to shoot yourself in the head with, when you grow weary of me," Helena told her future husband.

"What are you talking about, woman? What an idea!"

"Who can guess his intentions. . . ? He spends his life plotting."

In the days following the day when he told me they were to be married—Joaquín wrote in his *Confession*—*I felt as if my soul had frozen. And the icy cold pressed upon my heart, as if flames of ice were suffocating me. I had trouble breathing. My hatred for Helena, and even more, for Abel*—*and hatred it was, a cold hatred whose roots choked my heart*—*had become like a petrified growth, as hard as stone. Yet, it was not so much a poisonous plant as it was an iceberg which blocked up my soul; or rather, my soul itself was congealed in hatred. The ice of it was so crystalline that I could see into and through it with complete clarity. I was perfectly well aware that they were right, absolutely right, and that I had no right whatever to Helena; that one ought not, cannot, force a woman's love; that since they loved each other, they should be united. And still, confusedly I felt that it had been I who had brought them, not only together, but to the point of love; that they had come together because they both wished to spurn me; that Helena's decision was largely determined by an urge to see me suffer and rage, to set my teeth on edge, to humiliate me before Abel; on his part I sensed a supreme egotism which never allowed him to take notice of the suffering of others. Ingenuously, he simply did not pay any attention to the existence of others. The rest of us were, at most, models for his paintings. He did not even hate, so full of himself was he.*

I attended the wedding, my soul frost-bitten with hatred, my heart coated with bitter ice, and seized with the apprehension, the mortal terror, that when I heard their "I do," the ice would crack, and my heart would break, and I would die then and there, or turn into an idiot. I went to the wedding as one goes to one's death. And what happened was more mortal than death itself; it was worse, much worse than dying. I wish I might have died instead.

She was completely beautiful. When she greeted me I felt as if an icy sword was plunged into the ice which froze my heart; it was her insolent smile of compassion which cut through me. "Thank you," she said; "poor Joaquín." I understood. As for Abel, I do not know whether he even really saw me. "I understand your sacrifice," he said, merely to say something. "No, no," I hastened to say, "there is none involved; I told you I would come and I came; you see how reasonable I am; I could not have failed my eternal friend, my brother." My attitude must have seemed interesting to him, though scarcely very picturesque. I was like the Comendador in Don Juan, *a guest made of stone.*

As the fatal moment drew near I began to count the seconds. "In a very short time," I told myself, "everything is over for me." I believe my heart stopped. Clearly and distinctly I heard each "I do," his and hers. She looked at me as she uttered the words. And I grew colder than ever, not through any sudden clutching at my heart or any palpitation, but rather as if what I had heard did not concern me. This very fact filled me with an infernal terror and fear of myself. I felt myself to be worse than a monster; I felt as if I did not exist, as if I were nothing more than a piece of ice, and as if this would be true forever. I went so far as to touch my skin, to pinch myself, to take my pulse. "Am I really alive? Am I myself?" I asked myself.

I do not wish to recall everything that happened that day. They took leave of me and started out on their honeymoon journey. I sank back into my books, my studies, my practice, for I was beginning to have one. The mental clarity which resulted from this irreparable blow, the discovery within myself that there is no soul, moved me to seek in study, not consolation —consolation I neither needed nor wanted—but instead the basis for an immense ambition. I must crush Abel's budding fame with the fame of my own name from now on. My scientific discoveries, a work of art in their own way, of true poetry, must put his paintings in the shade. Helena must one day come to realize that it was I, the medical man, the antipathetic one, who could surround her with an aureole of glory, and not he, not this painter. I plunged headlong into my studies. I even went so far as to believe I might forget the newly wedded pair! I wished to turn science *into a narcotic, at the same time that I used it as a stimulant.*

VI

Soon after the couple returned from their honeymoon, Abel fell gravely ill, and Joaquín was summoned to examine and attend him.

"I am very worried, Joaquín," Helena told him; "he was delirious all night; in his delirium he called for you constantly."

Joaquín examined his friend with every care and attention, and then, looking straight at his cousin, he told her:

"It's serious, but I think I will be able to save him. I'm the one for whom there's no salvation."

"Yes, save him for me," she exclaimed. "And you know that . . ."

"Yes, I know!" And Joaquín took his leave.

Helena hurried to her husband's bedside, and laid her hand on his forehead. He was burning with fever, and Helena began to tremble. "Joaquín, Joaquín," Abel called out in his delirium, "forgive us, forgive me!"

"Be quiet," Helena said, almost in a whisper, "be quiet; he's been to see you and he says he will cure you, he says he will make you well. . . . He says you should be quiet. . . ."

"He'll cure me? . . ." the sick man repeated mechanically.

When Joaquín reached his house he, too, was feverish, with a kind of icy fever. "And if he should die? . . ." he thought to himself. He threw himself on the bed fully dressed, and began to imagine what would happen if Abel were to die: Helena's mourning, his own meetings and conversation with the widow, her remorse, her discovery of his true character and of his burning desire to avenge the wrong done him, of his violent need of her, of her falling into his arms at last in the realization that her other life, her betrayal, had been only a nightmare, the bad dream of a coquette; she would know that she had always loved him, Joaquín, and no other. "But he will not die," he told himself. "I will not let him die, I must not let him, my honor is at stake, and . . . I need to have him live! He must live!"

And as he said "he must live!" his soul trembled, just as the foliage of an oak tree trembles in the lashing of a storm.

They were atrocious days, those days of Abel's sickness—Joaquín wrote in the *Confession*—*days of incredible torture. It was in my power to let him die without anyone suspecting, without leaving any telltale evidence behind. In the course of my practice I have known strange cases of mysterious death which later I have seen illuminated in the tragic light of subsequent events, as, by the remarriage of the widow, or similar developments. I struggled then, as I had never struggled with myself before, against that foul dragon which had poisoned and darkened my life. My honor as a doctor was at stake, my honor as a man, and my mental well-being, my sanity itself was involved. I understood that I struggled in the clutches of madness; I saw the specter of insanity and felt its shadow across my heart. But in the end, I conquered. I saved*

Abel from death. I never worked more successfully, more accurately. My excess of unhappiness allowed me to be most happy and correct in my diagnosis.

"Your . . . husband is completely out of danger," Joaquín reported to Helena one day.

"Thank you, Joaquín, thank you." She grasped him by the hand; and he permitted his hand to rest in her two hands. "You don't know how much we owe you. . . ."

"And you don't know how much I owe you both. . . ."

"For God's sake, don't act that way. . . . Now that we owe you so much, let's not start that again. . . ."

"No, I am not starting anything again. I owe you a good deal. This illness of Abel's has taught me a lot, really a great deal. . . ."

"Ah, you look on it as one more case?"

"No, no, Helena; it's I who am the case!"

"But I don't understand what you mean."

"Nor do I, completely. And yet, I can tell you that in these days of fighting to save your husband . . ."

"Say 'Abel,' call him by his name!"

"Very well, fighting for his life, then, I studied my own sickness along with his, and decided . . . to marry!"

"Ah! But do you have the girl?"

"No, not yet, but I will find her. I need a home. I will look for a wife. Or, do you think, Helena, that I will not find a woman to love me?"

"Of course you will find her, of course you will!"

"A woman who will love me, I mean."

"Yes, I understand, a woman who will love you, yes!"

"Because as far as a good match is concerned . . ."

"Yes, there is no question but that you are a good

match . . . young, not poor, a good career ahead of you, beginning to make a name, good and kind. . . ."

"Good . . . yes, and unappealing, isn't that so?"

"No, no, not at all; you're not lacking in appeal."

"Oh, Helena, Helena, where shall I find another woman?"

". . . who will love you?"

"No, who will simply not deceive me, who will tell me the truth, who will not mock me, Helena, who will not mock me! . . . Who may marry me in desperation, perhaps, merely because I will support her, but who will tell me . . ."

"You were quite right when you said you were ill, Joaquín. You should marry!"

"And do you think, Helena, that there is anyone, man or woman, who might love me?"

"There is no one who cannot find someone to love him."

"And will I love my wife? Will I be able to love her? Tell me."

"Why, nothing would be more likely. . . ."

"Because, really, Helena, the worst is not to be unloved, or to lack the faculty to be loved; the worst is not to be able to love."

"That's what Don Mateo, the parish priest says about the devil, that he cannot love."

"And the devil is right here on earth, Helena."

"Be quiet; don't say such things."

"It's worse for me to say them to myself."

"Then don't say anything!"

VII

FOR HIS OWN salvation, and in the need to assuage his passion, Joaquín devoted himself to searching for a woman, a wife in whose motherly arms he might take refuge from the hatred he felt, a lap where he might hide his head, like a child afraid of the dark, afraid to look at the hellish eyes of the ice-dragon.

Poor, unfortunate Antonia!

Antonia had been born to be a mother; she was all tenderness and compassion. With superb instinct, she divined the invalid in Joaquín, a man sick of soul, possessed; and, without knowing why, she fell in love with his misfortune. The cold, curt words of the doctor who had no faith in the goodness of others held a mysterious attraction for her.

Antonia was the only daughter of a widow who was being treated by Joaquín. "Will my mother come through this crisis?" she asked Joaquín.

"It's a very difficult case, very difficult. She is very tired, poor thing, very run down; she must have suffered a good deal. . . . Her heart is very weak. . . ."

"Save her, Don Joaquín, save her! If I could I would give my life for hers."

"That cannot be done. Besides, who knows? Your own life, Antonia, may be more needed than hers. . . ."

"My life? What for? Who for?"

"Who knows! . . ."

The death of the poor widow occurred inevitably.

"It could not have been otherwise, Antonia," Joaquín told her. "Science is powerless."

"Yes, God wished it so."

"God?"

"Ah!" Antonia gazed through her tears at the dry, steely eyes of Joaquín: "You don't believe in God?"

"I? . . . I don't know! . . ."

The sharp twinge of pity which the unfortunate orphan felt for the doctor momentarily made her forget the death of her mother.

"If I did not believe in Him, what would I do now?"

"Life finds answers for everything, Antonia."

"Death finds more! And now . . . so much alone . . . without anyone . . ."

"That's so, loneliness can be terrible. But you have the memory of your saintly mother, and a life to devote to commending her to God. . . . There is a much more terrible loneliness!"

"What is it?"

"The loneliness of a person who is despised and mocked by everyone . . . The loneliness of a person to whom no one will tell the truth."

"And what truth is it that you want to be told?"

"Would you tell me the truth, now, at this moment, over the still-warm body of your mother? Would you swear to tell me the truth?"

"Yes, I would tell you the truth."

"Good . . . I am a disagreeable person, isn't that so?"

"No; that is not so!"

"The truth, Antonia . . ."

"No, it isn't so."

"Well, then, what am I? . . ."

"You? You are an unfortunate man, a man who suffers. . . ."

The ice in Joaquín began to melt and tears came to his eyes. Once again he trembled to the roots of his soul.

It was not very long afterwards that Joaquín and the recently orphaned girl became engaged, planning to marry as soon as her year of mourning was over.

My poor little wife—Joaquín was to write years later in his *Confession*—*she struggled to love me and cure me, to overcome the repugnance that I must have aroused in her. She never told me this, she never even let it be understood. But, could I have failed to arouse repugnance in her especially when I revealed to her the leprosy of my soul, the gangrene of my hatred? She married me as she would have married a leper—I have no doubt of this at all—from motives of pity, a divine pity, and from a Christian spirit of abnegation and self-sacrifice, in order to save my soul, and thereby save her own. She married me out of the heroism of saintliness. And she was a saint! . . . But she did not cure me of Helena, and she did not cure me of Abel. Her saintliness was for me just one more source of remorse.*

Her gentleness irritated me. There were times when—*God forgive me!*—*I would have wished her wicked, hot-tempered, disdainful.*

VIII

MEANWHILE ABEL'S fame as an artist continued to spread. He had become one of the best-known painters in the entire nation, and his name was making itself known across the border. And the growing fame of Abel brought Joaquín the chill sense of icy desolation left behind by a hailstorm. "Yes, he is a very *scientific* painter; he is a master of technique; he knows a good deal, a good deal; he is exceedingly clever"; thus spoke Joaquín of his friend, in words that somehow hissed. It was a way of seeming to praise him, by denigrating him.

Because, in truth, it was Joaquín who presumed to be the artist; a true poet in his profession, a diagnostician of genius, creative, intuitive; he even dreamed of abandoning his practice in order to dedicate himself to pure science, to theoretical pathology, to research. But, then, he was earning so much! . . .

And yet, it was not profit—he wrote in his posthumous *Confessions*—*which most prevented me from devoting myself to scientific investigation. On the one hand, I was drawn to it by a desire to become renowned, to build a great scientific reputation which would overshadow Abel's artistic fame and thereby humiliate Helena, avenging myself on them both, and on everybody else as well—it was my wildest hope. On the other hand, this same murky passion, this extravagant grudge and hatred, deprived me of all serenity of soul. No, I did not have the will to study, the pure and tranquil spirit which was necessary. My practice distracted me, moreover.*

My practice distracted me, and yet there were times when I trembled, thinking that my state of inner distraction prevented me from paying the strict attention required by the ills of my poor patients.

Then a case occurred which shook me to my foundations. I was attending a poor woman who was rather dangerously, but still not desperately, ill. Abel had painted a portrait of her; a magnificent portrait, one of his best, one of those which have remained as definitive among his works. And it was this painting which was the first thing that came into my sight—and into my hate—as soon as I entered the sick woman's home.

In the portrait she was alive, more alive than in her bed of suffering flesh and bone. And the portrait seemed to say to me: Look, he has given me life forever! Let's see if you can prolong this other, earthly life of mine! At the bedside of the poor invalid, as I listened to her heart and took her pulse, I was obsessed by the other woman, the painted one. I was stupefied, completely stupefied, and as a result the poor woman died on me; or rather, I let her die, in my stupefaction, in my criminal distraction. I was convulsed with horror at myself, my miserable self.

A few days after the woman's death, I found it necessary to go to her house to visit still another sick member of the family, and I entered firmly resolved not to look at the portrait. But it was useless, for the portrait looked at me, regardless of whether or not I looked at it, and it drew my gaze perforce. As I took my leave, the recently bereaved husband accompanied me to the door. We paused at the foot of the portrait, and I, as if I had been impelled by some irresistible and fatal force, exclaimed:

"A magnificent portrait! It is one of the greatest things Abel has done."

"Yes," answered the widower, "it is the greatest consolation left me now. I gaze at it for hours. It seems to speak to me."

"Oh yes, yes," I added, "Abel is a wonderful artist!"

As I went out, I said to myself: "I let her die, and he resurrected her!"

Joaquín suffered a great deal whenever any of his patients died, especially if they were children; the deaths of certain others, however, left him almost indifferent. "Why should such a person want to live . . . ?" he would ask himself about someone. "I would actually be doing him a favor to let him die. . . ."

His powers of observation as a psychologist had grown sharper as his spirit languished, and he was quick to intuit the most hidden moral lacerations. He perceived, behind all the falsity of convention, how husbands foresaw the death of their wives without any sorrow whatsoever—when they did not consciously desire it—and how wives longed to be free of their husbands, longed even to take other husbands already chosen beforehand. In the same year in which a patient named Alvarez died, his widow married Menéndez, the dead man's dear friend, and Joaquín said to himself: "That death was really quite strange. . . . Only now do I see it all clearly. . . . Humanity is absolutely vile! And that lady is a 'charitable' lady, one of the most 'honorable' ladies. . . ."

"Doctor," one of his patients said to him once, "for God's sake, will you kill me? Kill me without telling me anything, for I cannot go on. . . . Give me something which will make me sleep forever. . . ."

"And why should I not do what this man wants me to do," Joaquín asked himself, "if he lives only to suffer? It makes me grieve! What a filthy world!"

His patients were not infrequently mirrors for him.

One day a poor woman in his neighborhood came to him; she was wasted by her years and work; and her husband, after twenty-five years of marriage, had formed a liaison with a miserable adventuress. The rejected woman had come to tell the doctor her troubles.

"Ay, Don Joaquín! Let us see if you, who are said to know so much, can give me a remedy to cure my poor husband of the philter which this loose woman has given him."

"But what philter, my good woman?"

"He is going to live with her; he is leaving me, after twenty-five years. . . ."

"It would have been even stranger if he had left you when you were newly married, while you were still young and even . . ."

"Oh, no sir, no! The fact is that she has given him some kind of love potion which has turned his head. Otherwise, it just could not be. . . ."

"A love potion," murmured Joaquín, "a love potion? . . ."

"Yes, Don Joaquín; yes, a love potion. . . . And you, who have so much knowledge, let me have some sort of remedy against it."

"Ah, my good woman, the ancients searched in vain to find a liquor which would rejuvenate. . . ."

And when the poor woman went away in desolation, Joaquín said to himself: "But doesn't this unfortunate woman look at herself in the mirror? Doesn't she see the ravages of years of hard work? These country-born people attribute everything to potions or jealousies. . . . For instance, they don't find work. . . . Jealousy is to blame. . . . Some scheme doesn't come out right. . . . Jealousy. The person who attributes all his disasters to the envy of others is in reality an envious person. Aren't we all? Haven't I perhaps been given a potion?"

During the next few days he was obsessed with the idea of a philter, a potion. At length he said to himself: "That is the original sin!"

IX

Joaquín married Antonia in his search for shelter; the poor woman guessed at her mission from the first, the role she was to play in her husband's heart, as a shield and a source of consolation. She was taking a sick man for a husband, a man who was perhaps an incurable spiritual invalid; her duty would be that of a nurse. And she accepted her destiny with a heart full of compassion, full of love for the misfortune of the person who was joining his life with hers.

Antonia felt that between her and her Joaquín there was an invisible wall, a crystalline and transparent wall of ice. That man could not belong to his wife, for he did not belong to himself, he was not master of himself, but was, instead, both alienated and possessed. Even in the most intimate transports of conjugal relations, an invisible shadow of prophetic melancholy fell between them. Her husband's kisses seemed to her stolen kisses, when they were not the kisses of madness.

Joaquín avoided speaking of his cousin Helena in front of his wife, and Antonia, who noticed his self-conscious avoidance at once, did not fail to bring her into the conversation at every turn.

This was at the beginning, for a little later she avoided mentioning her any more.

One day Joaquín was called to Abel's house in his capacity of doctor. There he learned that Helena was already bearing the fruit of her marriage to Abel, while Antonia showed no sign of such fruitfulness. The unhappy doctor was assaulted by a shameful suggestion which arose to humiliate him; some devil was taunting him: "Don't you see? He is even more of

a man than you are! He, who through his art resur-
rects and immortalizes those you allow to die because
of your dullness, he is to have a child, he is to bring
into the world a new being, a work of his own, created
in flesh, and blood, and bone, while you . . . You
probably are not even capable of . . . He is more of
a man than you!"

He arrived at the shelter of his own home down-
cast and brooding.

"Have you come from Abel's house?" his wife
asked.

"Yes. How did you happen to know?"

"It's in your face. That house is your torment. You
should not go there. . . ."

"And what should I do?"

"Excuse yourself from going! Your health and
peace of mind come first. . . ."

"These are only apprehensions of yours. . . ."

"No, Joaquín, don't try to conceal it from me . . ."
—and she was unable to continue, the tears drowning
her voice.

The unfortunate Antonia sank to the ground. Her
sobs seemed torn from her body by the roots.

"What is the matter, woman, what is all this? . . ."

"Only tell me, Joaquín, what afflicts you. Confide
in me, confess yourself to me. . . ."

"I have nothing to accuse myself of. . . ."

"Come, will you tell me the truth, Joaquín, the
truth?"

For a moment, he hesitated, seeming to struggle
with an invisible enemy, with his Guardian Devil,
and then, his voice animated with a sudden, desperate
resolution, he almost cried out:

"Yes, I will tell you the truth, the entire truth!"

"You love Helena. You're still in love with Helena."

Chapter IX

"No, I am not! I am not! I was, but I am no longer."

"Well then? . . ."

"Then what?"

"What is this torture in which you live? Why is that house, Helena's house, the source of your misery? That house does not let you live in peace. It's Helena. . . ."

"Helena, no! It's Abel!"

"Are you jealous of Abel?"

"Yes, I am jealous of him! I hate him, I hate him, I hate him"—and Joaquín clenched his fists and gritted his teeth as he spoke.

"If you are jealous of Abel . . . then you must love Helena."

"No, I don't love her. If she belonged to someone else, I should not be jealous of that person. No, I don't love Helena. I despise her, I despise that peacock of a woman, that professional beauty, the fashionable painter's model. Abel's mistress. . . ."

"For God's sake, Joaquín, for God's sake! . . ."

"Yes, his mistress . . . his legitimized mistress. Do you think that the benediction of a priest changes an affair into a marriage?"

"Listen, Joaquín, we're married just as they are. . . ."

"As they are, not at all, Antonia, not at all! They got married only to demean me, to humiliate and denigrate me; they married to mock me; they married to hurt me."

The poor man burst into sobs which choked him, cutting off his breathing. He seemed to die.

"Antonia . . . Antonia . . . ," he whispered in a little smothered voice.

"My poor child!" she said, embracing him.

She held his head in her lap as if he were a sick child, caressing him while she said:

"Calm yourself, my Joaquín, calm yourself. . . . I am here, your wife is here, all yours and only yours. And now that I know all your secrets, I am yours more than before and I love you more than ever. . . . Forget them . . . scorn them. . . . It would have been all the worse if such a woman had loved you."

"Yes, but it's he, Antonia, it's he. . . ."

"Forget him!"

"I can't forget him. . . . He pursues me. . . . His fame, his renown haunt me. . . ."

"If you work, you will have fame and renown, for you are not any less than he. Leave your practice, we don't need it. We can go to Renada, to the house which belonged to my parents, and there you can devote yourself to what you like best, to science, to making discoveries of the sort that will earn you notice. . . . I will help you in every way I can. . . . I will see that you are not distracted . . . and you will be more than he. . . ."

"I can't, Antonia, I can't. His success prevents me from sleeping and would not allow me to work in peace. . . . The vision of his awesome paintings would come between my eye and the microscope and would prevent my seeing anything others have not seen. . . . I can't. . . . I can't. . . ."

Then, lowering his voice like a child, stammering almost, as if stunned by his fall into the abyss of humiliation, he sobbed:

"And they are going to have a child, Antonia. . . ."

"We will have one also," she whispered in his ear, covering it with a kiss; "the Holy Virgin will not deny me, for I ask her every day. . . . Or the holy water of Lourdes . . ."

Chapter X

"Do you, too, believe in potions, Antonia?"

"I believe in God!"

" 'I believe in God,' " Joaquín repeated when he was alone—alone with the other presence, with his obsession. "What does it mean, to believe in God? Where is God? I shall have to find Him!"

X

When Abel had his child—Joaquín wrote in his *Confession*—*I felt hatred welling in me. He had invited me to attend Helena in her labor, but I had excused myself by saying that I did not attend deliveries, which was true, and that I would not be able to maintain my sangfroid, the necessary cold-bloodedness— benumbed-bloodedness, I should have said—where my cousin was concerned, should she run any risk. And yet, my own evil spirit suggested a ferocious temptation: attend her and smother the child surreptitiously. I was able to overcome myself and suppress this revolting thought.*

This new triumph of Abel's, of Abel the man and not the artist only—for the child was a beauty, a masterpiece of health and vigor, a little angel, as everyone said—bound me all the more to Antonia, from whom I was expecting a child of my own. I longed to make of my wife, I needed to make of this poor victim of my blind rage—the real victim even more than I was myself—I needed to make of her, to make her be, the mother of my children, flesh of my flesh, heart of my heart, entrails of my devil-tormented entrails. She would be the mother of my children and for that reason superior to the mothers of the children of others. She, unhappy woman, had chosen me, the disagreeable, the despised, the affronted one; she had taken up what another woman had refused with disdain and scorn. And she even spoke well of them to me!

Abel's child, little Abelín—for they gave it the same name as the father, as if to continue his lineage and fame—the young Abel, who would with the passage of time be the instrument of my revenge, was a marvel of a child. I needed to have one like him— but one even more beautiful.

XI

"WHAT ARE YOU working on these days?" Joaquín asked Abel one day. The doctor had come to Abel's house to see the child, and had then gone to visit the painter in his studio.

"Well, next I shall paint a historical piece, specifically a scene from the Old Testament; at the moment, I am doing research for it. . . ."

"How is that? Looking for models from the period?"

"No; reading the Bible and commentaries on it."

"I am well advised to call you a scientific painter. . . .

"And you are an artistic doctor, isn't that so?"

"But worse than a scientific painter, you're a literary one! Beware of making literature with your brush!"

"Thanks for the advice."

"And what will the subject of your painting be?"

"The death of Abel at the hands of Cain, the first fratricide."

Joaquín turned paler than ever; gazing fixedly at his first friend, he asked in a half-suffocated voice:

"How did you happen to think of that?"

"Very simply," Abel answered without perceiving his friend's meaning; "it was the suggestiveness of the name. Since my name is Abel. . . . I had made two nude studies. . . ."

"Nude of body . . ."

"Even of soul . . ."

"You mean to paint their souls?"

"Of course! The soul of Cain, the soul of envy. And the soul of Abel . . ."

"What is he the soul of?"

"I wish I knew. I'm trying to find out, but I can't put my finger on the right expression. I want to paint him before his death, thrown to the ground and fatally wounded by his brother. I've got Genesis here, and I'm reading Lord Byron's *Cain*; do you know the book?"

"Byron's *Cain* I don't know. What have you gotten from the Bible?"

"Very little . . . you'll see," and, taking up the book, he read: " 'And Adam knew Eve his wife: who conceived and brought forth Cain, saying: I have gotten a man through God. And again she brought forth his brother Abel. And Abel was a shepherd, and Cain a husbandman. And it came to pass after many days, that Cain offered, of the fruits of the earth, gifts to the Lord. Abel also offered of the firstlings of his flock, and of their fat: and the Lord had respect to Abel, and to his offerings. But to Cain and his offerings he had no respect. . . .' "

"And why was that?" interrupted Joaquín. "Why did God look with respect on the offering of Abel and look with disfavor on Cain and his offering? . . ."

"It isn't explained here. . . ."

"And haven't you asked yourself the question before setting out to paint your picture?"

"Not yet. . . . Perhaps because God already saw in Cain the future killer of his brother, the envious. . . ."

"If he was envious it was because God had made him so, and had given him a philter. Go on with the reading."

" 'And Cain was exceedingly angry, and his countenance fell. And the Lord said to him: Why art thou angry? And why is thy countenance fallen? If thou do well, shall thou not receive? But if ill, shall not sin forthwith be present at the door? But the lust thereof shall be under thee, and thou shalt have dominion over it. . . .' "

"Instead, sin dominated him," interrupted Joaquín again, "because God had abandoned him. Go on."

" 'And Cain said to Abel his brother: Let us go forth abroad. And when they were in the field, Cain rose up against his brother Abel, and slew him. And the Lord said to Cain . . .' "

"That's enough! Don't read any more. I'm not interested in what Jehovah told Cain after there was no help for the matter."

Joaquín rested his elbows on the table, his face between the palms of his hands. He fixed a sharp, frozen stare on Abel, who became alarmed at he knew not what. And then Joaquín said:

"Have you ever heard of the joke they play on children who learn Sacred History?"

"No."

"Well, they ask them, 'Who killed Cain?'; and the children, all confused, answer: 'His brother Abel.'"

"I didn't know that."

"You do now. And tell me, since you are going to paint this biblical scene—and how like the Bible it is!—hasn't it occurred to you that if Cain had not killed Abel, it would have been Abel who would have ended up killing Cain?"

"How can you think of such a thing?"

"Abel's sheep were acceptable to God, and Abel the shepherd found grace in the eyes of the Lord, but neither the fruits of the earth offered up by Cain, the husbandman, nor Cain himself found favor with God. His favorite was Abel. The God-forsaken was Cain. . . ."

"And what fault was that of Abel's?"

"Ah, you think, do you, that the fortunate, the favored, are not to blame? The truth is that they are to blame for not concealing—and not concealing it as a shameful thing, which it is—every gratuitous favor, every privilege not earned on proper merit; for not concealing this grace instead of making an ostentatious show of it. For I have no doubt but that Abel flaunted his favor under the snouts of Cain's beasts, or that he taunted him with the smoke of the sheep he offered to God. Those who believe themselves to be of the company of the just tend to be supremely arrogant people bent on crushing others under the ostentation of their 'justice.' As someone once said, there is no worse canaille than 'honorable' people. . . ."

"And are you sure," asked the painter, who had become apprehensive over the serious aspect the conversation had assumed, "are you sure that Abel boasted of his good fortune?"

"I have no doubt of it, or of the fact that he showed

no respect for his elder brother; I do not suppose, either, that he asked the Lord to show his elder brother some favor too. And I know something else: and that is that Abel's successors, the Abelites, have invented Hell as a place for the Cainites, because, if there were no such place, the Abelites would find all their glory insipid. Their pleasure is to see others suffer while they themselves do not suffer at all."

"Joaquín, Joaquín, how very sick you are!"

"You're right. And no one can doctor himself. . . . Let me have this *Cain* of Lord Byron's, I want to read it."

"Take it."

"And tell me, doesn't your wife supply you with any inspiration for this painting? Doesn't she provide you with any ideas?"

"My wife? . . . There was no woman in this tragedy."

"There is in every tragedy, Abel."

"Perhaps Eve. . . ."

"Perhaps. . . . Perhaps the woman who gave them both the same milk; or potion. . . ."

XII

J O A Q U Í N R E A D Lord Byron's *Cain*. And later he wrote in his *Confession*:

The effect made upon me by reading that book was dreadful. I felt the need to give vent to my feelings, and so I took some notes, which I still have and which are now here before me. And I wonder now if I took them down merely to unburden myself? No, I undoubt-

*edly thought to make use of them some day in writing
a great book. Vanity consumes us. We make a spectacle of our most intimate and vile disabilities. I can
imagine the existence of a man who would want to
have a pestiferous tumor such as no one has ever
had before, solely in order to vaunt it about, and to
call attention to the struggle he was waging against
it. This very* Confession, *for instance, isn't it something more than a mere unburdening of the soul?*

*I have sometimes thought of tearing it up, so as to
free myself from it. But would that free me? No! It
is better to make a spectacle than to consume oneself.
After all is said and done, life itself is no more than
a spectacle.*

The reading of Byron's Cain *struck me to the core.
How right Cain was to blame his parents for having
taken the fruits of the tree of knowledge instead of
those of the tree of life! For me, at any rate, knowledge has not done more than exacerbate the wound.*

Would that I had never lived! *I say with Cain.
Why was I created? Why must I live? What I do
not understand is why Cain did not choose suicide.
That would have been the most noble beginning for
the human race. But then, why didn't Adam and Eve
kill themselves after the fall and before they gave
birth to children? Ah, perhaps because Jehovah would
have created other such beings as they, another Cain
and another Abel? Isn't this same tragedy perhaps repeated in other worlds, up there among the stars?*

*Perhaps the tragedy has been performed elsewhere,
the first-night performance on earth not having quite
sufficed. Was it opening night, after all?*

*When I read how Lucifer declared to Cain that he,
Cain, was immortal, at that moment I began to wonder fearfully if I, too, and my hatred with me, were*

immortal. Do I have a soul? *I asked myself.* Is my hatred a soul? *And I came to think finally that it could not be otherwise, that such a hatred could not be the property of the body. That which I could not find in others with a scalpel I now found in myself. A corruptible organism could not hate as I did. Lucifer had aspired to be God, and I, ever since I was very young, had I not aspired to reduce everyone else to nothing? But how could I have been so unfortunate, unless I was made that way by the creator of all misfortune?*

It required no effort for Abel to take care of his sheep, just as it required no effort for the other Abel to paint his pictures; for me, on the contrary, a very great effort was needed to diagnose the ills of my patients.

Cain complained that Adah, his own beloved Adah, his wife and his sister, did not understand the mind which overwhelmed him. But my Adah, my poor Adah understood my mind well enough. In all truth, she was a Christian. But then, I did not, in the end, find any sympathy either.

Until I read and reread the Byronic Cain, *I, who had seen so many men die, had not thought of death, had not* discovered *it. I began to wonder if I would die with my hate, if my hate would die with me, or outlast me; I wondered if hate outlived the haters, if it were something material, transmissible; I speculated as to whether hatred were not the soul, the quintessence of the soul. And I began to believe in Hell, and in Death as a being, as the Devil, as hatred made flesh, as the God of the soul. Everything that science did not explain, the terrible poem of that great hater, Lord Byron, made clear to me.*

My Adah, too, would taunt me gently when I did

not work, when I could not work. And Lucifer stood between my Adah and myself. "Walk not with this spirit!" my Adah cried. Poor Antonia! And she begged me to save her too from the spirit. My poor Adah did not go so far as to hate these influences as much as I did. But then, did I go so far as truly to love my Antonia? Ah, if only I had been capable of loving her I would have been saved. She was for me another instrument of my revenge. I wanted her as the mother of a son or a daughter who would avenge me. Although I did think, quite naïvely, that once I became a father, I would be cured of all this. Still, hadn't I gotten married simply to produce hateful beings like myself, to transmit my hatred, to immortalize it?

The scene between Cain and Lucifer in the Abyss of Space remained engraved in my soul as if it had been burned into it. I saw my science in the light of my sin and the wretchedness of giving life in order to propagate death. And I saw clearly that this immortal hatred constituted my soul. This hatred, I thought, must have preceded my birth and would survive after my death. I was shaken with horror to think of living always so as to abhor always. This was Hell. And I had so scoffed at belief in it! It was a literal Hell!

When I read how Adah spoke to Cain of his son, of Enoch, I thought of the son, or the daughter I would surely have; I thought of you, my daughter, my redemption and my consolation; I thought of how you would come one day to save me. And as I read of what Cain said to his own sleeping, innocent son, who knew not that he was naked, I wondered if it had not been a crime in me to have engendered you, my poor daughter! Do you forgive me for having created you? As I read what Adah said to her Cain, I remembered my own years in paradise, when I was not yet on the hunt for rewards, when I did not dream of surpassing all the others. No, my daughter, no; I did not offer up my studies to God with a pure heart; I did not seek truth and knowledge, but instead sought prizes, and fame, and the chance to be more than he was.

He, Abel, loved his art and cultivated it with a purity of purpose, and never strove to impose himself on me. No, it was not he who took away my peace. And yet I had gone so far, demented as I was, as to think of overturning Abel's altar. The truth was I had thought only of myself.

The narrative of Abel's death as it is given us by that terrible poet of the Devil blinded me. As I read I felt everything grow dark, and I think I suffered a fainting spell, and a kind of nausea. And from that day on, thanks to the impious Byron, I began to believe.

XIII

ANTONIA PRESENTED Joaquín with a daughter. "A daughter," he told himself; "and *he* has a son!" But he soon recovered from this new trick of his demon. And he began to love his daughter with all the force of his passion, and through her, her mother as well. "She shall be my avenger," he said to himself at first, without knowing what it was she was to avenge him for; but later: "She shall be my salvation, my purification."

I began to keep this record—he wrote in the *Confession*—*a little later, for my daughter's sake, so that once I was dead, she might know her poor father, and feel for him, and love him. As I watched her sleeping in her cradle, innocently dreaming, I thought how in order to bring her up and educate her in purity I should have to purify myself of my passion, cleanse myself of the leprosy of my soul. And I decided to make certain she should love, love everyone, and love them in particular. There, upon the innocence of her dreams, I swore to free myself from my infernal chains. I vowed to be the chief herald of Abel's greatness.*

Abel Sánchez completed his historical canvas and entered it in a large exhibition. There it received widespread acclaim and was hailed as a true masterpiece; inevitably, he was awarded the medal of honor.

Joaquín went often to the exhibition hall to view the painting and to look into it, as into a looking glass, at the painted Cain, and to watch the eyes of the people, to see if they looked at him after looking at the other figure.

I was tortured by the suspicion—he wrote in the *Confession*—*that Abel had thought of me when he was painting his Cain, that he had sounded all the depths in the conversation we had held at his house at the time he first told me of his intention to paint his subject and when he had read the passages from Genesis—when I had so completely forgotten him and so completely bared my sickened soul as I thought only of myself. But no, there was not in Abel's Cain the least resemblance to me; he had not thought of me in the painting; he had not attempted to attack me, to denigrate me, nor had Helena apparently influenced him against me. It sufficed them to savor the future triumph, the triumph they were anticipating. They did not even think of me now!*

And this idea that they did not even think of me,

did not even hate me, tortured me more than the other idea had. To be hated by him, with a hatred such as mine for him, would have been something after all, and could have been my salvation.

And so Joaquín surpassed himself, or simply delved deeper into himself, and conceived the idea of giving a banquet to celebrate Abel's triumph. He, Joaquín, Abel's everlasting friend, his "friend from before they knew each other," would arrange a banquet for the painter.

Joaquín had a certain fame as an orator. At the Academy of Medicine and Sciences it was he who overawed the others with his cold and cutting words, usually over-precise and sarcastic. Most often, his speeches had the same effect as a stream of cold water poured over the enthusiasm of the newcomers; they were dour lessons in pessimistic skepticism. His usual thesis was that nothing was known for certain in medicine, that everything was hypothetical and a matter of constant raveling and unraveling, that distrust was the most justified emotion. For these reasons, when it became known that it was Joaquín who was giving the banquet, most people joyously made ready for an inevitably double-edged address, a pitiless dissection—in the guise of a panegyric—on the subject of scientific, documentary painting; at best, it would be a sarcastic encomium.

A malevolent anticipation titillated the hearts of all those who had ever heard Joaquín speak of Abel's painting. And they warned the latter of his peril.

"You are mistaken," Abel told them. "I know Joaquín and do not believe him capable of such a thing. I know something of what is going on within him, but he has a profound artistic sense, and whatever he says will probably be well worth hearing. I should like next to paint a portrait of him."

"A portrait?"

"Yes, you don't know him as I do. He is a fiery, turbulent soul."

"Such a cold man . . ."

"On the outside. In any case, fire burns, as they say. For my purposes, he couldn't be better, a face made on purpose. . . ."

This opinion of Abel's reached the ears of his subject, who once more sank into the sea of speculation. "What must he really think of me?" he asked himself. "Does he really think me to be a 'fiery, turbulent soul'? Or does he in reality see that I am a victim of a whim of fate?"

At this time he went so far as to do something for which he was later deeply ashamed. It happened that a maid entered his service who had formerly served in Abel's house, and he made overtures to her, confidentially importuning her—without compromising himself—for the sole purpose of ascertaining what she might have heard about him in the other house.

"Come now, is it possible that you never heard them speak of me?"

"They said nothing, sir, absolutely nothing."

"Didn't they ever speak of me?"

"Well, they did talk, just talk; but they said nothing."

"Nothing, nothing ever?"

"I didn't hear them speak very much. They spoke very little while I served them at table, just about those things usually spoken of at the table. About his paintings . . ."

"I understand. But nothing, never anything about me?"

"I don't remember anything."

As he left the maid he was seized with a profound self-aversion. "I'm making an idiot of myself," he said to himself. "What must this girl think of me!" He was so humiliated by his action that he contrived the girl's dismissal on some small pretext. "But suppose she goes back now into Abel's service," he asked himself then, "and tells him all this?" So that he was on the point of asking his wife to summon her back. But he dared not. And thereafter he shuddered at the thought of meeting her in the street.

XIV

THE DAY OF the banquet arrived. Joaquín had not slept the night before.

"I am going to the battle, Antonia," he told his wife as he left the house.

"May God light your way and guide you, Joaquín."

"I should like to see our little girl, our poor little Joaquinita. . . ."

"Yes, come and see her. . . . She's sleeping. . . ."

"Poor little thing! She doesn't yet know the Devil exists! But I swear to you, Antonia, I shall learn to tear him from me. I will tear him out, I will strangle him, and I will throw him at the feet of Abel. . . . I would give her a kiss if I weren't afraid of waking her. . . ."

"No, no! Kiss her!"

The father bent over and kissed the sleeping child, who smiled in her dreams as she felt herself kissed.

"You see, Joaquín, she blesses you too."

"Goodbye, my wife!" And he kissed her, with a very long kiss.

Antonia was left behind to pray before the statue of the Virgin Mary.

A malicious undercurrent of expectation ran through the conversation at the banquet table. Joaquín, seated on Abel's right, was very pale; he scarcely ate or spoke. Abel himself began to feel some trepidation.

As the dessert was served, some of the diners began to hiss as a call for silence, and a hush fell, in which someone said: "Let him speak." Joaquín stood up. He began to talk in a muffled, trembling voice; but soon it cleared and began to vibrate with a new accent. His voice filled the silence, and nothing else was to be heard. The surprise was general. A more ardent, more impassioned eulogy had scarcely ever been heard, or one more filled with admiration and affection for both the artist and his work. Many felt tears welling up in their eyes as Joaquín evoked the days of his childhood shared with Abel, when neither of them yet dreamed of what they would one day become.

"No one has known him more intimately than I," he said; "I believe I know you," addressing Abel, "better than I know myself, with more purity, because looking into one's own heart one tends to see only the dust from which one has been created. It is in others that we see the best part of ourselves, a part which we can love; and thus we give our admiration. He has accomplished in his art what I should like to have accomplished in mine; for this reason, he is one of my models; his glory is a spur to my work and is a consolation for the glory which I have not been able to gain. He belongs to us all; above all he is mine, and I, enriched by his work, try to make this work as much mine as he made it his by the act of creation. Thus am I able to be a satisfied subject of my mediocrity. . . ."

From time to time his voice cried out. His audience was under his spell, obscurely aware of the titanic battle between this soul and its demon.

"And behold the face of Cain"—Joaquín let the fiery words form like single drops—"the tragic Cain, the roving husbandman, the first to found cities, the father of industry, envy, and community life. Behold his face! See with what affection, with what compassion, with what love the unfortunate is painted. Wretched Cain! Our Abel Sánchez *admires* Cain just as Milton admired Satan, he is enamored of his Cain just as Milton was of his Satan, for to admire is to love and to love is to pity. Our Abel has sensed all the misery, all the unmerited misfortune of the one who killed the first Abel, and who, according to biblical legend, brought death into the world. Our Abel makes us understand Cain's guilt, for guilt there was, and he makes us pity him and love him. . . . This painting is an act of love!"

When Joaquín finished speaking, there was a heavy silence, until a salvo of applause thundered out. Abel stood up then; pale, shaking, hesitatingly, with tears in his eyes, he addressed his friend:

"What you have said, Joaquín, is worth more, has greater value, much greater, than my painting, than all the paintings I have done, than those I shall ever do. . . . Your words are a work of art, and of the heart. I did not know what I had accomplished until I heard you. You, and not I, have made my painting, you alone!"

The two eternal friends embraced amid their own

tears and the clamorous applause and cheers of the assembly, which had risen to its feet.

In the middle of the embrace his demon whispered to Joaquín: "If you could only crush him in your arms! . . ."

"Stupendous," they were saying. "What an orator! What a great speech! Who would have thought . . . ? It's a shame there were no reporters present!"

"Prodigious!" said one man, "I don't expect to hear another such speech ever again."

"Chills ran through me as I listened," said another.

"Just see how pale he is!"

Such was indeed the case. Joaquín, as he resumed his seat following his success, felt overcome, overwhelmed by a wave of sadness. No, his demon was not yet dead. His address had been a success the like of which he had never before enjoyed, nor would be likely to enjoy again, and now the idea came to him of devoting himself to speaking as a means of gaining a fame which would obscure the fame of his friend in painting.

"Did you see how Abel wept?" one man asked as he came out.

"The truth is that this address by Joaquín is worth all the paintings of the other. The speech made the painting. It will be necessary to call it 'The Painting of the Speech.' Take away the speech, and what's left of the painting? Nothing, despite the first prize."

When Joaquín arrived home, Antonia came out to open the door and to embrace him:

"I already know, they've already told me. Yes, yes! You're better than he, much better. He must know that if his painting is to have value it will be because of your speech."

"It's true, Antonia, it's true, but . . ."

"But what? Do you still . . . ?"

"Still! I don't wish to tell you the things my demon whispered while Abel and I embraced. . . ."

"No, don't tell me!"

She closed his mouth with a long, warm, moist kiss, as her eyes clouded over with tears.

"Let's see if you can draw the demon out of me this way, Antonia; let's see if you can suck him out."

"Should I absorb him then, so that he stays in me?" the poor woman asked, trying to laugh.

"Yes, draw him in, for he can't harm you; in you he will die, he will drown in your blood as in holy water. . . ."

At his home, Abel found himself alone with Helena. She said:

"I've been told all about Joaquín's oration. He's had to swallow your triumph . . . he's had to swallow it! . . ."

"Don't talk like that; you didn't hear him."

"It's just as if I had."

"His words came from his heart. I was deeply moved. I must tell you that even *I* did not know what I had painted until I heard his exposition."

"Don't trust him . . . don't trust him . . . when he eulogizes you like that, it must be for some reason. . . ."

"Maybe he said what he felt."

"You know he is dying of envy. . . ."

"Be quiet!"

"Dying, yes, almost dead, with envy of you. . . ."

"Be quiet, woman, be quiet!"

"No; and it's not jealousy, for he no longer loves me, if he ever did . . . it's envy . . . envy. . . ."

"Be quiet!" roared Abel.

"All right, I'll be quiet, but you'll see. . . ."

"I've already seen and heard, and that's enough. Be quiet, now!"

XV

A N D   Y E T , that heroic act did not restore poor Joaquín.

I began to feel remorse—he wrote in his *Confession* —*of having said what I had, of not having let my evil passion pour forth and thus gotten free of it, of not having broken with him artistically, denouncing the falsity and affectation of his art, his imitativeness, his cold, calculated technique, his lack of emotion. I was sorry for not having destroyed his fame. By so doing I would have freed myself, told the truth, and reduced his prestige to its true scale. Who knows but that perhaps Cain, the biblical Cain, who killed the other Abel, began to love his victim as soon as he saw him dead. And it was at this juncture that I began really to believe: one of the results of my testimonial speech was my own conversion.*

The conversion alluded to by Joaquín in his *Confession* proceeded from the fact that his wife Antonia, seeing her husband was not cured—fearing that he was perhaps incurable—induced him to seek help in prayer, and in the religion of his fathers, the religion which was hers, the religion which would be their daughter's.

"You should first go to Confession."

"But I haven't been to church for years."

"All the same. . . ."

"But I don't believe in these things. . . ."

"You believe you don't. But the priest has explained to me how it is that you men of science believe you don't believe, and all the same believe. I know that the things your mother taught you, the things I shall teach our daughter . . ."

"All right, all right, leave me alone!"

"No, I will not. Go to Confession, I beg you."

"And what will the people who know my ideas say?"

"Oh, is that it? Is it out of social considerations. . . ?"

However, Joaquín's heart was touched, and he asked himself if he really did not believe; moreover, he wanted to see if the Church could cure him, even if he did not believe. And he began to frequent the services, almost too conspicuously, as if by way of challenge to those who knew his irreligious convictions; finally, he sought out a confessor. And, once in the confessional, he poured out his soul.

"I hate him, Father, I hate him with all my heart, and if I did not believe as I do, or as I want to believe, I would kill him. . . ."

"But that, my son, that is not necessarily hatred. It is more like envy."

"All hatred is envy, Father, all hatred is envy."

"You should change it into noble emulation, into a desire to succeed in your profession, and in the service of God, to do the best you can accomplish. . . ."

"I cannot, I cannot, I cannot work. His fame and glory keep me from it."

"You must make an effort . . . it is for this purpose that man is free. . . ."

"I do not believe in free will, Father. I am a doctor."

"Still . . ."

"What did I do that God should make me this way, rancorous, envious, evil? What bad blood did my father bequeath me?"

"My son . . . my son. . . ."

"No, I do not believe in human liberty, and whoever cannot believe in liberty is surely not free. And I am not! To be free is to believe oneself free!"

"It is evil of one to doubt God."

"Is it evil to doubt, Father?"

"I don't mean to say that, but simply that your evil passion comes from your doubting God. . . ."

"Is it evil, then, to doubt God? I ask you again."

"Yes, it is evil."

"Then I doubt God because he made me evil. Just as he made Cain evil, God made me doubt. . . ."

"He made you free."

"Yes, free to be evil."

"And to be good!"

"Ah, why was I born, Father?"

"Ask rather to what end. . . ."

XVI

ABEL HAD painted a Virgin and Child: the painting was in fact a portrait of Helena, and the child, Abelito. It had been well received, was reproduced and, before a splendid photograph of it, Joaquín prayed to the most Holy Virgin, asking her to protect and save him.

But while he prayed, in a low-toned murmur, as if to hear himself, he fought to stifle another voice more profound, which welled from deep within him saying: "If he would only die! If he would only leave her free for you!"

"So," Abel hailed him one day, "you have become a reactionary."

"I have?"

"Yes, they tell me you have given yourself up to the Church and go to Mass every day. Since you never did believe either in God or the Devil—and it can scarcely be a matter of having made a conversion just like that—well, then, you must have turned reactionary!"

"What does it all matter to you?"

"I'm not calling you to account, you understand. But, well, now . . . do you really believe?"

"I need to believe."

"That's something else again. I mean do you really believe?"

"As I've already told you, I need to believe. Don't ask me again."

"For my part, art is enough. Art is my religion."

"Still, you have painted Virgins. . . ."

"Yes, Helena."

"Who is not precisely a virgin. . . ."

"For me, it's as if she were. She is the mother of my child. . . ."

"Only that?"

"And every mother is a virgin by virtue of being a mother."

"You're entering the realms of theology!"

"I don't know about that, but I hate stupid conservatism and prudery, which is something born merely of envy, it seems to me, and it surprises me to find signs of it in you. I had faith in your being able to withstand the mediocrity of the vulgar, and I am surprised to see you wearing their uniform."

"What do you mean, Abel? Come, explain yourself."

"It's clear enough. Common, vulgar spirits are never distinguished, and, unable to bear the fact that others are, they attempt to impose upon others more fortunate the uniform of dogma—which is a kind of dull fatigue uniform—so that the uncommon may appear undistinguished. The origin of all orthodoxy, in religion as in art, is envy, have no doubt of it. If we were all to dress as we pleased, there would be one among us who would think up some striking mode of dress which would accentuate his natural elegance; if it were a man who did this, women would naturally be attracted to him; and yet if a vulgar, common individual were to do the same thing, he would merely look ridiculous. It is for this reason that the vulgar, that is to say, the envious, have invented a kind of uniform, a manner of dressing themselves like puppets, which comes to be the fashion—for fashion, too, is another matter of orthodoxy. Don't deceive yourself, Joaquín, those ideas which are called dangerous, daring, impious, are merely those that never suggest themselves to impoverished, mediocre intelligences, the people who don't even have a grain of personal initiative or originality, but do have 'common sense'— and vulgarity. Imagination is what they most hate— especially since they don't have any."

"Even though this be the case," Joaquín exclaimed, "don't those we call vulgar, common, mediocre have the right to defend themselves?"

"On another occasion, at my house, you remember, you defended Cain, the envious; then, later, in that unforgettable speech which I shall repeat till I die, in that speech—to which I owe a good deal of my reputation—you showed us, at least you showed me,

Cain's soul. But Cain was scarcely a mediocrity, a vulgarian, a common man. . . ."

"But he was the father of all the envious."

"Yes, but of another kind of envy, not the envy of the bigots. . . . Cain's envy was something grandiose; the envy of the fanatical inquisitor is picayune and miserably small. And it shocks me to see you on the side of the inquisitors."

"Can this man read my thoughts, then?" Joaquín asked himself as he took leave of Abel. "He doesn't seem to notice what I suffer, and still . . . he talks and thinks in the same way he paints, without knowing what he says or paints. He works unconsciously, no matter how much I try to see in him the thoughtful technician. . . ."

XVII

JOAQUÍN FOUND out that Abel was involved with one of his former models; this information corroborated his suspicion that Abel had not married Helena from motives of love. "They married," Joaquín told himself, "to humiliate me." And he added: "And Helena doesn't love him, nor is she capable of loving him . . . she doesn't love anyone, she's incapable of affection; she's no more than a beautiful shell of vanity. . . . She married from vanity and disdain for me, and from vanity or caprice she is capable of betraying her husband . . . even with the man she didn't want as husband." A spark glowed among the embers of recollections, a live coal which he had thought extinguished under his ice-cold hatred: it was his old love for Helena. Yes, in spite of everything he was still enamored of this female peacock, this co-quette, this artist's model to her husband. Antonia was very much superior to her, without any doubt, but the other was the other. Then, there was revenge . . . and revenge was so sweet! So warming to a frozen heart!

In a few days he went to Abel's house, carefully choosing an hour when Abel himself would be out. He found his cousin Helena alone with her child, Helena before whose image made divine he had vainly sought protection and salvation.

"Abel has told me," Helena said to him now, "that you've taken up going to church. Is it because Antonia has dragged you there, or do you go there to escape Antonia?"

"What do you mean?"

"You husbands tend to become holy men either while tracking down a wife, or escaping her. . . ."

"There are those who escape their wives, but not precisely to go to church."

"Oh?"

"Yes. But your husband, who has borne this tale to you, doesn't seem to know something else, which is that the church is not the only place where I pray. . . ."

"Naturally not! Every devout man should say prayers at home."

"And I do. And my chief prayer is to the Virgin, to ask her for protection and salvation."

"That strikes me as very sensible."

"And do you know before whose image I ask this?"

"Not unless you tell me. . . ."

"Before the painting made by your husband. . . ."

Helena turned away abruptly, her face deeply flushed, toward the child sleeping in a corner of the sitting room. The suddenness of the attack had disconcerted her. Composing herself, however, she said:

"This is an act of impiety on your part, Joaquín, and proves that your new devotion is no more than a farce, and perhaps something worse. . . ."

"I swear to you, Helena. . . ."

"The second commandment—don't take His holy name in vain."

"Therefore I truly swear to you, Helena, that my conversion was sincere; I mean that I have wanted to believe, I have wanted to defend myself with faith against a passion that devours me. . . ."

"Yes, I know your passion. . . ."

"No you don't know it!"

"*I know it.* It is that you cannot endure Abel's existence."

"Why can't I endure him?"

"That is something only you could answer. You have never been able to endure him, not even before you introduced him to me."

"That's untrue, utterly untrue!"

"It's the truth! The utter truth!"

"Why should I not be able to endure him?"

"Because he is becoming well known, because he has a reputation. . . . Don't you have a good practice? Don't you make a good living?"

"Listen, Helena, I am going to tell you the truth, all of it! I am not satisfied with what I have. I wanted to become famous, to find something new in my science, to link my name to some scientific discovery. . . ."

"Well, then, apply yourself to it, for it's not talent you lack."

"Apply myself . . . apply myself. . . . Yes, I could

have applied myself, Helena, if I had been able to offer up the triumph at your feet. . . ."

"And why not at Antonia's feet?"

"Please, let's not speak of her."

"Ah, have you come for this, then! Have you waited until my Abel"—and she emphasized the *my* —"was gone, so that you could come for this?"

"Your Abel . . . your Abel . . . a precious lot of attention your Abel is paying you!"

"Oh? Do you also play the role of informer, tattle-tale, gossip?"

"Your Abel has other models besides you."

"What of it?" Helena retorted, bridling. "And what if he does have them? It's a sign that he knows how to win them! Or, are you jealous of him for that too? Is it because you haven't any recourse but to content yourself with . . . your Antonia? Ah, and because he has shown that he knew how to find himself another, have you thought of coming here today to find yourself another, too? And do you come to me like this, to bring me these tales? Aren't you ashamed? Get away from me! Get out! The sight of you makes me sick."

"O my God! Stop, Helena, you're killing me . . . you're killing me!"

"Go, go to church, you hypocrite, you envious hypocrite; go and let your wife take care of you and cure you, for you are very sick."

"Helena, Helena, only you can cure me! In the name of all you love most, remember you are condemning a man and losing him forever!"

"Ah, and in order to save you, you would have me lose another man, my own?"

"You won't lose him; you've already lost him. He's not interested in any part of you. He's incapable of loving you. I, I am the one who loves you, with all my soul, with a love that you can't conceive of even in your dreams."

Helena stood up, went over to the child and, awakening him, took him in her arms; then she turned around to Joaquín and said: "Get out! This child, the son of Abel, orders you from his house. Get out!"

XVIII

JOAQUÍN WORSENED. Wrath at having laid bare his heart before Helena and despair at the manner in which she had rejected him finally withered his soul. He succeeded in mastering himself for a time and he sought consolation in his wife and daughter. But his home life grew more somber, and he more bitter.

At this time he had a maid in his house who was very devout, who managed to attend Mass every day, and who passed every moment which domestic service permitted her shut up in her room saying her prayers. She went about with her eyes lowered and fixed on the ground, and she responded to everything with the greatest meekness, in a somewhat sniveling voice. Joaquín could not bear her, and was constantly scolding her without any pretext whatever. She habitually replied: "The master is right."

"What do you mean, I'm right?" Joaquín burst out on one occasion. "I'm not right at all!"

"Very well, sir, please do not be angered. You're not right then."

"Is that all?"

Chapter XVIII

"I don't understand, sir."

"What do you mean, you don't understand, you prude, you hypocrite! Why don't you defend yourself? Why don't you answer back? Why don't you rebel?"

"Rebel? I, sir? God and the Blessed Virgin keep me from any rebellion, sir."

"What more can you want," interposed Antonia, "if she admits her own shortcomings?"

"She doesn't admit them at all. She is steeped in arrogance!"

"In arrogance, I, sir?"

"You see? The hypocrite is proud of not admitting anything. She is simply using me, at my expense, to do exercises in humility and patience. She uses my fits of temper as a kind of hair shirt to exercise the virtue of patience in herself. At my expense, mind you! No, it shall not be; not at my expense. She can't use me as an instrument to pile up good marks in heaven! That's real hypocrisy for you!"

The poor little maid wept, as she prayed between her teeth.

"But it's really true that she is humble. . . . Why should she rebel? If she *had* rebelled, you would have been even more irritated."

"No! It's a gross breach of faith to use the foibles of someone else as a means of exercising one's own virtue. Let her answer me back, let her be insolent, let her be a human being . . . and not just a servant. . . ."

"In which case, Joaquín, you would be much more annoyed."

"No, what really irritates me most are all these pretensions to greater perfection."

"You are mistaken, sir," said the maid without

lifting her eyes from the ground; "I don't think I am better than anyone."

"You don't, eh? Well I do! And whoever doesn't think himself better than another is a fool. You probably think yourself the greatest woman sinner of all time, isn't that it? Come on now, answer me!"

"These things cannot be asked, sir."

"Come now, answer me, for they say that Saint Aloysius Gonzaga believed himself the greatest sinner among men, and you, answer me yes or no, don't you think you're the greatest sinner among women?"

"The sins of other women are not on my soul, sir."

"Idiot! You're worse than an idiot! Get out of here!"

"God forgive you, sir, as I do!"

"For what? Come back and tell me. For what? What will God have to forgive me for? Come on, tell me!"

"Very well. For your sake, ma'am, I am sorry to go, but I shall leave this house."

"That's the way you should have begun . . . ," Joaquín concluded.

Later, alone with his wife, he said to her:

"Won't this innocent hypocrite go around now saying that I am mad? Antonia, am I not, perhaps, mad? Tell me, am I mad, or not?"

"For God's sake, Joaquín, don't become . . ."

"Yes, yes, I believe I am mad. . . . Send me away. All this will put an end to me."

"You must put an end to *it*."

XIX

JOAQUÍN NOW lavished all his ardor upon his daughter, in raising her, in educating her, in keeping her free of the world's immoralities.

"It's just as well she is the only one," he would say to his wife. "It's just as well that we didn't have another."

"Wouldn't you have liked a son?"

"No, no, a daughter is better; it's easier to isolate a girl from this vile world. Besides, if there had been two, jealousies would have developed between them. . . ."

"Oh, no!"

"Oh, yes! Affection cannot be divided equally between several; what is given one is taken away from another. Each one demands everything for himself, and for himself alone. No, no, I shouldn't want to see myself in God's plight. . . ."

"What is that, now?"

"The one of having so many children. Isn't it said that we are all children of God?"

"Don't say these things, Joaquín. . . ."

"There are healthy people so that there may be infirm. . . . One has only to look at the way illness is distributed!"

Joaquín did not want his daughter to have anything to do with people. He brought a private teacher to the house, and he himself, in moments of leisure, gave her instruction.

Joaquina, the poor girl, saw in her father an invalid, a sick man, a patient rather than a doctor. Meanwhile, from him she received a somber view of the world and of life.

315

"I tell you," Joaquín continued the argument with his wife, "that she is enough, alone, so that we need not divide our affection. . . ."

"They say that the more it is divided, the more it grows. . . ."

"Don't believe it. You remember poor Ramírez, the solicitor? His father had two sons and two daughters and very few resources. In their house they ate appetizers and soup, but never a main course. Only the father, Ramírez senior, ate a main course; from time to time, he would share a little with one of the sons and one of the daughters, but never with the others. When they 'celebrated,' on special occasions, they were served two entrees to be divided among the family, plus one for him, since, as master of the house, he had to be distinguished in some way. The hierarchy had to be preserved. And at night, as he retired to sleep, Ramírez senior would kiss one of his sons and one of his daughters, but not the remaining two."

"How awful! Why did he do that?"

"How do I know? . . . Perhaps the two favorites looked more attractive. . . ."

"It sounds like the case of Carvajal, who can't bear his youngest daughter. . . ."

"That's because the last child was born six years after the other and at a time when he was low in funds. She was just one more burden, an unexpected one. That's why they call her The Intruder."

"Good God, how horrible!"

"Such is life, Antonia, a seedbed of horrors. And let us thank God that we don't have to distribute our affection."

"Don't say that!"

"I'll say no more."

And she made him keep quiet.

XX

ABEL'S SON was studying medicine and his father made a habit of keeping Joaquín informed on the progress of the boy's studies. Joaquín himself spoke to the boy a few times and gradually grew attached to him, or simply "fond" of him, as he thought at the time.

"How does it happen that you prepare him for medicine instead of for painting?" Joaquín asked the father.

"I am not preparing him, he is preparing himself. He doesn't feel any vocation toward art. . . ."

"I see, and to study medicine one needs, of course, no 'vocation'. . . ."

"I didn't say that. You always take everything the worst way. He not only does not feel any vocation toward art, but he is not even curious about it. He scarcely stops to see what I am painting, or to look into it at all."

"Perhaps it's better that way. . . ."

"Why do you say that?"

"Because if he had devoted himself to painting he would necessarily become a better or a worse painter than you. If worse, it would not do, nor could he have endured it, to be called, not merely Abel Sánchez, the younger, but Abel Sánchez the Bad, or Sánchez the Bad, or Abel the Bad. . . ."

"And if he were better than I?"

"Then it would be you who could not endure it."

" 'The thief thinks that everyone else is a thief.' "

"Oh, that's it. Turn on me with an insult. No artist can tolerate the fame of another, especially if it is a son or brother. Better the fame of a stranger. That one of the same blood should triumph . . . never!

How explain it? . . . You do well to train him for medicine."

"In any case, he will earn more."

"Do you mean to imply that you don't make a good income from painting?"

"I make something."

"Yes, and have fame besides."

"Fame? For whatever that's worth . . . as long as it lasts."

"Money doesn't last either."

"It's a little more substantial."

"Don't be a fraud, Abel, and pretend to despise fame."

"I assure you that what concerns me now is to leave my son a fortune."

"You will leave him a name."

"There is no market quotation on a name."

"On yours, there is!"

"On my signature, but it's only . . . Sánchez! And he might very well decide to sign himself Abel S. Puig, or some such thing. Let him be Marquis of the house of Sánchez. The Abel takes away the sting from the Sánchez. And Abel Sánchez sounds well enough."

XXI

FLEEING FROM himself, and, so as to suppress in his sick and melancholy consciousness that ever-present image of Abel which haunted him, Joaquín began to frequent a nightly gathering at his club. The light conversation would serve as a narcotic, and he hoped he might even be intoxicated by it. Do not some men give themselves up to drink so as to drown the passion which devastates them, and to allow their frustrated love to flow away with the wine? And so he would give himself up to the talk in the club, listening rather more than taking an active part, so as to drown his passion.

Only, the remedy turned out to be worse than the ill.

He always went prepared to keep himself in restraint, to laugh and joke, to gossip pleasantly, to appear as a kind of disinterested spectator of life, generous as only a professed skeptic can be, heedful of the fact that to understand is to forgive, prepared never to allow the cancer of hatred which consumed his will to show through. But the evil escaped through his lips, in his words, when he least expected it, and the odor of wickedness was perceived by all. He would return home exasperated with himself, reproaching himself for cowardice and his lack of control, and would resolve to return no more to the club gatherings. "I will not go again," he would tell himself, "I must not. All this only worsens the matter, aggravates it. The atmosphere there is poisonous, the air is filled with suppressed evils and passions. No, I shall not return there. What I need is solitude, solitude. Blessed solitude!"

And yet he would go back.

He would go back because he was unable to endure his solitude. For in solitude he never managed to be alone, the other one was always present. The other one! He went so far as to catch himself in a dialogue with him, supplying the other's words for him. The other, in these solitary dialogues, these monologues in dialogues, spoke to him without rancor of any kind, of indifferent matters, even sometimes of pleasant things. "My God, why doesn't he hate me?" Joaquín came to ask himself. "Why doesn't he hate me?"

One day he even found himself on the point of addressing God, of asking Him in a diabolic speech to infiltrate some hatred into Abel's heart, hatred toward himself, Joaquín. Another time he burst out: "Oh, if he only envied me . . . if he only envied me." And this idea, which flashed lividly across the black clouds of his bitter spirit, brought him a relaxing joy, a joy which caused him to tremble in the marrow of his tremulous soul. "To be envied! . . . Only to be envied! . . ."

"But," he asked himself, "doesn't all this simply prove that I hate myself, that I envy myself?" He went to the door, locked it with a key, looked about him and, certain that he was alone, fell to his knees. In a voice scalded by tears he murmured: "Lord, you have told me to love my neighbor as myself, and I cannot love him at all, for I don't love myself, I don't know how to love myself. I cannot love myself. What have you done with me, Lord?"

He went then and got his Bible, and opened it to where it reads: "And Jehovah said to Cain: Where is thy brother Abel?" Slowly he closed the book, murmuring: "And where am I?"

At this moment he heard sounds outside, and he hastened to open the door. "Papa! Papa!" his daughter was joyfully shouting, as she came in. Her fresh, young voice seemed to bring him back into the light. He kissed the girl and then grazing her ear with his lips he told her in a low voice, so that no one else might hear: "Pray for your father, my daughter."

"Father, Father!" cried the girl, throwing her arms about his neck.

Chapter XXII

He hid his head in the girl's shoulder and burst into tears.

"What is the matter, Papa, are you sick?"

"Yes, I am sick. . . . But you mustn't ask any more."

XXII

A N D H E R E T U R N E D to the club. It was useless to fight against going back. Every day he invented another pretext for going. And the mill of conversation continued to grind.

One of the figures there was Federico Cuadrado, an implacable man, who, when he heard anyone speak well of another would ask: "Against whom is that eulogy directed?"

"I can't be fooled," he would say in his small, cold, cutting voice. "When someone is vigorously praised, the speaker always has someone else in mind whom he is trying to debase with this eulogy, a second someone who is a rival to the praised party. This is true when it's not a matter of deliberately trying to vent one's scorn on the person mentioned. . . . You can be sure that no one eulogizes with good intentions."

"Wait a minute," interjected León Gómez, who took a great delight in making the cynic talk; "there's Don Leovigildo, now, whom no one has ever heard say a word against another. . . ."

"Well," a provincial deputy put in, "the fact is Don Leovigildo is a politician, and politicians must remain on good terms with everybody. What do you say, Federico?"

"I say that Don Leovigildo will die without having

spoken badly or thought well of any man. . . . He would not give, perhaps, the slightest little push to send another sprawling, even if no one were to see it, because he not only fears the penal code, but also Hell. But if the other person falls and breaks his crown, he will wallow in the sheer joy of it all. And in order to enjoy his pleasure in the broken skull to the fullest, he will be the first to go and offer his sympathy and condolences."

"I don't know how it is possible to live with such sentiments," interposed Joaquín.

"What sentiments?" Federico caught him up. "Don Leovigildo's, mine, or yours?"

"No one has mentioned me in this conversation!" Joaquín spoke with acerbity.

"I do, now, my good fellow, for we all know each other here. . . ."

Joaquín felt himself turn pale. The phrase "My good fellow," which Federico, inspired by his guardian devil, lightly bestowed upon anyone into whom he dug his claws, had pierced Joaquín in his innermost self.

"I can't understand why you have such an aversion to Don Leovigildo," blurted out Joaquín, who was sorry as soon as he had spoken, for he felt he was stirring up sputtering, dangerous fire.

"Aversion? Aversion, I? For Don Leovigildo?"

"Yes. . . . I don't know what harm he could have done you."

"In the first place, my good fellow, it is not necessary for someone to harm you for you to take a dislike to him. When you have a dislike for someone, an 'aversion,' it becomes easy to invent some harmful or malevolent action, that is to say, to imagine that the harm had been done one. . . . In the second place, I don't have any greater 'aversion' toward Don Leovigildo than I have for anyone else at all. He's a man, and that's enough. Moreover, he's an 'honorable' man!"

"Just as you are a professional misanthrope . . . ," began the provincial deputy.

"Man is the rottenest and most indecent vermin there is; I've said so a thousand times. And the 'honorable' man is the worst of the lot."

"Come on now," said León Gómez; and then, addressing the deputy: "What do you say to that, you who were talking the other day about honorable politicians, referring to Don Leovigildo?"

"An honorable politician," Federico burst out. "Oh, no, not that! That's completely impossible!"

"Why?" exclaimed three voices at once.

"Why, you ask? Because he himself has belied it in his own words. He had the audacity in the course of a speech he was delivering to call himself honorable. And it is not honorable to declare oneself so. The Gospel says that Christ our Lord . . ."

"Don't mention Christ, I beg you!" Joaquín interrupted.

"What, does Christ hurt you too, my good fellow?"

There was a short silence, bleak and cold.

"Christ our Lord," reiterated Federico, "said that he should not be called good, for only God is good. And yet there are Christian swine who dare to call themselves honorable."

"*Honorable* is not exactly the same as *good*," interpolated Don Vicente, the magistrate.

"Ah, now you have said it yourself, Don Vicente.

Thank the Lord for the opportunity to hear a sentence like that, both reasonable and just, from a magistrate!"

"So that one must not confess oneself to be honorable, is that it?" asked Joaquín. "But how about confessing oneself a rogue?"

"That isn't necessary."

"What Señor Cuadrado wants," said Don Vicente, the magistrate, "is for men to admit they are scoundrels, and continue on in their normal course, isn't that it?"

"Bravo!" exclaimed the provincial deputy.

"I shall tell you, my good fellow," answered Federico, considering his reply. "You must certainly know what constitutes the excellence of the sacrament of Confession in our most wise Mother the Church. . . ."

"Some other barbarity, now," interrupted the magistrate.

"Not at all a barbarity, but a very wise institution. Confession allows for more graceful, more tranquil sinning, since one knows that one's sins will be forgiven. Isn't that so, Joaquín?"

"Yet, if one does not repent . . ."

"Oh, yes, my good fellow, yes, one must repent, and then again sin and once again repent, knowing while one is sinning that one will repent, and knowing when one repents that one will sin again, so that finally one is both sinning and repenting at the same time. Isn't that true?"

"Man is a mystery," said León Gómez.

"There is no need for inanities!" replied Federico.

"Why is that inane?"

"Any 'philosophical' maxim, stated just like that, any off-hand maxim, any solemn, general statement, put in the form of an aphorism, results in an inanity."

"And philosophy, then?"

"There is no other philosophy than what we are doing here right now. . . ."

"You mean flaying our fellow men?"

"Exactly. Man is best when flayed."

After the club gathering, Federico approached Joaquín to ask if he were going home, for he would have liked to accompany him for a short distance; but when Joaquín told him he was not going home, but simply going on a visit close by, Federico said:

"I understand. The business about the visit is just a blind. What you want is to be left alone. I understand."

"How do you understand it?"

"One is never better off than when one is alone. But, when solitude weighs on you, call upon me. You will find no one who will better distract you from your burdens."

"What about your own?" Joaquín blurted out.

"Bah! Who cares about them? . . ."

Whereupon they parted company.

XXIII

There roamed about the city a poor needy man, an Aragonese, father of five children, who earned a living as best he could, as a scribe or at whatever turned up. The poor man frequently appealed to friends—if such men as he can indeed be said to have any—petitioning them under a thousand pretexts for the advance of two or three five-peseta notes. The saddest aspect of the whole thing was that he sometimes sent around one of his children, or even his wife, who appeared at the homes of acquaintances bearing little begging letters. Joaquín had occasionally helped him, especially when he had sent for him as a doctor to treat someone in his family. For Joaquín found a singular satisfaction in helping the poor man; he saw in him a victim of human badness.

Once Joaquín asked Abel about him.

"Yes, I know him," the latter said. "I even gave him work for a while. But he's an idler, a vagrant. With the excuse that he is drowning his sorrows, he doesn't let a day go by without showing up at the café, even though at home the stove can't be lit. Nor will he be without his little packet of cigarettes. He wants to turn his troubles into smoke."

"That isn't the whole story, Abel. It would be necessary to examine the case from within. . . ."

"Listen, don't be absurd. Something I can't tolerate is that line about 'I'll return this loan as soon as I can. . . .' Let him ask for alms and be done with it! It would be more open and noble. The last time, he asked me for fifteen pesetas and I gave him five, but told him: 'Not to be paid back!' He's a loafer!"

"How can you blame him? . . ."

"Come now, here we go again: 'Whose fault is it?' "

"Exactly! Whose fault *is* it?"

"All right, then. Let's forget it. If you want to help him, please do so; I won't stand in the way. I'm sure that I will give him what he wants if he asks me again."

"I knew that without your telling me, for underneath it all you are . . ."

"Let's not go 'underneath it all.' I am a painter and I don't paint the person underneath. Even more, I'm convinced that all men show everything they are inside on the outside."

"Well, then, for you, a man is no more than a painter's model. . . ."

"Does that seem a small matter to you? For you, he is no more than a sick man, a patient. You're the one who goes about looking into men, auscultating them, listening in. . . ."

"Yes, a dire routine . . ."

"How so?"

"Because when one is accustomed to looking into people, one ends up looking into oneself, auscultating oneself, listening in. . . ."

"There's an advantage in that. I have enough when I look at myself in the mirror. . . ."

"Have you ever really looked at yourself in the mirror?"

"Naturally! You must know that I've painted a self-portrait."

"A masterpiece, no doubt. . . ."

"Well now, it's not altogether bad. . . . And you, have you examined yourself thoroughly?"

The day following this conversation Joaquín left the club with Federico because he wanted to ask him if he knew the poor man who roamed about begging in a shameful fashion. "And tell me the truth now, for we're alone. None of your ferocious statements."

"Well, look, he's a poor devil who should be in jail, where he would at least eat better than he does and where he would live more calmly."

"But what has he done?"

"No, he hasn't done anything. He should have, and that's why I say he should be in jail."

"What is it he should have done?"

"Killed his brother."

"Now you're starting up again!"

"I shall explain it to you. This poor man is, as you know, from the province of Aragon, and there, in his native region, absolute liberty in disposing of property still exists. He had the misfortune to be the first-born son and legitimate heir, and then he had the misfortune to fall in love with a poor girl, comely and honorable though she was to all appearances. The father opposed their relationship with all his might, threatening to disinherit him if he went so far as to marry the girl. And our man, blind with love, first compromised the girl seriously, thinking thus to convince the father, and ended by marrying her and leaving home. He stayed on in the town, working as best he might at the home of his in-laws, hoping to soften his father. And the latter, a good Aragonese, grew more and more unyielding, and died disinheriting the poor devil and leaving his estate to the second son; and a rather fair-sized estate it was, too. When his in-laws died a little while later, the poor man appealed to his brother for help and work; and his brother denied him; and, so as not to kill this false brother—which is what his natural anger urged him to do—he has come here to live from alms and cadging. This, then, is the story; as you see, very edifying."

"So very edifying!"

"Had he killed his brother, that species of Jacob, it would have been an evil; and not killing him, was an evil too. . . . Perhaps a worse one."

"Don't say that, Federico."

"It's true, for he not only lives wretchedly and shamefully, a parasite, but he lives hating his brother."

"And if he had killed him?"

"Then he would have been cured of his hatred, and today, repentant of his crime, he would be honoring his brother's memory. Action liberates one and dissipates poisoned sentiment, and it is poisoned sentiment which sickens the soul. Believe me, Joaquín, for I know it very well."

Joaquín looked at him deliberately:

"And you?" he spat out.

"Me? You wouldn't want to know things that don't concern you, would you, my good fellow? Let it be enough for you to know that all my cynicism is defensive. I am not the son of the man everyone takes to be my father; I am the child of an adultery, and there is no one in this world whom I hate worse than my own father, my natural father, who was the ruin of the other one, the father who out of cowardice and baseness gave me his name, this indecent name which I bear."

"Still, the father is not the one who begets, but the one who raises the offspring. . . ."

"The truth is that this other father, the one you think raised me, did no such thing, but instead weaned me to the venom of hatred which he bears my natural father, who engendered me and who forced him, the man who raised me, to marry my mother."

XXIV

ABELÍN, ABEL'S son finished his studies and his father called on Joaquín to see if he would take on the boy to practice with him as his assistant. Joaquín accepted him.

I accepted him—Joaquín wrote later in the *Confession* dedicated to his daughter—*from a strange mixture of curiosity, abhorrence of his father, and affection for the boy (who at that time seemed to me to be a mediocrity) coupled with a desire to free myself by this means from my evil passion. At the same time, deeper down in my heart, my demon whispered that the failure of the son would negate the preeminence of the father. So that on the one hand, I wanted to redeem myself of my hatred for the father by my affection for the son, and, on the other, I took a secret delight in anticipating that though Abel Sánchez triumphed in painting, another Abel Sánchez of his own blood would fail in medicine. I never would have been able at that time to imagine how deep a love I would come to feel for the son of the man who embittered and darkened the life of my spirit.*

And thus it came to pass that Joaquín and the son of Abel felt drawn to each other. Abelín was quick-witted and he avidly followed the precepts of Joaquín, whom he addressed as "maestro." His teacher proposed to make a good doctor of him, entrusting him with the wealth of his clinical experience. "I will lead him," he told himself, "to make the discoveries which this misbegotten restlessness of spirit has prevented me from making."

"Maestro," Abelín said to him one day, "why don't you assemble all the scattered observations, all the random notes you have shown me, and write a book? It would be enormously interesting and highly instructive. There are scatterings of genius throughout the material, and extraordinary scientific wisdom."

"The truth is, Son" (it was thus he habitually addressed him), "I can't, I simply can't. . . . I don't have the taste for it, I don't have the will, the courage, the serenity, the I-don't-know-what. . . ."

"It would merely be a question of getting start-ed. . . ."

"Yes, Son, of course; it would merely be a question of getting started, but as many times as I've thought of it I've never come to the point of making a decision. To set myself to write a book . . . here in Spain . . . on medicine . . . ! No, it wouldn't be worth the effort. It would be like writing in the sand. . . ."

"No, your work wouldn't be in vain, I'm sure of it."

"What I should have done is precisely what you must do: abandon this insufferable practice and dedi-cate yourself to pure research, to true science, to physi-ology, histology, pathology, and not to the paying sick. You, who have some little means—your father's paintings must assure you of some—must devote yourself to that."

"You may well be right, sir; but this does not alter the fact that you ought to publish your memoirs as a diagnostician."

"Look! If you like, we will arrange something. I will give you my notes, all of them. I will amplify them orally, I will answer all your questions. And you will publish the book. Does that appeal to you?"

"Wonderful! It would be wonderful. I have taken notes, ever since I have been assisting here, of every-thing I have heard and learned."

"Very well, my son, very well." And he embraced the boy with deep feeling.

Later, Joaquín said to himself: "This boy shall be my handiwork! Mine, and not his father's. In the end he will venerate me and understand that I am more worthy than his father, that there is more art in my practice of medicine than in his father's painting. And then, I will take him away from him. He took Helena away from me, and I will take away his son from him. Abelín will become my son, and who knows? . . . perhaps he will finally renounce his father, when he finally knows him and finds out what he did to me."

XXV

"BUT TELL ME," Joaquín asked his disciple one day, "how did you really come to study medicine?"

"I am not sure. . . ."

"Because it would have been most natural for you to have been attracted to painting. Young men usually feel called upon to practice their fathers' professions; from a spirit of emulation . . . the very ambience . . ."

"Painting never did interest me."

"Your father told me. . . ."

"My father's painting even less."

"What do you mean by that?"

"I don't feel it, and I don't know whether he does either. . . ."

"That's very serious. Would you explain? . . ."

"There is no one to hear what I say, and you, sir, you are like a second father to me . . . a second . . . Well, then. . . . Besides, you are his oldest friend, before you had either one reached the age of reason, and you are almost like brothers. . . ."

"Yes, yes, that's true enough. Abel and I are like brothers. . . . Go on."

Chapter XXV

"Well, then, today I would like to open my heart to you."

"Do so. Whatever you tell me will never be known."

"Yes, the truth is that I doubt that my father has any feeling for what he paints—or for anything else. He paints like a machine. He has a natural gift for it. But feeling? . . ."

"This is what I have always believed."

"Why, it was you, according to everyone, who contributed the largest impetus to his fame with that famous address which is still spoken of."

"How else could I have spoken?"

"That is what I say to myself. In any case, I think that my father feels neither painting nor anything else. He is made of cork."

"I wouldn't say that, son."

"Yes, cork. He lives only for his own glory. All that talk about his despising fame is a farce, pure farce. On the contrary, he seeks only applause. And he is an egotist, a perfect egotist. He doesn't love anyone else."

"Well, now . . . no one else . . . that's pretty strong."

"It's true, no one else. I don't even know how he came to marry my mother. I doubt that it was for love."

Joaquín turned pale.

"I know," the youth continued, "that he has had entanglements and affairs with some of his models. But they have been a matter of caprice, and a little bit of showing off. He doesn't really care for anyone."

"But it seems to me that you are the one who should . . ."

"He has never paid any attention to me. He has supported me, has paid for my education and studies, he has not stinted nor does he now stint me with respect to money. And still, I scarcely exist as far as he is concerned. Whenever I have asked him something, in regard to history, art, technique, painting, his travels, or anything else, he has said to me: 'Leave me alone, leave me in peace.' Once he said: 'Learn it yourself! Learn it, as I did! There are the books.' How different that is from you!"

"It might be that he didn't know, my son. Parents sometimes act unjustly toward their children simply because they do not want to admit they are more ignorant or slower than the youngsters."

"No, it wasn't that. . . . And there is something worse."

"Worse? What can that be?"

"Yes, worse. He has never reprimanded me, no matter what I may have done. Although I am not, nor ever have been, either dissolute or wild, still everyone who is young has his slips and falls. Nevertheless, he has never inquired into them, and, even if he knew about them, has said nothing."

"That shows respect for your integrity, confidence in you. . . . It is probably the most generous and noble way to bring up a son, and it demonstrates faith. . . ."

"No, it is nothing like that, in this case. It is simply indifference."

"Don't exaggerate, it isn't indifference. . . . What could he say to you that your conscience wouldn't have already told you? A father can't be a judge."

"But he can be a comrade, an adviser, a friend, or a teacher like you."

"And yet there are things which decorum forbids mentioning between father and son."

"It is only natural that you, his greatest and oldest friend, almost his brother, should defend him even though . . ."

"Even though what?"

"May I tell you everything?"

"Yes, tell everything."

"Well, then, I have never heard him speak otherwise than well of you, too well, but . . ."

"But what?"

"That's just it. He speaks too well of you."

"What do you mean by speaking too well?"

"For instance, before I came to know you, I thought of you as someone completely different from what you really are."

"Explain yourself."

"For my father you are a kind of tragic being, with a soul tortured by profound passions. 'If one might only paint the soul of Joaquín,' he has often said. He speaks as if there were a secret operating between you and him. . . ."

"These are merely suspicions of yours. . . ."

"No, they are not."

"And your mother?"

"Ah, my mother . . ."

XXVI

"LISTEN, JOAQUÍN," Antonia said to her husband one day, "it seems to me that one of these fine days our daughter will leave us, or be taken away from us. . . ."

"Joaquina? Where to?"

"To the convent!"

"Impossible!"

"On the contrary, highly possible. You have simply been engrossed in your own affairs, and now you are taken up with this son of Abel's, whom you seem to have adopted. . . . Anyone would say you were more fond of him than of your own daughter. . . ."

"The point is that I am trying to save him, to redeem him from his antecedents. . . ."

"No, what you are really trying to do is to take revenge. How vengeful you are! You neither forgive nor forget! I fear that God will punish you, will punish us. . . ."

"Oh, and is that the reason Joaquina wants to enter a convent?"

"I didn't say that."

"But I do, and that's the same thing. Is she going because she is jealous of Abelín? Is she afraid that I will grow to love him more than I do her? Because if that's the reason . . ."

"That is not the reason."

"What, then?"

"I don't know. . . . She says she has a vocation, that God calls her there. . . ."

"God? God? Her confessor, more likely. Who is he?"

"Father Echevarría."

"The one who was my confessor?"

"The same."

Joaquín seemed crestfallen. He began to ponder. On the following day he called his wife aside and told her:

"I believe I have uncovered the motives for Joaquina's impulse to enter the cloister, or rather, the motives for Father Echevarría's inducing her to become a nun. Do you remember how I sought help and refuge in the church against that wretched obsession which takes possession of my whole soul, against that spitefulness which through the years grows older—harder and more stubborn, and do you remember how, despite all my efforts, I did not succeed in my purpose? No, Father Echevarría did not give me any help, he could not. For that evil there is no remedy but one, only one."

He was silent for a moment, as if expecting a question from his wife, and, as she kept quiet, he went on:

"For that evil there is no remedy but death. Who knows? . . . I was almost born with it, and perhaps I shall die with it. Well then, this little priestling, who could not help me nor convert me, is now, without a doubt, pushing my daughter, your daughter, our daughter, toward the convent, so that there she may pray for me, so that she may save me by sacrificing herself. . . ."

"But it is not a sacrifice . . . she says it is her vocation. . . ."

"That's not true, Antonia; it's a lie. Most of those who become nuns, do so to escape work, to lead a poor, but easy life, a mystic *siesta*. Either that, or they are running away from home. Our daughter is running away from home, from us."

"It must be from you. . . ."

"Yes, she is running away from me. She has guessed my secret."

"And now that you have formed this attachment for that . . ."

"Do you mean to tell me that she is running away from him too?"

"From your capriciousness, your new caprice. . . ."

"Caprice? Caprice, you say? I am anything but capricious, Antonia. I take everything seriously, every-thing, do you understand?"

"Yes, too seriously," added the woman, dissolving into tears.

"Come now, don't cry, Antonia, my little saint, my good angel, and forgive me if I have said any-thing. . . ."

"What you say isn't the worst, it's what you don't say."

"Listen, for God's sake, Antonia, for God's sake, see to it that our daughter doesn't leave us. If she goes into a convent, it will kill me; yes, it will kill me, it will simply kill me. Make her stay here, and I will do whatever she wants . . . if she wants me to send Abelín away, to dismiss him, I will do it. . . ."

"I remember when you said you were glad we had only the one daughter, because that way we did not have to divide our affections or spread them. . . ."

"But I don't divide them!"

"Something worse then. . . ."

"Antonia, our daughter wants to sacrifice herself for my sake, and she doesn't know that if she enters a convent she will leave me in despair. This house is her convent!"

XXVII

Two days later Joaquín took counsel in his study with his wife and daughter.

"Papa, it's God's will!" Joaquina said to him reso-lutely, gazing at him squarely.

"It isn't God who wills it, but that little priestling

of yours," her father replied. "How does a child like
you know what God wills? When have you communicated with Him?"

"I go to Communion every week, Father."

"And you think that the attacks of dizziness which
come from your fasting stomach are revelations from
God?"

"A fasting heart breeds worse delusions."

"This decision cannot stand. God doesn't will it,
He can't. I tell you He can't will it!"

"I don't know what God wants, but you, Father,
know what He doesn't want, is that it? You may know
a good deal about things of the body, but about things
of God, of the soul . . ."

"Of the soul is it? So you think I know nothing of
the soul?"

"Perhaps you know something it would be better
not to know."

"Are you accusing me?"

"No. It is you, Father, who accuse yourself."

"You see, Antonia, do you see, didn't I tell you?"

"And what did he tell you, Mama?"

"Nothing, my child, nothing. Suspicions and imag-
inings of your father. . . ."

"Well, then," exclaimed Joaquín, like a man who
has come to a decision, "you are entering a convent
in order to save me, isn't that true?"

"Perhaps you are not too far from the truth."

"And what is it you want to save me from?"

"I am not sure."

"Would I know? . . . From what, from whom?"

"From whom, Father, from whom? Why, from the
devil or from yourself."

"And what do you know about it?"

"For God's sake, Joaquín, for God's sake . . . ,"

Antonia's voice was tearful; she was frightened by her husband's tone and appearance.

"Leave us, Antonia, leave us alone, the two of us. This does not concern you!"

"How can it not concern me? . . . She is my daughter. . . ."

"She's mine, you mean! She's a Monegro, and I'm a Monegro. Leave us. You don't understand, you couldn't understand these things. . . ."

"Father, if you continue to treat Mother in this way in front of me, I am leaving. Don't cry, Mother."

"But do you believe, my daughter? . . ."

"What I believe, and know, is that I am as much his daughter as yours."

"As much?"

"Perhaps more."

"Don't talk like that, for God's sake," the mother burst out, in tears, "if you go on I will leave the room."

"That would be best," added the daughter. "Alone, we would be better able to see each other's faces, or rather, souls, we Monegros."

The mother paused to kiss her daughter before leaving the room.

"Well now," began the father coldly, as soon as he found himself alone with his daughter, "to save me from what or from whom are you going to a convent?"

"From whom or from what I don't know, Father; I know only that you must be saved. I don't know either what is wrong in this house, between you and my mother, I don't know what is wrong with you, but there is certainly something wrong. . . ."

"Did the little priestling tell you that?"

"No, the little priestling did not tell me that; he hasn't had to tell me; no one has told me, I have simply breathed it in since I was born. Here in this house we live as if in spiritual darkness!"

"Nonsense! That's something you've read in a book!"

"Just as you have read other things in your books. Or do you really believe that only those books which deal with the insides of the body, those books of yours with the ugly illustrations, are the ones to teach the truth?"

"Very well. And this spiritual darkness which you talk about, what is it?"

"You should know better than I, Father. In any case, don't deny that something is taking place here, that a sadness hangs over us like a black cloud and penetrates everywhere, that you are never satisfied and are suffering, as if you bore a great weight on your back. . . ."

"Yes; original sin," said Joaquín maliciously.

"Truer than you think," answered his daughter. "You haven't yet expiated it."

"I was baptized. . . ."

"That doesn't make any difference."

"And as a remedy for all this you propose to stick yourself in a nunnery, is that it? Well, the first thing to have done would have been to find out what the cause was. . . ."

"God forbid that I should judge you and my mother."

"But you don't object to condemning me?"

"Condemn you?"

"Yes, condemn me; your going off in this fashion is a condemnation. . . ."

"What if I went off with a husband? If I left you for a man? . . ."

"It would depend on the man."

There was a brief silence.

"The truth is, my daughter, I am not well," Joaquín resumed. "I do suffer, I have been suffering nearly all my life. There is a good deal of truth in what you have guessed. Nevertheless, your decision to become a nun is the finishing blow, it exacerbates and heightens my pain. Have compassion on your father, your bedeviled father. . . ."

"It's from compassion . . ."

"No, it's from egotism. You're running away. You see me suffer and you run away. It's egotism, indifference, lack of affection which leads you to the cloister. Suppose I had a contagious and prolonged disease, leprosy for example, would you leave me to go off to the convent and pray to God to cure me? . . . Come now, answer, would you leave me?"

"No, I wouldn't leave you; I'm your only child, after all."

"Well, imagine that I am a leper. Stay and cure me. I'll place myself in your care, and do what you order."

"If that's the way it is . . ."

The father rose and gazed an instant at his daughter through his tears before he embraced her. Then, holding her in his arms he whispered in her ear:

"Do you want to cure me, my daughter?"

"Yes, Papa."

"Then marry Abelín."

"What!" exclaimed the girl, detaching herself from her father and staring into his face.

"Does it surprise you?" stammered the father, surprised in his turn.

"Me, marry Abelín, the son of your enemy? . . . "

"Who called him that?"

342

"Your silence through the years."

"Well, that's the reason—because he is the son of the man you call my enemy."

"I don't know what there is between you, I don't want to know, but lately . . . seeing how you grew attached to his son, I became frightened, I feared . . . I don't know what. To me your affection for Abelín seemed monstrous, something infernal. . . ."

"No, my daughter, it was not that. In him I sought redemption. And believe me, if you succeed in bringing him into my house, if you make him my son, it will be as if the sun were at last to shine in my soul. . . ."

"But do you, my father, want me to court him, to solicit him?"

"I don't say that."

"Well, then? . . ."

"If he . . ."

"Ah, so you already had it planned between the two of you, without consulting me?"

"No, I hadn't thought it out, I, your father, your poor father, I . . ."

"You grieve me, Father."

"I grieve myself. And now I am responsible for everything. Weren't you thinking of sacrificing yourself for me?"

"That's true, yes, I will sacrifice myself for you. Ask whatever you like of me!"

The father went to kiss her, but she, breaking away from him, exclaimed:

"No, not now! When you deserve it. Or do you want me, too, to quiet you with kisses?"

"Where did you hear that, Daughter?"

"Walls have ears."

"And accusing tongues!"

XXVIII

"Ah, to be you, Don Joaquín," said the poor disinherited Aragonese father of five to Joaquín one day, after he had succeeded in extracting some money from his benefactor.

"You want to be me! I don't understand."

"Yes, I would give everything to be you, Don Joaquín."

"What is this 'everything' you would give, now?"

"Everything I can give, everything I have."

"And what is that?"

"My life!"

"Your life to be me!" To himself Joaquín added: "I would give my own to be someone else entirely!"

"Yes, my life in order to be you."

"This is something I can't very well understand, my friend. I can't understand anyone's being ready to give up their life to be someone else. To be someone else is to cease to be oneself, to cease to be the person one is."

"Doubtless so."

"Which is the same as ceasing to exist."

"Doubtless."

"And with no guarantee of becoming another . . ."

"Doubtless. What I mean to say, Don Joaquín, is that I would cease to exist, with a very good will, or more clearly, that I would put a bullet in my head or throw myself in the river, if I could be sure that my family, who keep me tied to this miserable life, who don't allow me to take my life, would find a father in you. Don't you understand now?"

"Yes I do understand. So that . . ."

". . . what a wretched bit of attachment I have to

this life! I would be very glad to give up being myself and to kill off my memories, if it were not for my family. Although, in truth, there is something else which restrains me, too."

"What?"

"The fear that my memories, my story, my history might accompany me beyond death. Ah, to be you!"

"And suppose motives just like your own, my friend, keep me alive?"

"Impossible, you're rich."

"Rich . . . rich . . ."

"A rich man never has cause for complaint. You lack nothing. A wife, a daughter, a good practice and reputation . . . what more could you want? You weren't disinherited by your father, you weren't put out of your house to beg by your brother. You weren't obliged to become a beggar! Ah, to be you, Don Joaquín!"

When Don Joaquín found himself alone later he said to himself: "Ah, to be me! That man actually envies me, he envies *me*! And I, who would I like to be?"

XXIX

A FEW DAYS later Abelín and Joaquina were betrothed. And, in the *Confession*, dedicated to his daughter, Joaquín wrote not long afterwards:

It is scarcely possible, my daughter, to explain to you how I brought Abel, your present husband, to the point of proposing to you. I had to make him think you were in love with him or at least wanted him to be in love with you; I had to do this without the slightest hint of the talk you and I had held when your mother told me you wanted to enter a convent for my sake. I saw my salvation in this marriage. Only by linking your fate with that of young Abel, the son of the man who had poisoned the fountain of my life, only by mixing our two blood lines could there be any hope for my salvation.

And yet, it occurred to me that perhaps your children, my grandchildren, the children of his children, his grandchildren, the heirs to our blood, might some day find themselves warring within themselves, bearing hatred in their seed. Still, I thought, isn't hatred toward oneself, toward one's very blood brother, the only remedy against hating others? The Scripture says that Esau and Jacob were already fighting in the womb of Rebecca. Who knows but that some day you will conceive twins, one with my blood and the other with his and that they will hate each other and fight, beginning in your womb, before coming out into the air and into consciousness. This is the human tragedy, and like Job, every man is a child of contradictions.

And I have trembled to think that I had perhaps joined you together, not for a union of your blood, but instead to separate the two lines even more and perpetuate a hatred. Forgive me! . . . I am prey to a certain delirium.

But it is not only my blood and his that are involved; there is also Helena's. . . . The blood of Helena! This is what most disturbs me: the blood which blooms in her cheeks, her forehead, her lips, that sets off her glance; that blinded me through the tissue of her skin!

And then there is another blood line . . . Antonia's; the blood of the unfortunate Antonia, your blessed

346

mother. This blood is like baptismal water. It is the blood of redemption. Only your mother's blood, Joaquina, can save your children, our grandchildren. It is this spotless blood which can redeem us.

Antonia must never see this journal; she must not see it. Let her leave this world, if she outlives me, without having more than guessed at our mystery— and our corruptibility.

The betrothed quickly grew to understand and appreciate each other and to feel genuine affection. They came to realize that each was a victim of his own home, and of their individual ambience, both unfortunate: the one home frivolous and unfeeling, the other impassioned and stifling. They both sought support in Antonia. They felt a profound impulse to establish a home, a center of serene and self-sufficient love, of love which would be all-encompassing and would not romantically fix its gaze elsewhere or moon after other loves; their need was for a castle of solitude, where love could unite the two unfortunate families. They would make Abel, the painter, come to realize that the intimate life of the home is an imperishable reality of which art is but a bright reflection, when it is not a shadow. They would show Helena that perpetual youth is the property of the spirit able to submerge itself in the vital current of the family and its inheritance. Joaquín would be made to realize that although name and identity are lost with the loss of one's blood they are lost only to be joined in the new name and the new blood.

Antonia did not need to be shown anything for she was a woman who had been born to live in the sweetness of custom.

Joaquín did in fact undergo a rebirth. He spoke of his old friend Abel with emotion and affection, and even confessed that it had been a stroke of good fortune to have lost Helena once and for all through Abel's intervention.

Once when he and his daughter were alone, he told her: "Now that everything seems to be taking a different and better turn, I can speak quite frankly. I did, at one time, love Helena. Or, at least I thought I did, and I courted her, to no avail. And the truth is she never gave me the slightest reason to hope for anything. Then I introduced her to Abel, who will now be your father-in-law, your second father, and the two of them were immediately drawn together. I took the entire episode as an affront, a mortal insult. . . . But what right did I have to her?"

"That's true. But men are like that in their demands."

"You're right, Daughter. I have acted like a madman, brooding upon a fancied insult, an imagined betrayal. . . ."

"Is that all, Father?"

"How do you mean, is that all?"

"Is that all there was to it, nothing more?"

"To my knowledge . . . no!" But as he said this, he closed his eyes and was unable to control the beating of his heart.

"Now you will be married," he went on, "and you will live with me. Yes, you will live with me, and I will make your husband—my new son—a great doctor, an artist in medicine, a complete artist, who at the very least will equal his father's fame."

"And he will record your work as he has told me."

"Yes, he will write what I have not been able to. . . ."

"He has told me that your career has demonstrated

genius and that you have developed practices and made discoveries. . . ."

"Adulation on his part. . . ."

"He has told me privately. You are not known, not esteemed at your true worth, and he wants to write this account so that your work will become known."

"High time, at that. . . ."

"If fortune is good, it's never too late."

"Ah, Daughter, if instead of burying myself in patients, in this cursed practice which doesn't allow time to breathe or learn, if instead I had devoted my-self to pure science, to research, the discovery for which Dr. Alvarez y García is so much lauded would have been my work, for I was on the verge of develop-ing it. But this business of working for a living . . ."

"We weren't in straits, you didn't have to do it."

"Yes, but . . . I don't know. Anyway, it's all past now and a new life begins. Now I shall give up my practice."

"Really and truly?"

"Yes, I shall give it over to your future husband, and simply keep an eye on how it goes. I shall lend him a guiding hand, and I will devote myself to my own work. We will all live together, and make an-other life. I can begin to live again and I will be another man, another person. . . ."

"What a pleasure it is to hear you talk this way, Father. At last!"

"Does it please you to hear that I shall be another person?"

Joaquín's daughter looked at him closely as she sensed the undertones implicit in the question.

"Does it make you happy to hear that I shall be someone else?" the father asked the girl again.

"Yes, Father, it makes me happy!"

"In other words, the actual person, the person that I really am, strikes you as unfortunate?"

"And how does it strike you, Father?" the girl asked him resolutely, in her turn.

"Oh, don't let me say any more," he cried out.

And his daughter stopped his mouth with a kiss.

XXX

"You already know why I've come," Abel said to Joaquín as soon as they were alone in Joaquín's office.

"Yes, I know. Your son has announced your visit."

"My son and soon yours. You don't know how happy it makes me. This is the way our friendship should culminate. My son is now nearly yours too. He already loves you as he would a father, and not just as a teacher. I'm ready to say he loves you more than he does me. . . ."

"No, no, not that. Don't say that."

"And what of it? Do you think I am jealous? I am incapable of jealousy. And listen, Joaquín, if there was something standing between us before . . ."

"Please, Abel, don't say any more about . . ."

"I must. Now that our two bloodlines will be united, now that my son is to become yours, and your daughter is to become mine, we must settle that old score. We must be absolutely frank."

"No, no, nothing of the kind. And if you talk of it I'll leave."

"All right, then. But in any case I shall not forget what you said about my work the night you spoke at the supper."

"I wish you wouldn't talk about that either."

"About what shall I talk then?"

"Nothing of the past; nothing. Let's talk only about the future. . . ."

"Well, if you and I, at our age, are not to talk of the past, what are we to talk of? Why, we haven't anything left but the past."

"Don't say that," Joaquín almost cried out.

"We can't live now except from memories."

"Abel, please be quiet."

"And if the truth were known, it's better to live from memories than from hopes. The former have some basis in fact, but the latter . . . one cannot even know whether they'll ever be."

"But let's not go over our past," Joaquín insisted.

"We can talk of our children, then; in short, of our hopes."

"That's it. Let's talk of them, rather than of ourselves. . . ."

"In you my boy will have a teacher and a father. . . ."

"In any case, I hope to leave him my practice, give him at least those patients who are willing to make the change and whom I have already prepared for it. In serious cases I will be there to assist."

"Wonderful. Thank you, thank you."

"Then I will also give Joaquina a dowry. But they will live with me."

"My son has already told me. Still, I think it would be better if they had their own home: there is no house big enough for two families."

351

"No, I cannot be apart from my daughter."

"But you think we can live apart from our son, is that it?"

"You already live apart from him. . . . A man scarcely lives at home, a woman scarcely lives outside it. And I need my daughter."

"All right then. . . . You see how amenable I am."

"This house will be yours, and Helena's. . . ."

"I appreciate your hospitality. It's something understood between us."

There followed a long discussion in which they arranged everything which concerned their two children's establishment as a family. When it was time to separate, Abel offered Joaquín his hand in a gesture of complete sincerity; he looked at his friend's eyes, and from the depths of his heart cried "Joaquín!" Tears came to the eyes of the doctor as he took the proffered hand.

At the end of a long moment Abel said: "I haven't seen you cry since we were boys, Joaquín."

"We shan't be boys again, Abel."

"And that's the worst of it."

And they took leave of each other.

XXXI

THE SUN, albeit an autumn sun, seemed to warm Joaquín's cold house following the marriage of his daughter. Joaquín himself seemed to quicken and come alive. He began to transfer his patients to the care of his son-in-law; serious cases he kept under his own care, and he let it be known that he acted in a consultative capacity in all matters.

The young Abel, Abelín, using the notes he had gotten from his father-in-law (whom he now called Father, addressing him familiarly) and availing himself of the oral help of the doctor, had launched on the compilation of the volume which set forth the medical work of Joaquín Monegro. The youth had approached his subject with a veneration which would not have been possible on the part of the doctor himself. "It is better this way," Joaquín thought, "to have someone else write this account, as Plato did for Socrates." He himself could not, in good conscience and without seeming presumptuous and avid for the unattainable applause of posterity, detail his knowledge and skill. He would reserve his literary energies for other endeavors.

And it was at this point that he began the serious composition of his *Confession*, the intimate account of his struggle with the passion which consumed his life, the struggle against the demon which had possessed him from the first stirrings of awareness to the present moment. He wrote the account so that after his death his daughter might know of his effort. He addressed the narrative to his daughter; but he was so permeated with the profound tragedy of his life of passion, so self-centered in the story of it, that he entertained the hope that his daughter, or his grandchildren, would one day make the narrative known to the world, to a world which would be seized with both wonder and horror at this darkly afflicted hero who had lived and died in its midst without revealing the depths of his suffering to those around him. For the truth was that Joaquín thought of himself as an exceptional spirit and, as such, more tormented and prone to pain than anyone else, a spirit marked by God with the sign of those predestined to greatness.

My life, dear daughter, has been one long passion —he wrote in the *Confession*—*and yet I would not have exchanged it for another. I have hated as no one else ever has, for I have felt more than anyone the supreme injustices of the world's favors. The way the parents of your husband acted toward me was neither human nor noble; what they did was infamous; but even worse, much worse, were the acts of every human being upon whom I have relied for love and support since the days of my childhood when I trusted everyone. Why have they rejected me? Why do they prefer the light-headed, the fickle, the egotists? My life has been made bitter by these people. And I have realized that the world is naturally unjust, and that I have not been born among my own. That was my chief misfortune, not to have been born among my own. The vulgarity, the common baseness of those surrounding me, led me to my downfall.*

At the same time that he put together his *Confession*, he was preparing, in case the first effort did not come to fruition, another literary endeavor which would make him eligible for the pantheon of immortals of his people and caste. The second work would be titled *Memoirs of an Aging Doctor*, would be the harvest of a knowledge of the world, of passions, of life, joy and sadness, even of secret crimes, in short, the harvest he had gathered in his years of medical practice. It would be a mirror to life, but revealing the very entrails, the darkest corners of it; a descent into the abysses of human vileness. Into the book he would pour his soul, without speaking of himself; in it, by way of denuding the souls of others, he would denude his own; in it he would take vengeance on the vile world in which he had been forced to exist. When people saw themselves thus exposed and naked they would at first be astounded, but in the end they would admire and respect the author of the exposure; and in it, in this book, he would paint the definitive portraits—their names slightly altered in fictional guise—of Abel and Helena, and these portraits would be the ones to stand for all time. His portrait of that pair would be worth all the portraits Abel had ever painted. And Joaquín savored the satisfaction of knowing that if he were successful in creating this literary portrayal of Abel Sánchez he would immortalize his subject more surely than all Abel's own painting would do, so that critics and commentators in a remote time would easily discover the actual person of the painter as soon as they penetrated the thin veil of fiction.

"Yes, Abel," Joaquín told himself, "your best opportunity of attaining what you have so long struggled for, the only thing for which you have striven, the only thing which interests you, for which you denigrated me, and even worse, ignored me, the best chance you have to perpetuate your memory does not lie with your paintings but rather with me, with whether or not I succeed in painting you just as you are, with my pen. And I will succeed, because I know you, because I have withstood you, because you have burdened me all my life. I shall unmask you for all time, and you will no longer be Abel Sánchez, but whatever name I give you. And when you are spoken of as the painter of your paintings, people will say rather: 'Ah, yes, that character of Joaquín Monegro's.' For in that sense you will be my creation, and you will live only as my work lives, and your name will follow along the ground behind me, dragged along in the mud at my heels, as the names of those put in the Inferno were dragged along by Dante. And you will be the perfect symbol of the envious man."

Of the envious man! For Joaquín persisted in believing that whatever passion animated Abel beneath his apparently impassive exterior of egotist, whatever feeling moved him was based on envy, his particular type of envy, and that from envy he had usurped, even as a child, the affection of playmates from Joaquín, and from envy had taken Helena from him later. And yet, why then had Abel allowed his own son to be taken away from him? "Ah," Joaquín told himself, "he simply is less concerned with the boy than with the renown of his own name. He doesn't believe in living on in his blood descendants, but only in those who admire his paintings, and he abandons his son to me so he may enjoy fame without competition from someone else with his name. But I shall unmask him."

He was disquieted by his age as he took up the writing of these *Memoirs*, for he had already reached his fifty-fifth year. Still, had not Cervantes begun his *Quixote* in his fifty-seventh year? And he bethought himself of all the other authors who had written their masterpieces after having passed his present age. Moreover, he felt strong, complete master of his mind and will, rich in experience, mature in judgment, his deep feelings and passion—which had been aroused for so many years—subdued and yet ebullient.

Now, in order to complete the work, he would hold himself steadily in check. Poor Abel, what a fate awaited him! He began to feel scorn and compassion for the painter. He looked upon him as a model and as a victim; he studied and observed him carefully, though the opportunity to do so was not very great, for Abel came very seldom to visit his son in his new home.

"Your father must be very busy," Joaquín would say to his son-in-law; "he scarcely shows up here. Does he have some complaint against us, I wonder? Have we offended him, Antonia, or my daughter, or I, in some way? I would regret it if . . ."

"No, no, Father" (for Abelín now addressed his father-in-law in this manner), "it is nothing of that sort. He doesn't stay at home either. Haven't I told you that he is not interested in anything but his own affairs, and these affairs center around his paintings and whatever . . ."

"No, Son, don't exaggerate, there must be something else."

"No, that's all there is to it."

And, in order to hear the same explanation again, Joaquín would ask the same question again.

"How does it happen," he would ask Helena, "how does it happen Abel doesn't come here?"

"Oh, he is the same about going anywhere!" she would reply. For Helena, on the other hand, did visit her daughter-in-law at her home.

XXXII

"BUT TELL ME," Joaquín said to his son-in-law one day, "why did it never occur to your father to train you in painting, to stir your interest in that direction?"

"I've never cared for it."

357

"That's beside the point. It would seem natural for him to have wanted to initiate you in his art. . . ."

"On the contrary, he was annoyed whenever I showed any interest in it. He never urged me or encouraged me to do even what other children do as a matter of course, to make drawings and figures."

"That's strange, very strange. And yet . . ."

The young Abel was disturbed by the expression on his father-in-law's face, by the unnatural glare in his eyes. He felt that something writhed within him, something painful which he wished to be rid of, some poisonous secretion. And Joaquín's words were followed by a silence charged with bitterness, a silence which Joaquín broke by saying:

"I simply do not understand why he did not wish to make you into a painter. . . ."

"No, he simply did not want me to be what he was. . . ."

Another silence followed, which Joaquín again suddenly broke, as if with heavy regret and with the air of a man who has decided to make a clean breast of things:

"By heaven, I do understand it!"

Young Abel was shaken, without knowing well why, by the tone with which his father-in-law uttered these words. "Why then . . . ?" he asked.

"No, nothing." Joaquín appeared to have recovered and withdrawn into himself.

"But you must tell me," the youth exclaimed, using the familiar form of address again, as if talking to a friend—a friend or an accomplice. He was fearful, nevertheless, of hearing what he asked to hear.

"No, no, I don't want you to say later . . ."

"This way it's worse, Father, than telling me directly, whatever it is. Besides, I think I already know. . . ."

"What . . . ?" Joaquín asked, directing a piercing glance at his son-in-law.

"That he perhaps feared I would some day eclipse him, his own name. . . ."

"Yes," said Joaquín in a wrathful voice, "that's it exactly. Abel Sánchez the son, or Abel Sánchez the Younger—that he could not stand. And that later he should be remembered as your father rather than you remembered as his son. This is a tragedy which has happened more than once within a family. . . . For a son to outshine his father . . ."

"But that is simply . . . ," Abel broke off.

"That is simply envy, Son, envy pure and simple."

"Envy of a son! . . . On the part of a father?"

"Yes, and that is the most natural kind. Envy cannot exist between two persons who scarcely know each other. A man from another country or another time is not envied. The outsider, the foreigner is not envied, only the man from the same town; not the man of an older generation, but the contemporary, the companion. And the greatest envy is between brothers. Witness the legend of Cain and Abel. . . . Certainly the most terrible jealousy is that of a man who thinks his brother desires his wife, the sister-in-law. . . . And then there is the jealousy between fathers and sons. . . ."

"But what of the difference in age in this case?"

"It makes no difference. The fact that a being whom we created should come to obscure our own existence proves too much."

"And between master and disciple, then . . . ?"

Joaquín remained silent. For a moment he fixed his

gaze on the floor; then he spoke, as if to the ground beneath his feet:

"Decidedly, envy is a form of family relation." And he added: "But let us talk of something else; and forget all this as if it had never been spoken. Do you hear?"

"No!"

"How do you mean, no?"

"I mean I did not hear what you said before."

"I wish neither of us might have heard it."

XXXIII

H E L E N A   W A S in the habit of going to her daughter-in-law's home with the purpose of introducing there, in this bourgeois home lacking in distinction, a more refined tastefulness, a touch of greater elegance, or so she thought. She took it upon herself to correct, according to her lights, the deficiencies in the education of poor Joaquina, who had been brought up by a father filled with an unreasoning arrogance and an unfortunate mother who had to bear with a man rejected by another woman. And every day she expounded some lesson in manners and smart taste.

"All right, just as you wish." Antonia was always agreeable.

Joaquina's reaction was different: though she burned inwardly, she resigned herself; nevertheless, she felt that some day she would rebel; if she restrained herself, it was because of her husband's entreaties.

"It will be as *you* wish," she said once, emphasizing the formal form of address which she had never ceased to use with Helena; "I don't understand these matters, nor do they concern me. In all this, it will be as you please. . . ."

"But it is not as I please, Daughter, but simply a matter of . . ."

"It's all the same! I have been brought up in this house, a doctor's house, and when it's a question of hygiene, of health, or when later the child comes, and it's a question of raising it, I know what must be done; but now, in these niceties which you call matters of taste and refinement I must submit to one who has been formed in the house of an artist."

"But you mustn't get yourself into this state. . . ."

"Not at all, it's not that I get into a state. It's simply that you are always throwing it in our faces that what we do should not be done our way but some other way. After all, we are not arranging evening parties or tea dances."

"I don't know where you have picked up this pretended scorn. . . . Yes, pretended, I say it's pretended. . . ."

"I have not said anything to indicate, madame . . ."

"This pretended, this feigned scorn of all good form, of all social convention. A fine fix we would be in without them! . . . It would be utterly impossible to live!"

*   *   *

Joaquina had been advised by both her father and her husband to take long walks, to expose her flesh and blood which was forming the flesh and blood of the coming child to the sun and air. Since the two men could not always accompany her and Antonia did not like to leave the house, Helena was usually the one to go with her. The mother-in-law was pleased to take these walks, to have Joaquina at her side like a younger sister (which was what people who did not know them took her to be), to overshadow her with the splendid beauty which the years had left intact. Beside her, her daughter-in-law was effaced, and Helena remained the object of the insistent stares of the passersby. Joaquina's attraction was of a completely different sort: it was a charm to be relished slowly by the eyes. Helena, on the other hand, dressed herself to dazzle the gaze of anyone who might be distracted. "I'll take the mother!" a passing young gallant provocatively murmured one day at Helena's side as he heard her call Joaquina "Daughter"; the older woman breathed more heavily, moistening her lips with the tip of her tongue.

"Listen, Daughter," she would tell Joaquina, "you must do your best to hide your condition. It is very unbecoming for a girl to let it be seen she is pregnant. It looks like a bit of stubborn brazenness."

"I'm simply trying to be as comfortable as possible, and not pay any attention to what people think or don't think. . . . Even though I am in 'an interesting condition,' as ridiculous people say, I don't pretend I am interesting or interested, in their sense, no matter what other women may have done while in this condition. I am not concerned. . . ."

"Well, you have to be concerned. You live in the world."

"And what difference does it make if people *do* know? . . . Or don't you want them to know, Mother, that you are on your way to becoming a grandmother?"

Helena was piqued both by the insinuation and the thought; but she controlled herself. "Well, listen, as far as age is concerned . . ."

"Yes, as far as age is concerned, you could be a mother all over again," said Joaquina, wounding the other woman to the quick.

"Yes, of course," said Helena, choked and surprised, disarmed by the sharp attack on her. "But the idea that they should see you . . ."

"No, you can rest easy on that score, because it's you they look at rather than me. People remember that wonderful portrait of you, that work of art. . . ."

"Well, if I were in your place . . . ," began her mother-in-law.

"You in my place, Mother? And supposing you could join me in this same condition, would you?"

"Look, if you go on in this vein, we will return to the house at once, and I shall never go out with you again, nor set foot in your house, in your father's house, that is. . . ."

"My house, madame, mine, and my husband's . . . and yours, too!"

"Where in heaven's name have you gotten this temper of yours?"

"Temper, is it? Ah, of course, temperament belongs only to artists."

"Oho, listen to our harmless little mouse, the one who was going to become a nun before her father hooked my son for her. . . ."

"I have already asked you, madame, not to repeat this lie. I know well enough what I did."

"And my son does too."

"Yes, he too knows what he has done. And let's not talk of it again."

XXXIV

A N D T H E S O N of young Abel and Joaquina, in whom was mingled the blood of Abel Sánchez and Joaquín Monegro, was born into the world.

The first battle occurred over the name which should be given the child. The mother wanted the boy to be called Joaquín; Helena wanted his name to be Abel. The decision was left to Joaquín by Abel, by his son Abelín, and by Antonia. A veritable struggle took place thereupon in the soul of Monegro; the simple task of naming a new human being took on for him the character of a fateful augury, a magical determination; it was as if the future of the new spirit were being decided.

"His name should be Joaquín, the same as mine; after a while it would be written Joaquín S. Monegro, and eventually the S. would be left out, the S. which was the only remnant of the Sánchez, and *his* name, his son's name and his entire line would be absorbed into mine. . . . And yet, wouldn't it be better if his name were Abel Monegro, Abel S. Monegro, so that the Abel might be thus redeemed? Abel is his grandfather, but an Abel is also his father, my son-in-law, who has now become the same as a real son to me, my own Abel whom I have created. And what difference does it make if the new child is called Abel, if his other grandfather will not be remembered as Abel but as whatever I call him in my fictional memoirs, by whatever name I brand on his forehead? . . . But then again, . . ."

And while he thus wavered, it was Abel Sánchez the painter who finally decided the issue:

"Let him be called Joaquín. Abel the grandfather,

Abel the father, Abel the son, three Abels. . . . It's just too much. Besides, I don't like the name; it's the name of a victim. . . ."

"You were glad to give the name to your own son," Helena objected.

"It was your idea, and rather than make any objection . . . But imagine what would have happened if instead of taking up medicine he had become a painter. . . . Abel Sánchez the Elder and Abel Sánchez the Younger. . . ."

"And there cannot be more than one Abel Sánchez," interposed Joaquín, amused to have been proven so completely right in his conjecture.

"As far as I am concerned there could be a hundred of them," replied Abel. "I would always be myself."

"Who could doubt it?" asked his friend.

"An end to it, let him be called Joaquín. It's decided!"

"And let him not take up painting, eh?"

"Nor medicine either," Abel concluded, pretending to follow along with the pretended jest.

And the child was called Joaquín.

XXXV

THE NEWBORN child's grandmother Antonia, who was the one to take care of it, would hug the infant to her breast as if to protect it from some imagined danger and whisper: "Sleep, my child, sleep, for the more you sleep the better, especially in this house, where it is better to be asleep than awake, and you will grow strong and healthy, and let us pray God that the two warring bloods do not quarrel; for otherwise what will become of you?"

And the child grew; he grew along with the written pages of the *Confession* and the *Memoirs* of his maternal grandfather, and with the artistic fame of his paternal grandfather. Abel's reputation as a painter was never greater than it now became; and he, for his part, seemed to occupy himself very little with whatever did not deal with this fame.

One morning, when he saw his grandchild sleeping in its cradle, he fixed his gaze on the infant with more than usual intensity and exclaimed: "What a beautiful study this would make!" And taking out a notebook he set about making a pencil sketch of the sleeping child.

"What would you call a finished drawing of such a subject?" Joaquín asked him. "A study of innocence?"

"The habit of giving titles to paintings is peculiar to the literati; something like the doctors' habit of giving names to diseases they can't cure."

"And whoever told you that the real purpose of medicine was to cure illnesses?"

"What is it then?"

"Knowledge, a knowledge of disease. The end of all science is knowledge."

"I had thought it was knowledge in order to cure. What use otherwise our having tasted the fruit of the tree of the knowledge of good and evil, if not to free ourselves of the evil?"

"And the end of art, what is it? What is the end purpose of this sketch you have just made of our grandchild?"

"That is its own end; it contains its purpose. It is an object of beauty and that's enough."

Chapter XXXVI

"What is the beautiful object, your sketch or our grandchild?"

"Both of them!"

"Do you perhaps think that your drawing is more beautiful than the little Joaquín?"

"Oh, now you're off on your mania! Joaquín, Joaquín!"

Antonia the grandmother came and took the child from its cradle and carried it off, as if to defend it from each of the grandfathers. Meanwhile she whispered to him: "Ah, my little one, my little one, my sweet lamb, sun of this house, pure sweet angel, let them leave you alone, and not draw you or treat you! Don't you be a model for any painter, or a patient for any doctor. . . . Let them have their art and their science, and you come with your grandmother, my little pet, my tiny baby. You are my darling, my angel, the sunshine warming this house. I will show you how to pray for your two grandfathers, and God will hear you. Come with me, my little darling, you pure sweet lamb, little lamb of God." And Antonia would not even stop to glance at Abel's sketch of the child, nor did she care to see it.

XXXVI

J O A Q U Í N   A N X I O U S L Y followed, with his sickly anxiety, the growth in body and spirit of his grandson Joaquinito. Whom did he take after? Whom did he resemble? Which family was uppermost in him? He watched him all the more anxiously once he began to talk.

Joaquín was disturbed that the other grandfather, Abel, spent more and more time in his house, his son's house, now that the grandchild had been born, and he was amazed that the painter also saw to it that the child was frequently brought to his own home. Abel, that great and grandiose egotist—for such did his own son and his fellow parent-in-law consider him— seemed to have become intensely human, even somewhat like a child himself, in the presence of the newborn. He soon began to make drawings especially for the child, and gradually these began to delight the young Joaquín. "Little grandfather, Abelito, make saints!" And Abel never tired of drawing dogs, cats, horses, bulls, human figures. The child would ask for a horseman one time, two boys boxing another time, a boy running away from a dog which ran after him, or a repetition of all the previous scenes.

"Never in all my life have I been happier to do something," Abel said. "This is pure pleasure; the rest is nonsense."

"You can put together an album of drawings for children," Joaquín added.

"No, there would be no charm in that, not for children. . . . That wouldn't be art, but rather . . ."

"Pedagogy," interposed Joaquín.

"It would be that, whatever else it might be, but certainly not art. This is most like art, these drawings which our grandchild will tear up within half an hour."

"And if I were to save them?"

"Save them? What for?"

"I've heard of a book recently published containing drawings of this type which added greatly to the artist's reputation."

"I'm not making these drawings for publication, do

you understand? And as regards reputation, which is one of your great preoccupations, you might as well know that I don't give a fig for it."

"Hypocrite! Why, it's the only thing that really does concern you. . . ."

"The only thing? It doesn't seem possible that you should accuse me of that. What concerns me now is this child, and that he may become a great artist."

"That he may inherit your genius, you mean?"

"And yours too."

The child watched the duel between his two grandfathers without comprehending, although he could guess at something amiss from their attitudes.

"What can be happening to my father," Abel's son asked Joaquín, "that he has become so crazy about his grandson? He never paid me the slightest attention. I don't recall, either, that he ever made me such drawings when I was a child."

"It's just that we are becoming old," Joaquín answered, "and age teaches one a great deal."

"The other day, when the child asked him some question or other, I even saw him conceal some tears. The first tears I've ever seen from him."

"Oh, that's merely a cardiac reaction."

"How?"

"The truth is that your father is worn by the years and by work, by the effort of artistic endeavor and by his emotions. In short, he has a very weak heart, and any day . . ."

"Any day what?"

"He will give you, that is to say us, a great shock. . . . I am actually glad that the occasion to tell you this has arrived. You might as well prepare your mother too."

"It's true he does complain of fatigue, of dyspnea. . . . Can it be . . . ?"

"Exactly. He has had me examine him without your knowledge, and I have done so. He needs attention."

And thus as soon as the weather began to get raw Abel stayed home and had the grandchild brought to him, a circumstance which embittered the other grandfather's entire day. "He is spoiling the child," Joaquín complained; "and he's trying to steal all his love; he wants to be first in his affection, and make up for all his son's affection for me. He is doing it for revenge, yes, for vengeance. He wants to take away this last consolation from me. It's always he, the same one who took away my friends when we were children."

Meanwhile, Abel was instructing the child to love his other grandfather.

"I love you more," the child said to him one time.

"No, no. You mustn't love me more. You must love all of us the same. First, mother and father, and then your grandparents, and each one the same. Your grandfather Joaquín is a very good man, he loves you very much, he buys you toys. . . ."

"You buy me toys too. . . ."

"He tells you stories. . . ."

"I like your drawings better. Will you make me a bull now, and a picador on horseback?"

XXXVII

ONE DAY Joaquín came to see Abel. "Look, Abel,"
Joaquín said grimly as soon as they were alone, "I've
come to talk to you about a serious matter, very serious, a matter of life and death."

"My illness?"

"No. But if you will, mine."

"Yours?"

"Yes, mine. I've come to talk to you about our
grandchild. Rather than beat about the bush, let me
say that I think you should go away, far enough so
that we don't see each other. I pray you, I beg you
to do this. . . ."

"I, go away? Are you mad? Why should I go
away?"

"The child loves you and not me. That's clear. I
don't know what you do to him. . . . I don't want to
know. . . ."

"I bewitch him, no doubt, or give him a potion. . . ."

"I don't know. Some perverse hold. . . . Those
damned drawings of yours exert a fascination, the
perversity of your diabolic art. . . ."

"The drawings are evil too, then? You're not well,
Joaquín."

"It may be that I am not well, but that no longer
matters. I am not at an age to be cured. And if I am
unwell, you should make allowances, show me some
consideration. . . . Listen, Abel, you made my youth
miserable, you have hounded me all my life. . . ."

"*I* have?"

"Yes, you, you."

"I never knew it, then."

"Don't pretend. You have always despised and denigrated me."

"Look, if you continue in this way, I am leaving the room, because you will make me really ill. You know well enough that I am not in a condition to listen to madness of this sort. Go away yourself, go to an institution where they can treat you or take care of you, and leave us alone."

"Abel, for the sole purpose of humiliating me, for the sole purpose of debasing me, you deprived me of Helena, you took her away from me. . . ."

"And haven't you had Antonia?"

"No, it was not for her sake you did it. It was an affront on your part, scorn, mockery. . . ."

"You're not well, Joaquín. I repeat, you are not well."

"You are worse off."

"As regards my body, that's true. I know I have not long to live. . . ."

"Too long."

"Ah, you want my death then?"

Joaquín's manner changed quickly. "No, Abel, no, I didn't say that." And then, with a plaintive note in his voice he added: "But please do go away from here. You can live somewhere else. Leave me the child . . . don't take him away from me . . . for the little time you have left. . . ."

"For the little time I have left then, let him stay with me."

"No, you pervert him with your tricks, you lure him away from me, you alienate him, you teach him to despise me. . . ."

"That's a lie! He has never heard from me, nor ever will, anything disparaging about you."

Chapter XXXVII

"It's sufficient that you sway him in some way, that you beguile him."

"And do you think that if I went away, that if I were to step out, he would therefore love you? Even if one wants to, Joaquín, it's impossible with you, it's impossible to love you. . . . You repel everyone, you reject them. . . ."

"You see, you see . . ."

"And if the boy does not love you as you want to be loved, to the exclusion of everyone else or more than anyone else is loved, it's because he senses the danger, because he fears . . ."

"What does he fear? . . ." hissed Joaquín, turning pale.

"The contagion of your bad blood."

It was then that Joaquín rose, livid with anger. He came at Abel, and his hands went out like two claws for the sick man's throat.

"You thief!" he shrieked.

He had scarce laid hands on the victim before he drew back in horror. Abel gave a cry, clasped his hands to his chest, and murmured, "I'm dying!"

"An angina attack," thought Joaquín, "there's nothing to be done. It's the end!"

At that moment he heard the voice of the grandson calling, "Grandfather, grandfather." Joaquín turned around.

He heard his own voice: "Whom are you calling? Which grandfather do you want? . . . Is it me you want?" The child was before him now, but was stricken dumb by the mystery lying there before him. "Come, tell me. Which grandfather were you calling? Was it me?"

The boy at length replied: "No. I was calling grandfather Abel."

"Abel was it? Well there you have him . . . dead. Do you know what that means, dead?"

Almost mechanically Joaquín raised the dead man's head and arranged his body in the armchair in which he had died. Then he turned to his grandson once more; he spoke in an unearthly voice:

"Yes, he's dead. And I killed him. Abel has been killed again by Cain, by your grandfather who is Cain. And now you have the power to kill me if you want. For he wanted to steal you away from me. He wanted to take away all your affections. And he has succeeded. . . . The fault was his." He was weeping now. "He wanted to rob me of you, who were the only consolation left for the poor Cain. Won't they leave Cain anything? Come to me now, and put your arms around me."

The child fled uncomprehending. He fled as if from a madman. And as he fled he called his grandmother Helena.

Alone, Joaquín continued to speak: "I killed him, but he was killing me. For over forty years he has been killing me. He poisoned all the walks of my life with his lording it over me, his triumphs and his celebrations. He wanted to steal the child from me. . . ."

On hearing hurried footsteps Joaquín took hold of himself and turned. It was Helena who entered.

"What has happened? . . . What does the child mean? . . ."

"Your husband's sickness has come to a fatal end," said Joaquín coldly.

"You!"

"I was not able to do anything. One is always too late in this type of case."

Helena fixed him with steady eyes: "You . . . It was you!"

Then, shaken and white, but maintaining her composure, she went to her dead husband's side.

XXXVIII

A YEAR PASSED during which Joaquín fell into a profound melancholy. He abandoned his *Memoirs*, and avoided seeing anyone, including his children. The death of Abel would have seemed a natural end to his gnawing disease, but a kind of blight had settled upon the house. For her part, Helena found that mourning and black suited her; she set about selling the remaining paintings left by her husband; she also seemed to have developed a certain aversion toward her small grandson. Meanwhile, another child had been born, so that there was now a granddaughter as well.

Joaquín himself was finally brought to bed by the onslaught of some obscure complaint. He felt himself slipping, at the boundary of death, and one day he summoned his family, his son-in-law's, his wife, and Helena.

"The child told you the truth," he blurted out at once, "it was I who killed Abel."

"Don't say such things, Father," his son-in-law pleaded.

"There's no time for either interruptions or falsehoods. I killed him. Or just as well killed him, for he died in my hands. . . ."

"That's another matter."

"He died when I seized him by the throat. It was all like a dream. My entire life has been a dream. But this was like a nightmare which happens just at the moment of waking, at dawn, between sleep and consciousness. I have not really lived nor slept . . . not even when awake. I no longer remember my parents; I don't want to remember them, and I trust that now that they are long dead, they have forgotten me. . . . And God, too, perhaps will forget me . . . in eternal forgetfulness perhaps there is peace. And you, too, my children, must forget me."

"That is not possible," exclaimed his son-in-law, and he took the doctor's hand and kissed it.

"Don't touch me! These are the hands which were at your father's throat when he died. Don't touch them. . . . But don't leave me yet. . . . Pray for me."

"Father, Father," cried his daughter, unable to say more.

"Why have I been so envious, so bad? What did I do to become that way? What mother's milk did I suck? Was there a philter, a potion of hate mixed with it? A potion in the blood? Why must I have been born into a country of hatred? Into a land where the precept seems to be: 'Hate thy neighbor as thyself.' For I have lived hating myself; and here we all live hating ourselves. Still . . . bring the child."

"Father!"

"Bring the child!"

When the child was brought, he had him come near: "Do you forgive me?" he asked.

"There is nothing to forgive," interrupted Abel.

"Tell him you do," said the child's mother. "Go to your grandfather and tell him you do."

"Yes . . . ," whispered the boy.

"Tell me clearly, my child, tell me you forgive me."

"Yes, I do," said the child innocently.

"That's it. It's only from you I need forgiveness, from you who have not yet reached the age of reason, who are still innocent. . . . And don't forget your grandfather, Abel, who made you drawings. Will you forget him?"

"No!"

"No, don't forget him, my child, don't forget him. . . . And you, Helena. . . ." Her gaze fixed before her, Helena was silent.

"And you, Helena . . . ," the dying man repeated.

"I, Joaquín, have forgiven you a long time ago."

"I didn't mean to ask you that. I only wanted to see you next to Antonia, Antonia. . . ."

That poor woman, her eyes swollen with tears, threw herself down on the bed by her husband as if seeking to protect him.

"It is you, Antonia, who have been the real victim. You could not cure me, you could not make me good. . . ."

"But you have been, Joaquín. . . . You have suffered so much!"

"Yes, from a phthisis, a tuberculosis of the soul. But you could not make me good because I have not loved you."

"Don't say that!"

"I do say it, I must say it, I say it here before everyone. I have not loved you. If I had loved you I would have been saved. I have not loved you, and now it pains me that this was so. If we could begin all over again. . . ."

"Joaquín, Joaquín!" cried the poor woman from the depths of her broken heart. "Don't say such things.

Have pity on me, have pity on your children, on the grandson who is listening to you even though he doesn't seem to understand, . . . perhaps tomorrow. . . ."

"That's why I've said it, out of pity. No, I have not loved you. I haven't wanted to love you. . . . If we were to start all over again! . . . Now, for it's now that . . ."

His wife did not let him finish. She covered his dying mouth with her own, as if she wished to recover his last breath.

"I will save you, this will save you, Joaquín."

"Save me? What do you call salvation?"

"You can still live a few more years, if you want to. . . ."

"What for? So as finally to grow old, really old? No, old age isn't worth it, egotistic old age is no more than a state of infancy with a consciousness of death. An old man is a child who knows he will die. No, no, I don't want to become an old man. I would fight with my grandchildren from pure jealousy. I would grow to hate them. . . . No, no . . . enough of hatred! I could have loved you, I should have loved you, it would have been my salvation, but I did not."

He fell silent. He could not, or did not want to continue. He kissed the members of his family. A few hours later he gave his last weary breath.

IT IS WRITTEN

How to Make a Novel

Prologue

Mihi quaestio factus sum

As I WRITE these lines, at the end of May 1927, nearing sixty-three years of age, here in Hendaye, on the very frontier with Spain, in my native Basque homeland, within tantalizing view of Fuenterrabía, I cannot recall without a shudder those infernal mornings of Paris loneliness in the winter of my summer of 1925, when in the little room in the pension at 2, rue de la Pérouse I was consumed in writing the narrative which follows. I hope never again to go through a more tragic experience of mind. I was revived only to be tortured anew with a delicious torture (Saint Teresa spoke of "delicious pain"), the torture of a desperate production, the kind which seeks to find salvation in work, and I think of how I felt—through every hour—"the tragic sense of life." Upon me I felt the weight of my entire life, which has been and is my death. I felt the weight not only of my sixty years of individual physical life, but more, much more than that: I felt the weight of centuries of a silent tradition borne in the innermost layers of my spirit, the weight of unspeakable and unconscious memories from the other side of the cradle. For our desperate unhoping hope of a personal life the other side of the tomb is nurtured on a dim recollection of our rootedness in the eternity of history.

What mornings those were in my Paris solitude!

After I had read, as was my custom, a chapter of the New Testament, whichever one came in its turn, I began to wait and to hope for the mail from my home and country. And, after I had received it and been disillusioned, I set myself to ruminating on the shame and humiliation of my poor stultified country laboring under a most cowardly, vile, and uncivil tyranny.

Once the sheets of paper were covered, feverishly and at top speed, I would read them first to the Peruvian Ventura García Calderón and then to the Frenchman Jean Cassou—who is as Spanish as he is French. The latter took them to translate into French for some journal. For various reasons I did not want the Spanish text to appear first, especially since it could not be published in Spain, where a degrading military censorship prevails, a censorship worse than illiterate, in the hands of those who hate truth and intelligence. Thus, once translated by Cassou, the work appeared under the title of *Comment on fait un roman*, with a prefacing *Portrait d'Unamuno* by the translator, in the 670th issue (their 37th year) of the *Mercure de France*. When it was published, I was already here in Hendaye, where I had arrived at the end of August, 1925. And here I have remained, as my answer to the attempt made by the Praetorian tyranny of Spain to influence the government of the French Republic into moving me away from the frontier, in the course of which attempt I was visited by the emissary of Monsieur Painlevé, the then President of the French Cabinet. My visitor was none other than the Prefect of the *Basses-Pyrénées*, who came from Pau specifically for the purpose of applying pressure on me, but who failed, naturally, to convince me to move on. Some day I will tell the detailed story of the repugnant farce mounted along this frontier, which faces Vera, by the abject Spanish police at the service of that poor epileptic, the mad General Don Severiano Martínez Anido, still Minister of the Interior and Vice-President of the Council of assistants to the Spanish Tyranny, who made up a story about a supposed Red uprising—a bogeyman!—in order to exert pressure on the French government to intern me. Even now, as I write these lines, those poor devils in the pay of the so-called Dictatorship have not given up their efforts to move me out of here.

When I left Paris, Cassou was busy translating. After he completed the task and sent in to the *Mercure*, I failed to ask him to send me back the MS (which was in pen, for I avoid the typewriter). And now that I have finally decided to see it printed in my own language, in the only language in which I know how to present my thought plain, I have no wish to recover the original text. I am not at all sure how I would react to the sight of all those prophetical pages which I covered with words in that little room where I lived out the solitudes of my Paris solitude. I would rather retranslate from Cassou's French translation, and that is what I propose to do. But is it feasible for a writer to retranslate one of his own works from a translation already made into another language? It is not so much a matter of thus resurrecting a work, but rather of killing it, or it is a mortician's job, or one of re-mortification. Or even of killing the work again.

So-called literary production is really a matter of consumption, not merely market consumption, but consumption in the pathological, medical sense. Whoever sets down his thoughts, his dreams, his sentiments, murders them one after the other. So soon as one of our thoughts is fixed in words, expressed, crystallized, it is left for dead and is no more "ours" than our own skeleton will be after it is under ground. History, the uniquely alive, is the eternal present, the fugitive moment which remains in passing, which passes as it remains, and literature is nothing but death. It is a death from which others can take life. For whoever reads a novel can live it, relive it (and "novel" stands for story, history), and whoever reads a poem, a "creature" (a poem is a creature and poetry is creation), can re-create it. Among those who can do so is the author himself. Does an author, whenever he rereads a work of his own, always find again the eternity of that past moment which makes the present eternal? And, reader, have you not chanced to meditate before a picture of yourself taken or painted twenty or thirty years before? The eternal present is the tragic mystery, the mysterious tragedy, of our historical or spiritual life. And thus the tragic torture in trying to redo what is already done, that is, undone. Retranslation of oneself comes under this head. And yet . . .

Yes, I must, in order to live, to relive, to take firm hold of that past which is all my future reality, I must retranslate myself. And I am going to retranslate myself. But, as I do so I must also live my present history, the story of my today, and even my entire history since the day I handed the original over to Jean Cassou. And therefore it will not be possible for me to be faithful to that past moment in time. The text that follows will not agree entirely, then, with that published in the *Mercure de France*. The differences should be of interest to no one, unless it be some scholar of the future.

Since the text was preceded in the French by a *Portrait d'Unamuno* by way of prologue, I will also translate that, and comment on it briefly afterwards.

Portrait of Unamuno

SAINT AUGUSTINE WAS seized with a species of frenzied anguish as he contemplated what he must have been like before he "awoke" in his consciousness. Later on he was astounded by the death of a friend who had been another one like himself, another Augustine. I do not believe that Miguel de Unamuno, who is in the habit of pausing at any and all points in his reading, has ever cited either of these two passages. Nevertheless, he would find himself face to face with himself in them. There is something of Saint Augustine in him, and something of Jean Jacques, something of all those who, absorbed in the contemplation of their own miracle, cannot stand being mortal.

The prideful instinct to delimit oneself, to bring the whole of creation within one's own scope, is gainsaid by two unfathomable, deeply disturbing mysteries: a birth, and a death, both of which we share with other living beings and through which we embark on a common destiny. It is this unique drama which Unamuno has explored in all its meanings, in all its nuances.

He must penetrate into an absorbing world very much his own, a world whose cardinal virtues and sins are not precisely those of orthodox theology. He is obsessed with its qualities and its vices, its imperious solitude, its avarice—an avarice proper to the Basque terrain—and envy, an envy which is a daughter of the Spanish Cain whose shadow, as a poem of Machado's puts it, falls over the desolation of desert Castile. He is imbued with a certain passion, sometimes called love, which in him is a terrible need to propagate the flesh that we are assured is to be resurrected on the final day—a consolation more direct than the idea of immortality of the soul. It is his own humanity whom he confesses, whose confession he hears ceaselessly, for whom he claims and proclaims the right to live on, thinking thus to confer on this humanity a form of existence not subject to the usual laws, to create a humanity of whom nothing would be lost, whose aggregate would remain forever in substance and form—a divine organization, a deification, an apotheosis.

It is through this sublimation of self, these perpetual analyses, that Miguel de Unamuno testifies to his own eternity: he is eternal as all things are eternal in him, as the offspring of his spirit, as that character in *Mist* who appears before him to throw in his face that terrible cry of "Don Miguel, I don't want to die!" Eternal, also, as Don Quixote, who is more alive than the poor cadaver called Cervantes; as eternal as Spain, not the Spain of the princes, but his own, Don Miguel's Spain, which he carries with him into his exile, a Spain he makes, day after day, which he uses to make each of his works, in its language and thought, a Spain of which he can finally say that she is his daughter rather than his mother.

Miguel de Unamuno comes to add his experience, his effort, to that of all those who have tried to retain something of the humanity which slips through everyone's hands in such a vertiginous way, to that of Shakespeare and Pascal and Nietzsche, noble names alongside whom his work does not pale, for it signifies the same desperate avidity and longing.

He will not accept the fate of Polonius, he cannot countenance being dragged away, dragged from the scene, as Hamlet dragged a rag-doll Polonius off by the armpits: "Come now, good Sir!" Unamuno protests. His protest rises to God. Not to that chimera constructed out of Alexandrian abstractions by metaphysicians inebriated on logomachy, but to the Spanish god, the Christ with the glass eyes, natural hair, articulated body, made of earth and wood, bloodstained, dressed in a gold-embroidered skirt to hide his privy parts, a Christ who has lived among everyday things and is to be found, as Saint Teresa attests, even among the kitchen pots and pans.

Such is the agony of Don Miguel de Unamuno, warrior, man of battle, battling with himself, battling with his people and against his people, a hostile man, an advocate of civil war, a tribune without advocates, a solitary, alone, expatriated, savage in speech, preacher in the desert, *provocateur*, vain, confounding, paradoxical, implacable, unyielding, enemy of nothingness, whom nothingness fascinates and devours, torn between life and death, dying and resurrecting at the same time, dead and resurrected, invincible and forever vanquished.

* * *

He would not be pleased to have a study of him include any attempt to analyze his ideas. Of the two approaches habitual in that kind of essay—the Man and his Ideas—he could not conceive of any but the first approach. Ideocracy is the most terrible of the dictatorships he has tried to overthrow. In studying a man, it is better to consider his words rather than his ideas. "Meanings," Pascal said before Buffon, "receive their dignity from words. They do not give words their dignity." Unamuno does not have ideas: he is, himself, the ideas which the ideas of others have become—are made—in him, the resulting eventuality of chance encounters, the random destiny of his wanderings around Salamanca, where he meets Fray Luis de León and Cervantes; the fortuitous fruits of those spiritual journeys which take him to Port Royal, Athens or Copenhagen, home-country of Sören Kierkegaard; the fate which brought him to Paris, where he played a part, innocently and without astonishment, in our carnival.

This absence of ideas, in the context of a perpetual monologue in which all the ideas in the world are made into a batter for his personal use, which he kneads into live passion, white-hot proof, pathetic egotism, has not failed to surprise the French, lovers of conversation and the exchange of ideas, of a prudent dialectic in which agreement is generally reached favoring the discreet veiling of individual nonconformity, so that it is overlooked and finally forgotten, eventually lost altogether. The French are great believers in press interviews and inquiries, in the course of which the spirit of a man yields to the suggestions of some journalist who knows his public and also knows all about the general—and burning—problems of the day, for which some solutions must be found, and who knows what issues should provoke general outcry and which issues should be damped down altogether. Where in such a performance would there be room for the soliloquy of an old Spaniard who does not wish to die?

The evolution of our species seems to involve a perpetual and saddening deterioration of energy. As every generation unfolds there is a more or less con-

stant loss of human sensibility, of the human absolute.
The only ones overawed by the process, terrified of it,
are a certain few individuals who, avid for completion,
not only would refuse all loss, but even insist on total
gain, on winning all. Pascal's complaint was that he
could not understand anyone's letting himself be distracted from this striving-to-win-all. The great Spaniards have shared this same complaint: for them, ideas
and everything that constitutes a provisional economy
—moral or political economy—is of no interest whatever. They are interested only in the economy of the
individual—and therefore of the eternal. Thus, for
Unamuno, to act politically is, still, to save himself;
is, still, to be saved. It is to defend his person, affirm
it, have it enter history forever. It is not a matter of
asserting a certain doctrine, of securing the victory of
this doctrine or that party, of expansion of the national territory, or of overthrowing any social order.
And so whenever Unamuno enters the political arena,
he finds no political figure with whom he can get
along. He disappoints them all, and his polemical ora-
tory is lost in the confusion, especially because it is
against himself that he is making his points. The
King, the Dictator: he would be delighted to turn
them into characters in his own drama, produce them
and put them on the boards of his own theater, stage
them at will, just as he has done with the man Kant
and with Don Quixote.

Naturally, Unamuno finds himself in a state of
continuous conflict with all his contemporaries. As
politician, all the formulas of interest to the generality
mean nothing and say nothing to him. As novelist and
dramatist, everything to be said relating to the observation of reality, to the play of passions, strikes him
as laughable. As poet, he cannot conceive of an ideal

sovereign beauty. Ferocious, lacking magnanimity, Unamuno ignores all systems, all principles, everything objective and outside himself. His thought, like that of Nietzsche, is unable to find expression except discursively. Like that of the poet-philosopher, his thought is subject to the most diverse influences, it is haphazard—though he does not quite manage to compress it in aphorisms or forge his statement by hammer blows. His determinism is purely personal, he reacts only to events that concern him; he requires being aroused and finding resistance. His thought is essentially exegetical. Since he has no doctrine of his own, he writes only books of commentary: commentaries on *Don Quixote*, commentaries on the Christ of Velásquez, commentaries on the speeches of Primo de Rivera. And his commentaries on all these things have mainly to do with how they affect the integrity of Don Miguel de Unamuno, his self-preservation, his terrestrial and future life.

In the same way, Unamuno the poet is completely a poet of circumstance—in the most ample sense of that word, naturally. He is—always—saying something about something specific. Unlike Góngora, for example, he cannot find sustenance in pure poetry, he cannot live on the ideal, poetry-in-itself, nor give it anything of his own. Tempestuous and arrogant, like a proscript of the *Risorgimento*, Unamuno is moved to clamor, in a lyric form, proclaiming his faith, his hopes, his first memories, the woe of his exile. The art of versifying is not for him an excuse for abandon. On the contrary, it is a high occasion, a withdrawal and a necessity—and he makes use of it merely to restate his case. In the vast perspectives of his oratorical poetry—hard, robust, and romantic—he remains always himself, only more powerfully so, savoring his victory over words-as-matter and over time.

We have made a canon of art, a canon to imitate, a norm to achieve or a problem to resolve. And once we have put forth and established our postulate, we are not pleased to have anyone ignore it. Are the works written by this man then admissible? For they bristle with, and in, disorder. At the same time they are undelimited, monstrously amorphous; they cannot be classified, belong to no genre. At every turn we are stopped short by personal observations, all of them made in a tone of truculent familiarity and insolence. It is difficult to follow the course of his philosophic fiction or philosophic aesthetic, even though from time to time we find ourselves on the point of coming to agreement with him.

They say that Luigi Pirandello, whose idealism has often been criticized for its Unamuno-like ironies, kept his insane mother by his side day after day. Something of the same can be said of Unamuno: he has lived his entire existence in the company of a crazy man, the most divine madman of them all, our Lord Don Quixote! That is why Unamuno cannot stand any kind of servitude whatsoever. He has rejected them all. After a close look at everything possible, this prodigious humanist has decided that the two most horrible sciences possible are sociology and pedagogy. And the reason he so decided is that those two sciences presume to subject the formation of the individual, along with what is irreducible in him and least expendable, to an *a priori* construction. If one wants to follow what Unamuno is saying, one must discard from one's thought everything alien to his ineradicable way of looking at things, and be prepared to accept the sudden peculiarities and irregularities of language through which his uniqueness must assert

its flexibility and assure itself that it is in good working order. For the rest of us, not to accept the rules
is to risk making fools of ourselves. Don Quixote, for
his part, cares nothing for such a risk, and ignores it.
Unamuno, too, would ignore it. He is aware of all
the other pitfalls, but not of this one. Rather than
submit to the smallest form of servitude, he prefers
to risk falling into the abyss of ridicule, where the
belly laughs resound.

Once we eliminate from any portrait of Unamuno
everything that is not Unamuno himself, we can situate ourselves at the center of his resistance: he appears before us in his physical reality, all of a piece.
He marches straight ahead, carrying with him, wherever he goes, whether in his *paseo* around the lovely
Baroque plaza at Salamanca or about the streets of
Paris or along the roads of the *pays Basque*, his inexhaustible monologue, always the same despite the
wealth of variants. Well built, dressed in what he calls
his civilian uniform, his head firmly upon those
shoulders which had never been able to bear, even
in snowy weather, the bother of an overcoat, he
presses straight on, indifferent to the quality of his
audience, much in the manner of his teacher, Don
Quixote—who spoke to shepherds in the same manner he addressed dukes—ever intent on the tragic
play of words, a play which he never allows to catch
him by surprise. He attributes transcendental importance to everything, even to the art of *origami*, to the
paper birds he triumphantly folds into existence. Does
he really think that his philological play will express
and all-the-longer prolong his concept-ism? With Unamuno we reach the rock bottom of Spanish nihilism.
We are made aware that this world depends on dream

so thoroughly that there is no point even in dreaming it systematically. If the philosophers have ventured to do so, it is doubtless from an excess of innocence on their part. They have fallen prey to their own traps. They have failed to notice how much of their personal dream, of themselves, they have put into their systems. In his lucidity Unamuno has felt the need at every instant to stop and contradict himself, to gainsay himself. Because he dies.

Yet: why should the combinations and permutations of the world have produced this accident, Miguel de Unamuno, if it was not so that he should last and be eternalized? Swinging between the opposing poles of nothingness and permanence, he goes on waging the daily battle of existence, on a battlefield where the slightest event assumes the most tragic importance. No one of his moves can be judged in accord with the objective and customary ordinances by which we regulate our own. His are made in dependence to a higher duty: he relates them to his awesome need to persist.

Nothing is vain, useless, or lost in the minutes or hours among which he stirs and bestirs himself. The most ordinary of instants, where the world takes over and we are swept along, are moments which he uses to be himself. His anguish never lets go of him, and neither is he ever free of that pride which lends splendor to everything he touches. His passionate concern never allows him to escape, to sink into a self-forgetting annihilation. Always wakeful, he sleeps only to gather strength for the dream of waking and its pleasures. Threatened on all sides, he considers the threats with a certain bitter clarity, and maintains an attitude which appears to welcome all conflict, all woe, all litigation. Reduced to utter solitude and self-recourse, he is the most human of men, rich in all true virtues. For there is no denying he has managed to reduce all questions and problems to the simplest and most natural one; and nothing stands in the way of our looking at ourselves in him as in an exemplary man: by so doing we will be rewarded. We need but to let go of the social ritual of our ant heap, of its temporal considerations, of its dogmas and customs. A man is going to vanish: that is all—and everything. If he can go on, minute after minute, doggedly refusing to take his departure, he may yet save us. In the last analysis, it is us he is defending by defending himself.

JEAN CASSOU

Commentary

AH, MY DEAR Cassou! Your portrait of me forces me to unloose my tongue. And the reader will understand that if I include the *Portrait* in this book—and translate it from the French in order to do so—I include it to give me the opportunity to gloss it, to add a commentary on it. Cassou states that I write only commentaries anyway. The truth is I do not understand the difference between writings that are commentaries and those that are not. Still, I am assuaged by the thought that the *Iliad* is perhaps no more than a commentary on one episode from the Trojan war, and that the *Divine Comedy* is simply a commentary on the escatological doctrines of medieval Catholic theology as well as on the turbulent history of Florence in the thirteenth century and the struggles between the Papal State and the Empire. For Dante was merely a poet of circumstance, according to the priests of Pure Poetry. (I read, not long ago, the aesthetic commentaries of the Abbé Henri Bremond.) Of course, the Gospel and the Pauline epistles are merely circumstantial writings also.

Now that I have gone over Cassou's *Portrait*, I see myself with some surprise, looking into his lines as if into a mirror, but I seem to see the mirror itself better than the person in the mirror. I pause, first, at the passage where he finds it odd that, though I tend to pause so frequently at every point of my reading, I never seem to have paused at the two passages cited by my portraitist. It is probably forty years since I read the *Confessions* of the African and, oddly enough, I never have read them again; and now I do not remember what effect those two passages produced on me in my youth. My mind was taken up with such other concerns at the time! My most urgent concern was to marry, at once, the woman who is forever the mother of my children and, in her own way, my mother too. Yes, I like to pause (though I should really use some word more vitally personal and less aesthetic than "like"), I do like to pause, not only at every point of my reading, but at every moment in time, at every moment, because I am passing. People talk about "the book of life" just to hear themselves talk, although it is a phrase as pregnant with meaning as almost all those phrases that reach the high status of a commonplace. This phrase, like its companion "the book of nature," means, to most of those who use it, absolutely nothing. The truth is that these poor people have not understood, assuming they ever heard of it, the passage in Apocalypse, in the Book of Revelation, where the Spirit commands the Apostle to eat a book. Whenever a book is a living thing, it must be eaten, and, whoever eats it, if he is alive, if he is truly living, relives, is revivified by the meal. But for writers—and the sad fact is that the only people who read books any more are those who write them—for writers a book is only a piece of writing, nothing sacred or living or revivifying or eternalizing, as are the Bible, the Koran, the Discourses of Buddha, or like our Book, the Book of Spain, *Don Quixote*. And only those who realize how the Word was made flesh at the same time it was made Letter, who sense how we eat, in the bread of eternal life, Eucharistically, that flesh and that Letter, only those who understand that fact can understand how apocalyptic, how much of a revelation eating a book can be. And the Letter we eat, which is flesh, is also the Word, which does not mean it is also idea, that is, skeleton. It is impossible to live on skeletons: no one can find nourishment from a skeleton. That is the reason I tend to pause at random in my reading of books of all kinds, among them the book of life, the history I am living, and the book of nature, and at every vital point.

The Fourth Gospel (John 8:6-9) tells us (and now the ideologues are upon us, claiming that the passage is apocryphal), that when the scribes and Pharisees brought the woman taken in adultery before Jesus, the Master "stooped down, and with his finger wrote on the ground," without reed or ink, in the dust, with his bare finger, and as they continued to question him, he again stooped down and wrote on the ground, after telling them that whoever felt he was without sin should cast the first stone upon the woman, and thereupon her accusers went away in silence. What did they read in the dust in which the Master had written? Did they read anything at all? Did they pause in the course of that reading? For my part, I go along the roads of country and city, of nature and history, striving to read—in order to comment on it—what the bare invisible finger of God has written in the dust which the wind of revolution— natural revolutions and historical revolutions—carries away. And God stoops to earth to write. And what God has written is our own miracle, the miracle of each one of us—Saint Augustine, Jean Jacques, Jean Cassou, you, reader, or I who am writing this commentary with pen and ink—the miracle of our conscious human solitude and eternity.

Solitude! Solitude is the marrow of our essence

and, by gathering in groups, forming in flocks, we only deepen it. Our gregariousness merely makes our solitude more profound. Our solitude, our radical, deep-rooted solitude, and nothing else, has given rise to our envy, the envy of Cain, whose shadow extends —my Antonio Machado put it so well—across the solitary desolation of the high Castilian desert-plateau. This envy of ours, the dregs of which the present Spanish tyranny has stirred up, and which is nothing but the fruit of Cainite envy, especially that barrack and conventual envy—military and monkish— that envy natural to herds and droves subjected to regulation, that inquisitorial envy which has made Spanish history into a tragedy. For the Spaniard hates himself.

Ah, yes, there is another humanity within that sheeplike humanity, within that herded humanity, a humanity whom I confess and for whom I clamor! And with what verbal felicity Cassou wrote "il faut lui donner une organisation divine!" A divine organization? What we must do is to organize God!

The Augusto Pérez of my *Mist* asked me not to let him die, true enough, but just at the same moment that I heard his plea—and I heard it just as I was writing him down according to what he dictated —I could also hear the future readers of my book, who, while they were eating it, devouring it perhaps, were asking me simultaneously not to let *them* die. And everyman, everyone with whom we deal in our mutual spiritual human commerce, all of us, want not to die, try to avoid dying: I want not to die in you, reader who reads me, and you want not to die in me who writes this for you. And poor Cervantes, who is something more than "the poor corpse" Cassou calls him, also sought not to die when he wrote down the words Don Quixote dictated, and thereby narrated the hero's life—so as not to die himself. And as regards Cervantes, I want to point out that when he claims to have taken the Knight's history from a book in Arabic by Cide Hamete Benengeli, he means to say that the tale was not a mere figment of his imagination, not fiction or fantasy. The invention of Cide Hamete Benengeli encloses a profound lesson, one which I expect to develop at a future date. At the moment, I must press on, in obedience to the chance developments of a commentary.

Cassou comments on my often-repeated statement that my Spain is as much my daughter as my mother. My daughter because she is my mother, and mother because daughter. That is: my wife. For the mother of our children is our mother and our daughter as well. Mother and daughter! We are torn, rent from our mother's womb, without consciousness, to look, by the light of the sun, at the earth and the sky, at the blueness and the greenness. And what greater consolation, in the end, than to be able to rest our head against the breast of an understanding daughter and there die with eyes open to gaze a last fill, by way of viaticum, on the eternal greenness of the country of birth!

Cassou says that my work does not fade. Thank you, Cassou. The reason it doesn't is that it is always the same. And because it is made in such wise that it can be another book for whoever eats it in the reading. What difference does it make to me, reader, if you don't read what I tried to put into the book, so long as you read something there that sets you ablaze in your life? That an author should allow himself to get distracted by explaining what he meant to say has always struck me as idiotic; what concerns us is what he did say, not what he meant to say; or, better, what we heard him say. Cassou goes on to call me, in addition to savage—and if by that he means I am a sylvan man, I accept the epithet—paradoxical and implacable. I have been called paradoxical numberless times and now I no longer know what those who apply the adjective to me mean by "paradox." The word paradox, like the word pessimism, has lost all meaning in our land of sheeplike conformity. Implacable? Me? Thus are legends made. But let us leave the matter there.

Then Cassou says I am dead and resurrected at the same time: *mort et ressuscité ensemble.* When I read that I felt a shudder of anguish. And that was because I suddenly remembered the narrative in the Fourth Gospel, where "the chief priests" planned to put the resurrected Lazarus to death because, on account of him, many of the Jews believed in Jesus (John 12:10). It is a terrible thing to be resurrected, all the more so among those who have a name that they live, but are dead (Rev. 3:1). The poor walking dead, who talk and gesticulate and react, and who lie down in the dust in which the bare finger of God wrote, and who read nothing there, and since they read nothing in it do not dream. Nor do they read anything in the verdure, the greenness of the countryside. Have you never paused, reader, before that abysmal poetic moment in the same Fourth Gospel where we are told that when a great multitude followed Jesus over beyond Lake Tiberias, in Galilee, and it was needful to find bread for them all when they had scarcely any money, and Jesus told his apostles "Make the men sit down"; and the text adds "Now there was much grass in the place" (John 6:10). Much green grass, much country verdure, there where the multitude, hungering for the words of the Word, of the Master, were to sit down to hear him, to eat of his words! Much grass! They did not sit in the dust which the wind carries away but upon the green grass which is moved by the breeze. There was much grass!

Cassou next says I have no ideas. But I think what he means is that ideas do not have *me*. And he makes some commentaries which are suggested, surely, by a certain conversation I sustained with a French journalist and which was published in *Les Nouvelles Littéraires*. How I have regretted having agreed to that interview! For, in truth, there is nothing I can say to a journalist who knows his public and knows all about the general problems of the day—which, by reason of their being the least individual, are also the least universal and least eternal—problems to which an answer must be supplied through a journalist who knows when to cause a scandal or when to damp down the issue altogether. A scandal! But, what kind of scandal? Not, of course, the Gospel scandal, the stumbling block, the scandal of which Christ speaks when he says there must be scandal, but woe to him upon whom it falls! Not Satanic or Luciferian scandal, which is archangelic and infernal, but the miserable scandal of meddlesome literary cliques, of those seedy, mean literati who do not know how to eat a book—they can barely read one—nor do they know how to knead an eatable book out of their flesh and blood, knowing only how to write one down with pen and ink. Cassou wonders, correctly, what these journalistic interviews can mean for any man, Spanish or not, who does not want to die and who knows that the soliloquy is the preferred manner of speech for those souls who feel the divine solitude. For what difference does it make what Peter thinks of Paul or what Andrew makes of John?

No, I am not interested in the so-called problems of the present moment, which are nothing of the sort. For the true present, the ever present, is the eternal present. In these tragic times for my poor Spain, I often hear people ask: "And what will we do tomorrow?" No, it should be: what shall we do now? Or better, what am I going to do now? What is each one of us going to do right now? The present and the individual, the here and the now. In the concrete case of the present Spanish political—or rather apolitical: in-civil—situation of my country, my reply, whenever I hear talk about the "political future" or Constitutional reform, is that the first step is to get rid of the present wretchedness, of the present tyranny: put it on trial and condemn it to death. And the rest can wait. When Christ was on his way to the house of Jairus to cure the dying daughter, he encountered the woman "having an issue of blood twelve years," and he tarried with her, for that was matter of the moment. And the other, the dying girl, the dead girl, could wait (Luke 8:41-56).

Generalizing from my own case, Cassou says all the great Spaniards find everything that constitutes a provisional economy—moral or political economy—of no interest whatever; that they care only for the economy of the individual, and therefore, of the eternal; and he adds that for me to act politically is to save myself, to defend my person, affirm it, have it enter history forever. To which my response is: first, that the provisional is the eternal, that the *here* is the center of infinite space, the focus of infinitude, and the *now* is the center of time, the focus of eternity; then, that the individual is the universal (in logic individual judgments are assimilated to universal judgments) and therefore the eternal; finally, that there is no other politics but that of saving individuals in history. Unless it be for saving the souls of individual men, nothing is worth anything, neither the triumph of a doctrine or a party, or the expansion of the national territory, or the overthrow of any social order whatsoever. Additionally, I would like to say that I can get along with politicians—and have gotten along with some of them more than once—with any and all politicians who feel and understand the infinite, eternal value of individuality. Even if the politicians call themselves socialists: perhaps precisely because they do. Yes, one must enter history forever, *à jamais*. Forever! The true father of historical history, of political history, the profound Thucydides—Machiavelli's true master—said that he was writing history "for ever": εἰς ἀιεί. And to write history for ever is one way, perhaps the surest, of entering history for ever, to make history for ever. And if human history is what I have repeatedly said it is, namely, God's thought on man's earth, then to make history, and to make it for ever, is to make God think, to organize God, to amass eternity and knead it. Not for nothing did another of the great disciples and continuators of Thucydides, Leopold von Ranke, say that each human generation is in direct contact with God. For the Kingdom of God, for whose advent simple souls pray every day—"Thy Kingdom come!"—the Kingdom within us all, comes to us from moment to moment, and the Kingdom is its own eternal coming. And all of history is a commentary on divine thought.

A commentary? Cassou says I have written only commentaries. And what has everyone else written? In the narrow, academic sense in which Cassou seems to use the word, I'm not sure that my novels and dramas are indeed commentaries. My *Peace in War*, for example, is that a commentary? Ah, yes, a commentary on the political history of the Carlist Civil War, 1873-1876. But the point is that to make commentaries is to make history. Just as narrating how to make a novel is to make it. Is the life of any one of us anything more than a novel? Is any novel as novelesque as an auto-biography?

I would prefer to pass over what Cassou says of my being a topical poet. So is God a poet of circumstance. And he comments on my poetry to call it "oratorical" and "hard, robust, and romantic." I have recently been reading about pure poetry: pure as distilled water, and equally undrinkable; distilled in a laboratory still and not from the clouds that hover in the air and sunlight. As far as "romanticism" goes, I am ready to add this term to the words "paradox" and "pessimism." I mean: I don't know what it means —any more than those people who abuse it know.

In the next breath, Cassou asks if my works are admissible, for they bristle with, and in, disorder, are undelimited and monstrously amorphous, and cannot be classified in any category or assigned to any genre. "*Classer*," to class or classify, and "genre," category (kind of goods, too): there's the key to it all! And he speaks of the reader as on the point of being in agreement, "*nous allions nous mettre d'accord*," as to the correct course of the narrative being presented to them. But why now does the reader have to come to any agreement with what the writer is telling him? For my part, when I begin to read someone, I don't do it in order to come to any agreement with him. I don't ask for anything of the sort. Whenever one of those impenetrable readers, one of those who don't know how to eat books, nor go beyond themselves, tells me that he has just read something of mine and adds, "I don't agree with you! I don't agree at all!" I reply, curbing my compassion as best I can, "And what difference does it make, my dear sir, either to you or to me, whether or not we are in agreement, whether or not we are in accord?" For my part, I am not even always in accord with myself and, what is more, I tend to be in accord with those who are not in agreement with me. It is only proper to a living individuality, an individuality who is always present, always changing and always the same, one which aspires to live forever—and this aspiration is its essence—an individuality which really is such, which is and exists, it is only proper that it find in other, different, individualities a source of nourishment and that it serve in turn to nourish them. It is this consistence that sustains an individuality's ex-istence, and to resist is to desist from eternal life. And now: Cassou and the reader can see to what dialectic games— so conceptist, so Spanish—I am led by my playing with etymology, as in ex-ist, con-sist, re-sist, and de-sist. (And we must include, in-sist, for insistence, some say, is a basic characteristic of mine.) Despite everything, I believe I do as-sist my neighbors, my brothers, my fellow men, assist them to find themselves, and to enter history forever, and to make their own novel. But in some agreement, in mutual accord? Nonsense! Some animals are herbivorous, and some plants carnivorous. Everything sustains itself on its opposites.

Cassou cites the most intimate, most human, most felt-in-the-guts part of that dramatic novel which is the life of Luigi Pirandello: the fact that he kept his mad mother by his side day after day. What was he supposed to do with her, throw her into a madhouse? When I realized Cassou's analogy, I shuddered. For I keep, close to my heart, pressed against it, through the days of my everyday life, my poor mad mother, Spain. It is not correct of Cassou to say that I keep only the mad Don by my side, no, for I keep Spain with me as well, a Spain which is as mad as Don Quixote: mad with grief, mad with shame, mad with despair and, who knows, perhaps also mad with remorse. Is the crusade upon which Spain has been launched by King Alfonso XIII, that representative of Hapsburgian spiritual foreignism, anything but madness? And not, unfortunately, a Quixotic madness.

As for Don Quixote, I have already said so much about him . . . ! He has made me say so much about him . . . ! A madman, yes, although not the most divine madman of them all. The most divine madman was and still is Jesus, the Christ. The second Gospel, the one according to Saint Mark, relates that Christ's people, his own—*hoi par' autou*—the members of his house and family, his mother and his brothers, as we are told later, went to get him, saying he was beside himself—*hoti exeste*, alienated, mad (Mark 3:21 and 31). And it is a curious fact that the Greek term used here for being mad should indicate one's being outside oneself, and is analogous to the Latin *ex-sistere*, exist. The truth is that existence is a madness and the person who exists, who is outside himself, who gives of himself, who transcends—this person is a madman. And we have the holy madness of the Cross, over against which stands sanity, which is nothing but stupidity, a condition of being in oneself, staying within oneself, being reserved and "all there." Those Pharisees who reproached Jesus and his disciples on the sabbath for plucking ears of corn and rubbing them in their hands by way of threshing, and reproved Jesus for healing a man with a withered hand on another sabbath, those Pharisees were, according to the Third Gospel, "filled with madness" (Luke 6: 11), but their madness was *anoias*, dementia or folly, not true madness. These liturgical, observing Pharisees were demented fools, not truly mad. Although Paul of Tarsus, the mystic discoverer of Jesus, began by being a Pharisee, the praetor Festus in the end cried out, in a loud voice: "Paul, thou art beside thyself; much learning doth make thee mad" (Acts 26: 24). Festus did not use the evangelical term used by Christ's family, and say that Paul was beside himself, but used rather the word *mainei*, indicating his mind had wandered and he had fallen into mania. He used a term which has come down to us. In the eyes of Festus, Paul was a maniac; much learning, much reading, had done him in, turned his head—whether or not his brain had been dried up, as in the case of Don Quixote, the madman out of the books of chivalry.

And why should reading make one mad, as in the case of Paul of Tarsus and Don Quixote de la Mancha? Why should one go mad eating books? There are so many ways of going mad! And just as many more to get stupefied! The most common way of getting stupefied is to read books *without* eating them, swallowing the Letter without assimilating anything, failing to turn one's reading into spirit. Fools sustain themselves—maintain themselves in their stupidity—by subsisting on the bones of doctrine and not on its flesh. Fools are those who say: "No one is going to laugh at me!" Which are the words of General M. Anido, chief hangman of Spain, who does not mind if he is hated so long as he is feared. "No one laughs at me!" And God laughs at him; and at all the folly he perpetrates in the name of fighting Bolshevism.

I would prefer to say nothing at all about the final touches to my portrait by Cassou, but I cannot resist saying a few words about the rock bottom of Spanish nihilism which I am said to represent. I do not like the word. "Nihilism" sounds Russian, it has a Russian flavor although a native Russian would prefer *nichevism*, for the word nihilism was applied to Russia from outside. The root, *nihil*, is Latin. In Spanish, we would be better off using "*nadismo*," from our endlessly resounding and abysmal word *nada*. *Nada* which first meant "*cosa nada*," nativity of something, something born and therefore an everything, an all, has come to mean (as *rien* in French, from *rem* = thing) the no thing, the nothing, nothingness (and the same process can be observed with French *personne*). The plentitude of being has given way to its void.

Life, which is everything and, because it is everything, is reduced to nothing, is a dream, or perhaps the shadow of a dream, and perhaps Cassou is right when he says there is no point in dreaming it systematically. Of course not! System, which is consistence or consistency, destroys the essence of the dream and with it the essence of life. And, as he says, philosophers have not noticed what part of themselves, of the dream that they are, they have put into their attempt to systematize life and the world and existence. There is no profounder philosophy than the contemplation of how one philosophizes. The history of philosophy is the perennial philosophy.

Finally, I must thank my Cassou—my Cassou: have I, the portrayed, not made him, the portraitist,

made him the author of my portrait?—for recogniz-
ing that, in the final analysis, in defending myself I
am defending my readers, especially those of my readers who defend themselves against me. And thus,
when I tell them how a novel is made, how to make
a novel, that is, how I am making the novel, the story,
of my life, I lead them into making their own novel,
the novel which is the life of each one of them. How
unfortunate they are if they have no novel! If your
life, reader, is not a novel, not a divine fiction, not
a dream of eternity, then leave off this book, let it go,
do not read further. Do not go on, because I'll give
you indigestion, you will have an attack of me and
will have to vomit me up, with no benefit either to
you or to me.

*　　*　　*

And now, to retranslate my narrative of how a
novel is made, how to make a novel! And since it is
impossible for me to revive it, restage it, without re-
thinking it, that is, without reliving it, I will be forced
to make further commentaries this time round. I
would like to respect as far as possible the person I
was during that winter of 1924 to 1925 in Paris, and
so I will put brackets around any added commentary, thus: [   ].

All these bracketed commentaries, and the three
connected narratives fitted together to form the whole,
are bound to remind some readers of one of those
lacquered Japanese boxes which contains another box,
and that box still another, and that one still another
again, each one carved and decorated according to
the artist's ability, and then one final, tiny box—
empty. But such is the world, such is life. Commentaries on commentaries and commentaries upon those

commentaries. And the novel? If by novel, reader, you mean the plot, there is no novel. Or, to put it another way, there is no plot. In the flesh is the bone and in the bone the marrow: but the human novel has no marrow, and lacks all plot. Everything is but little boxes, dreams. And what is truly novelistic is how the novel is made, how to make a novel.

How to Make a Novel

H E R E I A M staring at these blank pages—blank as the dark future: terrifyingly blank—striving to hold on to passing time, pin down the flighty day, in short, make myself eternal or immortal, although eternity and immortality are not one and the same. Here you have me before these blank white pages—my future —endeavoring to pour out my life in the hope of continuing to live, in the hope of giving myself life and tearing myself out of the hands of death every moment of the day. Meanwhile I am also endeavoring to console myself in my exile, in the expatriation from my eternity, in the expatriation from my heaven and earth.

Exile! Proscription! What profoundly personal, and even religious, experiences it has furnished me! Exile, first, on the island of Fuerteventura, God's sanctuary, which I will forever love in the depths of my soul, and then here in Paris, rich and overflowing with the universal experience of humanity, where I wrote those sonnets comparable in their origin and intention with the *Châtiments* written by Victor Hugo on his island of Guernsey against the tyranny of Napoleon le Petit. Yet these poems have not sufficed; I have not put my entire self-in-exile into them, and they are not enough to eternalize me in the fugitive present, in this threatening historical present—in History: the sum of all possible threats.

I receive very few people. I spend the greater part

of the morning alone in this cell by the Place des États-Unis. After lunch I repair to the Café de la Rotonde, in Montparnasse, at the intersection of Boulevard Montparnasse and Raspail, where a small group of Spaniards, young students in the majority, meet to comment on the scanty reports we receive from Spain, our Spain and their Spain. And every day we set about, anew, repeating the same saws, and building, as they say here, castles in Spain. Some people here still call the Rotonde "Trotsky's Café," because the Russian Bolshevik chief apparently went there when he was exiled in Paris.

How awful it is to live in expectation, wondering each day what the morrow will bring! I spend hours at a time, all alone, stretched out on the bed of my small hotel, or "family house," contemplating the ceiling of my room instead of the open sky and dreaming of my future and the future of Spain. Or: unraveling History. My insecurity prevents me from beginning any serious work, because I cannot be sure of being able to finish it in peace. Since I do not know whether this expatriation will last another three days or three weeks or three months or three years—I was about to add three centuries—I do not start upon anything lasting. Still, nothing lasts longer than whatever is done at the moment and for the moment. I recall my favorite expression: the *eternalization of momentaneity*. My own innate taste—and very Spanish it is—for antitheses and conceits would lead me to speak of the *momentanization of eternity*. Would that I could nail down the wheel of time!

[It is now almost two and a half years since I wrote those lines in Paris, and here I am in Hendaye, going over them, within sight of Spain, my Spain. Two and a half years later! Troubled Spaniards come to visit and ask me, referring to the tyranny: "How much longer will it last?" I answer: "As long as you want!" And if they say, "a long time, by the looks of it!" I say: "How long? Five years more? Twenty? Let us say twenty. I am sixty-three. In twenty years, I'll be eighty-three. I expect to live to be ninety. No matter how long it lasts, I'll last longer!" Meanwhile, I am in sight, tantalizing sight, of Spain, my Basque Spain, and I watch the sun rise and set over the mountains of my land. The sun rises over there, a little to the left these days of the Peña de Aya, of Las Tres Coronas, and from here in my room I can contemplate, falling down the shadowy slopes of that mountain, the horsetail formed by the waterfall of Uramildea. From this distance my anxious sight drinks in that fresh cascade. As soon as I can return to Spain, I will go, a liberated Tantalus, and dip into those waters of consolation.

And I watch the sun setting now, at the beginning of June, over the spur of Jaizquibel, atop the Guadalupe fort in which poor General Don Dámaso Berenguer, the Uncertain, was imprisoned. I am tempted daily by the city of Fuenterrabía—color-print on Spain's cover—lying at the foot of Jaizquibel, with its ivy-covered ruins of the castle of the Emperor Charles V, the son of Joanna the Mad of Castile and Philip the Handsome of Burgundy, Spain's first Hapsburg, who brought along with him—it was the Counter Reformation—the tragedy in which we still live. And the poor prince: Don Juan, the ex-future Don Juan III, with whom was extinguished the possibility of a Spanish dynasty, truly pure-blooded and home-bred!

And the Fuenterrabía bell! The sound of it stirs my innermost being. And just as in Fuerteventura and in

Paris I was given to writing sonnets, here in Hendaye
I am given to the *romance* form of Spanish versifica-
tion. One of the ballads is on the Fuenterrabía bell, on
Fuenterrabía a bell in itself:

> If you are not to return me to Spain
> God of singular good,
> if you are not to let me lie there,
> Thy will be done!
>
> In heaven as on earth,
> on mountaintop or at sea,
> Fuenterrabía of dreams,
> your bell resounds.
>
> The cry of Jaizquibel,
> where storms and winds are born,
> I hear within my heartbeat,
> Spain's own blood and bone.
>
> And you mirror-river
> Bidasoa flow out to sea
> to be lost, but carry my dreams
> to repose forever in God.
>
> Fuenterrabía the bell,
> stern tongue of eternity,
> sound the redeeming voice
> of the God of singular good.
>
> Make me, Lord, your bell,
> the bell of your truth,
> and may world's war
> mean eternal peace!

Now let us return to our narrative.]

In these circumstances and in this state of mind, it
occurred to me, some months ago, after having read
Balzac's terrible *Peau de chagrin*, the plot of which I
knew and which I devoured with growing horror,
here, in Paris and in exile, it occurred to me to put
myself into a novel which would constitute a kind of

autobiography. But are not all novels that eternalize themselves and last, and by lasting eternalize their authors and antagonists, are not all such novels, then, autobiographies?

In these middle July days of 1925—yesterday was July 14th, Bastille Day—I read the eternal love letters written by that proscribed exile Giuseppe Mazzini to Giuditta Sidoli. Another proscript Italian, Alceste de Ambris, lent them to me; he does not know what a favor he has done me. In one of these letters, written in October 1834, Mazzini replies, in answer to his Giuditta asking him to write a novel: "It is impossible for me to write a novel. You know well enough that I would not be able to separate the two of us or place myself in any kind of picture without revealing my love for you. . . . And then the moment I set my love down next to you, the novel would disintegrate." For my part I have put my Concha, the mother of my children, the living symbol of my Spain, of my dreams, and my future—for it is in these children that I am eternal—I have put her into one of my last sonnets and she is tacitly in all of them. And I have put myself into them. And, again, are not all novels that are born live essentially autobiographical? And is not this the reason they eternalize themselves? And let not my expression "born live" surprise anyone, for (a) one is born live and dies live, or (b) one is born dead and dies dead, or (c) one is born live to die dead, or (d) one is born dead to die live.

Yes, every novel, every work of fiction, every poem, when it is live is autobiographical. Every fictional being, every poetic personage whom an author creates helps create the author himself. And if the author puts a flesh and blood person whom he has known into his poem, he does so after he has made the person a part of his own flesh and blood. The great historians are also autobiographers. In describing the tyrants, Tacitus describes himself. This is obvious the love and wonder bestowed on them: we admire and even love what we curse and combat. (How the rebellious Sarmiento loved the tyrant Rosas!) And Tacitus appropriated the tyrants, made them part of himself. Flaubert's supposed impersonal objectivity is a myth. All of the poetic characters in Flaubert are Flaubert himself, and more than anyone else, Emma Bovary herself. Even Monsieur Homais is Flaubert, and if Flaubert mocks Monsieur Homais, it is so as to mock himself, from a sense of compassion, that is, from love for himself. Poor Bouvard! Poor Pécuchet!

All creatures *are* their creator. Never could God have felt more the Creator, more the Father, than when He died in Christ, when in Him, in his Son, He tasted death.

Those of us who are authors and poets put ourselves into our work, create ourselves in the poetic characters we create, even when we make history, when we make poetry, when we create people who are, we think, live flesh and blood people outside ourselves. Are not my Alfonso XIII de Borbón y Hapsburgo-Lorena, my Primo de Rivera, my Martínez Anido, my Conde de Romanones a parcel more of my creatures, parts and portions of myself, as much mine and part of me as my Augusto Pérez, my Pachico Zabalbide, my Alejandro Gómez, and all the other creatures of my novels? All of us who live chiefly from reading, by reading, and in reading cannot separate historical characters from poetic or novelistic characters. Don Quixote is as real and affective for us as Cervantes, or rather, the latter is as real as the former. For us, everything is the book and the reading of it. We may speak of the Book of History, the Book of Nature, the Book of the Universe. We are men of the Book, biblical. And we could say that in the beginning was the Book. Or History. For History begins with the Book and not with the Word, and before History, before the Book, there was no consciousness, there was no mirror, there was nothing. Prehistory is unconsciousness, nothingness.

[Genesis says that God created man in His own image and likeness. That is, He created him to be a mirror where God could see Himself, so that He might know Himself, create Himself.]

Mazzini is for me today as much as Don Quixote, no more and no less. He exists no less than Don Quixote and therefore he has existed no less than Don Quixote.

To live in history and to live history! And one way to live history is to recount it, to create it in books. And this kind of historian, a poet in his recounting, his creating, his inventing of events which men thought objectively verified, that is, proved outside their consciousness, in nothingness precisely, provokes further events. It is well said that to win a battle means to make one's own side and the other side too, friend and foe, believe it has been won. There exists a legend of reality which forms the substance, the inner reality of reality itself. The essence of an individual and of a people is its history, and history is what is called the philosophy of history as well as the reflection which each individual or every people create out of what happens to them and out of what happens in them. From events and happenings we get facts and feats, ideas made flesh and blood. But inasmuch as what I here propose is to explain how to make a novel, and not to philosophize or write history, I must not go any further afield and will leave it for some other occasion to explain the distance lying between the event and the fact, between what happens and passes away and what is made of it and remains.

In August 1917, just before seizing power, Lenin is said to have desisted from finishing a tract, very badly written, on *The State and Revolution*, because he decided it would be more opportune and practical to experience the revolution than to write about it. But is not writing about revolution a manner of experiencing it? Did not Karl Marx make the Russian Revolution as much as and more than Lenin? Did not Rousseau make the French Revolution as much as Mirabeau, Danton, and Company? The answers have been given thousands of times, but they must be repeated another thousand times so that they live on, since the conservation of the universe, according to the theologians, is a matter of continuous creation.

["When Lenin resolves a great problem," writes Karl Radek, "he does not think in abstract historical categories, he does not ponder the question of ground rent or surplus value or absolutism or liberalism. He thinks of live men, of the villager Isidore of Twer, of the worker in the Putiloff factories or of the policeman in the street, and he tries to picture how the decisions taken will affect the villager Isidore or the worker Onufri." All of which means only that Lenin was a poet, a novelist, a historian and not a sociologist or an idealogue; he was a statesman and not a mere politician.]

To live in history and to live history, to form myself in history, in my Spain, and to make my history, my Spain, and with it my universe and my eternity, such has been and continues always to be my tragic craving in exile. History is legend, as we already both

418*

know, as does everyone else, and this legend, this history devours me, and when it is finished I will be finished with it. And this is a tragedy more terrible than the tragedy of the tragic Valentin of *Peau de chagrin*. And it is not only my tragedy but also that of all those who live in history, for history, or from history, the tragedy of all citizens, that is, of all men— political or civil animals, as Aristotle would say—the tragedy of all those who write, of all those who read, of all those who read these lines. Thus the detonation of universality, omnipersonality and totalpersonality (*omnis* is not *totus*), the lack of "impersonality" in this narrative. For it is not an example of *ego*-ism but of *nos*-ism.

My legend! My novel! That is, the legend, the novel of myself, Miguel de Unamuno, the person we call by that name, which we have made together, myself and the others, my friends and my enemies, and the friend in me and the foe in me. And the reason I cannot look at myself for any length of time in the mirror is because my eyes immediately gaze behind my eyes, behind their likeness, and as soon as I gaze into my gaze, I feel myself being drawn out of myself, losing my history, my legend, my novel, returning to the unconscious, to the past, to nothingness. As if the future was not also nothing! And yet the future is our all.

My novel! My legend! The Unamuno of my legend, of my novel, the one we have made together, the friend in me and the foe in me and all the others, my friends and enemies, this Unamuno gives me life and death, he creates me and destroys me, he sustains me and stifles me. He is my agony. Am I as I think I am or as I am thought to be? And thus these lines become a confession before my unknown I, my unknowable I: unknown and unknowable to me. And thus I create the legend in which I must be buried. But now I will come to the point of my novel.

*   *   *

For I had conceived the idea, some months ago, of writing a novel, of making a novel in which I would put down the most intense experiences of my exile and thereby create myself, eternalize myself under the sign of banishment and proscription. And I am convinced that the best way to make this novel is to relate how it should be made. It will be a novel of a novel, a creation of a creation. Or God of God, *Deus de Deo.*

The first step was to invent a central character who would be, naturally, myself. And then a name would be needed. I would call him U. Jugo de la Raza. U. is the initial letter of my surname; Jugo is the surname, the first, paternal, surname of my maternal grandfather and of the hamlet at Galdácano, in the Basque country, whence he came; Larraza is the name, also Basque—like Larra, Larrea, Larrazabal, Larramendi, Larraburu, Larraga, Larreta, and so many others—of my paternal grandmother. I write it in two words, La Raza, The Race, for the play on words that is in it—a taste for conceits—though in truth Larraza in Basque means pasture. I don't know what Jugo means in Basque, but I do know it does not mean what it does in Spanish: marrow, substance, pith, juice.

U. Jugo de la Raza is beset with a sovereign ennui —and what ennui besets a sovereign!—because he no longer lives except in himself, in the poor "I" under the sway and spell of history, in the saddened man who has not made himself a novel. And that is why he likes novels. He likes them and he uses them to live in others, to be someone else, to eternalize himself in another. At least that is what he thinks he does, but the truth is that he uses novels to discover himself, to live in himself, to be himself. Or better, in order to escape from his unknown and unknowable "I," unknown and unknowable even to himself.

[When I spoke of sovereign or sovereign's ennui, here and elsewhere, many times, I was thinking of our poor king, Don Alfonso XIII de Borbón y Hapsburgo-Lorena, whom I have always thought to be suffering a sovereign ennui and even to have been born bored—the heritage of dynastic centuries!— and I have assumed that all his imperial dreams, of which the latest and the worst was the Moroccan crusade, were to fill the vacuum produced by ennui, by the tragic solitude of the throne. It is like his mania for speed and his horror for what he calls pessimism. What kind of inner life, intimate life of a proper subject of God, could this poor lily in a thousand-year-old flowerpot boast?]

U. Jugo de la Raza, wandering along the banks of the Seine, down the length of the quays, among the stalls of old books, comes upon a novel which he scarce has time to examine for possible purchase before he is completely won over, drawn out; he identifies himself with the main character of the novel— a novel in the form of a romantic autobiographical confession—and the novel identifies him: gives him an immediate history, in short. The vulgar world of reality, of the age, disappears before his eyes. When, for an instant, he looks up from the pages of the book and fixes his gaze on the waters of the Seine, the river appears to him to be fixed too, unflowing, and the Seine is converted into an immobile mirror;

he looks away in horror and returns to the pages of the book, the novel, where he may find himself, where he may come to life. And then he comes upon a passage, an eternal passage, where he reads these prophetic words: "When the reader comes to the end of this painful story he will die with me."

Then Jugo de la Raza thought the letters of the words in the book were being erased before his eyes, as if the waters of the Seine were spilling over them, as if he himself were being drowned. He felt hot at the base of his skull and cold all over the rest of his body. His legs shook and the shadow of the specter of angina pectoris, which had been an obsession years before, fell across his soul. As he held onto the book his hands trembled. He was forced to lean for support against the quayside stall. At last he put the book down where he had found it and went off, following the river toward his house. He had felt the flurry of wind from the wingbeat of the Angel of Death blowing across his forehead. He arrived home, his home in that boardinghouse, house of passage, stretched out on the bed, and there he fell into a prolonged and swooning trance; he thought he would die and he suffered the most intense anguish.

"No, I won't touch that book again, I won't read it, I won't buy it and finish it. It would mean my death. . . . O, it's all foolish, of course, I know. That phrase was merely a grim fantasy of the author's, but it almost killed me. He is a stronger man than I am. And then when I had to cross the Pont de l'Alma —the Bridge of the Soul!—I felt an urge to throw myself into the Seine, into that mirror. I had to hold onto the parapet. And I recalled other such temptations, long ago now, and imagined again the fantasy of that born suicide who lived to be eighty constantly longing to kill himself and killing himself daily in thought. Is that life? I will not read that book. No, no more. Not that book or any other. And I will not walk along the banks of the Seine any more, nor among the bookstalls."

But poor Jugo de la Raza could not live without the book, without that book. His life, his inner existence, his reality, his true reality was now definitively and irrevocably joined to that of the central figure of the novel. If he continued reading it, living it, he ran the risk of dying when the central figure of the novel died. But if he did not read any further, if he did not live the book any longer, would he live at all? And, after all these doubts, he walked along the banks of the Seine once again. He passed the same bookstall once more, and as he did so he glanced with immense love and immense horror upon the fateful book. Then he gazed on the waters of the Seine and . . . prevailed! He prevailed. Or was he prevailed upon? He passed on without opening the book, murmuring: "How does the story develop? What can the outcome be?" He was convinced that one day he would not be able to resist any longer, that he would find himself forced to take up the book and go on with the reading even if it meant his death at the end.

Thus did the novel of my Jugo de la Raza evolve, my novel of Jugo de la Raza. And meanwhile I, Miguel de Unamuno, a novelistic figure also, scarcely wrote a line, scarcely worked at anything from fear of being devoured by my acts. From time to time I wrote political letters against Don Alfonso XIII and against the Praetorian tyrannizers of my poor country; but those letters, which were making history in my Spain, were devouring me. And there, in my Spain, my friends and my enemies were saying I was not a political man, that I did not have the temperament, and even less the temperament of a revolutionary, and that I should devote myself to writing verse and fiction and leave off politics. As if engaging in politics was different from writing poetry, and as if writing poetry was not another manner of engaging in politics!

But the worst of it was that I was not writing anything of great import; I was sunk into a state of worrisome inactivity, living in expectation, meditating on what I might do or say or write if this, that, or the other thing happened, dreaming of the future, which is the same as wasting it. And I would read whatever books fell into my hands by chance, without any plan or harmony, merely to indulge the awful vice of reading, the unpunished vice, of which Valery Larbaud speaks. Unpunished. But, wait now! It is exquisitely punished! The vice of reading is punished with continuous death!

Most of my projects—among them, three pages on how to make a novel—remained in abeyance. I had published my sonnets here, in Paris, and in Spain they had published my *Teresa*, written before the dishonorable coup d'état of September 13, 1923, before beginning my history of exile, the history of my exile. And yet it was necessary for me to live, in the usual sense of the word, to earn my livelihood by writing! And even so! . . . The courageous Buenos Aires daily, *Crítica*, had asked me to be a contributor on a regular well-paid basis. And yet, though I was without an excess of funds, and far away from friends and family, I was unable to put pen to paper. I stopped —and still have not renewed—my contributions to the Buenos Aires weekly *Caras y Caretas*. I had no wish—and do not now wish—to contribute to any newspaper or journal in Spain: I reject the humiliation of military censorship. I will not allow my writing to be censored by illiterate soldiery debased and degraded by training-camp discipline and reared to hate intelligence above all else. I know that after letting pass some harsh judgments of mine, judgments which in their own minds would seem felonious, they would edit out some innocent word merely to show their power. Censorship by orderlies? Never!

[Since coming here to Hendaye from Paris, I have acquired new evidence of the incurable stupidity of the censorship which serves the unfathomable idiocy of Primo de Rivera, and more evidence of the panic-stricken fear of truth displayed by poor insane Martínez Anido. It would be worth writing a book about the censorship, for the wild humor that is in it—if it were not all so terribly depressing. What that crowd fears, above all, is irony, the ironic smile, in which they see disdain, contempt. "Nobody, but nobody, laughs at us!" So they proclaim. I shall cite an instance. A lively, wide-awake lad, well informed and of an ironic mind, a product of liberal arts education, one of those "quota" recruits, as we call them, who have enough money to shorten their military service and gain certain privileges, was attached to a company whose captain, moved both by dislike and a certain fear, did his best to avoid any confrontation. However, he was obliged on one occasion to address the troops and to deliver one of those prescribed patriotic speeches. The poor captain could not stop himself from watching the lively lad, scrutinizing the expression of his mouth and eyes, and as he did so he found it difficult to make any sense of his own platitudes, until finally, getting rattled and then excited, losing control of himself, he stopped and addressed that particular soldier directly: "Is that a smile on your face?" The boy replied: "No, Captain, not at all, sir." But the captain insisted: "Yes, you've a smile inside you." And in our ill-fated Spain, whenever these Cainites, fit material to supply an armed band or a patrol of inquisitors for the Holy Office, unfortunate souls in uniform, whenever they encounter someone they mockingly call an "intellectual," they likewise scrutinize their eyes and mouth and read there a hidden smile of disdain and also suspect a smile hidden inside, an inner laughter directed at them. This is the worst sort of tragedy. And this is the pack the present tyranny has set loose.

Here on the frontier I have learned more of the radical perversion of the police, more about this institution of hangman's helpers. But I do not want to make my blood boil by writing further about these people, and so I return to my former narrative.]

Let us continue with the novel of Jugo de la Raza, the novel of his reading of a novel. What had to happen was that one day poor Jugo de la Raza was no longer able to resist: he was overcome by history, that is, by life, or better, by death. He went along the Seine, came to the bookstall, bought the book, pocketed it, and began to run, back along the length of the river toward his house, running with the book as if it were a stolen object, in fear it would be stolen from him. His flight made him lose his breath, he had to fight for air, and then the almost extinguished specter of angina pectoris reappeared before his eyes. He was forced to halt, and then, after first gazing around him on all sides, at the passersby and, even more intensely into the Seine, that flowing mirror, he opened the book and read a few lines. But he quickly closed it again. He was prey again to what, years before, he had called cerebral dyspnea, breathlessness, or perhaps the "X" sickness of MacKenzie, and he even thought he felt the fateful tingle down the length of his left arm and between the fingers of his hand. On other occasions he used to say to himself: "On reaching that tree there I shall fall down dead," and then, once he had passed it, a tiny voice from the bottom of his heart would whisper: "Perhaps you are really already dead. . . ." And so he arrived home.

He arrived home; he ate, all the while striving to prolong the meal—hurriedly prolonging it—and afterward climbed the stairs to his room; he took off his clothes and lay down as if to sleep, as if to die. His heart reverberated like an alarm bell. Stretched out on his bed, he first recited a Paternoster and then an Ave Maria; he paused at "Thy will be done on earth as it is in heaven" and then at "Holy Mary, mother of God, pray for us sinners now and at the hour of our death." He repeated it three times, crossed himself, and waited until his heart calmed down before opening the book. He felt time was consuming him; that the future of the novelistic fiction would swallow him, the future of that creature of fiction with whom he had identified himself; he felt he was sinking into himself.

Finally, somewhat composed, he opened the book and resumed reading. He forgot himself completely; and he could truly have said he had died. He dreamed of the Other or rather the Other was a dream he dreamed in himself, a creature of infinite solitude. A stabbing pain in his heart woke him. The novel's main character had just repeated to him: "I must tell my reader again that he will die with me." This time the effect was frightful. The tragic reader lost consciousness in his bed of spiritual agony. He left off dreaming the Other and he stopped dreaming himself. And

427*

when he came to, he hurled the book away, turned off the light, and attempted, after crossing himself once more, to fall asleep, to leave off dreaming. Impossible! From time to time he had to get up to drink water: it occurred to him that he was drinking the Seine, the mirror. "Am I crazy?" he asked himself. "No, for when someone asks if he is crazy it's a sign he's not. And yet . . ." He got up, started a fire in the fireplace, and burned the book. Hurriedly he went back to bed. And at length he managed to fall sleep.

The passage which I had planned for my novel, in the event that I had written it, where I would show the hero burning the book, recalls what I just finished reading in the letter which Mazzini, the great dreamer, wrote from Grenchen to his Giuditta on May Day of 1835: "If I go down into my heart I find ashes and an extinguished hearth. The volcano has burned itself out and nothing is left of it but the heat and the lava moving along the surface, and when everything has frozen over and all is fulfilled, nothing will be left, nothing but a vague memory of something which might have been and was not, the memory of what should have been done to achieve happiness and of how all was lost in inertia when titanic desires were rejected from within, before they were ever poured out, of how the soul was thus mined of hope, the memory of anguish, of fruitless vows . . . and then—nothing." Mazzini was an exile, an exile from eternity. [Mazzini was an outcast like Dante: Dante the great outcast—the great scorner. And before Dante, Moses and Saint Paul were proscribed outcasts, and scorners too; and after Dante, there was Victor Hugo. And all of them, Moses, Saint Paul, Dante, Mazzini, Victor Hugo, and so many others, learned in proscribed exile from their country, learned in the desert, where they sought their country, sought the meaning of their exile from out of eternity. It was in exile from his Florence that Dante was able to see that Italy was enslaved and the abode of sorrow:

Ahi serva Italia, di dolore ostello.]

As regards the idea of having my Jugo de la Raza, my reader of the novel, ask "Am I crazy?": I must confess that the greatest faith I ever had in my own sound judgment has come to me whenever I observed others around me, while watching what they did and did not do, while listening to what they said, and did not say, and it was in such moments that I had the fleeting suspicion that I might be mad.

To be mad is to have lost one's reason, they say, one's reason but not one's truth, for there are madmen who declare the truths that others silence because it is neither rational nor reasonable to proclaim them, and thus the truth-tellers are said to be mad. And what is reason? Reason is what all of us, or at least a majority of us, agree on. Truth is something else again. Reason is social; truth, ordinarily, is completely individual, personal, and incommunicable. Reason unites us; truth separates us.

[But now I see that it is perhaps truth which unites us and reason which separates us. And I realize how all that murky philosophy of reason and truth and madness was a response to a state of mind alien to me at times of greater spiritual calm. And, even though my battle with the authorities has intensified, here on the frontier, in sight of the mountains of my native country, my spirit has become more serene in its depths. And not for one moment does it occur to me that I might be mad. For if, at the risk of life and limb perhaps, I mount an attack against windmills as if they were giants, I do so in the full knowledge that they are windmills. But inasmuch as other people, those who consider themselves wise, believe the windmills to be giants, it is only right to undeceive them.]

Sometimes, in the intervals in which I believe myself to be a creature of fiction and in which I make my novel, in which I play a role, before my own eyes, I have dreamt that either almost all other people, especially in my Spain, are mad, or that I am. Since all the others cannot be mad, I must be. Listening to the judgments passed on my statements and writings and acts, I think: "Do I not perhaps utter other words than those I hear myself uttering, or am I heard to utter other words than those I utter?" And at such moments I never fail to conjure up the figure of Don Quixote.

[Later, here in Hendaye, a poor devil accosted me to say that in Spain I was considered a madman. It turned out that he was a policeman: he told me so himself, and he added that he was drunk. Being drunk, of course, is not the same as being mad. For example, Primo de Rivera does not go mad when he gets drunk, which he does at every critical juncture, but he merely exacerbates his *idiotitis* (cf. appendicitis, pharingitis, laryngitis, otitis, enteritis, phlebitis), which is an inflammation of his congenital and constitutional idiocy. His insurrectionary *pronunciamiento* had nothing Quixotic about it, nothing to do with sacred madness. It was a piece of speculative slyness accompanied by a vulgar *manifiesto*.]

At this point I ought to repeat a a question I think I raised in regard to Our Lord Don Quixote, and that was to ask what his punishment would have been if instead of dying when he recovered his reason—that reason common to anybody and everybody, thereby losing his truth, his own truth—what would have happened, if instead of dying as was only proper, he had lived a few years longer? And what would have happened is that all the madmen in Spain at the time— and there must have been a good plenty, for the terrible new disease had just been brought back from Peru—would have repaired to see him, asking for his help; when they saw it refused, they would have covered him with abuse and denounced him as an impostor, a traitor, and a renegade. For there exists a horde of madmen suffering from persecution mania, which quickly turns into a persecutory mania, and these madmen would begin to persecute Don Quixote as soon as he refused to persecute the alleged persecutors. But what did I do, my good Don Quixote, to have become a magnet to attract all the madmen who think themselves persecuted? Why do they turn to me? Why do they cover me with praise, if in the end they are to cover me with insult?

[When this same Don Quixote of mine had freed the galley slaves who were being transported as prisoners by the Holy Brotherhood, he was then stoned by the felons he had liberated. But even though I know that perhaps one day the galley slaves will stone me, not for that reason will I relax my efforts to combat the power of the patrolmen of the present-day Holy Brotherhood in my Spain. I cannot tolerate, even if my intolerance be considered madness, the process by which the hangmen give themselves the status of judges and by which the end-purpose of authority— which is justice—is suffocated by the so-called principle of authority, which is the principle of power, or so-called order. Nor can I tolerate the actions of a stunted and mean-spirited bourgeoisie, which out of a panic fear, an unreflecting fear, of the communist conflagration, a nightmare dreamt by men driven mad by fear, hands over house and wealth to firemen who lay it waste more surely than the conflagration itself. In Spain it is the firemen themselves, in fact, who start the conflagration, so as to live from the work of extinguishing it. For even though assassination in the streets has almost ceased (those which do occur are hushed up) since the advent of the praetorian police tyranny, it is only because the assassins are on the payroll of the Home Office and in the employ of the Ministry itself. Such is the nature of a police regime.]

Let us return once more to the novel of Jugo de la Raza, the novel of his reading of a novel [of the reader as actor, of the reader for whom to read is to live what he reads]. When he awoke the next morning, in his bed of spiritual agony, he found himself grown calmer; he got up and briefly contemplated the ashes of the fated book of his life. And those ashes seemed to him, like the waters of the Seine, another mirror. His torment was now renewed: how did that story end? And he went back to the quays along the Seine to search for another copy of the book, knowing he would not find one and knowing why he should not find one. And he suffered from not being able to find it: he suffered death. He made up his mind to travel about, to travel in God's world; perhaps God would forget him, leave him to his story. For the moment he went to the Louvre, to contemplate the Venus de Milo, as a means of freeing himself of his obsession. But the Venus de Milo seemed like the Seine and like the ashes of the book he had burned, another mirror. And so he decided to go away, to the sea and the mountains, for contemplation; to look long at aesthetic and architectonic wonders. Meanwhile he asked himself: "How does the story end?"

And I asked myself something similar, when I imagined that passage in my novel: "How will the story of the Directory end, and what will be the fate of the Spanish monarchy and of Spain itself?" And I devoured—as I still devour—the newspapers, and waited for letters from Spain. And I wrote the lines of Sonnet LXXVIII in my *De Fuerteventura a París*:

> Revolution is a comedy
> the Lord devised against ennui.

For is not the oppressiveness of history compounded of tedium? For my part I was also burdened with the displeasure of my fellow countrymen.

I understand perfectly the sentiments expressed by Mazzini in his letter to his Giuditta dated March 2, 1835, from Berne: "If I were to let myself go, I would hurl the lie and heap scorn on my Italian-speaking countrymen, but I would also savage with a vengeance any foreigner who would allow himself, in my presence, to guess my sentiments." I fully understand his "furious indignation" in dealing with other men, especially with his compatriots, who judged him so poorly and understood him so little. How great his truth, the truth of that "scornful soul," twin to the soul of Dante, that other great proscript, that other great scorner!

There is no way of divining, of vaticinating rather, how it will all turn out, over there in my Spain. No one believes in what they claim to be: the Socialists do not believe in socialism, nor in the class struggle, nor in the iron law of wages or any other Marxist symbology; the Communists do not believe in the community [and even less in Communion]; the Con-

servatives do not believe in conservation; the Anar-
chists do not believe in anarchy; the Praetorians do not
believe in the Dictatorship . . . O Nation of beggars!
And does anyone believe in himself? Do I believe in
myself? "The people are silent!" Thus ends Push-
kin's tragedy *Boris Godunov*. The people do not believe in themselves. And God is silent! And He is silent because He is an atheist.

Let us return, again, to the novel of my Jugo de la
Raza, to the novel of my reader, to the novel of his
reading, to my novel.

I thought to make him go on a trip, have him leave
Paris in search of oblivion, in order to forget history.
He would have wandered about, pursued by the ashes
of the book he had burned, and he would pause to
gaze into the waters of the rivers and seas. I thought
to have him wander, weary with history's anguish,
along the canals at Ghent and Bruges, or in Geneva
along the banks of Lake Leman, and to cross, enveloped in melancholy, the bridge at Lucerne which
I myself crossed thirty-six years ago now, when I was
twenty-five. I would have included recollections of my
wanderings: I would have written of Ghent and Geneva and Venice and Florence and . . . then, on his
arrival at one of these cities, my poor Jugo de la Raza
would have sought out a bookstall and there he would
have found another copy of the fateful book and, all
a-tremble, he would have bought it and carried it off
to Paris, prepared to take up where he left off, reading until his curiosity was satisfied, to the point where
he could foresee the end without getting to it, until
he could have said: "Now I can guess how all this
will end. . . ."

[When I wrote these lines in Paris, almost two
years ago now, it would not have occurred to me to

have my Jugo de la Raza wander anywhere but Ghent and Geneva and Lucerne and Venice and Florence. . . . Now I would have him wander through this idyllic *Pays Basque* which combines the sweetness of *la douce France* with the sweetness of my bittersweet Biscay. He would walk along the quiet banks of the humble Nivelle, where it runs between emerald meadows at Ascain at the foot of Larrún—another derivative of *larra*, pasture—and he would gaze about the soothing greenness of his native land, thick as it is with a thousand-year-old silence which annihilates deceitful history. He would wander among those clusters of ancient houses which gaze into the waters of a quiet river; and he would gradually begin to hear the silence in the human abyss.

I would have him go as far as St.-Jean-Pied-de-Port, birthplace of Doctor Huarte de San Juan, who wrote the *Examen de Ingenios*, and the city whence the River Nive flows down to St.-Jean-de-Luz. And there in the old Navarrese city, at one time Spanish and now French, if he were to sit on a stone bench in Eyalaberri, in that ambit of peace, he would hear the eternal murmur of the river. And he would go to the riverbank, and see the stream flowing beneath the bridge leading to the church. And the surrounding fields would speak to him in Basque, in children's *Eusquera*, childlike Basque, and they would speak to him like children in simple peace and trust. Should his watch stop, he would repair to a watchmaker, who would tell him, when Jugo de la Raza declared that he did not speak the Basque tongue, that languages and religions separate men. As if Christ and Buddha had not spoken to God in a like way, even if in different languages.

My Jugo de la Raza would walk in meditation

along the street of the Citadel which climbs from the church up to the castle, the work of Vauban; the majority of the houses date from before the French Revolution, and in them three centuries have slept their sleep. The automobiles of the collectors of kilometers cannot, thank God, climb that street. And on that street of peace and quiet he would visit the *prison des evesques*, the St.-Jean bishops' jail, an Inquisition dungeon. Behind it the old walls give shelter to small confined orchards. The old jail, vine-covered now, lies in the background.

Then my poor tragic reader would contemplate the waterfall formed by the Nive, and he would see how those waters, never for a moment the same, form a kind of wall: a mirrorlike wall, a mirror of history. And he would follow the river down toward Uhartlize, where he would pause in front of the house whose lintel announces:

> Vivons en paix
> Pierre Ezpellet
> et Jeanne Iribar
> ne. Cons. Annee 8^e
> 1800

And he would dream of living in peace—Let us live in peace!—like Pierre Ezpellet and Jeanne Iribar in the days when Napoleon was filling the world with the clamor of his history.

Wanting to take in with his eyes the green of his own land's hills, my Jugo de la Raza would go as far as the bridge at Arnegui, on the frontier between France and Spain. Over that insignificant bridge, on the second day of Carnival, 1875, the pretender Don Carlos de Borbón y Este, Carlos VII for the Spanish Carlists, crossed as the last civil war ended, a war which engendered the one now put upon us by the praetorian guard of Alfonso XIII, a Carlist war of its own, just as the *pronunciamiento* of Primo de Rivera was Carlist. And it was on February 21, 1924, fifty years to the day from when I heard one of the first shells fired by the Carlists against my native Bilbao fall beside the house where I was born, that I was taken out of my Salamanca house to be shipped into exile and confinement on the island of Fuerteventura in the Canaries. And there, beside the humble bridge at Arnegui, Jugo de la Raza might have mulled over the fact that the villagers thereabouts no longer know about Carlos VII, the king who crossed the bridge declaring, as he looked back on Spain: "I will return!"

The legendary Charlemagne must have crossed over this same bridge or one near it. This is the route to Roncesvalles, where the trumpet of Roland—who was no Orlando Furioso—sounded; today silence reigns among these hedgerows of shaded peace. And Jugo de la Raza might well bring together, link together in his imagination, in his everyman's sacred imagination, where centuries of time and continents of space are merged, where periods of time become eternity and the horizon extends to infinity, he might well bring together, link together Carlos VII and Charlemagne. And then he would link them to Alfonso XIII and the first Spanish Hapsburg, Carlos I of Spain—who was the Emperor Charles V of Germany and of the Holy Roman Empire—and he would recall the day that he, Jugo, visited Yuste and contemplated, in lieu of any other water mirror, the pond in which the Emperor was said to fish tench from a balcony. And amid all the others, beside Carlos VII the Pretender and Charlemagne, Alfonso XIII, and

Carlos I, he would make out the pale enigmatic shade of Don Juan, the prince who died of "phthisis" at Salamanca before he could gain the throne, the ex-future Don Juan III, son of the Catholic Monarchs Ferdinand and Isabel. Meditating on them all as he walked from the bridge at Arnegui back to St.-Jean-Pied-de-Port, Jugo de la Raza would ask himself: "And how will all this end?"]

But I must interrupt this novel so as to return to the other. I devour all the news I receive here concerning my Spain, especially all reports on the Moroccan campaign, and I ask myself if the outcome of this war will allow me to return to my own country, there to make my history and its history, to return to die there, to die there and be buried in the desert. . . .

To these questions, people here react by asking whether I can or cannot return to my Spain, whether there is any law or provision of public authority which would prevent my return. I find it very difficult to explain to anyone, especially non-Spaniards, the reason why I cannot and should not return as long as the Directorate and General Martínez Anido remain in power, since I would find it impossible to keep quiet, to desist in my attacks and accusations against them. If I return to Spain and shout my accusations in the streets and plazas, proclaim the truth, my truth, then my freedom and even my life would be in danger, and if I were to lose either one, neither my so-called friends nor the so-called friends of liberty and life would lift a finger. When I do explain my situation to people, some of them smile and exclaim: "Ah, yes, I see, a question of honor!" And behind their smile I read their thoughts: "How careful he is to play out his role. . . ."

And would they not to some extent be right? Am I not on the point, perhaps, of sacrificing my most personal I, my divine individuality, whatever I am in God, the person I should be, to the "Other," the other I, the historic I, the I which moves and acts in its own history and with its own history? Why do I obstinately persist in not returning to my Spain? Am I not in the course of creating my own legend, the legend which will accompany me to the grave, as well as helping to create the legend which my friends and enemies are fashioning? The point is that if I do not make a legend for myself, I will die altogether. And if I do make myself one—the same fate awaits me anyway.

Here you have me making my own legend, my novel, and making their novel, the novel of Primo de Rivera, the novel of Martínez Anido, figments of my imagination, creatures of fiction. Do I lie when I attribute certain intentions and feelings to them? Do they exist as I describe them? Do they even exist at all? Do they exist, in any way at all, outside of me? Insofar as they are my creations, they are creatures of my love even if that love is disguised as hatred. I said that Sarmiento admired and loved the tyrant Rosas; I will not say that I admire our king, but that I love him I will admit, for he is mine, I made him. I would like him out of Spain, but I like him, I love him. Perhaps I even love that simpleton of a Primo de Rivera, who regrets what he did to me, just as underneath it all he regrets what he did to Spain. And as for that poor epileptic Martínez Anido (who during one of his attacks and while frothing at the mouth and wracked with tremors called for my head), I feel a compassion which amounts to tenderness, because I suspect that he desires nothing more than he desires my pardon, especially if he guesses that every day I pray, "Forgive us our debts as we forgive our debtors." But Ah! my role! I must return to the stage! To the comedy!

[Well now, no! When I wrote those lines I was carried away; I wrote them in a moment of depression. I might well pardon them for what they have done to me, but I am not the one who can pardon them for what they have done and continue to do to my unfortunate country. And it is not a matter of playing a role. And as to whether that loud-mouthed Primo de Rivera now regrets his actions, that may well be, but what he calls his honor will not allow him to say so. His is the terrible cavalier honor, described for all time in the quatrain from Guillén de Castro's *Las mocedades del Cid*:

> Try always to be right
> in honor ever strong
> but if your course prove wrong
> defend it sans respite.

Which does not mean that Primo de Rivera is honorable or strong, or even less that in the pronunciamiento issued at his *coup* he made any attempt to be right.]

Giuditta Sidoli wrote to her Giuseppe Mazzini to tell him of "feelings which turn into necessities," and of "work done from the material need to produce work, and for reasons of vanity" and the great exile spoke out against this view. Mazzini wrote from Grenchen on May 14, 1835: "There are hours, solemn hours, hours which have roused me these ten years, in which I *see us*. I see life. I see my heart and the hearts of others, but then at once . . . I come back to the illusions of poetry." Mazzini's poetry was history, his history, the history of Italy, which was his mother and daughter both.

Hypocrite! Greek for actor; I know, since I am a Hellenist breadwinner: it was my chair of Greek with which the Directory played the comedy of taking it away from me by reserving it for me. Hypocrites? No! My role is my truth, and I must live my truth, which is my life.

These days I play the role of a proscript. Even the careless negligence in my personal appearance, my obstinacy in not changing my apparel, in not having a new suit made, partly depend—with the aid of a certain native avarice which now that I am alone encounters no obstacle—on the role I play. When my wife came to visit me with my three daughters in February 1925, she took charge of my linen, refurbished my clothes, provided me with new stockings. Now they are full of holes, in tatters, perhaps so that I might be able to say to myself what Don Quixote, my Don Quixote said to himself, when he saw that his stockings had unraveled: "Oh poverty, poverty!" I sensed this passionately when I was commenting the quixotic history in my *Life of Don Quixote and Sancho*.

Could I be playing a role in a comedy, a comedy even for my friends? But no! My life and my truth are my role. When I was exiled without a word of explanation—I still do not know the reason—without so much as a pretext, I told my people, my family, not to come with me, to let me go alone. I had need of solitude, and moreover I was aware that the real aim of those garrison tyrants was to ruin me, to force me to squander my modest possessions and those of my children; I knew that my exile was a species of confiscation, and so I decided to restrict my expenses and even not to pay them at all, and I acted accordingly. They could confine me to a desert island, but they could not do so at my expense.

I asked to be left alone, and my people—they are mine and I am theirs—understood me and truly cared for me and left me alone. Then, toward the end of my confinement on the island, after my eldest son had come with his wife to join me, a certain lady presented herself—accompanied by her daughter, who doubtless served by way of guard—a lady who had plagued me with her epistolary persecution. Perhaps she meant to use me as neither my wife nor my children had done. The lady in question is a woman-of-letters, and my wife, though she writes well, is not. But could that poor woman-of-letters, concerned about her name and fame, which she perhaps meant to join to mine, could that woman care for me more than my Concha, the mother of my eight children and my own true mother as well? My real mother, yes. In a moment of supreme, of abysmal anguish, when she saw me in the claws of the Angel of Nothingness, wracked with superhuman weeping, she cried out to me from the depths of her maternal being, superhuman and divine: "My child!" I discovered then all that God had done for me in this woman, the mother of my children, my own virgin mother, who has no novel but mine, my mirror of holy, divine unconsciousness and eternity. Naturally she left me alone on my island, while the other woman, the woman-of-letters, the woman of her own novel and not mine, came to me looking for gaudy emotions—or perhaps to live out a film script.

Still the poor woman-of-letters sought what she sought naturally, she sought what every writer seeks, and every historian, every novelist, every politician, every poet: to live on in lasting, permanent history, so as not to die. These days I have been reading Proust, the prototype of writers and recluses: what tragic solitude! He was afflicted by the sense of death, and so was able to fathom the abyss of the human tragedy because he felt death, but death at every instant, for he felt himself dying at every moment, so that he dissects the dead body of his soul: and with what minute concentration! In the re-search of time lost! Time is always lost. To gain time, as they say, is to lose it. Time: there lies the tragedy.

"I know the sorrows of artists as treated by artists: Theirs are the shadow of sorrow; ours, its substance," Mazzini wrote to his Giuditta on March 2, 1835. And Mazzini was an artist, no more and no less than an artist. He was a poet; as a politician he was a poet, no more than a poet. The shadow of sorrow and not its body. And there is the basis of the novelesque tragedy, of the tragic novel of history: sorrow is shadow and not body. The most painful sorrow, the sorrow which makes us cry out and makes God weep bitter tears is a shadow of ennui. Time is not corporal. Kant said it was an *a priori* form of sensibility. What a dream the dream of life . . . ! A dream without awakening?

[That last phrase I added just now, as I rewrite my words of two years ago. Just now, too, at the beginning of June 1927, when the praetorian tyranny in Spain is every day growing more vile and the ruffian who represents it best now vomits up, almost daily, the dregs of his drunken nights, vomits in the lap of Spain, I have just received the current issue of *La Gaceta Literaria* of Madrid dedicated to Don Luis de Góngora y Argote and to Gongorism by the cultured and cultist youths of castrated Spanish intellectuality. I read the issue here, in my mountains, which Góngora called "green ash of the Pyrenees" (*Soledades*, II, 759), and I see that these youths have "seized much Sea and little water." And the Sea, without water, is doubtless a pure cultist poetry. But, in short, these my memoirs, this narrative of how a novel is made, are "voices of blood and blood from the soul" (*Soledades*, II, 119).

Yet I myself, who detest Gongorist euphuism, who find no poetry—that is, creation, which is action—where there is no passion, where there is no body and blood of human sorrow, where there are no tears of blood, even I am prey to the most terrible, the most anti-poetic aspect of Gongorist euphuism: erudition. "The sea is not deaf. Erudition deceives" (*Soledades*, II, 172), Góngora wrote, but did not think, and thereby delineates himself. He was, that cleric from Córdoba, a scholar, a professor of poetry . . . a wretched profession!

All of this speculation results from considering Mazzini's view of the sorrows of the artist at the moment when a homage to Góngora is offered by the cultist youth in Spain. But Mazzini, the man who cried "God and Country!", was a patriot, a citizen, a civic man. Could as much be said for those cultist youths? I am forcibly reminded of our great mistake in placing culture above civilization, or rather above civility. Yes: before and above all else, civility!]

And now we return for the last time to the history of our Jugo de la Raza.

As soon as I would have brought him back to Paris, his fateful book with him, he would have to face the problem of either finishing the book that had become his life and consequently dying at its end, or renouncing it and living finally to die anyway. One kind of death or another: in history or outside it. I would have had him deliver a monologue in which he discussed these matters, which is one way of living, of animating oneself:

"But this is all no better than madness. . . . The author of this novel is making mock of me. . . . Or is it that I am making mock of myself? Why should I die just when I finish reading this book, when the autobiographical character himself dies? Why shouldn't I survive myself? Outlive myself and examine my dead body. I will go on reading a while until there is very little time left for the poor devil to live and then, when I have guessed the end, I will go on living in the thought that I will thus make him live a little longer. When old Don Juan Valera was suddenly stricken with blindness he refused to be operated and explained: 'If I am operated upon, I might be left blind for good, forever without hope of recovering my sight, while if I refuse an operation, I can live always with the hope that some operation or other will cure me.' But no, I will not go on reading this book. I will keep it within arm's length, on my night table, and while I sleep I can think that I could read it if I wanted to, but I won't read it. And yet, can I live like that? In any case, I must die, since every one dies. . . ." [The everyday expression in Spanish is that every god dies. . . .]

And so, meanwhile, Jugo de la Raza would have begun reading the book again, but without ever finishing it, reading it slowly, very, very slowly, syllable by syllable, spelling it out, stopping when he was only a line ahead, and then beginning again: advancing like a tortoise, a hundred steps forward and ninety-nine back, advancing and then retreating in equal proportion, always keeping in mind the frightful last step.

The words I would have placed in the mouth of my Jugo de la Raza about how every one dies [or in everyday Spanish, of how every god dies], are patently vulgar, of the greatest possible vulgarity, the most common of all commonplaces and therefore the most paradoxical of paradoxes. When we studied logic we were given as example of a syllogism "All men are mortal; Peter is a man, therefore Peter is mortal." And then followed the illogical anti-syllogism "Christ is immortal; Christ is a man, therefore every man is immortal."

[This anti-syllogism, whose major premise is an individual term, neither universal nor particular, but which attains maximum universality, for if Christ was resurrected any man may be resurrected—or as everyday Spanish would have it: any christ may be resurrected—this anti-syllogism is at the root of what I have called the tragic sense of life and it forms the essence of the agony of Christianity. All together it constitutes the divine tragedy.

The Divine Tragedy! Not what Dante, the medieval believer, the Ghibelline proscript, called his *Divine Comedy*, which was a comedy and not a tragedy because in it there was hope. In the twentieth canto of the *Paradiso* there is a tercet which reveals the light shining over this comedy. It is the passage which states that the kingdom of heaven suffers violence— according to the biblical sentence—the violence of warm love and live hope which together overcome the divine will:

> Regnum coelorum violenza pate
> da caldo amore, e da viva speranza
> che vince la divina volontate

And these lines are more than pure poetry or cultist erudition.

"Live hope overcomes the divine will!" To have that belief really is faith, poetic faith! Whoever hopes firmly, with full faith in his hope, that he will not die, will not die . . . ! In any case Dante's damned live in history and thus their damnation is not tragic, not a divine tragedy, but comic tragedy. On them, despite their damnation, God smiles. . . .]

Sheer vulgarity! And yet the most tragic passage in Mazzini's tragic correspondence is to be found in a letter of June 30, 1835, where he writes: "Everybody is dying: Romagnosi has died, Pecchio has died, and Vitorelli, who I thought was some time dead, has just died." And Mazzini perhaps said to himself one day: "I, who thought myself dead, am going to die." Just as Proust.

What am I going to do with my Jugo de la Raza? Inasmuch as what I am here writing, reader, is a true novel, a true poem, a creation which consists in telling you how a novel is made rather than how it is told—a novel, that is to say, a historical life—I am in nowise obliged to satisfy your frivolous interest in mere tale-telling. Any reader who in reading a novel concerns himself with the final destiny of the characters without concerning himself with his own does not deserve to have his curiosity satisfied.

As regards my own sorrows, which are perhaps incommunicable, perhaps I need only repeat what Mazzini wrote his Giuditta from Grenchen on July 15, 1835: "Today I should tell you, so that you do not tell me again that my sorrows belong to the realm of poetry, as you call it, that for some time past they have been in fact precisely that—poetry." And in another letter, of June 2 of the same year: "Everything strange to them they call poetry; they call poets mad until they drive them mad; they drove Tasso mad; they perpetrated Chatterton's suicide and others like it; they have even hounded the dead—Byron, Foscolo, and others—because these dead did not follow the right road. Our scorn upon them! I shall suffer, but I will not renege on my soul; I will not do wrong in order to placate them, though I would wreak evil if they were to deprive me of what they call poetry, for by dint of prostituting the name of poetry by means of hypocrisy they have succeeded in putting everything in doubt. For my part, I see things in my own light and call them by my own names, for me poetry is virtue, is love, is piety, is affection, is love of country, is unmerited lucklessness, is you, is your mother's love, is whatever is sacred on earth. . . ." I cannot go on listening to Mazzini. On reading these lines any reader's heart will hear the cry of an eagle wounded in flight as it soars in the sunlight, will hear the cry fall through the black clouds below, through the storm building up.

Poetry! Divine poetry! Lifetime solace! Yes, and poetry is all Mazzini says. And it is also polity. That other great proscript, doubtless the greatest of all proscribed citizens, the Ghibelline Dante, was and is and will go on being a high, a profound, a sovereign poet and politician and believer. Polity and religion and poetry were in him and for him one and the same thing, an intimate trinity. His sense of citizenship, his faith and his fantasy made him eternal.

[Just now, in the issue of the *Gaceta Literaria* in which the cultist youth of Spain offer their homage to Góngora and which I have just received and read, one of these youths, Benjamín Jarnés, in a piece-let cultistically called "Gold Beaten and Nectar Expressed" tells us that "Góngora does not have recourse to the fatuous fire of dyed-bluish fantasy or to the shimmering flame of passion but appeals to the perennial light of tranquil intelligence." Now is that what these intellectuals call poetry? A poetry without the fire of fantasy or the flame of passion? Then may they feed on the bread made from this beaten gold! And then the writer adds that Góngora "did not so much propose to repeat a fine story as to invent a fine language." But is there any language without a story, or any fineness of language without a story finely told?

All this homage to Góngora, given the circumstances in which it is offered, given the present state of my poor country, strikes me as a tacit and slavish homage to tyranny, a servile act, and in some of these intellectuals—not in all, of course—an act of beggary. And all this poetry they celebrate is no more than a lie. A lie and nothing but a lie . . . ! Góngora himself was a liar. Just listen to the way the man who said that "erudition deceives" begins his *Soledades*:

> It was in the year's flowing season
> when the feigning raptor of Europa . . .

The "feigning!" The feigning? Why did he think himself obliged to tell us that Jupiter's making off with Europa when he took on the character of a bull was a lie? Why did this learned cultist also feel himself obliged to give us to understand that his own fictions were lies? Lies and not fictions. Did he, the cultist artist, who was also a clergyman, a priest in the Roman Catholic Apostolic Church, believe in the Christ to whom he rendered public homage? Did he not, perchance, when he consecrated the Host in the Holy Mass, also act the cultist? I prefer the fantasy and passion of Dante.]

449*

There are people, simpletons, who advise me to leave off politics. They mean their brand of politics, and they speak with an air of pretended disdain, which is nothing but the fear felt by eunuchs or impotent men or by men as good as dead. And they assure me that I should stick to my teaching, my studies, my novels, my poems, my own life. They do not want to understand that my teaching, my studies, my novels, my poems *are* the essence of politics. They will not understand that it is a question of fighting, today, in my own country, for the freedom of truth, which is the supreme justice, of fighting to liberate truth from a terrible dictatorship which dictates nothingness, from an awful tyranny, the tyranny of stupidity and impotence and naked purposeless force. Mazzini, Dante's favorite son, made of his life a poem, a novel much more poetic than those of Manzoni, D'Azeglio, Grossi, or Guerrazzi. And the greater and better part of the poetry of Lamartine or Hugo was a result of their being as good poets as they were political men. But what about the poets who were never political? We should have to take a closer look at them; but in any case

non raggioniam di lor, ma guarda e passa.

Then there are others, the vilest of all: the so-called intellectuals, intellectuals by definition: technicians, savants, philosophers. On June 28, 1835, Mazzini wrote to Giuditta: "For myself, I mean to leave it all behind and go back to my own individuality, for I am full of bitterness toward all I love most, and disgusted with mankind. I disdain those who cull only abjectness from among the ruins and spoils of philosophy. Contemptuous of everyone, I am painfully outraged at myself, at the present and the future. I shall never be able to rid my hands of the doctrinal muck. May the curse of my country, the nation which will emerge from the future, fall upon them all!"

So be it! So be it, I say of the savants and philosophers who live in and off Spain, of the wise men who want to hear no yelps and raised voices, of those who would have us smile as we are spit upon by the vilest of the vile, who ask wherefore liberty. As for them, they would sell it. Prostitutes!

[Ever since I wrote those lines, two years ago, I have not had—God's curse!—any reason to change my mind. The degradation, the degeneration of Spanish intellectuals—let us call them by this name— continues apace. They submit to the censorship and bear in silence the officious dispatches in which Primo de Rivera almost daily outrages the dignity of the civil and national conscience of Spain. And they persist in their vapid dissertations.]

I shall now return again, after the last time, when I said I would not go on, to my Jugo de la Raza. Seething as he was with fateful anguish, with his ill-omened book always before his eyes and within hand's reach, unable to open it and take up his reading as a means of prolonging the agony which was his life, he seemed in danger of suffering an attack of hemiplegia or some other form of stroke. I wondered if he would not lose his willpower, his memory, or in any case the appetite for life. In the end he might forget the book, the novel, his own life, and he would forget himself: another form of dying, and of dying before one's time (assuming there is a time for dying or that one can die outside the appointed time).

This kind of denouement has occurred to me after seeing the latest photographs of poor Francos Rodríguez, journalist, former supporter of the Republic, and later government minister for the king. He looks hemiplegic. One of the pictures shows him leaving the Royal Palace, in the company of Horacio Echevarrieta, after calling on the king to request the latter to lay the first stone in the Casa de la Prensa, new headquarters for the newspapermen's association, of which Francos is president. In another, he is at the king's side in the course of the ceremony. His face shows us fright made flesh. And now I recall poor Don Gumersindo Azcárate, another supporter of the Republic, who was brought to the Palace, already in a state of mumbling dotage, a living corpse. At the ceremony, in which the king laid the first stone for the Casa de la Prensa, Primo de Rivera delivered a panegyric on Pi y Margall, a consistent and lifelong republican who died in the full use of his faculties as a citizen: that is, he died while still alive.

As I thought of this possible solution to the novel of my Jugo de la Raza, a natural solution if I were simply to tell his story rather than make it, I thought of my wife and children and of how I would never die an orphan, for my sons would be fathers to me and my daughters would be mothers. And if some day fear of the future should show itself in the flesh of my face, if I should lose my will and my memory, neither my sons nor my daughters, my fathers nor my mothers, need allow the slightest homage from others, nor need they allow a vengeful pardon, nor allow a tribute, panegyric, or eulogy from this tragic blusterer, this monster of frivolity, who once wrote that he would like to see me free of passion—that is to say: worse than dead. And if this be comedy, it is, like Dante's, divine comedy.

[On rereading these lines as I rewrite them, I am conscious, as reader of myself, of the deplorable effect on others of my saying that I do not want to be pardoned. This sentiment is one of Luciferian, near-Satanic, pride; it is not compatible with "forgive us our debts as we forgive our debtors." For if we forgive our debtors, why should we not be forgiven by those to whom we owe a debt? And I cannot deny that in the heat of battle I have offended them. But my bread and my wine have been embittered and poisoned by the sight of them imposing unjust and undeserved punishment, always in the thought of bestowing pardon. The most repugnant aspect of what they call the royal prerogative of pardon is that more than once—I myself have some direct experience of it—the royal power has violated the rights of the tribunals of justice, has used bribery, to force an unjust sentence with the sole end of then inflicting one of its spiteful royal pardons. The same purpose and end is sought by the absurd severity of the penalty which is heaped upon the supposed crime of affront to the king, the crime of *lèse-majesté*.]

On reading this cynical, perhaps immodest, confession along the lines of Jean Jacques, some reader will doubtless question my theory of divine comedy and indignantly claim that I am merely playing a part, that I have no notion of true patriotism and that the comedy of my life has been far from serious. But the truth is that such a reader is made indignant by the evidence that he himself in his turn is a comic character, a novelistic character no less, a character the like of whom I would situate squarely in his dream of life. Let him make his life from his dream, and he will be saved. Since all is comedy and novel, let him know that what strikes him as extra-scenic reality is the comedy of a comedy, the novel of a novel, and that the noumenon invented by Kant is about the most "phenomenal" possible and that substance is what is most formal. The essence of a thing is its surface.

And now, why put an end to the novel of Jugo? This novel, and for that matter all novels which must be made, and which do not satisfy in merely being told, do not, strictly speaking, come to an end. What comes to an end, is finished, is perfect, is death, and life cannot die. The reader in search of finished novels does not merit being my reader; he himself is finished before having read me.

The reader given to strange deaths, the sadist in search of the ejaculations of sensibility, the one who in reading *La Peau de Chagrin* feels himself swoon in a voluptuous spasm when Raphaël calls Pauline: "Pauline, come . . . !" and further on: "I love you, I adore you, I desire you . . . ," and sees her rolling, half nude, about the couch, and desires her in his final death agony, his agony which is his desire itself, through the choked sounds of his death rattle, and bites Pauline in the breast while she dies, too, tightly clutching him—such a reader may want me to give a similar ending to the agony of my protagonist; but, if he has not felt that agony in himself, what good would it do for me to extend myself further? Besides, there are requirements to which I would not answer. Let him look to himself alone, as best he can, alone and in solitude!

Despite everything, some reader will insist on asking: "And so, what end does this man come to? How does history dispose of him?" And what about you, now, reader? If you are no more than a reader, you will come to an end when you come to the end of your reading; but if you are a man, a man like me, that is, actor and author of yourself, then you should not read at all—for fear of forgetting yourself.

There is a famous story of how an actor who committed suicide hypocritically on the stage always drew great rounds of applause until, in the one and only representation in which he committed suicide theatrically but truly—something he could not repeat again, inasmuch as his suicide was genuine—then on this last and authentic appearance, he was jeered. Of course it would have been even more tragic if he had garnered smiles and laughter. Laughter, laughter: the abysmal tragic Passion of Our Lord Don Quixote! And that of Christ. To make men laugh in one's agony! "If thou be the king of the Jews, save thyself" (Luke 23:37).

"God is not capable of irony. And love is much too holy, much the purest aspect of our nature, not to come to us from Him. We must, then, either deny God, which is absurd, or believe in immortality." Thus wrote the agonic Mazzini—wonderful agonist! —from London to his mother—to his mother!—on June 26, 1839, thirty-three years before his definitive earthly death. But supposing History is no more than the laughter of God? And each and every Revolution but an outburst of His laughter? All of it peals of laughter resounding like thunder, as the divine eyes water from laughing.

In any case and for the rest, I do not care to die merely to please certain dubious readers. And you, reader, who have come this far: are you alive?

Continuation

A N D   S O   E N D E D the narrative about how to make a novel, which appeared in French in the *Mercure de France*, a narrative written almost two years ago now. And my own novel has gone on, continued, my novel, or history, or comedy, or tragedy, or whatever, and the novel, history, comedy or tragedy of my own Spain, and of Europe, and of all humanity, has gone on, continued. And over and above the anguish connected with the possible ending of my novel, over or under it, above or below, I continue to be anguished at the possible ending of the novel of humanity, in which one of the episodes, a mere episode, is the so-called decline and fall of the West and the end of our civilization.

Once more I recall the ending of Carducci's ode, *Su Monte Maris*, where the human race is exhausted

> until, withered at the Equator
> beneath the insistence of a terminal heat,
> the faded lineages produce one last
> man, one woman,
>   standing alone amid rent cliffs,
> dead woods, ash-colored and their eyes
> glazed, watching the sun go down
> across the immense ice.

Apocalyptic vision! And it recalls another, all the more terrible because comic, in a work by Courteline, wherein he depicts the end of the last of mankind, aboard a ship resembling a new Noah's Ark in a new universal deluge. Sailing along with the last of mankind aboard ship, is a parrot: the ship begins to sink, and the humans to drown, but the parrot climbs to the highest part of the mainmast and, as the mainmast is going under, now the last point left in the world, the parrot shrieks out to the sky the last cry: "Liberté! Egalité! Fraternité!" And so ends History.

This view of things is generally called pessimism. And yet, it is not the pessimism meant by the king of Spain—still king today, June 4, 1927—Don Alfonso XIII, when he says that the pessimists must be isolated. Thus, I was isolated for some months on the island of Fuerteventura, so that I might not contaminate my compatriots with my paradoxical pessimism. I was then pardoned that confinement or isolation, to which I had been taken without ever having been given—even yet—a reason or even a pretext. I came to France and ignored the pardon and took up residence in Paris where I wrote the preceding narrative, and at the end of August 1925 I came here from Paris, to Hendaye, to continue making a novel of life. And it is this part of my novel which I am now going to tell you, reader, so that you may continue seeing how a novel is made.

*   *   *

I wrote the above two days ago, and in all the time since, I have not put pen to paper, ruminating the while on how the novel being made might end. For now I would like to bring it to an end, rescue my Jugo de la Raza from the terrible nightmare of his fateful book, and come to the end of his novel as Balzac reached the end of the novel of Raphaël de Valentin. And I believe I will be able to do so, be able to finish making the novel, thanks to my twenty-two months in Hendaye.

I will not, of course, tell you reader, the story in detail, of my stay here, of my frontier adventures. I will save that for another place, where I will also detail the maneuvers of the abject tyrants of Spain to drive me out of here, to get the government of the French Republic to intern me. I shall also relate how the Ministre de l'Intérieur, Monsieur Schrameck, requested me to move away from the frontier because my stay here could create "certain difficulties" "*à l'heure actuelle*"—September 6, 1925. I was asked to leave so as "to avoid any incident likely to prejudice the good relations existing between France and Spain" and "to facilitate the task incumbent on the French authorities." And I shall relate how I answered the minister, and wrote at the same time joint letters to my friend Monsieur Painlevé, then president of the Council of Ministers, and to Señor Quiñones de León, the king's ambassador to the French Republic, refusing to quit this corner of my native *pays basque*, gateway to Spain—and all the other things that happened. The first was a visit from the Prefect of the Basses-Pyrénées who came from Pau on September 24: he attempted, in the name of Monsieur Painlevé, to talk me into leaving the frontier zone. I refused once again, and the Spanish tyranny, no longer satisfied with their triumph at interning me, mounted a police compaign. A band of Spanish police officers, directed by a certain Luis Fenoll, appeared in Hendaye, where they bought a number of pistols in a local shop; they then went off to the frontier zone around Vera, carried out a mock skirmish with an imaginary band of Communists—bogeymen!—and then got themselves lost! Eventually they ran into a detachment of the Spanish border-police and were brought before a captain, who chanced to be Don Juan Cueto, an old and dear friend of mine. The police chieftain, Fenoll, declared that he was on a "high political mission," under orders from the military to provoke, or rather to feign, a frontier incident, a kind of Communist invasion, which would justify my being forced out of the area. This singular maneuver failed because of the loyalty of Captain Cueto, now held for trial, who publicly denounced it, and because of the heavy-handedness characteristic of the police. Even then the abject petty tyrants of Spain—I would not call them Spaniards—did not cease in their endeavors to move me on. And someday I will relate the varied details of this struggle. For the moment, and in order to put an end to the narrative of this external and almost apparitional part of my life, I shall merely add that a little over a month ago, on May 16, I received another letter from the Prefect of the Basses-Pyrénées at Pau, in which he begged me to call on him as quickly as possible, "*le plus tôt possible*," in his office there, so that he might communicate the contents of a message from Monsieur le ministre de l'Intérieur. I answered that I would not, for very good reason, leave Hendaye, and therefore begged him to forward the message to me here—in writing. I have had no further news to this day. I was pretty sure they would not venture to put down anything in writing, for it would remain as evidence; for my part I shied away from the spoken word, which the wind carries off. And yet—does writing remain? Does the wind carry off the word? Does the word, which is the skeleton, possess a more lasting essence, more eternity, than the flesh? And here again we are at the center, the very core of the inner life, of the "inner man" as Paul would say (Eph. 3:16), and the marrow of my novel. And thus I am impelled to continue, to finish telling you, reader, how to make a novel.

Underneath, beneath the farcical police activity to which the petty tyrants reduce and degrade polity, I carry on my own brand of intimate politics, politics made religion and religion made politics, my novel of historic eternity, here in my Hendaye exile, in this frontier outpost of my native Basque country. Sometimes I go to the beach at Ondarraitz, to immerse the eternal childhood of my soul in the sight of the eternal childhood of the sea which speaks from before history, or rather from beneath history, and tells us of its divine substance. And other times, going up river along the banks of the Bidasoa, I pass the Island of Pheasants where the dynastic marriage was arranged between Louis XIV of France and the *infanta* of Spain, María Teresa, daughter of Philip IV of Spain, a Hapsburg, and the Family Pact was signed. "The Pyrenees are no more!" they said, as if mountains of age-old rock could be abolished by a pact. And I make my way to the little village of Biriatu, a haven of peace. There, I sit for a while at the foot of the tiny church facing the hamlet of Muniorte, a cluster of houses where, according to popular legend, some illegitimate descendants of Richard Plantagenet are said to live. Richard was duke of Aquitaine and might have been king of England; he was the Black Prince who went to the aid of Peter the Cruel of Castile. I look across the narrow gorge of the Bidasoa at the foot of Choldocogaña, thick with memories of our civil wars, where more history flows than water, and I envelop my exiled thoughts in the moist air of my maternal mountains. Sometimes I go as far as Urrugne, where an inscription on the sundial of the church belfry announces that every hour wounds and the last one kills—*vulnerant omnes, ultima necat.* Or I stray even further, to St.-Jean-de-Luz, in whose metropolitan church Louis XIV married the *infanta* of Spain and where the door they used for their entrance and exit was sealed up behind them. Other times I go as far as Bayonne, where I am brought back to my infancy, restored to my blessed childhood, to my historical eternity, for Bayonne brings me the essence of my native Bilbao as it was fifty years ago, that Bilbao which made my childhood and which my childhood made. The environs of Bayonne cathedral take me back to the basilica of Santiago of Bilbao, my basilica. Even the monumental fountain beside it is the same! And all these excursions have allowed me to foresee the ending of the novel of my Jugo.

My Jugo, finally, would renounce the fateful book, give up the idea of reading it to the end. In his wanderings about God's world in an attempt to escape the fateful word he would eventually return to his native land, the land of his childhood, and there he would find his own and very youth, his eternal childhood, that childhood in which he did not yet know how to read the word, when he was not yet a man of the book. And in that childhood he would find his inner man, the *eso anthropos.* Thus Paul in his Epistle to the Ephesians: "For this cause I bow my knees unto the Father of our Lord Jesus Christ, Of whom the whole family in heaven and earth is named." (And the Father's "whole family" could be translated, without undue violence, as "whole Fatherland.") "That he would grant you, according to the riches of his glory, to be strengthened with might by his Spirit in the inner man" (3:14-16). And this inner man encoun-

461

ters himself in his fatherland, his eternal fatherland, the fatherland of his eternity, on encountering his childhood. He discovers a sense, even more than a sense, an essence of filiation, on feeling himself a son and discovering his father: he feels the father in himself.

Just now, in the days devoted to writing these pages, a little book has fallen into my hands as if by divine—that is paternal—providence: *Gottes Kindschaft*, *God's Filiality*, by Johann Hessen, and in it I find: "Thus it should be clear that it is always and in every instant the child in us who believes. Just as seeing is a function of sight, so believing is a function of the sense of the childlike. There is as much potential in us for believing as there is in us a sense of the childlike." And naturally enough Hessen refers us to the Gospel of Matthew, where Christ, the Son of Man and Son of the Father, says: "Verily I say unto you, Except ye be converted, and become as little children, ye shall not enter into the kingdom of heaven" (18:3). The point is to become as children, to return to childhood. And therefore I "convert" my Jugo to childhood, return him to his childhood.

And the child, the son, discovers the father. And in the Epistle to the Romans (8:14-15)—to which Hessen also refers us—Paul tells us: "For as many as are led by the Spirit of God, they are the sons of God. For ye have not received the spirit of bondage again to fear; but ye have received the spirit of adoption, whereby we cry, *Abba*, Father!" That is: Papa! I cannot remember the time when I used the word in the days before I began to read or write; it was in some moment of my eternity, lost in the oceanic mist of my past. My father died when I was barely six. And every image of him has been erased from my memory;

art, artifice, has left me, in substitution, or perhaps
in erasure, the image of him in portraits, among others a daguerreotype of him as a young man, when he
was still no more than a son himself. Still, one image
remains, for I see him, confusedly as through an
oceanic mist, at the moment when I first sensed, as
a very young boy, the mystery of language. It was
in our paternal house in Bilbao, in a sitting room kept
like a sanctuary reserved for domestic liturgy, where
we children were not allowed to enter lest we mar the
waxed floors or rumple the seat covers on the overstuffed chairs. A small sphere formed of mirrors hung
from the ceiling, and in its glass sides one saw oneself
diminished and deformed. Prints of biblical scenes
lined the walls: one of them showed—the scene is
before me again!—Moses striking the rock to draw
forth water, much as I strike the eternal rock of my
childhood to draw forth these recollections. Next to
the sitting room there was a dark room where the
marmot hid: a strange mysterious being. One day I
managed to penetrate the solemn and forbidden room
and there I found my father—Papa!—who took me
into his arms: he was seated in one of the overstuffed
chairs, talking to a Frenchman, a Monsieur Legor-
geux, a subsequent acquaintance of my own. And he
was talking in French. What an effect on my childlike consciousness (I would not say imaginative fantasy, though perhaps it is the same as consciousness)
to hear my own father—Papa!—speaking an exotic
language, out of another world! And that is the image
which remains: my father speaking a mysterious and
enigmatic language, for French was still a language
of mystery.

I found my father speaking a mysterious language
and at the same time perhaps whispering kindly to

me in our own. Does the son ever discover the father? Is it not more likely the father who discovers the son? Is it the filiality we bear in our bones which reveals our paternity to us or is it not more likely the paternity in us which reveals our filiality? "The child is father of the man," as Wordsworth said once and for all. But is it not the sense of paternity, our sense of perpetuity in the future, which reveals to us the sense of filiality, our sense of perpetuity in the past? Is there not an obscure sense of perpetuity back into the past, of pre-existence, and with it at the same time a sense of perpetuity on into the future: a sense of pre-existence as well as of per- or super-existence? Thus among the people of India, an infantile and filial people, we find a belief in—or more than a belief in, the life-experience of—prenatal life, or a succession of previous lives, just as among many of us in the West there is a belief in, even a life-experience of, life after death, a desire for it, a vital hope and faith in it. And how, now, is the Nirvana toward which the Easterners make their way—and there is nothing but the way— different from our life after conception but before birth, life in the womb, a dream without dreams, an unconsciousness conscious of life? For my part, when I dream of a mystical experience against time, or better, back into time, I think of dying as a disparturition or being un-born, and of death as a new birth.

"Father, into thy hands I commend my spirit," the Son cried out (Luke 23:46) on being un-born, at the parturition of death. Or according to another Gospel (John 19:30) he exclaimed: *Tetélestai!* "It is finished!"

> "It is finished," He sighed and bent
> His head, a Nazarene bush,
> and gave up the ghost to God,

464*

gave birth in His loss:
for thus Christ was born on the Cross.
As He was born, He dreamt
back to when in a manger,
dying in Bethlehem He'd stood
beyond all evil, beyond all good.

"It is finished!" and "into thy hands I commend my spirit!" What is thus finished? And what spirit is it that was placed in the hands of the Father, into the hands of God? The Son's work was finished, and His spirit was His work. Our own work is our spirit; my work is myself, who am making, creating myself day after day, century after century, just as your work, reader, is yourself, who are making and creating yourself moment after moment, even at this moment listening to me as I spend my moment talking to you. For I do want to think you are listening to me rather more than you are reading me, just as I am talking to you rather more than writing to you. We are our own work, our deeds. Every man is the son of his deeds, as the saying has it, a popular saying repeated by Cervantes, the son of Don Quixote. But is not every man also the father of his deeds? And Cervantes thus also the father of Don Quixote? So that, without straining the figure of speech, every man may be said to be both son and father to himself, and his work the holy ghost. God Himself, so as to be the Father, had to become the Son, as we are taught: to be born as Father, He descended to die as Son. "Jesus saith . . . no man cometh unto the Father, but by me," we are told in the Fourth Gospel (14:16). And "Jesus saith . . . he that hath seen me hath seen the Father" (14:19). And in Russia the Son is called "our little father Jesus."

For my part I can say that I did not truly discover

my filial essence, my eternity of filiality, until I became a father, until I discovered my paternal essence. It was then I reached the inner man, the *eso anthropos*, the father and the son. It was then I felt myself a son, son of my children and son of the mother of my children. And herein lies the eternal mystery of life. The terrible Raphaël de Valentin in Balzac's *Peau de Chagrin* died on Pauline's breast consumed with desire, whispering in his death agony "*Je t'aime, je t'adore, je te veux. . . .*" But he is not un-born nor re-born, for he does not end his novel on the maternal bosom, the bosom of the mother of his children, of his mother. And now, after all this, am I to make my novel of Jugo de la Raza end with him experiencing filial paternity and paternal filiality?

But there is still another world, novelesque also; and there is another novel too. And it is not the world and novel of the flesh, but that of the word, of the word made letter. And properly speaking it is this novel which, like history, begins with the word, or rather, with the letter, since without a skeleton the flesh cannot be made to stand upright. And here we come to the dialectics of action and contemplation, of polity and the novel: action is contemplative, contemplation is active, polity is novelistic and the novel is politic. When my poor Jugo wandered along the margins—they can scarcely be called banks—of the Seine and came upon the fateful book of foreboding and proceeded to devour it and fell under its spell, he converted himself into a pure contemplator, a mere reader, which is an absurd and inhuman thing. He suffered the novel: he did not make it. And I would like to tell you, reader, how a novel is made: how you make a novel, and how you yourself must make your

own novel. When the inward man, the intra-man, becomes a reader, a contemplator, he must make himself, if he is among the truly quick, a reader and
contemplator of the character he is making and creating as he reads. He must, in short, be a contemplator,
a meditator of his own works. When the inward man,
the intra-man (who is more divine than the trans- or
super-man of Nietzsche), transforms himself into a
reader, he also makes himself author, that is, actor:
when he reads a novel he becomes a novelist, when he
reads history, a historian. And every reader who is an
inward human being is author of what he reads and
is now reading. What you are reading at this moment, reader, on this page, is something you are saying to yourself and it is as much yours as it is mine.
And if such is not the case, then you are not even
reading me. If that is the case, I beg your pardon,
reader, for my impertinent, even insolent, statement
to the effect that I had no intention of telling you how
the novel of my Jugo, my novel and your novel, ended.
And I beg my own pardon for this affront.

Do you understand me, reader? And I put the
question to you in this fashion so that I may con-
veniently quote now a passage from an Italian philosophical work I have been reading, one of those books
I read here in exile by chance. In his *Le sorgenti irrazionali del pensiero*, Nicola Abbagnano writes: "To
understand does not mean to enter into the intimate
thought of another, but merely to translate into one's
own thought, into one's own truth, the subterranean
experience in which one's own life is fused with the
life of another." But is that not perhaps the same as
breaking into the inner chambers of another's thought?
If I translate into my own thought the subterranean
experience in which my life and your life, reader, are

fused, or if you translate it into your own thought, if we succeed in understanding each other, in jointly taking each other's meaning, do I not thereby enter into your most intimate thought at the same time as you enter into the innermost chamber of mine, neither of which thought, however, is properly either yours or mine but common to us both? Does not my intra-man meet and merge with your intra-man, with the result that I live in you and you in me?

Do not be surprised, reader, that I thrust you by chance into my chance reading. I am most fond of such reading, chance reading and reading by chance, just as I am fond of a game of chance, a daily card game played for afternoon coffee at the Grand Café d'Hendaye with three other players. And life, too, is a card game! For life consists in knowing how to take best advantage of chance, of hazard. As Montesinos puts it so succinctly in *Don Quixote*: "Patience! And shuffle the cards!" Shuffle the deck! What quixotic wisdom! And be quick of hand and quick of eye when chance is involved. Yes, patience and shuffle the cards! Which is just what I am doing here on the frontier, my frontier, with the political—and religious—novel of my life. Patiently I shuffle my cards. That is my problem.

And do not reproach me, my reader—as I must not reproach myself as reader of myself—for making problems instead of showing you how to make a novel, as I had promised, making problems, and what was worse, problems in meta-politics and religion. Shall we stop to consider the idea of a problem, the word "problem" itself? You must forgive a Hellenist philologist's explaining the novel, that is, the etymology, of the word *problem*, which is the substantive representing the result of the action of the verb *proballein*, which itself signifies to put or throw something forward, present something, and is the equivalent to Latin *proiicere*, to project. So that saying "problem" is as good as saying "project." And of what is problem the project? Of action! The project for a building is a "construction project." And a problem presupposes not so much a solution—in the analytic, or dissolvent sense—as a construction, a creation. The resolution comes in the doing. Stated in other terms, a "project" is resolved in a "traject," a "pro-blem" in a "meta-blem," a change. And problems are resolved only through action. And action is contemplative, just as contemplation is active. And to think that polity can be made without a novel or a novel without polity is not to know what's what.

A truly great political man was Thucydides, Machiavelli's master teacher, as great a man as Pericles, and he left us "for ever"—"for ever"!: the phrase is his, and is his seal—the History of the Peloponnesian War. And Thucydides made Pericles as surely as Pericles made Thucydides. God save me from comparing the petty tyrants of Spain, the king Don Alfonso XIII, that clown Primo de Rivera, or the epileptic Martínez Anido, with a Pericles, a Cleon, or an Alcibiades, but I am convinced that I, Miguel de Unamuno, have made them do and say not a few things, including a good deal of nonsense. If they make me think and make myself in my thought—which is my work and my action—I make them act and perhaps think. And thus and meanwhile we go on being alive, they and I.

And that is how, reader, to make a novel, for ever.

Finished on Friday, June 17, 1927,
in Hendaye, Basses-Pyrénées, on
the frontier between France and Spain

Tuesday 21st

"Finished?" How fast I was to write that! For is it really possible to finish in any way a description, even if only a novel, of how to make a novel? Years ago, when I was very young, I remember my Wagnerian friends speaking of "infinite melody." I am not sure what the term means, but it must be like life and its novel—even like history—which never end.

Today I have received a copy of *La Prensa*, of Buenos Aires, dated May 22, 1927, in which I find an article by *Azorín* concerning Jacques de Lacretelle. The latter had sent the former a copy of his book *Aparté*, and Azorín writes about it. "The book is composed of a short novel titled *Colère*, along with a *Diary* in which the author explains how he wrote his novel, and some critical philosophical pages dedicated to the memory of Jean Jacques Rousseau at Ermenonville." I know nothing of Lacretelle's book beyond this notice by Azorín, but I find it both significant and symbolic that an author who writes a *Diary* in order to explain how he wrote his novel should evoke the memory of Rousseau, who spent his life explaining how he made the novel of his life, the representation of his life, which was a novel.

And Azorín adds:

"Of all these writings, doubtless the most interesting is the *Journal de colère*, that is, the notes which he made, if not daily at least very frequently, on the development of the novel he was working on. Only recently a diary of the same type was issued by the most subtle and elegant André Gide to explain the genesis and evolution of one of his own novels. The

470*

practice should be extended. Every novelist could write a second book based on some novel of his own to explain the mechanism of his fiction, and the second book would be an authentic, true novel. When I was a child—and I suppose the same holds true today for other children—watches were fascinating things. My father or some uncle would show me his timepiece; I would study it with detailed admiration, put it to my ear and listen to the precipitant and persistent ticking, watch the minute hand advancing with slow certainty; finally, after I had been shown the entire exterior, my father or uncle would open the watchcase, using a fingernail or a penknife for the purpose, and show me the complicated and cunning organism. . . . When novelists write books now to explain the mechanism of their novel, to demonstrate their manner of writing, what they are doing, simply, is opening the watchcase. Monsieur Lacretelle's watch is a lovely piece; I don't know how many rubies its machinery boasts, but the entire works are beautifully polished, brilliant. Let us contemplate these works and speak of what we there observe."

And all this merits commentary indeed.

First of all, the analogy with a watch is very far-fetched; it results from Azorín's concept of "the mechanism of his fiction." A fiction based on mechanism—mechanical in short—is not and cannot be a novel. For a novel to live, to be life, it must be, like life itself, an organism and not a mechanism. And it is no use opening watchcases because, before all else, a true novel, a live novel, has no case, and then because what there is to demonstrate is not machinery but hot-blooded entrails throbbing with life. And this quality is visible externally. It is like wrath itself, which can be seen, marked, in the face and eyes of the wrathful, so that it is unnecessary to open any case whatsoever.

A watchmaker, who is a mechanic, may open the case of a timepiece to let his client see the mechanism, but a novelist has no need to raise anything at all for the reader to sense the throbbing entrails of the live organism which constitutes a novel. The entrails are those of the novelist, the author; and they are also those of the reader who has identified with him through reading.

On the other hand the watchmaker knows, reflexively and critically, the mechanism of his watch. Can the novelist be said to know in a like manner the organism of his novel? If the novel were encased, the novelist would be encased as well. The best novelists do not know what has gone into their novels. And if they set themselves to writing diaries of how they have written the novels, it is only so as to discover themselves. The men of diaries or autobiographies or confession—Amiel, Rousseau, Saint Augustine—spent their lives seeking themselves, seeking God in themselves, and their diaries, autobiographies, or confessions have been no more than a record of their search. And their search cannot end except with the end of life.

The end of life? Not even then! For their inner life, their interior, novelistic life continues on in their readers. Just as it began there. For, after all, does our own inner, interior, novelistic life really begin with each one of us? Still, I have already spoken on this head and why repeat something so obvious? And then again—why not? To repeat is only proper to the man of the diary, the man who confesses. For him every day is the same day.

And—beware of the diary! The man who falls into

the habit of keeping a diary, like Amiel, becomes a man of the diary, and lives for it. He no longer notes in his diary what he daily thinks, but thinks now in order to note the thought down. And yet—is it not all the same in the end? One plays with the notion of "the book of the man" and "the man of the book": but are there any men who are not of the book? Even among those who do not know how to read or write? Every man, every authentic man, is the son of a legend, either written or oral. And there is nothing else but legend, that is, novel.

We are left with the conclusion, then, that the novelist who relates how a novel is made is relating how a novelist is made, that is, how a man is made. And such a novelist reveals his human essence, eternal and universal, without any need to open any watchcase whatsoever. All this opening up of watchcases is a matter best left to littérateurs—and they are not exactly novelists.

Watchcases, indeed! Children disembowel a doll, especially if it is a mechanical doll, to see the works inside, to see its intestines. In order to know how a doll, a puppet, a mechanical homunculus functions, one must disembowel it, one must open the watchcase. But what about a historical human being, an authentic human being, an actor in the drama of life, the subject of a novel? One need only look in the face of such a one to know what he bears within. Or to speak in other terms, his entrails (from *intranea*, innards) are his extrails (from *extranea*, outtards), so that his form is his content. Thus, every expression of a historical and authentic human being is autobiographical. And that is why a historical and authentic human being is not encased. Even though he be a hypocrite. In fact it is precisely the hypocrites whose faces show most clearly what they bear within. They are encased all right, but the case is made of glass.

Thursday 30-VI

I have just finished reading how Frédéric Lefèvre, the man who published a set of conversations with public men in *Les Nouvelles Littéraires* (I was myself the subject of one of them), asked Georges Clemenceau, when he was a youth of eighty-five, if he were ready to write his Memoirs, and was answered: "Never! Life was made to be lived, not to be told." And yet, Clemenceau, in his long quixotic life as a guerilla-fighter of the pen, did nothing else but tell his life.

Is not telling one's life, retelling it, one way—and perhaps the most powerful way—of living it? Did not Amiel live his life in the telling? Is not his *Diary* his life? When will people cease counterposing action and contemplation? When will it become clear that action is contemplative and contemplation active?

There is that which has been made and there is what is to be made. The way to "the invisible things" of God is through what has been made, *per ea quae facta sunt*, according to the canonical Latin version, a not very literal rendition of the original Greek of a passage in Paul (Rom. 1:20): but this is the way of nature, and nature is dead. There is the way of history, and history is alive; and the way of history toward the invisible things of God, His mysteries, is via what is being made, *per ea quae fiunt*. Not by poems, which is the precise Pauline expression, but through poetry; not through understanding, but by intellection, or better, by intention, and more properly, *intension.* (Since we say *extension* and *intensity*, why not *intension* and *extensity*?)

Here and now I live my life in telling it. And here and now is the present, which sustains as it fuses the sequence of time, just as eternity envelops and joins it.

Sunday 3-VII

Reading today in a history of mystical philosophy of the Middle Ages, I came once again upon the sentence from Saint Augustine in his *Confessions* (Bk. 10, ch. 33, 50) where he says he has made himself a problem in himself, *mihi quaestio factus sum*: for I think *quaestio* must be translated as "problem." And I have made myself a problem, question, project of myself. How to resolve it? By making of the "project" a "traject," and of the "problem" a "metablem": by struggling. And thus struggling, civic-ly, delving in myself as question and problem of myself, I shall transcend myself, and do so inwardly, concentrating myself in order to irradiate myself, and I shall reach the present God, the God of history.

Hugh of Saint Victor, the 12th century mystic, said that to raise oneself to God was to enter into oneself, and not only to enter into oneself but to pass beyond oneself into the most inward part, *in intimis etiam seipsum transire*, in a certain ineffable way, and that the most intimate is the closest, the supreme and eternal. And through myself, passing through and beyond myself, I shall reach the God of my Spain in this experience of exile.

Monday 4-VII

Now that my family has come and I have settled down with them for the summer months in a villa beyond the hotel, I find myself resuming certain familiar habits. Surrounded by my own people I can amuse myself by playing, for example, a form of solitaire which the French call patience.

I enjoy a kind of solitaire which allows a certain margin of opportunity, even if only slight, for calculation on the part of the player. For instance, the cards are arranged vertically in eight lines of five, that is, in five lines of eight horizontally speaking—assuming that we can take the liberty of speaking of "vertical" and "horizontal" on a horizontal plane. The point is to take, from below, the aces and the deuces, placing the thirty-two remaining cards in four vertical lines, from higher to lower numbers and avoiding any two of the same suit in sequence; thus, a jack of diamonds, say, may not follow a seven of diamonds, but must be placed with any one of the other three suits. The result depends in part on the opening; and one must know how to take advantage of chance. And the same holds true for the art of life in history.

As I play, attentive to the rules, to the norms, with the most scrupulous normative conscience and a lively sense of duty as well as of obedience to the law of my own creation—games fairly played are the primal source of the moral conscience—while I play, I repeat, it is as if a silent music rocked me at my meditations concerning the history I am living and making. And as I handle the kings, queens, jacks, and aces of the pack, the real king, meanwhile, and the petty tyrants of my country, the executioners and bumbailiffs, the bishops and the entire deck in the farce of the Dictatorship, parade through the depths of my consciousness almost without my being aware of them. And I plunge into the game and play with chance. If nothing works out, I begin again, shuffling the cards, and that is a pleasure.

Shuffling cards is something like, on another level, sea-gazing: watching the waves break on the sand of the shore. And both speak to us of nature in history, of hazard and chance in liberty.

I am not impatient if the play is drawn out; and I do not cheat. All of it teaches me to wait on the outcome of the historical game being played out in my Spain, to wait without growing impatient for a solution, to shuffle the cards in this larger game of solitaire, of patience. The days come and go as the waves of the sea come and go; men come and go, sometimes they go and come, just as the cards come and go, and this coming and going constitutes history. Out there in the distance, even though I do not hear it consciously, the music of the frontier-sea resounds along the beach. The waves come up from Spain, lapping along the Spanish coast.

How suggestive the four kings, with their four knaves, kings of hearts and diamonds and spades and clubs, four chiefs of four columns of the winning order! Order!

Patience! And shuffle the cards!

Tuesday 5-VII

Still thinking of solitaire, of history. Solitaire represents the play of chance. A good mathematician could calculate the probability of a game's working out. And if two individuals were to set themselves to solving the problem competitively, the natural result would be that they would both find the same percentage of solutions to the same game. But the point of the competition should be to determine who can find more solutions in a given time. The best player is not the one who plays the fastest, but the one who breaks off the most games at the earliest moment, as soon as he foresees their lack of solution. In the supreme art of taking advantage of chance, the superiority of a player consists in his being able to make up his mind to abandon one game in time to start another. The same goes for politics and life.

Wednesday 6-VII

Am I about to fall into the habit of *nulla dies sine linea*, not a day without writing something for others —but most of all for oneself—and for ever? For ever for oneself, the forever of oneself, of course. Such practice means to fall into the habit of the man of the diary. To fall? And what is "to fall"? Those who speak of decadence, of decline, will know. For, the Latin for decline, *ocasus* (Spanish *ocaso*), from *occidere*, to die, is a derivative of *cadere* (Spanish *caer*), to fall. To fall is to die.

And I am reminded of those two immortal heroes —yes, heroes!—of Flaubert's decline, who remade him, Flaubert, the model for all other novelists (what a novel, his Correspondence!), and they remade him when he was in decline forever. Bouvard and Pécuchet. After Bouvard and Pécuchet had traveled all the regions of the universal human spirit, they ended their days as scribes. And now as regards my Jugo de la Raza, would it not be better if I brought his novel to a close by making him, once he had given up the fateful book, dedicate himself to playing solitaire, waiting in this fashion for the book of life to be brought to a close? The book of life and of the Way (of *vita* and *via*), the book of history, which is passage.

The Scholastic mystics spoke of *via* and *patria*, that is: history and the beatific vision. But are the two different? Is not *patria* the *via*, the fatherland the way? And will not the true *patria*, the celestial and eternal fatherland, the kingdom of God for whose coming we daily ask—those of us who ask—will not this *patria* eternally be a way?

But, in short, Thy will be done on earth as it is in heaven! Or, as Dante, the great exile, sang

e la sua volontate è nostra pace

E pur si muove! Ah, there is no peace without war!

Thursday 7-VII

The way, yes, *via*, which is *vita*, life, and to pass it playing solitaire—such is the novel. But solitaire is played in solitude, for oneself alone. No one else participates in one's solitaire. And the *patria* behind this *via* of solitaire is a *patria* of solitude—of solitude and a void. How to make a novel, well and good! But why, wherefore is it made? And the wherefore is the why. Why or wherefore is a novel made? So that the novelist may make himself. And wherefore is the novelist made? In order to make the reader, in order to make himself one with the reader. And only by the novelist and the reader of the novel making themselves one do they save themselves from their radical solitude. In the degree that they make themselves one they become actual and present and thereby eternal.

The medieval mystics, most notably Saint Bonaventure, the Franciscan, distinguished between *lux* and

*479**

lumen, between light and luminosity. Light remains in itself, luminosity shines out and illuminates. And a man may enlighten, and be enlightened; he may illuminate, and shine.

A spirit shines, but how can we know it shines unless it illuminates us? And there are men who shine, as we say. And those who shine do so with their own complaisance: they made themselves evident in order to shine. Does the person who shines know himself? Seldom. Since he seldom bothers to illuminate or enlighten others, he does not illuminate or enlighten himself. But the man who not only shines, but who also enlightens others, enlightens himself as he shines. No one knows himself better than he who takes care to know others. And, since to know is to love, we might perhaps modify the divine precept to read: love yourself as you love your neighbor.

What are you profited, if you gain the whole world, and lose your own soul? Good enough, but what are you profited if you gain your soul and lose the whole world? Let us substitute here, in place of the whole world, the human communion, the human community, in short, the common community.

And here is where religion and politics become one in the novel of life in the present. The Kingdom of God—or as Saint Augustine preferred, the City of God—is, insofar as it is a kingdom or a city, a matter of politics, and insofar as it is of God, a matter of religion.

For my part, in my exile here at the door of Spain, like its doorman, I do not illuminate or shine, but am here to enlighten myself by enlightening, in order to make the novel, the history, of Spain, our Spain. And when I say I am here to enlighten myself, I do not mean, reader, by "myself" myself alone, or refer merely to my *I*, but to your *I* as well, to our mutual *I*. For our *I* is not the same as *us*, *we* is not the same as *I* in the plural.

The wretched dictator Primo de Rivera thinks he shines. But does he enlighten himself? In the vulgar and metaphoric sense, he gets "lit up"; still, he is anything but one of the Illuminati. And neither does he enlighten anyone. He is an *ignis fatuus*, a feeble light casting no shadow.

Hendaye in 1927

Notes

Notes

xii. *Joyce turned pale*: The version given here is Dublin Apocrypha, viable Apocrypha. The account in Richard Ellmann's splendid monumental biography is doubly bookish, having been taken from another book, Burton Rascoe's *A Bookman's Daybook* (N.Y., 1929), p. 27, where the encounter with the unknown abominator took place in the Bois de Boulogne, "in the company of Nora Joyce and Djuna Barnes" (the Dublin legend alludes to the company of Sylvia Beach on the bridge), and concludes with Joyce, who "trembled and went white," saying, "That man, whom I have never seen before, said to me as he passed, in Latin, 'You are an abominable writer!' That is a dreadful omen the day before the publication of my novel." Richard Ellmann, *James Joyce* (N.Y. and Oxford, 1959), p. 538.

Foreword, by Jean Cassou

Translated from the French by Anthony Kerrigan and Martin Nozick.

xxi. *And the only one . . . justice*: see Ch. XXXI of *Mist*.

Américo Castro: (1885–1972), outstanding Spanish critic, philologist, and historiographer, who after the Spanish Civil War settled in the United States and wrote a series of epoch-making books and articles reinterpreting Spanish history.

xxiii. *nothing less than a whole man!*: paraphrase of the title of Unamuno's novella *Nada menos que todo un hombre* (1916), the third of *Tres novelas ejemplares y un prólogo* in *OC*, IX, 472–518.

xxiv. *Pérez Galdós*: Benito (1843–1920), generally considered to be the greatest Spanish novelist after Cervantes.

La Celestina: cf. note to *Mist*, p. 137.

Quevedo: Francisco de (1580–1645), poet, political writer, satirist, author of the picaresque novel *Vida del Buscón*, and one of the greatest figures of the Spanish Golden Age.

Pío Baroja: (1872–1956), outstanding Spanish novelist, much admired by Ernest Hemingway. Baroja's opinions of Unamuno are generally unfavorable.

xxv. *Tía Tula*: novel by Unamuno on the theme of virginal maternity, published in 1921; in *OC*, IX; Vol. 7 of this series.

xxvii. *André Spire*: (1868–?), French-Jewish poet, advocate of Zionism.

xxvii–xxviii. *His wife . . . "My son!"*: This famous episode is usually connected with Unamuno's religious crisis of 1897. Cf. note to *How to Make a Novel*, p. 442.

xxviii. *Romancero del destierro*: published in Buenos Aires in 1928, made up of thirty-seven poems in various meters plus eighteen ballads, inspired in the main by the political state of Spain. The line quoted reads: *Si caigo aquí, sobre esta tierra verde* (*OC*, XIV, 607).

xxix. *peau de chagrin*: the reference is to Balzac's novel of that name, translated into English as *The*

Fatal Skin. The fascination exercised by this book on Unamuno is reflected in *How to Make a Novel* (in this volume), *The Agony of Christianity* (Vol. 5 of this series), and in the death scene of *Nada menos que todo un hombre*, written in 1916.

MIST

Prologue

4. *my surname . . . ancestors*: Professor Geoffrey Ribbans tells us (*Niebla y Soledad, aspectos de Unamuno y Machado*, Madrid, 1971, p. 109 note): "According to a genealogical tree transcribed by Unamuno and to be found in the Unamuno museum-library in Salamanca, don Pedro de Goti, baptized 18 of October, 1650, was an ancestor (*quinto abuelo*) of Unamuno's on his mother's side. . . ." The "author" of this Prologue is Víctor Goti.

series . . . recently: Goti, the "author" of this Prologue, alludes to the Spanish magazine *Mundo Gráfico* and other similar publications.

6. *Taboada*: Luis (1848–1906), comic journalist who concentrated especially on the mores of the middle class of Madrid.

Quevedo: cf. note to Cassou's Foreword, p. xxiv.

'*Hardly had the rubicund Phoebus . . .* ': The quotation strays from the original which begins '*Apenas la blanca aurora había dado lugar a que el luciente Febo . . .* ' (*Don Quixote*, Part II, Ch. XX) which is translated by Walter Starkie (New York, 1964, p. 664) as "Scarcely had fair Aurora given shining Phoebus time to dry the liquid pearls on her golden hair with the heat of his rays . . . "

'*It must have been that of the dawn . . .* ': *Don Quixote*, Part I, Ch. IV.

8. *credei*: line 3, "A se stesso." The text has (OC^2 and 1925 ed.) *"ch'io eterno mi credea."*

Sénancour: Etienne Pivert de (1770–1846), whose novel *Obermann* was one of the books Unamuno quoted most frequently.

Quental: Antero de (1842–91), Portuguese poet whom Unamuno admired and translated.

Leopardi: Giacomo (1798–1839), great Italian poet whose *Canti* was one of the three books (the other two were the New Testament and the *Divine Comedy*) Unamuno took with him into exile in 1924.

9. *Vicente Pastor*: (1879–1966), famous bullfighter.

12. *Víctor Goti*: Geoffrey Ribbans (*op.cit.*, p. 109) tells us that the British Museum catalogue contains the name of Víctor Goti (without dates) as the author of one work—this prologue to *Niebla*! Goti is, of course, an invention of Unamuno.

15. *Praetorian Dictatorship*: the reference is to the dictatorship of General Primo de Rivera, 1923–1930. Unamuno was exiled in February of 1924 to the island of Fuerteventura in the Canaries; in the summer of the same year he escaped to Paris where he spent over a year, after which he moved to Hendaye where he remained until after Primo de Rivera's resignation on January 28, 1930; on February 9 of that year, Unamuno crossed the border and was back on Spanish soil.

my first rectorship of the University of Salamanca: Unamuno was appointed rector of the university in 1900, a post he was relieved of in 1914 without warning or explanation. In 1920 he was appointed vice-rector until his exile in 1924. After the establishment of the Republic in 1931 he was reappointed rector. Although he retired from his teaching duties in 1934 when he reached the age of 70, he continued as lifetime rector of the university, but was relieved of his post by the Republic in August 1936, and by the Nationalist (Rebel) government two months later to the day, thus making him a total proscript, banished by both sides in the Spanish Civil War.

the hypothetical revolution of 1931: the reference is to the fall of Alfonso XIII and the declaration of the Republic. Although Unamuno himself announced the fall of the monarchy to an assembled public in Salamanca, he soon showed his disillusionment with the new regime.

16. *That Augusto Pérez . . . ago*: the reference is to "Una entrevista con Augusto Pérez," dated October 1915, published in *La Nación* of Buenos Aires, *OC*, X, 333–43.

The Other: El otro (*misterio en tres jornadas y un epílogo*), completed in 1926. In *OC*, XII, Vol. 7 of this series.

I believe . . . Don Quixote: as Unamuno later explains, he is referring to his *Vida de Don Quijote y Sancho* (1905), translated and included in Vol. 3 of this series, *Our Lord Don Quixote*.

18. *Alejandro Plana*: (1889–1940).

19. *Peace in War*: Paz en la guerra, completed in 1897. In *OC*, II, Vol. 1 of this series.

Love and Pedagogy: Amor y pedagogía (1902), *OC*, II, a satire on supreme faith in science, as manifest in Don Avito Carrascal who hopes to educate his son "scientifically" to be a genius. The effort ends in the son's suicide. As Unamuno indicates, Don Avito turns up in *Mist*, Ch. XIII.

20. *The Mirror of Death*: El espejo de la muerte, a collection of short stories, *OC*, II.

Aunt Tula: La tía Tula, OC, IX, Vol. 7 of this series: the novel of a woman repelled by sex who yet wishes to become the mother of children conceived and born by others.

Eduardo Gómez de Baquero, *Andrenio*: (1866–1929), critic and academician, author of several books of criticism, among them *De Gallardo a Unamuno* (1928).

23. *Pedro Antonio and Josefa Ignacia*: the parents in *Paz en la guerra* (*Peace in War*), Vol. 1 in this series.

Augusto Pérez, Eugenia Domingo, and Rosarito: in *Mist*, in this volume.

Alejandro Gómez . . . Julia: principal characters in *Nada menos que todo un hombre* (*Nothing Less Than a Complete Man*), included in *Tres novelas ejemplares y un prólogo* (*Three Exemplary Novels and a Prologue*), *OC*, IX.

Joaquín Monegro, Abel Sánchez, and Elena: from *Abel Sánchez*, in this volume.

Saint Manuel Bueno . . . Carballino: in *San Manuel Bueno, mártir, OC,* XVI, Vol. 7 in this series.

Don Sandalio: from *La novela de Don Sandalio, jugador de ajedrez* (*The Novel of Don Sandalio, Chessplayer*), *OC,* XVI, Vol. 7 in this series.

Emeterio Alonso: protagonist of the novelette *Un pobre hombre rico o El sentimiento cómico de la vida* (*A Poor Rich Man, or The Comic Sense of Life*), *OC,* XVI. A good deal of the story consists of dialogue between Emeterio Alonso and his friend Celedonio Ibáñez.

Ricardo and Liduvina: protagonists of *Una historia de amor* (*A Love Story*), *OC,* XVI.

Cánovas: Cánovas del Castillo, Antonio (1828–97). Statesman and writer, prime minister several times, alternating with Sagasta, after the Restoration of the Bourbons in Spain at the end of 1874.

Sagasta: Práxades Mateo (1825–1903), politician and prime minister.

Primo de Rivera: Miguel (1870–1930), general and politician, responsible for the coup d'état of 1923 and dictator under the king until 1930.

Alfonso XIII: (1886–1941), last king of Spain, exiled in 1931 after the triumph of the Republic.

Galdós: Pérez Galdós, Benito (1843–1920), the greatest novelist of 19th century Spain, author of contemporary and historical novels, a liberal in politics and religion.

Pereda: José María de (1833–1905), important regional novelist and staunch defender of traditional Spanish values.

Menéndez Pelayo: Marcelino (1856–1912), the most important literary historian and critic of the 19th century in Spain, a defender of his country's political and religious traditions.

24. *died on me*: "se me han muerto": a frequent Spanish expression, even colloquially, very often used by Unamuno, translated literally here, a usage frequent enough in English as spoken by the Irish: cf. "She thinks that I am being affectionate, looking after her child, but the child has 'died on me', as they say in Ireland." Aidan Higgins, *Balcony of Europe* (London and New York, 1972), p. 237.

25. *Canticle of the Wild Cock: Cantico del gallo silvestre* from the *Operette Morali* (1st ed., 1827). Cf. *Leopardi: Poems and Prose*, ed. Angel Flores (Indiana U. Press, 1966), pp. 225–26.

47. *two solid, mortal, years*: Unamuno forgot that in Ch. II he had said that Augusto's mother had been dead only six months.

99. *Don Avito Carrascal*: one of the main characters in *Amor y pedagogía* (*Love and Pedagogy*, 1902), a novel by Unamuno.

130. *Manuel Machado*: (1874–1947), best known as co-author of plays with his more famous brother, the poet Antonio Machado (1875–1939). Manuel Machado's poems were also quite frequently quoted by Unamuno.

Eduardo Benot: (1822–1907), Spanish lexicographer.

137. *La Celestina*: the main character in one of the greatest works of Spanish literature, a novel in dialogue form originally known as *La tragicomedia de Calixto y Melibea*, but commonly referred to as *La Celestina*. Most probably written by a converted Jewish lawyer Fernando de Rojas (?–1541). The earliest known edition published in 1499, and the second edition of Seville, 1501, both contain sixteen acts. The 1502 edition of Seville has five more acts.

Celestina was a go-between in the tragic love affair of Calisto and Melibea, and her name has come to mean a procuress.

El Gran Galeoto: name of famous drama by José Echegaray (1832–1916), playwright and mathematician, engineer and cabinet minister, who (jointly with Frédéric Mistral) won the Nobel Prize for literature in 1904. *El Gran Galeoto* (1881) reveals how slander, through the power of suggestion, creates an adulterous passion, just as in Canto V of Dante's *Inferno*, the reading of the Lancelot romance led Paolo and Francesca to kiss and "read no more." Francesca explains that the book and he who wrote it were "a Galeotto" or pander, for in the Old French poem, Gallehault pandered to Lancelot and Guinevere.

164. *Campoamor*: Ramón de (1817–1901).

167. *Antolín S. Paparrigópulos*: The "S.," as Unamuno indicates, stands for "Sánchez," his father's surname. In order not to take away from the exceptional
qualities of both his given name and his second surname (Spaniards may use their father's surname and
their mother's maiden name), he reduces the very
common "Sánchez" to its initial. Juan López-Morillas
tells us (*Intelectuales y espirituales*, Madrid, 1961,
pp. 38–39) that Unamuno probably took the name Paparrigópulos from the Greek historian Konstantinos
Paparrigopoulos (1815–1891) and, according to the
same critic, Antolín is a "younger brother" to the
pedantic Don Fulgencio de Entrambosmares of *Love
and Pedagogy* (1902).

Both Entrambosmares and Paparrigópulos are lam-
poons of the school of the great historian and researcher Marcelino Menéndez Pelayo (1856–1912),
known for his nationalism, his conservatism and
staunch Catholicism, and—at least in his earlier period—for his disdainful attitudes toward the "misty"
thinking of the Germans.

168. *Becerro de Bengoa*: Ricardo (1845–1902),
Spanish writer.

171. *Prudentius*: Aurelius Prudentius Clemens
(348–c. 415), Christian Latin poet, born in Cala-
horra, Spain.

Lionnet's . . . caterpillar: Pierre Lyonnet (1707–
89), Dutch entomologist, whose greatest work is on
the caterpillar.

Kalilah and Dimnah: *Calila e Dimna*, a collection
of Oriental fables going back to Sanskrit sources, ultimately translated into Arabic and Syriac, Greek, Per-
sian, and Hebrew, from which they were put into

Latin. In 1251 they were translated into Castilian by order of the prince who would become Alfonso X of Castile (Alfonso el Sabio, 1221–85).

174. *Padre Isla . . . Gil Blas*: José Francisco de Isla (1706–81), a Jesuit priest exiled to Italy in 1767, after the expulsion of the Jesuits from Spain. His most important contribution to Spanish literature is his satire on the ridiculously ornate preaching of his period, *Historia del famoso predicador Fray Gerundio de Campazas, alias Zotes* (Part I, 1758; Part II, 1768). He also translated the *Gil Blas* of Alain René Lesage (1668–1747) and claimed to be restoring the novel to its original language.

175. *Justi's book on Velázquez*: Karl Justi (1832–1912), German art critic and author of *Diego Velázquez und sein Jahrhundert*.

177. *Averroes*: Abū al-Walīd Ibn Ruchd (1126–c. 1198), Arab physician and philosopher, born in Cordoba, author of commentaries on Aristotle.

180. *Pindar . . . happiness*: *Olympian Odes I*, in *The Odes of Pindar* (Loeb Classical Library, 1968), p. 9.

221. *Don Avito Carrascal . . . Don Fulgencio*: for the first, see note to Ch. XIII, p. 99; the second, Don Fulgencio de Entrambosmares, is the pedantic adviser to Don Avito in *Amor y pedagogía* (1902).

231. *Renan*: Joseph-Ernest (1823–92). *L'Abbesse de Jouarre*, a philosophical drama, was first published in Paris (1886), and then included in the *Drames philosophiques* (1888).

'*Food . . . healed*': the original Spanish proverb is in rhyme: "más mató la cena, que sanó Avicena." Avicenna (980–1037) was an Arab physician and philosopher.

ABEL SÁNCHEZ

318. *but it's only . . . Sánchez*: Sánchez is a very common name in Spanish, and since Spaniards bear both their father's name and mother's maiden name, Abel Sánchez could call himself Abel Sánchez Puig, and to avoid confusion with the many other Sánchez's, he could reduce his father's name to S. and thus be called Abel S. Puig.

A perfect example of this practice is found in the evolution of the signature of Pablo Picasso, who began by signing Pablo Ruiz (his father's surname, and thus his own first and customary surname), then went on to sign Pablo Ruiz Picasso (thus retaining his two surnames, his mother's unusual Italianate, or Balearic, surname alongside his father's—and his own—rather common first surname), to Pablo R. Picasso, in effect suppressing the Ruiz, and finally to Picasso, his mother's surname alone.

Joaquín S. Monegro: see note to p. 23.

HOW TO MAKE A NOVEL

Epigraph: *Mihi quaestio factus sum*: "I am now become a problem to myself." (Saint Augustine, *Confessions*, Book X, Ch. 33, 50.)

381. *nearing sixty-three years of age*: Unamuno was born on September 29, 1864.

Saint Teresa . . . "delicious pain": in *Life* (*Vida*), Ch. XXIX, where the saint refers to "esta pena tan sabrosa."

the tragic sense of life: the name of one of Unamuno's central works, *Del sentimiento trágico de la vida* (in this series, Vol. 4).

382. *my home and country*: Throughout the original Spanish text of the present book, omissions occur
in the various Spanish editions of the *Obras completas*,
the *Complete Works*, which we here designate (as in
the other volumes of our series in English) as *OC*¹
(Madrid, 1950, Vol. IV, which includes *Cómo se
hace una novela*), *OC*² (Barcelona, 1958, Vol. X),
and *OC*³ (Madrid, 1966, Vol. VIII). All the omitted
sentences or phrases have to do with the military
junta of General Primo de Rivera (1923–30) who
counted on the support of the king, Alfonso XIII.
The dictatorship was relatively benign, compared to
everything that came later, as Unamuno lived to learn.
But the military in command gave indications of crass
stupidity, and Unamuno was so outraged that he
clashed with it at every turn, was sent into a (relatively mild) exile in the Canaries, and from there
easily escaped, sailing away in a ship put at his disposition by French admirers. As explained repeatedly
in the text, the present work was written in Unamuno's French exile, first in Paris, and rewritten, or
translated back into his own Spanish by the author,
at Hendaye. In translating this book into English we
have used the integral text of the Argentine edition
(Buenos Aires, 1927), as well as the French version
of the book—of which his own Spanish is said by Unamuno to be a translation—in *Avant et après la révolution* (Paris, 1933). (As indicated by Unamuno,
this text was first published in the magazine *Mercure
de France*, 15 mai, 1926, No. 670, 37ᵉ année, tome
CLXXXVIII, naturally earlier in date.) Almost all
the sentences omitted in the Spanish texts are related
to the politics of the moment. It is in no way clear why
the various omissions were made: whether they were
the result of official censorship, or were omitted by

the publishers in a self-censorship of fear, or were omitted by Unamuno's editors. In any case, there is a progressive lessening of the amount of matter omitted. The OC^1 has the most matter omitted, the first printing of the OC^2 less, while a later printing of OC^2 as well as OC^3 includes practically every word omitted in the first two collections. In our version nothing is omitted.

382. *Ventura García Calderón*: (1886–1959), Peruvian writer and critic who spent most of his life in Europe, especially France.

M. Painlevé: Paul (1863–1933), mathematician and politician, Président du Conseil in 1917 and 1925.

383. *General Don Severiano Martínez Anido*: (1862–1938), captain-general of Barcelona after 1917, and member of the Primo de Rivera cabinet. Minister of Public Order for the Nationalists at the beginning of the Spanish Civil War.

385. *Portrait*: *Saint Augustine was . . . another Augustine.*: *Confessions*, Book First, Ch. I, and Book Fourth, Ch. IV, respectively.

Basque terrain: Although he spent most of his life in Salamanca, province of Castile, Unamuno was born in Bilbao and was always fiercely proud of being a Basque; he did not shy away, however, from criticizing his fellow Basques when the occasion called for it.

386. *Spanish Cain . . . Machado's puts it*: the reference is to the long somber poem *La tierra de Alvargonzález*, included in *Campos de Castilla* (1907–17), by Antonio Machado (1875–1939), the most famous poet of the Generation of 1898 and a great admirer of Unamuno.

387. *"Come now, good Sir!"* last lines of Act III of *Hamlet*:

"Come, sir, to draw toward an end with you.

Good night, mother."

Alexandrian: the museum or academy at Alexandria was a center of study and research sponsored by the state.

a Christ who has lived . . . pots and pans: "So come, then, my daughters, let there be no disappointment when obedience keeps you busy in outward tasks. If it sends you to the kitchen, remember that the Lord walks among the pots and pans and that He will help you in inward tasks and in outward ones too." From *The Book of the Foundations* (*Libro de las Fundaciones*, 1573–82), in *The Complete Works of Saint Teresa of Jesus*, tr. and ed. by E. Allison Peers (London and New York, fifth impression, 1957), III, 22.

Santa Teresa de Jesús (1515–82) was born Teresa Sánchez de Cepeda y Ahumada, was responsible for the reform of the Carmelite Order, founded many convents, and was the author of many books.

an advocate of civil war: it was Unamuno's contention, oft repeated, that men get to know one another more through friction than through its alternative, indifference, and that each man should live in conflict or struggle (agony) with himself.

387-88. "*Meanings . . . do not give words their dignity*": Unamuno translates a footnote by Cassou at this point: "The corollary to this thought: 'Words arranged in a different order yield different meanings and meanings differently arranged yield a different effect,' has been glossed in all the classic editions (Hachette), large and small, by the following examples, supplied by a Professor: 'Thus, the difference between *grand homme* and *homme grand*, between *galant homme* and *homme galant*, and so on.' This piece of monstrous foolishness would not outrage Unamuno, a Professor himself—another contradiction in this man who is a mass of antitheses—a professor who professes above all else a detestation of professors."

See Pascal, *Pensées* 50, in Hachette edition, edited by M. Léon Brunschvicg, the "Professor" referred to in the footnote: "Un même sens change selon les paroles qui l'expriment. Les sens reçoivent des paroles leur dignité, au lieu de la leur donner." Brunschvicg's "gloss" is a footnote to *Pensée* 23, which reads: "Les mots diversement rangés font un divers sens, et les sens diversement rangés font différents effets."

388. *Fray Luis de León*: (1527–91), Augustinian monk, writer, poet, scholar, and professor at the University of Salamanca. His statue stands facing the plateresque façade of the old university building, alongside the rector's home where Unamuno lived many years.

Port-Royal: center of French Jansenism, the religious movement to which Pascal adhered.

Sören Kierkegaard: (1813–55), Danish philosopher whom Unamuno started reading—in Danish—in 1900 and who exercised an enormous influence on the Spaniard.

389. *Kant and with Don Quixote*: for Kant, see Ch. I of *The Tragic Sense of Life*, Vol. 4 in this series; for Don Quixote, see Unamuno's *Life of Don Quixote and Sancho*, Vol. 3 in this series.

Commentaries on the Christ of Velázquez, commentaries on the speeches of Primo de Rivera: for the first, see Unamuno's long poem *El Cristo de Velázquez*, completed in 1920 and included in *OC*, XIII; for the second, see Unamuno's contributions to *Hojas Libres* and *España con honra*, periodicals published in

France during the Primo de Rivera dictatorship, and not yet collected.

390. *Risorgimento*: a resurgence of national feeling and activism in Italy dating from about the second half of the 18th century and culminating in the unification of Italy in 1870.

Góngora: Luis de Góngora y Argote (1561–1627), whose difficult works, the two *Soledades* and the *Fábula de Polifemo y Galatea* (both 1613) are synonymous with what is known as Spanish baroque. The subject of heated critical polemics, Góngora exercised a powerful influence on poets of the 17th century; his difficult poetry was scorned by some of the major critics of the 18th century, and although his fortune took a turn for the better in the 19th century, he was roundly condemned for his obscurity by the great historian, critic, and polygraph Marcelino Menéndez y Pelayo (1856–1912). In the early 20th century there were attempts at vindicating his reputation, which reached their apogee in 1927 when, on the occasion of the three hundredth anniverasry of Góngora's death, there was a series of ceremonies in his honor and the *Soledades* were explicated by Dámaso Alonso.

Góngora never was a favorite of Unamuno's, and the efforts of young writers of the so-called Generation of 1927, or the Generation of the Dictatorship, to exalt Góngora's reputation, angered the exiled Unamuno who felt that the times called for other things.

391. *Luigi Pirandello*: (1867–1936), famous Italian short-story writer, novelist, and playwright; received Nobel Prize for literature in 1934. Pirandello's most famous works are concerned with the conflicts of illusion and reality, and this has led some

commentators to see an analogy between him and Unamuno.

Unamuno is mistaken when he says that Pirandello kept his "insane mother" by his side. Actually, it was his wife, Antonietta Portulano, who was mad; Pirandello cared for her himself until 1918 when, shortly before her death, he had her committed to an asylum. The mistake may be considered a "Freudian slip" on the part of Unamuno, who thought of wives as mothers.

395. *Abbé Henri Bremond*: (1865–1933), French critic and historian, author of *Histoire littéraire du sentiment religieux en France* and of the work which Unamuno has in mind here, the essays on *La Poésie pure*.

396. *to eat a book*: Rev. 10:9.

398. *Antonio Machado*: cf. note for p. 130.

399. *Cide Hamete Benengeli*: "In the prologue to *Don Quixote*—which, like all prologues, including the present one, is merely literature—Cervantes reveals to us that he found the narrative concerning the heroic life of the Knight of the Sad Countenance among some Arabic papers of one Cide Hamete Benengeli. A profound revelation, this, in which the good Cervantes . . . discloses what we might call the objectivity, the existence (*ex-istere* means "to be outside") of Don Quixote and Sancho and his entire cast of characters outside the novelist's fiction and beyond it. For my part, I believe that Cide Hamete Benengeli was no Arab but a Jew, a Moroccan Jew, and that he did not make up the story either. In any case, this Arabic text of Cide Hamete Benengeli is in my possession." (*Our Lord Don Quixote*, in Vol. 3 this series, p. 6.) This ironic claim is by way of answer to a query re-

garding an erroneous citation from the original *Don Quijote*, a query put to him by Professor Homer P. Earle, the first American translator of *The Life of Don Quixote and Sancho*.

401. *certain conversation* . . . Les Nouvelles Littéraires: "Une heure avec Miguel de Unamuno," par Frédéric Lefèvre, *Les Nouvelles Littéraires, artistiques et scientifiques*, 2 août, 1924, pp. 1, 2. Frédéric Lefèvre (1889–1949) wrote a regular column called "Une heure avec . . ." in which he interviewed celebrated literary figures. Many of these interviews were later collected in books.

the gospel scandal . . . *must be scandal*: I Cor.: 1:23.

403. *enter history forever*: Unamuno includes *à jamais*. Cassou, however, translating back into the French has: ". . . il faut entrer pour toujours dans l'histoire. Pour toujours!" *Comment on fait un roman*, in *Avant et Après la Revolution* (Paris, 1933), p. 50, though in his "Portrait D'Unamuno" he had, indeed, written: "C'est . . . la faire entrer à jamais dans l'histoire" (p. 28).

Thucydides . . . *forever*: *Thucydides*, ed. Charles Forster Smith (Loeb Classical Library), Vol. I, Book I, xxii.4. "And, indeed, it has been composed, not as a prize-essay to be heard for the moment, but as a possession for all time" (p. 41).

Leopold von Ranke . . . *God*: von Ranke (1795–1886), one of the great German historians and philosophers of history, is identified with the beginnings of scientific historiography. "As early as 1820 he wrote a letter to his brother, 'God lives and is observable in the whole of history. Every deed bears witness of him, every moment proclaims his name, but especially do we find it in the connecting line that runs through history.' " (Quoted by Pieter Geyl, *Debates with Historians*, Meridian Books, 1958, p. 16.)

404. *Peace in War: Paz en la guerra* (1897), in *OC²*, II, in English in Vol. 1 of this series.

405. *felt in the guts: entrañable*: Unamuno was far in advance of the languages in using words which we might translate as "gut-reaction," "felt in the guts," "gut-felt," if it were not that these neologisms usually seem to be out of keeping with the general style of our version.

413. *In twenty years, I'll be eighty-three*: Unamuno lived to be seventy-two—thirty-six years in each of two centuries—not the ninety he had planned. But he *did* outlive the military dictatorship of Primo de Rivera, as he vowed he would.

General Don Dámaso Berenguer: (1873–1953), Spanish High Commissioner in Morocco, he captured the city of El Raisuli in 1920. In Annual, however, General Manuel Fernández Silvestre's troops were slaughtered by the Rifs under Abd-el-Krim, and in the summer of 1922, Spanish public opinion demanded that "responsibilities" be determined and Berenguer was replaced. These events eventually led to the *pronunciamiento* of September 23, 1923, and the dictatorship of General Miguel Primo de Rivera. When Primo became suspicious of some of his generals, among them Berenguer, they were imprisoned.

With the fall of Primo de Rivera in 1930, the king entrusted Berenguer with the formation of a government, and in February 1931, Berenguer announced the general elections which led to the abdication of the king in April of 1931.

And the poor prince . . . Don Juan III: Don Juan de Aragón, the only male heir to the throne of the

Catholic Sovereigns, Isabel of Castile and Ferdinand of Aragon, was born in 1478 and died in 1497. If he had inherited the throne he would have been Don Juan III, which title Unamuno ascribes to him as an "ex-future" or one who might have been.

Isabel died in 1504, leaving the crown of Castile to her daughter Juana, married to the Archduke Philip (the Handsome) of Hapsburg, son of Emperor Maximilian I of Austria and Mary of Burgundy. Philip died in 1506, and Juana went mad with grief (she is known in history as *Juana la loca* or Joan the Mad), and when Ferdinand died in 1516, the son of Philip and Juana, Charles I (better known as Charles V of the Holy Roman Empire) inherited the throne of Spain. Thus it was that the Hapsburg dynasty ruled in Spain until its extinction in 1700. Unamuno repeatedly held that the death of Prince Juan was a catastrophe for Spain, since the transference of power to the Hapsburgs was the beginning of foreign policies that ruined the country.

414. *romance*: *romances* are based on an octosyllabic meter and alternating assonance of the lines; of anonymous origin, they extend from the Middle Ages to García Lorca (*Romancero gitano*) and represent a thousand years of continuity in Spanish verse, a traditionalism perhaps unique in European literature; our English translation of Unamuno's use of the form here cannot pretend to reproduce the close structure of the original.

If you are not to return me to Spain: included in the poetry collection *Romancero del destierro* (Buenos Aires, 1927). To be found in *OC*, XIV, 663:

> Si no has de volverme a España
> Dios de la única bondad,
> și no has de acostarme en ella
> ¡hágase tu voluntad!

Como en el cielo en la tierra
en la montaña y la mar,
Fuenterrabía soñada,
tu campana oigo sonar.

Es el llanto del Jaizquibel,
—¡sobre él pasa el huracán!—
entraña de mi honda España
te siento en mí palpitar.

Espejo del Bidasoa
que vas a perderte al mar,
¡qué de ensueños te me llevas!
¡a Dios van a reposar . . . !

Campana Fuenterrabía,
lengua de la eternidad,
me traes la voz redentora
de Dios, ¡la única bondad!

¡Hazme, Señor, tu campana,
campana de tu verdad,
y la guerra de este siglo
deme en tierra eterna paz!

Fuenterrabía is a town; El Jaizquibel is a mountain rising behind it; the Bidasoa is a river.

415. *Giuseppe Mazzini*: (1805–72), political writer born in Genoa, champion of Italian unity and independence, spent most of his life in exile. The edition of Mazzini's letters to Giuditta Sidoli read by Unamuno is the *Lettere d'amore*, introduzione e note di Gaetano Gasperoni (Turin, Unione Tipografico-editrice Torinese, 1927).

Alceste de Ambris: revolutionary syndicalist and leader of the Italian Labor Union, once secretary to D'Annunzio; a collaborator of Mussolini's, but broke with him and died in exile in 1934, at age 70.

place myself: Unamuno is mistaken, since the Italian text says "metterti." Mazzini: *Lettere d'amore*, p. 14.

416. *Sarmiento*: Domingo (1811–88), Argentinian patriot, educator, statesman, writer, author of the classic *Facundo o civilización y barbarie* (1845), ambassador to the United States 1865–68, President of the Argentine Republic 1868–74.

Early in life Sarmiento joined in the revolt against the dictator Juan Manuel de Rosas (1793–1877), who enjoyed total power over Argentina from 1829 to 1852.

Poor Bouvard! Poor Pécuchet!: the foolish protagonists of Flaubert's novel *Bouvard et Pécuchet* (1881). They are a satire of bourgeois, democratic culture.

Martínez Anido: see note to p. 383 of Prologue.

Conde de Romanones: Alvaro de Figueroa y Torres (1863–1950), liberal politician and prime minister; arranged interview between the king and Unamuno in 1922, which some interpreted as a capitulation on the part of the writer.

Augusto Pérez: protagonist of *Niebla* (*Mist*), included in this volume.

Pachico Zabalbide: raisonneur in the novel *Paz en la guerra* (*Peace in War*), 1897; Vol. I in this series.

Alejandro Gómez: protagonist of the novelette *Nada menos que todo un hombre* (*Nothing Less than a Whole Man*), 1916, and included in *Tres novelas ejemplares y un prólogo* (*Three Exemplary Novels and a Prologue*), 1920.

418. *The State and Revolution*: Edmund Wilson says in *To the Finland Station* (N.Y., 1953, p. 452): "*State and Revolution* was written in the interval when he [Lenin] was in hiding in Finland in the summer of 1917, between the time of his first advent in Russia and the time of his return in the fall, and was interrupted by the events of October. 'It is pleasanter and more profitable,' he wrote when he brought it out

after the seizure of power, 'to live through the experience of a revolution than to write about it.' "

Karl Radek: (1885–1939). Born Sohelsohn, in Lvov (Lemberg), Radek first met Lenin in 1910, and later joined the Bolsheviks. He and Lenin disagreed sharply but they were reconciled after the Russian Revolution of March 1917. Radek accompanied Lenin and his party on the train from Switzerland but was stopped at the Russo-Finnish border while Lenin continued on to Petrograd. Worked for the Communist cause in Germany, was Trotsky's ally and friend, spent some time in China, broke with Trotsky, supported Stalin's "socialism in one country," but was nevertheless arrested in September 1936, was tried in January 1937, and was sentenced to ten years' imprisonment. In *The Gulag Archipelago* (I) (New York and London, 1973–74) Aleksandr Soltzhenitsyn, the undisputed authority and historian of these details to date, flatly calls Radek an early "stool pigeon" in the Stalinist apparatus (p. 370), a "plain provocateur" (p. 410), accuses him of making depositions against the Old Bolshevik Bukharin (p. 416), and states that he was shot, in 1939, "after 1937 show trial." (Also cf. Warren Lerner: *Karl Radek: The Last Internationalist*, Stanford, 1970.)

419. *the tragic Valentin of Peau de Chagrin*: Unamuno was well acquainted with Balzac's *Peau de Chagrin* (1832) or *The Fatal Skin*, for the death scene in his novelette *Nada menos que todo un hombre* (1916), is reminiscent of the end of Balzac's story. In Ch. VI of *La agonía del cristianismo* (*The Agony of Christianity*), Unamuno translates the half-mad words of Pauline to the old servant Jonathas who comes in to find the dead Rafaël de Valentin in her arms (p. 50 in Vol. 5 of this series).

It is not surprising that the slow ebbing away of

life, recorded by the "fatal skin" in Valentin's possession should have exercised a fascination on the Unamuno who was tormented by the desire for immortality.

421. *the Moroccan crusade*: In *The Agony of Christianity* (Vol. 5 of this series, p. 63), Unamuno writes: "Not long ago, the bishops of Spain in a collective document spoke of the war for the civil protectorate—civil! protectorate!—waged in Morocco by the Kingdom of Spain, not the Spanish nation, and called it a *Crusade!*"

422. "*. . . die with me*": Compare this with the inscription on the fatal skin possessed by Valentin in the *Peau de Chagrin* and which bears the inscription:

If thou hast me, thou wilt have everything.
Thy life, however, will be my possession.
God has so decreed. Wish what thou wilt,
All thy wishes shall be fulfilled.
But count thy wishes as thy life,
For it is measured thereby.
With every wish of thine
I shall grow shorter
Even as thy days.
Wilt have me?
Take me. God
will help thee!
So be it.

(*The Fatal Skin*, tr. Atwood H. Townsend, N.Y., 1963, pp. 35-36.)

Pont de l'Alma: the Alma for which the bridge is named is a small river in the Crimea where the Russians were defeated by the forces of the French and English during the Crimean War (1854). Coincidentally, *alma* in Spanish means "soul," and that is the way Unamuno prefers to read it.

424. *Valery Larbaud*: (1881–1957), French author and translator (co-translator of Joyce's *Ulysses*), admirer of Unamuno and one of those who protested his exile.

Actually, it was Stendhal who first referred to reading as an "unpunished vice."

I had published my sonnets . . . Teresa: Unamuno's *De Fuerteventura a París, Diario íntimo de confinamiento y destierro vertido en sonetos* (From Fuerteventura to Paris: Intimate Journal of Confinement and Exile Recorded in Sonnets), was published by Excelsior in Paris in 1925. *Teresa*, subtitled "Rimas de un poeta desconocido presentadas y presentado por Miguel de Unamuno" ("Rhymes by an Unknown Poet Presented and Brought out by Miguel de Unamuno"), was published by Biblioteca Renacimiento in Madrid, 1924.

427. *the "X" sickness of Mackenzie*: James Mackenzie (1853–1925), Scottish-English cardiologist, gave the name X-disease "to a syndrome of pathologic symptoms, including irregular respiration and pulse, sensitivity to cold, and dyspepsia, of unknown origin; also called *Mackenzie's disease*." (*Blakiston's New Gould Medical Dictionary*, N.Y., Toronto, London, 1956, p. 689.)

the Other: *El otro* (*The Other*), is the title of a drama Unamuno wrote in 1926, included in Vol. 7 of this series.

429. *Ahi serva Italia, di dolore ostello*: *Purgatorio*, VI, 76.

431. *Don Quixote . . . galley-slaves*: Part I, Ch. 22.

433. *De Fuerteventura a París*: In *OC*, XIV, 570.

> es la Revolución, una comedia
> que el Señor ha inventado contra el tedio.

The sonnet is dated 15-X-1924.

434. *the bridge . . . twenty-five*: In 1889, the young
Unamuno made a trip to Italy and France.

435. *deceitful history*: one of Unamuno's most reiterated beliefs was that recorded history represents
only surface movement, and beneath the agitated surface lies *intrahistoria* or "infrahistory," the humble
world of people who are born, suffer, reproduce, and
die, and are the same everywhere. He develops these
concepts most thoroughly in his *En torno al casticis-
mo*, first published in the form of five essays in 1895,
and in book form in 1902. In *OC*, III, 155-303.

Doctor Huarte de San Juan . . . Examen de Ingenios: Huarte de San Juan (1530?–?1591) was born
in the city of St. Jean Pied-de-Port, then San Juan
de Pie del Puerto, in what was Spanish Navarre. His
famous work was published in Baeza in 1575. The
first English edition (1594) by R. C., Esquire (Richard Carew) is called *The Examination of men's Wits.
In Which, by discovering the variete of natures, is
shewed for what profession each one is apt, and how
far he shall profit therein.*

Unamuno often refers to the Spanish work in his
The Life of Don Quixote and Sancho (Vol. 3 of this
series.)

436. *whose lintel announces*:

Let us live in peace
Pierre Ezpellet
and Jeanne Iribar
Year 8 of the New Constitution
1800

Don Carlos . . . Carlists: Don Carlos de Borbón y
Este (1848–1909), known to his followers as Car-
los "VII" and grandson of the first Carlist pretender
Carlos "V."

The original Carlists were the followers of the uncle of Isabel II of Spain. When Fernando VII died in 1833, leaving his throne to his three-year-old daughter Isabel under the regency of her mother, Fernando's brother Carlos invoked the Salic law to challenge the child-queen's right to the throne. The first Carlist War lasted from 1833 to 1840, the second from 1872 to 1876. The Carlist bombardment of Bilbao during the second of these civil wars is recorded in Unamuno's first novel *Paz en la guerra* (*Peace in War*, 1897).

The Carlists were ultra-conservatives, both in politics and religion, and their strength lay in the northern provinces.

437. *Roncesvalles . . . Orlando Furioso*: the allusion here is to the hero of the French epic *La Chanson de Roland*, who was killed in 778 as he led the rearguard of Charlemagne's forces in combat against the Basques at Roncevaux (Roncesvalles, Navarre). During the Renaissance, Roland became the protagonist of several epics, the most famous being the mock-heroic *Orlando Furioso* (*Roland Gone Mad*) of Ariosto (1516).

Yuste: monastery in the province of Extremadura, to which Carlos V (of the Holy Roman Empire, Carlos I of Spain) retired, leaving his throne to his son Philip (Felipe) II.

438. *Don Juan . . . Don Juan III*: see previous note.

440. *Las mocedades del Cid*: a play by Guillén de Castro (1569–1631). The quotation in the original reads (Act I, lines 662-65):

> Procure siempre acertalla
> el honrado y principal;
> pero si la acierta mal,
> defendella y no emendalla.

at once: Unamuno mistranslates Mazzini's "un'altra volta" (Mazzini, *Lettere d'amore*, p. 91) as "en seguida" or "at once" when it should be "once again."

441. *February 1925*: The editor of the *OC* says in a footnote to p. 884 of Vol. X that "the printed text says 1924 and the visit to which he refers was to Paris, the next year."

"*Oh poverty, poverty*": *Don Quixote*, Part II, Ch. XLIV. See *Our Lord Don Quixote*, Vol. 3 of this series, pp. 225ff. and p. 408.

442. *a certain lady*: Unamuno tells us elsewhere that the lady was Delfina Molina Vedia de Bastianini "my Argentine friend"—who arrived July 2 with her daughter and left on the 5th (*OC*, XIV, 546).

In a moment . . . "My child!": the reference is to Unamuno's spiritual crisis of Spring 1897, which came to a head one night as is briefly described in this passage and elsewhere in Unamuno's books and letters.

In one of his best letters, to his friend Pedro Jiménez Ilundain, dated January 3, 1898 (Hernán Benítez, *El drama religioso de Unamuno*, Buenos Aires, 1949, p. 260), Unamuno wrote: "What a terrible thing it is to cross the steppes of intellectualism, and then to come one day . . . face to face with the image of death and total annihilation! The crisis overcame me suddenly and violently. . . . And I took refuge in the childhood of my soul, and I understood the withdrawn life . . . my wife saw me weep and spontaneously cried out . . . , 'My child!' "

443. "*I know . . . March 2, 1835*: Mazzini writes (*Lettere d'amore*, p. 50): "Conosco questi dolori d'artisti trattati da artisti: è l'ombra del dolore: a noi il corpo."

Don Luis de Góngora y Argote: see note to p. 390.

444. *"seized much Sea and little water"*: from *Soledad Segunda*, v. 75.

Mazzini, the man who cried "God and Country!": Cf. Mazzini's "Ai Giovani d'Italia."

445. *Don Juan Valera*: (1825–1905), Spanish novelist, critic, and diplomat, was Spanish Minister to the United States from 1883 to 1886. His most famous novel *Pepita Jiménez* was published in 1874. In 1891 Valera was a member of the examining committee which granted Unamuno the Professorship of Greek in Salamanca.

447. *Everybody is dying . . . has just died*: p. 122 of Giuseppe Mazzini, *Lettere d'amore*. Footnotes on pp. 121–22 give the following information: Romagnosi (Gian Domenico), 1761–1835, jurist and philosopher; Pecchio (Giuseppe), 1785–1835, writer and exile; Vitorelli (Iacopo), 1749–1835, poet.

"Today I should tell you . . . poetry." On p. 127 of *op.cit*. Mazzini writes: "Oggi devo dirti, affinchè tu non mi scriva che i miei dolori appartengono alla poesia, come la chiami, che essi sono realmente tali da qualche tempo, e che devono almeno scusarmi, essendo pronto a confessare che il calcolo che io fo è cattivo, e che bene o male, malinconico o tranquillo, io devo scriverti sempre, almeno spiegare le mie irregolarità."

447-48. *June 2 of the same year*: *op.cit.*, p. 110.

448. *Benjamin Jarnés*: (1888–1950), novelist and man of letters. The article "Oro trillado y néctar exprimido," appeared in *La Gaceta Literaria*, June 1, 1927. Jarnés later edited two collections of Unamuno's works, *Páginas líricas* (México: Ediciones

Mensaje, 1943) and *Páginas escogidas* (México: Secretaría de Educación Pública, 1947).

449. *Soledades*: the lines quoted begin the *Soledad Primera*, the first of Góngora's two long poems, of which the second is incomplete.

450. *Manzoni*: Alessandro (1785–1873), Italian poet, playwright, and novelist, whose fame rests principally on his romantic historical novel *I promessi sposi*, published in its first form in 1827 and then again in revised form in 1840–42.

D'Azeglio: Massimo (1798–1866), Piedmontese author of two historical novels.

Grossi: Tommaso (1790–1853), poet, dramatist, and novelist, whose *I Lombardi alla prima crociata* furnished the basis of Verdi's opera of the same name.

Guerrazzi: Francesco Domenico (1804–73), patriot and author of romantic historical novels.

And the greater . . . political men: The French version by Cassou has: ". . . qu'ils étaient, tout poètes qu'ils étaient, des politiques.": which is, by reason of the commas, more logical: but in all the Spanish editions, where the sentence boasts no commas, the thought (or aesthetic nonsequitur) is more Unamunian.

non ragioniam di lor, ma guarda e passa: *Inferno*, III, 51.

451. *Francos Rodríguez*: José (1862–1931), Spanish doctor, journalist, and politician.

452. *Pi y Margall*: Francisco (1824–1901): author, politician, one of the presidents of the First Spanish Republic.

this tragic blusterer: one of Unamuno's derisive epithets for General Primo de Rivera.

453. *the royal power . . . royal pardons*: During World War I, Unamuno was anti-German while the

Spanish royal family's sympathies lay with the Axis. After the war, Unamuno's conflict with the king and his family was exacerbated and the author's references to the king's power and the pro-German activities of the Queen Mother led to a lawsuit. He was sentenced to sixteen years in prison for *lèse-majesté* and then pardoned. On many occasions, Unamuno claimed that he was condemned so that he could be pardoned.

456. *Carducci's ode, Su Monte Maris*: written January 1882, this poem is to be found in *Odi Barbare*, written between 1873 and 1889. Unamuno was a great admirer of the Italian critic and poet Giosuè Carducci (1835–1907), recipient of the Nobel Prize for literature in 1906, and his translation of the Italian poem in question entitled "Sobre el monte Mario," is in *Poesías* (1907), *OC*, XIII, 477–78.

Courteline: Georges Moinaux (1858–1929). Sometimes referred to as a modern, if minor, Molière, Courteline wrote twenty-eight satiric plays, most of them in one act.

459. *Don Juan Cueto . . . mine*: The editor of the *OC* points out in a footnote (*OC*, X, 903) that "Unamuno had written a prologue to his book *La vida y la raza a través del 'Quijote*,' " which is to be found in Vol. VII of the *OC*, pp. 368–74.

460. *beneath history*: see note to p. 435.

our civil wars: the Carlist wars. See note to p. 436.

462. *Johann Hessen*: born in 1889, Catholic priest, philosopher of religion, and professor at Cologne.

José Ferrater Mora's entry for Hessen in the *Diccionario de Filosofía* (5th ed.), Vol. I (Buenos Aires, 1971), p. 839, does not mention *Gottes Kindschaft* in the bibliography.

464. "*The child is father of the man*": from the poem (composed March 26, 1802, published 1807):

> My heart leaps up when I behold
> A rainbow in the sky:
> So was it when my life began;
> So is it now I am a man;
> So be it when I shall grow old,
> Or let me die!
> The Child is father of the Man;
> And I could wish my days to be
> Bound each to each by natural piety.

The Unamuno library contains a marked-up *Poetical Works of William Wordsworth* (London, n.d.).

465. "*It is finished!*": from *Romancero del destierro* (Buenos Aires, 1927). The poem, dated Hendaye, 3-VIII-1926 is included in *OC*, XIV, 638:

> "¡Queda cumplido!" suspiró y doblando
> la cabeza—follaje nazareno—
> en las manos de Dios puso el espíritu;
> lo dió a luz;
> que así Cristo nació sobre la cruz,
> y al nacer se soñaba a arredrotiempo
> cuando sobre un pesebre
> murió en Belén,
> allende todo mal y todo bien.

467. *Nicola Abbagnano*: (1901–), eminent Italian existentialist, author of the three-volume *Storia della filosofia* (1946–50, 2d ed. 1963), among other works. The quotation is from his *Le sorgenti irrazionali del pensiero* (Genoa, 1923), p. 166.

468. *Montesinos . . . cards*: *Don Quixote*, II, Ch. XXIII. Actually it is Durandarte, not Montesinos, who says "patience and shuffle the cards."

Hellenist philologist: Unamuno was Professor of Greek and History of the Spanish Language at the University of Salamanca.

469. *Thucydides . . . "for ever"*: Cf. note to p. 403.

470. *Azorín*: José Martínez Ruiz (1873–1967), essayist, playwright, novelist, one of the most important members of the so-called Generation of 1898.

Jacques de Lacretelle (1888–   ), novelist and member of the French Academy. The book referred to is *Aparté: Colère—Journal de colère—Dix jours à Ermenonville* (Paris, 1927).

André Gide . . . own novels: the reference is to the *Journal des Faux Monnayeurs* (1926).

474. *Frédéric Lefèvre*: Cf. note to p. 401.

475. *Hugh of Saint Victor*: (1096–1141), mystic and theologian, born in Saxony, died in Paris, abbot of the monastery "Sanct Victor."

479. *E'n la sua volontate è nostra pace*: *Paradiso*, III, 85.

Saint Bonaventure . . . lumen: Saint Bonaventure, born at Bagnorea in 1221, died at Lyons in 1274. *Lux* is the light of reason, *lumen* the illumination of faith: ". . . in Saint Bonaventure's view, philosophic truth implies an initial act of submission and humility, an admission by reason that it cannot achieve its own object unaided, and a final acceptance of the light above all lights, which is sufficient to itself, and which dispenses man from lighting a candle to look at the sun. (Etienne Gilson, *The Philosophy of St. Bonaventure*, tr. by Dom Illtyd Trethowan and F. J. Sheed, N.Y., 1940, p. 110.)